MW00710912

Granddaughters of the Holocaust

Never Forgetting What They Didn't Experience

Psychoanalysis and Jewish Life

The *Psychoanalysis and Jewish Life* book series has been established to promote scholarship, research, and a wide range of theoretical, textural, and clinical studies on the multiple interconnections between and mutual influence of Judaism and contemporary psychoanalysis. Its aim is broad, spanning a wide variety of subject areas: from the origins of psychoanalysis in Jewish circles in turn-of-the-century Vienna to clinical studies illuminating contemporary facets of Jewish identity and self-understanding; from explorations of psychological aspects of Jewish theology to psychoanalytic investigations of anti-Semitism; from studies of Jewish religious ritual to analyses of Hasidic mysticism and folklore; from psychoanalytic studies of pre-World War II Yiddish theater to the clinical practice of psychoanalysis in contemporary Israel. The *Psychoanalysis and Jewish Life* book series provides a home for fresh and intellectually challenging contributions across the spectrum of this interdisciplinary area of scholarship.

* * *

We are quickly approaching a time in which the survivors of the Shoah will no longer be with us to bear testimony to their experiences. As we approach this era, new studies have been undertaken not only of the second generation of the survivors' children, but now of the third generation, the survivors' grandchildren. The *Psychoanalysis and Jewish Life* Book Series is proud to publish *Granddaughters of the Holocaust: Never Forgetting What They Didn't Experience*, one of the first book-length studies of this kind. Nirit Gradwohl Pisano, herself the granddaughter of survivors, presents a qualitative study of in-depth interviews of Americans and Israelis who are part of this third generation. Dori Laub, one of the pioneers of qualitative research and psychoanalytic interviewing of survivors, contributes an introduction to this moving and insightful study, which will help facilitate further research and investigation of the intergenerational transmission of trauma and resilience.

—Lewis Aron

GRANDDAUGHTERS
OF THE HOLOCAUST

Never Forgetting What They Didn't Experience

NIRIT GRADWOHL PISANO

FOREWORD BY DORI LAUB

Boston 2012

Library of Congress Cataloging-in-Publication Data:
A catalog record for this title is available from the Library of Congress.

ISBN 978-1-936235-88-9

Book design and cover photo by Adell Medovoy

Published by Academic Studies Press in 2012
28 Montfern Avenue
Brighton, MA 02135, USA

press@academicstudiespress.com
www.academicstudiespress.com

אם אין אני לי, מי לי; וכשאני לעצמי, מה אני; ואם לא עכשיו, אימתי.
פרקי אבות, פרק א, משנה יד.

If I am not for myself, who will be for me?
If I am only for myself, what am I?
And if not now, when?
Ethics of the Fathers, 1: 14

ACKNOWLEDGMENTS

Since then, at an uncertain hour,
That agony returns,
And till my ghastly tale is told
This heart within me burns.
                    —Samuel Taylor Coleridge, 1798, p. 208

The Drowned and the Saved, Primo Levi's final memoir, which was first published months after his suicide in April of 1987, opens with the above quote. Twenty-two years later, in April of 2009, I arrived in Jerusalem for my grandmother's funeral. The shock and sorrow of her passing had taken residence in my throat. In a hurried visit to her modern, new apartment overlooking the ancient city, I was struck first by the light, and then by my grandmother's tangible presence in this home that I had not yet visited. I deeply and consolingly inhaled the familiar: the "Shalom" tile on her wall, bearing the image of a dove clutching an olive branch, which is now awkwardly hanging in my New York City apartment; the leftover pita, hummus, and Emek cheese stacked neatly in her refrigerator, which we heartbreakingly discarded moments later in preparation for Passover; the collage of my late grandfather's photos assembled in the bedroom, alongside pictures of her children, grandchildren, and great-grandchildren scattered throughout the apartment. And then I saw it. The sole item on her nightstand, embracing the edge of her bed, it appeared both horribly out of place yet entirely appropriate: Primo Levi's *The Drowned and the Saved*, as though she had been reading such books all along. In her final days, it seems, my grandmother courageously found her way back to the beginning.

Sensing the conclusion of my research on the horizon, and anxiously fantasizing how the final work might be received by my family, the presence of Levi's book confirmed on that day what I had unconsciously known: that my grandmother has accompanied me on this journey from the start, exploring the inexplicable, inviting the obscene, determinedly evolving our shared history. I offer my grandmother my deepest gratitude, admiration, and love. This study is dedicated to her, a pillar of strength and support, and to all of the extraordinary people who continue to reflect on their histories – ensuring that the most painful memories and frightening conversations are integrated in our ongoing collective narratives.

I would like to express my immense gratitude to the women who sat down for an interview and opened up their world. Their narratives provide a glimpse into history and remind us to "Never forget."

My sincerest appreciation goes to Michael O'Loughlin, my mentor and confidant, who gave me permission to discover the "research" that resonates with who I am. I look forward to our ongoing exploration of truth, and collaboration in the quest of bearing witness. Many thanks also to my editor, Lewis Aron, who provided the refueling push I needed to integrate my evolution and realize my place within this work.

Finally, I offer my deepest gratitude to my loving and supportive family, who joined me in my challenging journey through the world of history and psychology, and inspired me to uncover my own voice.

TABLE OF CONTENTS

FOREWORD

Dori Laub, MD

The greatest merit of this book is that it illuminates an arena we suspected existed, that we anecdotally described, and that we perhaps even published individual case studies about: the effects of the Holocaust on the third generation. An extensive body of literature exists on the second generation—they were the first absorbers of the shock—and clinicians have been looking with expectancy and fear for the effect on the third generation. In an era of globalization, of revolutionary changes in communication, and of an ever growing tendency to level differences and standardize life, do historical experiences still play a central role in one's psychological makeup?

The book, as it is written, is a passionate journey in the search for a truthful answer to this question. It examines the same history played out in a variety of plots, and it is this very variety which upholds the conclusion that such an effect is very much present and tangible. The book is not about a sweeping foreclosing generalization; it is rather about a tedious struggle for knowing, against traumatic erasure and muteness.

The methodology used—interpretative research of psychoanalytic interviews of ten granddaughters of survivors of the Holocaust and the concurrent reflections of the interviewer—allows for the creation of ten case studies in which three-dimensional, full-bodied, colorful, and nuanced characters emerge, who have a personality, a life, and a family history framed by very specific patterns of conflict and defense. This is by far more informative and enriching than the abstract themes that emerge in the studies utilizing content analysis or would-be quantitative analysis of traits that have until now been performed in this population. The ten granddaughters feel present in the room while one reads about them. They are not clichés. What is further stunning is the wealth of data that emerges from an interview of an hour and a half and a close recording of the interviewer's own reflections, associations, and countertransference observations. It is as if the course of a whole treatment has been captured in that one interview. Most likely it is the urge to give testimony, "the testimonial momentum," and the presence of a totally attuned listener that together drive the process to reach such extraordinary results.

All ten granddaughters acknowledge the powerful omnipresence of the historical trauma of the Holocaust in their current lives. The degree to which each one of them takes possession of it and makes a conscious decision regarding how to contain and address it varies. Some are fully aware of it and able to make life choices that are outside its impact; others are aware of it but cannot help letting it dictate various positions they take in life; still others, while powerfully aware of its emotional impact, cannot clearly define it, nor tease out the role it plays in their life. In the latter group, a vague fear that they are helpless to shape their lives and will inevitably succumb, so that future generations will continue to be affected, prevails.

It bears repeating that all of the ten granddaughters acknowledge the presence of the traumatic history of the Holocaust in their lives. It is this universe of undigested, unassimilated experiences, shards of a broken world, which ties them together. The word "camp" is perhaps the best that can be used to illustrate this tie. While for everyone else its connotation is to a summer camp, for them it reverberates with what their parents and grandparents have or have not told them about their WWII experiences.

This preface will highlight two topics: a) how the granddaughters differ in their experience of the Holocaust, and b) how they variably respond to these experiences. The Holocaust has transformed the everyday experiences of most of these individuals into events with traumatically layered meaning.

Bethany is struck by how little is verbally acknowledged. This phenomenon is discussed as "a shelter of silence that has become a Holocaust memorial." She speaks to the idea that "it is as though the Holocaust is being relived in silence." She has to call her father during the interview and apologizes profusely because he thought she had died when his call to come and pick her up was delayed. For Bethany, nothing else existed so long as Holocaust traumas did.

Yael feels almost cheated at having been born after the Holocaust and not having experienced it directly. Not knowing each other's whereabouts is very frightening to Yael, her mother, and her grandmother, resonating so much with the Nazi times, when people would just disappear.

Leah grew up with a paternal great aunt who kept dozens of suitcases packed, ready for an unexpected move, and with the ever-present image of a five-year-old son shot by the Nazis in the street, in front of her maternal grandmother.

Samantha and Jessica grew up with a grandfather, an Auschwitz survivor, who suffered from scleroderma and from a physically abusive bipolar wife who would hit him with a menorah. He tried to speak but could barely whisper. The murmurs of his memory were met with a refusal. His daughter, being the only caretaker of her suicidal parents, directed her rage at her children. While Jessica dissociated and suffers from explicitly non-Holocaust related nightmares that someone is trying to kill her, Samantha retained her clarity as to how the first and second generation reenacted the trauma, leaving the third generation dazzled and terrified. She is constantly on alert and anxious not to repeat it.

Miriam tried to establish boundaries by rebelling, binging and purging, and refraining from watching or reading Holocaust movies or books. Malka recognizes how events that occur in the present take the meanings of things that happened in the past, and that she is forever paying back something she does not owe. Briana, whose paternal grandparents are Holocaust survivors who felt very guilty for surviving—not good enough to deserve it—was always crying about it. Her grandparents' guilt was passed on to her father, who was never praised, and to Briana, who felt she had no right to feel pain because others suffered more. She has frightening dreams about the Holocaust—including feelings of terror at being found, at being buried alive, of Nazis all around, etc.

In response, each of them dealt with the intergenerationally transmitted Holocaust trauma very differently. In Briana's case, there were years of anorexia in response to her father's transgenerationally transmitted judgment of not being good enough, not deserving his survival. Her father wanted to make her eat, not talk about it. Leah's obsessive-compulsive rituals and routines were a way of putting order back into "something massive having gone off course"—the ghostly face of the 5-year-old boy who had been shot in front of his mother, appearing in every face of the family, and perhaps even in every human face. Yael's idealization of a heroic grandfather, who grasped that he had to place himself in the front of the wheelbarrow carrying the dead corpses from the gas chambers to the crematoria in order to not be shot, eclipsed everything else in her life. With his death, everything was lost. She suffers from a recurring nightmare of being chased by an army of Red Coats. Miriam, who chose a Slovak (whom she found extremely exciting) to be her first love, did so as a rebellion against both her grandmother's trying to forget her sadness and her mother's trying to recover and contain it.

Samantha struggles with food-related conflicts and panic attacks and Jessica lives in a hazy, elusive world. They are sisters, granddaughters of the above-mentioned severely abused and suicidal Auschwitz survivor. Their mother, his daughter, vacillated between excessive secrecy and excessive disclosure, particularly with Samantha. Their mother was exhausted and enraged at being the sole caretaker of her parents, and took it out on her children. While Samantha recognizes her own inability to fully bear witness to the overpowering nature of her experiences, she still feels that "everything could just end" and does all she can to avoid reenactments of "losing her cool." Her sister Jessica dissociates, feels she must have done something wrong to cause such fury in her mother, and cries all the time—especially in her therapy. A sense of helplessness prevails, knowing that she carries in her three generations of unexpressed feelings.

The larger the communicative gap, the more determined the refusal to listen; the more violent the clash, the more unbridgeable the divide. Although Rebecca kept asserting that "she is fine with it"—the interviewer felt she was treading lightly in the interview. Her senile grandfather called her mother a Nazi for proposing to transfer him from his current home to an assisted living situation. In return, he is described as being insane—a label that does not explore his experience of being relocated, institutionalized once again in his life. Growing up, his children refused to listen to stories, and the two generations lived in two separate worlds. Rebecca's flight is a flight into rationality. In an entirely different manner, Ruth, who also refused to hear her grandfather's stories, of how his baby sister Toni, age 12, was killed right away, is plagued by shame for not having spoken up when she saw a swastika in Madrid, Spain, and decides that it is her responsibility to carry on being a Jew and be proud of it. She has a strong sense of "history unfolding in the present."

Many of the granddaughters feel it is their function to continue or even to complete the "feeling work" that remains to be done to unlock the intergenerational trauma—to make conscious the "unthought known." They realize that "it is precisely in not knowing, in the utter lack of history, that trauma is transmitted". Their challenge is heightened by the denial and dissociation of the two preceding generations.

Bethany has become the "narrator" of the family who serves her grandparents and her father as a bridge back to life. She has dedicated herself to curing her ancestors' trauma, and she wants to live a life that will undo this history. Malka feels it is the women who are the carriers of the stories, handing them down from generation to generation. Her history is her "baby" and she is doing everything to keep it alive. She is the one who recognizes (and translates) how events that occur in the present take the meaning of things that happened in the past. Her father, even now, is coming in running in the middle of the night, to see if she is still there. Briana is the overly expressive member in the family who carries the emotions of various generations.

I have briefly reviewed the individualized unique experience of the Holocaust in each of the ten granddaughters and the equally unique response each one of them had to that experience. It goes without saying that history is very much alive and ongoing, and takes on a very personalized meaning in each one of them. One must read the book in its entirety in order to appreciate that.

Having taken testimonies of survivors myself, I can appreciate the hard work it took to carry out these interviews and, even more than that, to write them up and put them together. The level of self discipline required is simply exemplary. Repeatedly one has to pull back and avoid the pitfalls of a simplifying generalization and a premature foreclosure based on rushed and incomplete "understanding"; the latter comes to be a hugely powerful temptation when one attempts to unravel the convoluted and intertwined residual strains that remain in the wake of extreme traumatization.

PREFACE

As an Israeli-born, American-raised member of the third generation of the Holocaust, my identity is based on a mixture of Jewish and Israeli history, an amalgamation of past suffering and loss on the one hand, and emigration, hope, and renewal on the other. My paternal grandmother escaped Nazi Germany in 1938, at the age of seven, through the Kindertransport[1] to London. Aside from one sister, the remainder of her family perished in Auschwitz. Presumably, the younger girls were "lucky." The family members' parting on the train platform marked their eternal separation, and would continue to reverberate in my family's "goodbyes" for generations to come. At 16, my grandmother left her orphanage in London to make *aliyah*[2] and met my paternal grandfather, who would become the only rabbi in Bern, Switzerland, during the 1960s and 1970s. On my maternal side, my grandfather was born and raised in Amsterdam, and spent elementary school in a class with Anne Frank. He escaped to Switzerland via his father's Swiss passport in 1940, leaving his classmates behind. Throughout my life, I have recognized the value of my own Swiss passport, as it continues to provide a sense of relief, a kind of European "get out of jail card," (or get out of camp card), for my family and me.

My immediate family's relocation to the United States when I was seven years old was a world away from, yet highly reminiscent of, my grandmother's relocations at the same age two generations prior. In our life abroad, we cherished a sense of pride and resiliency, vehemently repeating the well-established Jewish motto, "Never again..." The intimately related but seemingly contradictory feelings of fear, guilt, and shame were left unacknowledged. We held three passports, spoke three languages, and successfully escaped the chaotic atmosphere of Israel, and more generally, of our past. While I had been taught a great deal

---

1   This is the rescue movement that took place in the months leading up to the outbreak of World War II. The United Kingdom took in approximately 10,000 Jewish children from Nazi Germany and the occupied territories.

2   The Hebrew word used to refer to Jewish immigration to Israel; literally "moving up." This is also the word used when a person is invited to recite a blessing over the Torah.

about the Holocaust, through stories, museums, books, and a personal trip to Auschwitz during high school, the sudden distance from my birthplace and its collective narrative further quieted the already faint memory of our traumatic history. I believe this distance provided me with an enhanced desire to seek out this topic and explore the manifestations of traumatic memory in the third generation. Along the way, I have discovered the ways in which my work serves as a testimony for my ancestors' experience.

My grandmother spent a lifetime shielding herself from the failure of language to depict her experience, and others from sharing her anguish. Understanding that some things must remain unsaid, her family attempted to "protect" their beloved wife and mother from her history. Of course, silence only further communicated her unimaginable suffering. Three generations following the event, as I sit with my interviewees, I invite them to share their historical curiosity, or lack thereof. "What are some of the questions you have always wanted to ask your grandparents?" I inquire. The questions imprinted in my mind, which I never successfully verbalized, include: What was it like to stand on a train platform at age seven, and wave goodbye to your family? How did you continue to exist following this separation? What happens now when you travel by train, interact with a seven-year-old, or say goodbye to a friend? I realize that what I am truly in search of are the forbidden feelings, the unspeakable and unfathomable emotions, which have been denied and transmitted in silence. While I never asked my grandmother these questions, and no longer have the opportunity to ask them, I am certain they will continue to shape who I am: "overly-sensitive," holding three generations' worth of unspoken emotions.

A number of issues arise from my brief familial account that I will address in this work, with the ultimate hope of better understanding the multifaceted and complex nature of identity formation vis-à-vis the intimate relationship between personal anecdote and collective memory. Of specific interest are the failures of language in communicating traumatic memory; the silence, myths, and taboos surrounding the Holocaust, during and after the birth of the State of Israel; and the unspoken but incessant transmission of traumatic memory following such catastrophe and humiliation. As can be seen in my own account, it is difficult to distinguish the origins of resiliencies from those of vulnerabilities, individual coping mechanisms from family and societal systems, or passion and pride from the intimately related experiences of fear, guilt, and shame. My individual story, merely one woman's narrative, simultaneously speaks to the struggle of a family, the development of a mentality, and the circumstances that impacted an entire civilization.

Contemporary Jews live in a world where the immediate memory of the Holocaust has faded, but culturally and psychologically transmitted residues of the Holocaust continue to manifest themselves. That is, while subsequent generations did not endure the horrors of the Holocaust directly, they did quite powerfully "absorb" the experiences, as stories pass from generation to generation, and communication transcends both verbal and nonverbal form. Unfathomable events are inevitably transmitted to and contained by the children and grandchildren of survivors.

The present work hones in on the intergenerational transmission of Holocaust trauma to the granddaughters of survivors. This group exposes the transmission pattern of Holocaust memories in a generation twice removed from the event itself, allowing for an additional perspective on family dynamics often unachieved by the children of survivors. The interviews conducted with these women offered an unencumbered space within which participants were asked to speak freely about their inheritance of Holocaust trauma and memory, and their responses to this legacy. Through words, behaviors, omissions, negations, and evasions, the resulting ten narratives provide startling evidence for the embodiment of ghostly echoes in the ways these women approach daily tasks of living and being. Thus, although the granddaughters of survivors did not themselves survive the Holocaust, they will, in a sense, "never forget what they didn't experience."

Unfortunately, silence surrounding historically traumatic events has the power to debilitate individuals and entire societies. Once a pattern of silence is established, shifting its contagious grip is a difficult undertaking, one that can span the realm of multiple generations. The act of narrating one's story—struggling to integrate thoughts and emotions in a coherent structure which feels accurate and acceptable to the narrator—is crucial for resilience to evolve. The nature of the narrative is secondary in importance: whether the narrator suppresses knowledge that exists beneath a thinly veiled surface, regurgitates a previously constructed account, or challenges herself in such a way that new narrative possibilities emerge, some type of story inevitably and remarkably unfolds. And, as content is disclosed and a process is revealed, even the unspeakable has a way of making its presence known. It is within this realm of language and beyond that the granddaughters of survivors can achieve a multi-generational perspective of their identities and bear witness as to what happened to their ancestors.

CHAPTER 1: REVIEW OF THE LITERATURE

Within reach, close and not lost, there remained, in the midst of the losses, this one thing: language. This, the language, was not lost but remained, yet in spite of everything. But it had to pass through its own answerlessness, pass through a frightful falling mute, pass through the thousand darknesses of death bringing speech. It passed through and yielded no words for what was happening—but it went through those happenings. Went through, and could come into the light of day again, "enriched" by all that.

—Paul Celan, 1958, p. 395

The Broken Link

Claude Lanzmann (1985), maker of the documentary *Shoah*, argued that any attempt to understand *Shoah*[1] is obscene. Nevertheless, as his film illustrates, engagement with the Holocaust and its legacy is essential. As Elie Wiesel noted, many survivors drew their will to survive from their belief in the importance of keeping memory of the exterminations alive. Attempts at narrating Holocaust memory can be found in works such as Wiesel's *Night* (1961), Spiegelman's *Maus* (1986, 1991), the writings of Améry, Borowski, and Levi, and in Lanzmann's *Shoah* (1985). These and the videotape archive collected by Dori Laub at Yale, and commentaries on that testimony (e.g., Langer, 1991), as well as the representational work being done at Holocaust museums worldwide, are attempts to symbolize an inexplicable event. As Holocaust archivist Dori Laub (1992) noted, *Shoah* is "An Event Without a Witness," in that anybody with a genuine understanding of the Holocaust was killed, and in that the Holocaust is incomprehensible and impossible to convey in words.

This sentiment is expanded in Davoine and Gaudillière's fundamental book, *History Beyond Trauma: Whereof One Cannot Speak, Thereof One*

---

1 The Hebrew word meaning "catastrophe," signifying the Holocaust.

Cannot Stay Silent (2004). The authors shed light on the complex nature of traumatic memories via a conceptualization of that which cannot be symbolized, an experience "outside the field of speech and beyond the mirror" (Davoine & Gaudillière, 2004, p. 45). As they explain, when a "catastrophe" falls beyond the scope of language—and words fail to even approach the horrific truths of history—distortions of memory are inevitable:

> The imminent catastrophe, the announced doomsday, has already happened but could not be inscribed in the past as past, since in this respect the subject of speech was not there. Nothing in the other was given him, no speech to name what happened there. Totally cut off, ignored, but also well known to everyone, sometimes uttered in history books and even advocated by the duty to remember though that made no difference, the truth was unable to be transmitted. The information has remained a dead letter, outside the field of speech (Davoine & Gaudillière, 2004, p. 29).

Within this framework, individuals suffering from psychosis are understood as desperately but often ineffectually attempting to merge the traumas of their personal histories with the traumas of history at large: because they do not possess the words for their experience, their existence unfolds outside of language. They cannot symbolize "what happened there," nor understand how "there" has overwhelmed the present, "here." Thus, in the absence of speech, their experiences have not been rightfully inscribed into the unconscious and then repressed; instead, they maintain the quality of being "erased, reduced to nothing, and yet inevitably existing" (Davoine & Gaudillière, 2004, p. 47). Along similar lines, survivors continue to live on condition that they repress or "cut out" their experiences and never look back, identified by Davoine and Gaudillière as "the cut out unconscious" (2004, p. 47). In order to achieve contact with this "cut out unconscious," there must be a willingness to engage in a new sort of "language game," a "silent language" in which one's story is shown, not spoken (Davoine & Gaudillière, 2004, p. 78-79). Yet, how can non-symbolic, nonverbal information be effectively communicated?

This conceptualization exposes the struggle of Holocaust survivors in a post-Holocaust world and challenges the relevance of survivors' *telling* of their tales. Langer's work, *Holocaust Testimonies: The Ruins of Memory* (1991), reveals the difficulty of conveying horrendous memories of the Holocaust in a contemporary world. A duality arises for survivors: on the one hand lies the "deep," "anguished," "humiliated," "tainted," and "unheroic" memory, and on the other hand, the "common" memory that clings to a benign sense of self and the world (Langer, 1991). Throughout their narratives and life experiences, survivors constantly shift back and forth between these two clashing existences: that of the traumatized self and that of the conventional self. While the latter position intermittently "restores the self" (Langer, 1991, p. 6), this constructive attitude is repeatedly disrupted by the haunting memories of devastating and unintegrated past events.

The sense of fragmentation therefore extends well beyond the act of telling a story for the sake of informing others, and is characteristic of survivors' attempts to exist in a post-Holocaust world. As one victim wonders, "After that, what are you supposed to do? You know what I'm saying? You're not supposed to see this; it doesn't go with life. These people come back, and you realize, they're all broken, they're all broken. Broken. Broken" (Langer, 1991, p. 136). The wounded identity and the shattered sense of agency further feed into this conflicted self:

> Witnesses remain divided between the knowledge that during their ordeal they were deprived of moral agency by their circumstances and their present need to see themselves then and now as the responsible agents of their own destiny and of those around them (Langer, 1991, p. 185).

Quite sensibly, then, Spiegelman's *Maus I and II* (1986, 1991) are founded on the idea that engagement with the Holocaust requires fictionalization: only the most absurd, nonsensical representations can symbolize the realities of this atrocity (Reilly, 1986).

Tarantelli (2003) writes of "a complete surrender to the process of disarticulation" during massive trauma, which "extinguishes even the most basic level of mental activity, contact with sensation, producing psychic and then psychogenic death" (p. 915). Tarantelli (2003) employs the metaphor of an "explosion" to capture the instantaneous psychological reaction to an external disaster (p. 916). Once something is completely destroyed and no existence is left, there is an "utter absence," an inability to observe that something because nothing remains to serve that purpose (Tarantelli, 2003, p. 916). This deadening void—in Grotstein's (1990b) terms "primary meaninglessness"—eliminates all other experience, such that the potential for meaning does not occur and the ability to register stimuli is impossible (Tarantelli, 2003). According to Matte Blanco (1988), "when we face emotions ... of an intensity which is felt as tending towards the infinite ... the experience of emotion leads one to feel the possibility of catastrophe, of disintegration" (p. 140; quoted by Tarantelli, 2003, p. 919). Thus, "psychogenic death" indicates a disruption of psychic energy and activity, wiping out consciousness, continuity, and any integration of self.

The process of disarticulation is unavoidable during massive psychic trauma, and the explosion eliminates a mind that might have endured the experience (Tarantelli, 2003). Even contact with physical sensation, which engages the mind's most primitive faculties, is entirely suspended under these circumstances. The explosion is all-pervading, such that the experience cannot be registered consciously by something outside of it because there is nothing outside of it (Tarantelli, 2003). In other words, the external and internal become one and the same. There is no "I-ness" (Ogden, 2001, p. 156; Tarantelli, 2003) that is separate from existence on the verge of extinction.

For a survivor of individual or collective trauma, experience unfolds outside of language, resisting symbolization. In her book, *The Unsayable: The Hidden Language of Trauma*, Rogers (2006) writes:

> What is so terrible about trauma is not abuse itself, no matter the brutality of treatment, but the way terror marks the body and then becomes invisible and inarticulate. This was the case even when someone could tell a story or reconstruct a memory. There was always something unsayable, too (p. 44).

Rogers (2006) beautifully portrays her work with victims of sexual abuse, illustrating her attempts to engage the silent communication of girls who were unwilling and unable to articulate their suffering.

Furthermore, she highlights the unspoken, unspeakable "language" of trauma, often observed through symptoms that manifest themselves on the body—symptoms which contemporary, categorical diagnoses fail to fully comprehend (Rogers, 2006).

The sayable versus "unsayable" is at the root of Lacanian views on language, in that language maintains the power to influence our "thoughts, demands, and desires" (Fink, 1999, p. 86). Lacan emphasizes the concept of "alienation" in language: "We have the sense, at times, that we cannot find the words to say what we mean, and that the words available to us miss the point, saying too much or too little. Yet without those words, the very realm of meaning would not exist for us at all" (Fink, 1999, p. 86). Because words are used as symbols within the realm of speech, a gap inevitably exists between the experience of a word and the actual thing it corresponds to. While for the neurotic patient language has been at least partly "subjectified," the psychotic patient constantly feels that he is "possessed" by language from the outside, as the symbols have not been truly absorbed (Fink, 1999, p. 87). This experience is familiar to the survivor of trauma. As explained by Davoine and Gaudillière, meaning depends on being able to find a place within language, successfully forming connections between thoughts and maintaining a social link with one's past (2004).

Boulanger (2005) highlights the "state of mindlessness" that characterizes the wounded self during massive psychic trauma: thoughts and reality become indistinguishable, such that connections between thoughts can lead to "terrifying meanings and untenable anxiety" (p. 23). Referencing Bion, Ogden, and Tarantelli, Boulanger reminds us of the value of "destroying links" during trauma, as dissociation can be self-protective during a time of overwhelming affects (2005, p. 23). Once broken, however, words lose their significance and the "unreflective world" takes over (Boulanger, 2005, p. 24). Alongside this break in contemplation and self-reflection, the mind loses its capacity to serve as a witness of events, a relater of testimony, and a bearer of meaning—for oneself, and, eventually, for future generations.

Intergenerational Transmission of Trauma

According to Davoine and Gaudillière (2004), a child easily and "paradoxically" becomes "the subject of the other's suffering, especially when this other is unable to feel anything" (p. 49). Through projective identification, the child thereby unexpectedly and unwillingly reenacts such a "hell" (Davoine & Gaudillière, 2004, p. 50). How does a child undertake her parents' suffering? In what way is trauma transmitted intergenerationally across families and entire communities? Can future generations heal the pain of a past they did not personally endure? Fraiberg, Adelson, and Shapiro's (1975) *Ghosts in the Nursery* examines these questions within a familial context, where members are "possessed by their ghosts ... while no one has issued an invitation, the ghosts take up residence and conduct the rehearsal of the family tragedy from a tattered script" (p. 165). The unspeakable past traumas experienced by the parents of Fraiberg et al's (1975) case studies were left unnamed and unprocessed, such that their mourning was foreclosed. The unmourned suffering silently escalated in power and magnitude, seizing lead roles in their lives and those of their children. Previous unresolved losses were thus transmitted to future generations.

What exactly happens with this powerful unmourned suffering? If the parent cannot recall it and will not speak of it, how does the child *know* its existence? In 1972, Judith Kestenberg initiated use of the term "transposition" to explain the psychological process of intergenerational transmission of massive trauma that occurs unconsciously (Kaplan, 1996). Transposition captures the phenomenon by which a parent's past experiences impinge upon the child's present being. Transposition has two distinct characteristics: first, it speaks to the immense "amount of psychological space" that the parent's history demands, and second, it refers to "reversals of ordinary time" between parent and child that leaves them in opposite chronological positions, with the child exceedingly an element of the parent's past (Kaplan, 1996, p. 224). Thus, the parent's history takes over the child's daily existence, forcing the child to abandon her right to live as an individual. Referencing a poem by Celan (1958), Kaplan writes: "the child suckles 'the black milk' of trauma, relishes and absorbs it, cultivates its bitter taste as if it were vital sustenance—as if it were existence itself" (1996, p. 224). Similarly, as Davoine and Gaudillière explain,

> Many small children have not received the words that would have allowed them to keep at bay the disasters experienced by their parents and ancestors. Rather, like

the children of Oedipus or Medea, they were abandoned, sacrificed on the battlefront of hatred, wars, and civil wars; they were armed with rifles, real or psychic, to be sent as human shields to protect the adults who remain in the rear (2004, p. 75).

That is, the child absorbs her parent's unmourned trauma as her own, devoting a lifetime to working through the internal devastation of their shared past. Because a transposition can arise at any given moment, the survivor parent's Holocaust history looms over the child's daily lifestyle:

> Though the mother still cannot remember her starvation, she transmits the emotional experience of starvation through her preoccupation with buying, preparing, serving, and eating food. The father transmits the physical degradations he endured by being preoccupied with cleanliness and the elimination of feces (Kaplan, 1996, p. 226).

At times, specifics such as a child's age may serve to trigger the reenactment of history in present time; for example, Kaplan (1996) describes a hypothetical scenario of a girl who is "innocently competing with her mother for her father's attention" (p. 226), but happens to do so at the exact age that her mother was when she arrived in the Nazi camps. In Kaplan's example, the mother impulsively reacts by cutting off her daughter's ponytail, as this was done to her by Nazi soldiers. In response to this injury,

> The daughter develops an unconscious fantasy that she has been selected by her mother to perform a special mission. She, and she alone, can repair her mother's trauma by sacrificing her own desires and longings. She becomes obese, thus effectively concealing her beauty under layers of fat. Or she starves herself until her body is transformed into the body of a concentration camp survivor (Kaplan, 1996, p. 226-227).

A survivor parent who has lost family members in the Holocaust consciously wishes that her new, post-Holocaust family will replace the family members that were killed; the parent's unconscious wish, however, is that each new child or spouse will serve to reinstate the deceased (Kaplan, 1996, p. 234). For the child of a survivor, "the memorialization of the dead entails his resurrection ... The revenant knows she must fall into the interrupted biography of the dead one and complete it before she can carry on with her own life" (Kaplan, 1996, p. 234). In *Maus I and II*, Art Spiegelman (1986, 1991) skillfully captures the memorialization of the dead in telling the personal tale of his upbringing by a Holocaust survivor. Art, the post-Holocaust son, acts as a surrogate for his father's late son, Richieu, to such an extent that Art reports feeling throughout his life that he was in competition with a ghost. Indeed, in the final scene, his father calls Art "Richieu." Similarly, Vladek's new wife, Mala, endlessly falls short of reinstating his late wife, Anja. The enactments are rampant throughout both books: Art mutters that Vladek is a "murderer" for having destroyed his dead first wife's, Anja's, wartime diaries; Vladek yells at Art for making a mess with cigarette ash while talking about his experience of being yelled at by SS officers for making a mess in the camps; finally, Art's distance from Vladek sustains in him a sense of guilt for "mistreating" his father (Spiegelman, 1986, 1991).

Beyond all other vehicles, tormented silences serve as the main channel through which parents' unimaginable suffering can be witnessed by their children. Kaplan (1996) captures this immense authority of silence: "At first the child knows only that one or both parents are hiding some terrible secret. And the child wonders, 'What is the meaning of the absence, the silence? What is the truth that must never be spoken?'" (p. 219). Within this context, a survivor's child lives a "double life," in that present experiences bear the undercurrents of past events (p. 231). Everyday situations and mundane occurrences become instantaneously linked to both past and present:

> A loop of cord hanging from a lamp becomes a hangman's noose to the survivor. The child hears the parent gasp and sees the parent frantically rearranging the cord. A policeman approaches on the street; the mother has a panic attack. She clutches the child's hand tightly and stands as still as a statue. Nothing is said, but the child registers the mother's reactions and knows "something"

is wrong. The child comes to know that existence is pre-
carious (Kaplan, 1996, p. 231).

Kaplan (1996) suggests that a child who senses her parent's terror,
guilt, and shame" about something unfathomable is compelled to recreate such scenarios in order to concretize and ultimately cure the parent's trauma (p. 232). In a sense, Kaplan (1996) believes that it is only
the survivor's children who can bear witness to their parent's history.
Furthermore, a parent's secrecy can, in effect, drive the child's impulse
to piece together what happened to the parent. "The parent unwittingly
and against her conscious will positions her trauma within the child;
the child sets out to cure the parent and undo her trauma by placing
himself in the parent's position" (Kaplan, 1996, p. 224). Thus, it is the
child's role to cure the parent's suffering through a number of contradictory tasks: "On the one hand, she is fighting to reinstate visions of
love and goodness. On the other hand she represents the concretization
of hatred" (Kaplan, 1996, p. 234-235). As a result, "She is expected to
carry out and perform for her parent the unfinished work of mourning.
Yet she is also expected to avenge the parents for the crimes committed
against them by enacting the silenced hatred and rage" (Kaplan, 1996,
p. 235).

Clearly, such duties take a toll on the child. At best, the child does
not receive the necessary help in integrating her own experiences. At
worst, deficits in a parent's empathic attunement to the child result
in the child's experiences of overwhelming affect, impaired symbolization of experience, and a complete lack of meaningful integration
of her feelings (Charles, 2003). Insufficient emotional development is
passed along the generations, as affect remains a foreign and threatening experience. Furthermore, repeated exposure to shameful affects
may lead to suppression or denial of those experiences through external tools such as compulsive eating and substance abuse (Charles,
2003). For these reasons, traumatic memories and familial reactions to
history may only come to light over the course of several generations
(Auerhahn & Laub, 1998, p. 22). "The barrage of experiences that pa-
tently ignore the child's perceived needs or feelings generates a sense
of helplessness and meaninglessness before the hands of a cold and
unseeing destiny, as the child who is not loved loses himself"—thus,
the cycle is repeated (Charles, 2003, p. 72). Finally, because children's

self-concepts are shaped by the circumstances of their upbringing, Charles (2003) argues that enactments reveal one's "helplessness in the face of destiny" (p. 73).

Auerhahn and Laub (1998) discuss ten forms of knowing massive psychic trauma, organized along a continuum that reflects the degree of psychological distance from, integration of, and ownership over the traumatic experience. These range from "not knowing"; to the replacement of disturbing memories with factual but less traumatizing ones; to states in which events are reenacted in an "altered state of consciousness"; to "compartmentalized, undigested fragments" of experience with "no conscious meaning or relation to oneself"; to "transference phenomena"; to a partial manifestation of the trauma in one's narrative; to its appearance in "compelling, identity-defining, and pervasive life themes"; to the integration of the trauma as a "witnessed narrative"; to its development as a "metaphor"; and to "action knowledge," where experience becomes consciously significant in such a way that it influences future decisions (Auerhahn & Laub, 1998, p. 23). Auerhahn and Laub maintain that survivors know mostly through fragments or transference phenomena, that children of survivors often know through life themes, and that people not directly impacted know about trauma through experiencing dilemmas in its communication (1998, p. 23). That is, as Davoine and Gaudillière (2004, p. xxvii) explain, "*a-letheia*," the "very name of truth," is synonymous with "non-forgetting." Whether or not people choose to know the massive traumatic event is inconsequential; they will hold on to the attempted wipe-out in all its truth and suffering. Below, they powerfully capture the impossibility of erasing "facts and people" from memory:

> Our work brings into existence zones of nonexistence wiped out by a powerful blow that actually took place. But whatever the measures chosen for erasing facts and people from memory, the erasures, even when perfectly programmed, only set in motion a memory that does not forget and that is seeking to be inscribed. In Greek, non-forgetting is, literally, *a-letheia*: this is the very name of truth, at stake in this specific memory as in the scientific approach. Hence we do not have to choose between the minute detail and the global fact. Sometimes a

fit of madness tells us more than all the news dispatches about the leftover facts that have no right to existence (Davoine & Gaudillière, 2004, p. xxvii).

Jewish Americans and the Holocaust

The development of a national identity is based on transmission of collective memory. Yet what is collective memory? How do subsequent generations continue to incorporate accounts of other people's past experiences into the narratives they construct as memory? In Maurice Halbwachs' (1992) work on this subject, he discusses how all memory is conceived within a social context. While identifications vary between groups, historical memory is adjusted and transmitted within groups in order to advance the present needs and desires of its members (Halbwachs, 1992). That is, historical memories are shaped by a social framework that is relevant to the present time. For example, Halbwachs (1992) elucidates that the story of Massada, based on a battle between the Roman army and Jewish revolutionaries in 73 A.D., did not receive much attention or significance in Jewish history for almost 2,000 years. However, it gained value for Palestinian Jews in the 1920's, as it became a key symbol of military heroism and unwavering loyalty, and a courageous declaration of "resistance and resilience" (Coser, 1992, p. 33). In this way, Halbwachs emphasizes the selective assimilation of historical memories into present identities (1992).

In his article entitled, "The American National Narrative of the Holocaust: There Isn't Any," Novick (2003) discusses the absence of an American national statement about the Holocaust. Due to both geographical and psychological distance from events overseas, Novick (2003) suggests that America was not affected by the atrocity of the Holocaust in the same way as countries in Europe and Israel. Considering the devastation and destruction surrounding the Holocaust in Europe, he claims few non-Americans can truly understand its limited influence in America (Novick, 2003, p. 29). The American national narrative of World War II, he argues, relates to the widely recognized image of American soldiers triumphantly raising the flag on Iwo Jima, the shocking attack on Pearl Harbor, or the "mushroom cloud" over Hiroshima (2003, p. 29-30). Furthermore, while Europe witnessed an "absence which is a presence" following the extermination of most of its Jews, Americans experienced a mounting Jewish presence in society (Novick, 2003, p. 30). Thus, despite the fact that a growing number of states mandate teaching about the Holocaust in public schools and Holocaust museums are spreading nationwide, Novick (2003) concludes that the Holocaust is not a part of the collective national narrative.

Regarding an "American *Jewish* narrative" (Novick, 2003, p. 31), however, the development of the Holocaust as an integral part of its collective identity followed a similar pattern as that of its Israeli counterpart. Having considerably restricted the Holocaust from their awareness during the 1940s and 1950s, Americans underwent a transformation in subsequent decades which highlighted this collective trauma (Cole, 2002). Two reasons have been suggested for this change: first, the 1973 Yom Kippur War reminded Americans of Israel's vulnerability, and second, the Holocaust served as a symbol of unity, a "common denominator" for American Jews (Novick, 1999, p. 7). Novick (1999) further suggests that Americans' marginalization of the Holocaust until this time was less about the survivors' inhibition of memory than about Jewish-American leaders' attempts at assimilation. Indeed, the survivors' silence and the societal suppression of perceived weakness in favor of attempted "normalcy" were identical to that of the young Israel.

Cole's (2002) question of "use versus abuse" of Holocaust history in American society traces the entrance of the Holocaust into popular culture, specifically through the movie *Schindler's List* (p. 129). He discusses the terms "exceptionalist" and "constructivist," first proposed by Mintz (2001) to distinguish between two divergent approaches in depicting the Holocaust (Cole, 2002, p. 130). The "exceptionalist" voice in Holocaust studies views the Holocaust as a defining moment in history that requires a staunch and blunt telling of events (Cole, 2002). The "constructivist" suggests that even an event as extraordinary as the Holocaust must be understood through pre-existing categories that capture history in a manner appropriate for a specific audience (Cole, 2002). These opposing methods summarize an ongoing controversy regarding how to fairly discuss and depict the Holocaust in modern-day society. Indeed, we continue to grapple with the incomprehensible.

Doneson (1996) clearly struggles with the constructivist approach:

> Therefore, in American fiction films and films for television that deal with the Holocaust, it is necessary to

revert to American symbols and language in order to convey a comprehensible, Americanized perception of the (European) Holocaust. Among the identifying characteristics common to American commercial film are the much maligned soap opera format and the happy, upbeat ending. Are these traits suitable for dramatization of the Holocaust, or do they tend to trivialize the attempted genocide of European Jewry? (p. 71).

As Doneson (1996) herself asserts, writers such as Lawrence Langer find this "upbeat" representation to be in stark contrast to the "reality of doom" surrounding the Holocaust (p. 71). Yet, regardless of this inconsistency, any attempt to grasp the unknowable will inevitably fail to capture the actual event. Doneson (1996) asks, "Is it necessary to ready oneself for sadness in preparation for a visit to Auschwitz? Should one take snapshots of the gas chambers and crematoria? Is this a trivialization?" (p. 72). She concludes that "It is indeed a daily occurrence, though one whose purpose, presumably, is meant to be noble—an attempt to fathom the nightmare of Auschwitz" (Doneson, 1996, p. 72). Even Claude Lanzmann's *Shoah*, which attempts to "penetrate forbidden territory," must do so within the confines of media: "More than explaining history, Lanzmann wants to grasp it, to live it, to enter into it. But he cannot. And how many others are even willing to try?" That is, memories cannot capture the actual truth, and commemorations cannot depict historical events as they were (Doneson, 1996, p. 76). Perhaps the most we can hope for is a continued identification with Holocaust memories, an ongoing meeting between ourselves and our history.

Shoshana Felman (Felman & Laub, 1992) captures Lanzmann's position as the "creator" of *Shoah*, addressing his "triple role as the narrator of the film ... as the interviewer of the witnesses ... and as the inquirer" of the testimonies (p. 216). While Lanzmann serves as the sole continuous voice throughout the movie, Felman describes the ways in which he succeeds in taking himself entirely out of it by speaking solely what he hears and refraining from communicating his own perspective (Felman & Laub, 1992). This "silent" narration allows the accounts to be told by others, and indeed the stories "speak for themselves" (Felman & Laub, 1992, p. 218). In a sense, the absence of a storyteller creates space for bystanders of the atrocities to share their personal anecdotes.

At the same time, Felman (1992) does not intend to say that the interviewer remains silent or separates himself from the dialogue. Instead, Lanzmann engulfs himself in concrete, specific questions, entirely reversing the barrier of silence surrounding the enormity of the Holocaust through "small steps," or "concrete particulars" (Felman & Laub, 1992, p. 219). Yet, most striking about Felman's description of the narrator's role is his strength as an "echo"; while many witnesses worked to evade, reject, or simply ignore Lanzmann's questions, "the narrator is precisely there to insure that the question, in its turn, will go on" ((Felman & Laub, 1992, p. 221). That is, Lanzmann serves as an eyewitness to the question he posed and the frequent disconnect between the inquiry and the response (Felman & Laub, 1992, p. 221).

Felman writes, it "is the story of the liberation of the testimony through its desacralization; the story of the decanonization of the Holocaust for the sake of its previously impossible historicization" (Felman & Laub, 1992, p. 219). As the struggle for the "liberation of the testimony" continues, the lives of second, third, and fourth generations of survivors unfold in a world distinct from, yet forever linked to, the Holocaust. Neusner's (1973) belief that the second generation of Holocaust survivors exists in a more "complicated" world than the survivors themselves is debatable, but driven precisely by the awareness of the Holocaust's imprint and the way it has been inextricably woven into Jewish identity. Neusner writes of the second generation:

> They know about events, but have not experienced them. And what they know they perceive through their experience of a very different world. The story that gives meaning and imparts transcendence to the everyday experiences of being Jewish simply does not correspond to the reality of the generations born since 1945 (Neusner, 1973, p. 296).

The Incorporation of the Holocaust in Israeli Identity

Since the emergence of the State of Israel, the place of Holocaust memories in its national narrative has been controversial and inconsistent. Arad (2003) recognizes the Holocaust as "a double-edged taboo; often in juxtaposition with one another, it was regarded on the one hand as 'uncanny' and 'dangerous,' and on the other hand as 'sacred' and 'conse-crated'" (p. 5) Bar-On (1995) describes an atmosphere in 1950's Israel in which Holocaust emotions were unwarranted and rebuffed. Indeed, the catastrophe of the Holocaust seemed to clash with the bold identity of the *Sabras*² and the emerging Zionistic identity based on independence, self-sufficiency, and strength: "It was believed that beginning anew in a sovereign Jewish state would result in a 'normalized' existence for the Jews, provided this catastrophic history, as epitomized by the *Shoah*, would be plowed under" (Arad, 2003, p. 7). Silence regarding past trauma was therefore promoted, out of fear that any recognition of past struggle would undermine the current quest for a "normal" existence. It was perhaps unsurprising that survivors—plagued by their traumatic experiences and filled with guilt that they survived while others did not—adhered to the notion of silence as a solution (Arad, 2003). Thus, the Holocaust was restricted from becoming part of the Israelis' modern collective consciousness. As survivor and writer Aharon Appelfeld is quoted as saying:

> The first years in Israel were years of repression and denial, of constructing a personality with no trace of what you went through and who you were ... The inner world was suppressed, as if it did not exist; it shrunk and sunk into deep sleep ... Whoever survived and came here brought with him much silence. It was tacitly accepted not to speak about certain matters and not to touch certain wounds (Arad, 2003, p. 7).

Langer (1991) places the Israeli response within a larger scope, suggesting that Westerners struggle to understand situations which are somehow outside of man's control.

> The concept of "you cannot do nothing" is so alien to the self-reliant Western mind (dominated by the idea of the individual as *agent* of his fate) that its centrality, its *blameless* centrality to the camp experience continues to leave one morally disoriented. The very principle of

---

2   Native-born Israelis.

blameless inaction by former victims is foreign to the
ethical premises of our culture, where we sometimes
confuse such inaction with cowardice, self-indulgence,
or indifference (Langer, 1991, p. 85).

Unfortunately, the societal disavowal of the realities of the Holocaust
was a powerful trend. In a 1952 article entitled "Israeli Culture and
Society," Samuel Koenig describes the "patterns of life" among the Jewish community of Palestine; the trends he considers "most important"
include "socialism, the glorification of the laborer and labor, pioneerism
(*halutziut*), Westernism, secularism, and democracy" (Koenig, 1952,
p. 160). No mention is made of the Holocaust, and survivors remain
altogether unidentified within the larger category of "immigrants."
Koenig does, however, comment that many of these immigrants arrived
"psychically scarred and physically weakened," but only as indication
that the immigrants "show little, if any, inclination or ability to become
pioneers, to go on the land, or to engage in other difficult but necessary
tasks" (Koenig, 1952, p. 165). Such an obvious disregard of Holocaust
experience and survival, while shocking to read today, was unremarkable
and, in fact, encouraged at the time. It was not until the circumstantial
arrival of war criminal Adolf Eichmann in Israel in 1961-1962, the 1967
Six-Day War, and the 1973 Yom Kippur War, that Israelis began to integrate the realities of their recent past.

Numerous changes occurred in Israel between the 1940s and 1970s,
and survivors' experiences were slowly but increasingly tolerated. Politi-
cally, the Eichmann trial was an unplanned eye-opener for Israeli society:
as a public trial in which survivors were asked to testify, opportunity
was created for Israeli citizens to listen to horrifying and heartbreaking
life stories for the first time (Arad, 2003). Immediately, the Holocaust
was transformed from a message endorsing "Zionist" philosophy to a
trauma of real individuals (Arad, 2003, p. 12). The younger generation
was particularly moved by these accounts and began to identify with
survivors' past suffering (Arad, 2003, p. 12). As Tom Segev writes in
his comprehensive book, *The Seventh Million* (1991), "The trial of Adolf Eichmann served as therapy for the nation, starting a process of
identification with the tragedy of the victims and survivors, a process
that continues to this day" (p. 11). Furthermore, accompanying the
identification with Holocaust survivors was the internalization of what

Arad (2003) calls "holocaustal anxiety" and Solomon (1993) labels "ex-istential anxiety"—Israelis' belief that the threat of extermination was real at any moment of vulnerability. During the 1967 Six-Day War, this sentiment established a widespread terror that losing the war might mean the end of the Jewish people. Victory represented defeat of both current and past enemies. Finally, the impact of the 1973 Yom Kippur War further consolidated the integration of past and present: Israelis experienced first-hand what it was like to be caught off guard, to feel defenseless and out of control, to undergo extensive loss (Arad, 2003, p. 16). The seemingly stark contrast between Holocaust survivors and non-survivors was dimmed.

Bar-Tal (2001) further discusses the crucial role of fear in Israeli society, and identifies fear as easily overriding hope because it occurs "automatically" and "unconsciously," and is fueled by past experiences (p. 605). Bar-Tal writes about the current Middle Eastern conflict when he says, "The society provides the contexts, information, models, em-phases, and instructions that influence the emotions of its members" (Bar-Tal, 2001, p. 605). However, this social basis of emotion is also descriptive of the influence of fear on Israel's early rejection of and identification with Holocaust survivors. In a dramatic attempt to start "new" and be "normal," *Sabras* struggled to bridge the gap between a past full of fear, shame, and humiliation, and a present filled with hope, pride, and strength. The fragile identity of the young nation was at risk of further fragmentation by the victims. As Langer (1991) writes of Holocaust victims,

> Self-esteem is crucial to the evolution of heroic memory; the narratives in these testimonies reflect a partially traumatized or maimed self-esteem, lingering like a non-fatal disease without cure. Heroic memory is vir-tually unavailable to such witnesses, because for them remembering is invariably associated with a jumbled terminology and morality that confuse staying alive with the intrepid will to survival (p. 176).

Davoine and Gaudillière (2004) reaffirm the human need for control when they write, "it is better to assume that one is oneself the cause of an inexplicable event, or to unload it onto the other, than to confront an event without a reason." (p. 72). Fear of the unknown is the most crippling of all.

With the negative impacts of fear aside, Bar-Tal (2001) elucidates a number of positive consequences of fear in stressful situations: it encourages groups to prepare for danger, it calls attention to cues that suggest impending threat, it enhances unity among group members, and it pushes people to act in support of the group (p. 609). As Holocaust narratives were incorporated into Israelis' identities, and the contagion of fear evolved out of political and historical tumult, group identity simultaneously flourished. Today, the communication and transmission of these fears can be pinpointed in Israeli media, art, literature, and politics. As Segev writes,

> The Seventh Million concerns the ways in which the bitter events of the past continue to shape the life of a nation. Just as the Holocaust imposed a posthumous collective identity on its six million victims, so too it formed the collective identity of this new country—not just for the survivors who came after the war but for all Israelis, then and now. This is why I have called them the seventh million (1991, p. 11).

Combat and Loss, Solidarity and Pride

Parallel to the collective sense of fear, the continuous political chaos, and the quest for a common narrative, Israeli pride evolved. Combat in and of itself served to enhance Israelis' solidarity by uniting their efforts around a mutual cause: the survival of the State of Israel. Even amongst authors who focus on the difficulty of inscribing one's traumatic past within the present, combat is recognized as a powerful source of integration: "Combat evokes in those who are fighting side by side a passion for taking care of the other physically and psychically, equivalent to the earliest and deepest family relationships ... For the bond of combat erases the distinction between oneself and the other" (Davoine & Gaudillière, 2004, p. 154-155). In Israel, the placement of military cemeteries inside and alongside civil cemeteries symbolizes the rallying around a "military community" (Weiss, 1997, p. 92) and the creation of a familial atmosphere. Soldiers continue to be viewed as the "silver platter" which makes Israelis' lives possible, and thus receive the highest form of respect and appreciation (Solomon, 1993, p. 251).

From this standpoint, it is unimportant whether "oneself" and "other" have faced similar or divergent life experiences, so long as they work together towards a current, common goal. Amongst Holocaust survivors as well, active involvement in a mutual cause seems to have the potential for additional reparatory effects in terms of the reestablishment of agency and the mending of a wounded identity. For example, in the case of "Nathan A.," "Still a teenager at the end of the war, he made his way to Israel, fought in its many wars, was wounded, but clearly reclaimed some of his lost dignity by actively participating in a common effort in behalf of Jewish freedom" (Langer, 1991, p. 137). On the other hand, as revealed in the case of "Alex H.," the effect of combat is illusory in that it establishes "a paradox of his post-Holocaust life: he is unhappy that this should have made him happy. There is, he now realizes, no vindication, no connection, no compensation for the state to which circumstances reduced him during those years" (Langer, 1991, p. 145). In other words, present combat cannot undo past trauma, but might assist to some extent in the renewal of one's agency and the reestablishment of oneself as a "dignified," "active" human being (Langer, 1991).

In a study examining the development of identity via projective drawings of Palestinian and Israeli Arab children in the West Bank and Gaza, Elbedour, Bastien, and Center (1997) differentiate between three levels of identity: 1) "individualized/personal identity" (where the self is "I"-centered), 2) "cultural identity" (where the self is characterized by the collective "we"), and 3) "conflict/political identity" (where the self is integrated along themes of "us-them") (p. 221). Results revealed that "the children raised in the greatest conflict identify most with the conflict while the children raised in relative peace are more likely to depict an individuated personal identity" (Elbedour et al, 1997, p. 225). Although this study did not include any Jewish-Israeli children, this finding is relevant in terms of collective identity and trauma, as it speaks to the tangled relationship between conflicts, fears, and solidarity. Furthermore, in a country where group cohesion provides the individual with a greater sense of pride, Israel faces the challenge of concurrently fostering individual tasks and needs. Reminiscent of Alex H.'s misconception that fighting for a common cause might undo his past circumstances (Langer, 1991), combat alone cannot do the work of "working through" and the necessary integration of past and present.

Beyond the act of combat, "bereavement and commemoration" of those killed in war is a key promoter of national solidarity (Weiss, 1997, p. 92). Weiss (1997) identifies a sort of "cult of the fallen" in Israeli society, where death is idealized as a heroic sacrifice (p. 91). Weiss points out that Israel's Remembrance Day—the memorial day for soldiers killed in combat—takes place exactly seven days following Holocaust Memorial Day and one day prior to Israel's Independence Day; thus, she elucidates a national narrative that leads "from destruction (holocaust) via sacrifice (the fallen) to salvation (independence)" (Weiss, 1997, p. 92). Furthermore, as the implementation of Remembrance Day proceedings targets the entire population, "it transforms the whole nation into one bereaved family" (Weiss, 1997, p. 93). The sense of family and communal mourning is intensely unifying, and reflects a community sitting Shiva together on a national level. Coser (1992), as well, argued that people do not remember historical events directly, but rather "history can only be stimulated in indirect ways through reading or listening or in commemoration and festive occasions when people gather together to remember in common the deeds and accomplishments of long-departed members of the group" (p. 24).

Zahava Solomon, who served in the Israeli Defense Forces as head of the Research Branch in the Medical Corps for over a decade, discusses the concept of "reactivation" of trauma that occurs through repeated wars (1993, p. 189). In her analyses on combat stress reaction (CSR), formerly known as shell shock, Solomon found that one CSR reaction frequently signifies impending CSR reactions in future wars. That is, current trauma does not "heal" past trauma; rather, it "deepens" it (Solomon, 1993, p. 209, quoting Berman, 1985). This effect extends to the second generation of Holocaust survivors, although they did not personally witness the Holocaust. In a three-year longitudinal study, Solomon (1993) found that "the passage of time did not have the same healing effect on the PTSD of the second generation as on that of other soldiers" (p. 232); instead, the second generation maintained a heightened sensitivity to stress and to combat's damaging consequences (p. 233). More generally, offspring of survivors have been found to react with high levels of anxiety to various situations, displaying "high narcissistic vulnerability, survival guilt, and conflicts over the expression of aggression" (Solomon, 1993, p. 229). Indeed, the aftereffects of the Holocaust continue to manifest themselves on both personal and societal levels.

Segev quotes the editor in chief of *Maariv*[3] as asking, "'What will I say to my loved ones, my burned ones, my murdered ones when they come to me at night, and as they continue to come forever?'" (1991, p. 206). As his chapters trace history, beginning with "Hitler," "Holocaust," "Israel," and "Restitution: How Much Will We Get for Grandma and Grandpa?" Segev (1991) illuminates the inseparable connection of past, present, and future, and concludes his book with chapters entitled "Growing Up: From War to War" and "Memory: The Struggle to Shape the Past." He writes, "Israelis are obsessed with history. They are the offspring of a nation, a religion, and a culture that has dismissed the present and left the future in the hands of faith and fate. The past thus becomes an object of worship" (Segev, 1991, p. 513). This "obsession," he explains, remains forever linked to Israel's ongoing "need to justify—to the rest of the world, and to itself—its very right to exist" (p. 514). The Holocaust, Israel, and Jewish identity continuously blend in the collective narrative of Jews worldwide. This study therefore aims to examine the transmission of Holocaust trauma and memories amongst the third generation of survivors, in the hope that the present will no longer be "dismissed."

The Third Generation of the Holocaust

Over the past two decades, researchers and clinicians alike have grown curious about the impact of the Holocaust on the lives of its third generation descendants. Nevertheless, the literature regarding grandchildren of survivors remains sparse, and repeatedly points to "contradictory" hypotheses and conclusions yielded by pertinent studies in the field. While many inquiries trace the long-sensed and increasingly recognized intergenerational transmission of Holocaust trauma and memory (Felsen, 1998; Rubenstein, Cutter, & Templer, 1989-1990), others underscore survivors' and their offspring's "resilience in the face of adversity" (Sigal, 1998, p. 582). Although "resilience" rightfully honors the struggle and endurance of survivors and their descendants in a post-Holocaust world, it is often interpreted as an absence of Holocaust themes, sensitivities and reverberations in their day-to-day lives. For example, a number of

---

3   A popular daily newspaper published in Israel.

researchers suggest that the transgenerational transmission of trauma has altogether ceased by the third generation (Bachar, Cale, Eisenberg, & Dasberg, 1994). Such conclusions invite questions about the concept of intergenerational trauma and the apparent efforts to either prove or refute its existence; the hunt for psychopathology versus the pursuit of a broader psychodynamic understanding of the third generation experience; and the implications of tracing "trauma trails" (Atkinson, 2002) two generations following such horrors.

Inconsistent findings have been accounted for by differences in sample, procedure, measures, and other methodological details. In an attempt to "resolve the divergence of the clinical and non-clinical findings on intergenerational transmission of trauma, between qualitative and quantitative approaches, and between methodologically more robust versus less robust studies," Sagi-Schwartz, van IJzendoorn, and Bakermans-Kranenburg (2008, p. 106) conducted a meta-analysis of research on the third generation. However, despite their defined objective, Sagi-Schwartz et al (2008) excluded all qualitative publications from their investigation, noting that such studies "do not fit into a meta-analysis paradigm" (p. 111). Furthermore, they acknowledged their attempts to retain a more "homogenous" group by including only non-clinical samples, thereby allowing their findings to be more "robust" (Sagi-Schwartz et al, 2008, p. 111). Thus, their conclusion that "participants showed no evidence for tertiary traumatization in Holocaust survivor families" must once again be understood within the margins of their research questions and criterion (Sagi-Schwartz et al, 2008, p. 105). Sagi-Schwartz et al (2008) recognize at the start of their paper that "the field still seems to beg for further systematic examination of third generation effects..." (p. 107); indeed, with the completion of their work, this yearning persists.

Alongside others, Bar-On (2008) addresses the deductions of quantitative analyses such as those described above, emphasizing the ways in which these studies "undermine what voices within the second and third generations tell us, and the echoes these stories have within us" (p. ix). He elucidates the problem with the notion of "methodologically more robust" studies (Sagi-Schwartz et al, 2008, p. 106), impelling us to question whether or not such models exist; for example, Bar-On (2008) questions the concept of "control groups," often comprised of "families of Jewish European descent who did not live under Nazi occupation," as a contrast to experimental groups of Holocaust survivors and their offspring (p. xi). Specifically, he emphasizes that members of "control groups" may have fled from Nazi-controlled territories, lost family members and friends in the Holocaust, and themselves wrestled with a complex experience of bereavement:

> So, they go through processes of mourning, of silencing these losses, as they "have no right to feel effected" in the eyes of the survivors, or in their own eyes, and in my view therefore cannot be counted as a control group in any deeper psychological meaning (Bar-On, 2008, p. xi).

Bar-On further addresses the refutation of intergenerational trauma, linking this impulse to the shame and silence that surrounded one's identity as a Holocaust survivor during the emergence of the State of Israel (2008, p. x). That is, the persistence of this historically-rooted dynamic may motivate individuals to deny the ongoing impact of the Holocaust in an attempt to assimilate with the "normal" lifestyle and mentality of the collective consciousness surrounding them. In addition, Bar-On (2008) suggests that the disavowal of intergenerational trauma transmission may reflect researchers' apprehension about imposing an additional, multi-generational burden or responsibility on survivors. He states of these researchers:

> They may have reacted to the assumption that relational aftereffects can be seen as some kind of an accusation toward the survivors who suffered so much, who were stigmatized enough, that they should not be burdened with any unnecessary additional stigma. This approach puts the survivors' assumed needs to be protected above those of their children and grandchildren (Bar-On, 2008, p. x).

Yet, what is the value of "protecting" survivors from recognizing the long-lasting impact of their traumatic experiences? Litvak-Hirsch and Bar-On (2006) depict grandchildren's increased opportunity to achieve "psychological freedom," particularly through their unique ability to address "undiscussable" themes within their families (p. 475). In doing so, these grandchildren are able to initiate new narrative possibilities amongst family members, breaking down the "double wall" of silence (Bar-On, 1995, p. 20) created by survivors and their children. Furthermore, the needs of the third generation are highlighted in *Echoes of the Trauma*, which explores the second generation's upbringing by survivor parents as well as survivors' children's experience of parenting their own adolescent children (Wiseman & Barber, 2008). While Wiseman and Barber (2008) emphasize the ways in which the second generation's "quest to heal the echoes of the parental past is a powerful motivator for generational change," they simultaneously recognize that amending one's "intergenerational transmission of problematic parenting" is not a simple pursuit (p. 227). They describe a conflictual scenario between a second generation parent and her third generation adolescent child, noting: "In some cases the communication was portrayed as more open through their parents' eyes than through the adolescent's eyes, perhaps representing the gap between the parents' explicit attitudes and actual behavior" (Wiseman & Barber, 2008, p. 226).

Regardless of awareness or intent, therefore, residues of the Holocaust persist. Scharf (2007) examined whether grandchildren of Holocaust survivors differed from a comparison group during the transition period in which adolescent males depart home to enter a three year compulsory military service in the Israel Defense Force (IDF). Findings revealed that boys whose parents were both offspring of survivors reported a less positive sense of self and perceived their parents as "less accepting and less encouraging independence" (Scharf, 2003, p. 603). In addition, a measure given to their peers indicated that sons of two second generation parents showed "inferior emotional, instrumental, and social functioning" (Scharf, 2007, p. 617-618). Scharf concluded: "It is recommended that researchers and clinicians develop awareness of the possible traces of trauma in the second and the third generation despite their sound functioning in their daily lives" (2007, p. 603).

As a follow up to Scharf's (2007) study, Berant and Hever (in press) focused on granddaughters of the Holocaust from their maternal side. Berant and Hever (in press) explored three non-clinical samples of young women facing distinct stages of separation-individuation: the draft to the IDF and the accompanying separation from their families, the transition to first-time motherhood, and the group voyage to concentration camps in Poland. Of particular significance were their discrepant findings based on the type of measure utilized; that is, when relying on self-report measures, Berant and Hever (in press) discovered that granddaughters of survivors did not endorse struggling more than their counterparts during these life changes. However, in an attempt to capture internal mental representations by asking granddaughters to describe their mothers in writing, for example, they found that women at all three stages showed "less positive maternal representations than the control group"; specifically, these women revealed "more ambivalence" towards their mothers, who "were perceived as less benevolent and less ambitious" (Berant & Hever, in press, p. 17). In reflecting on the inconsistencies in their own findings, Berant and Hever note, "...at a more subtle level, one can trace the distant influences of their grandparents that have led to specific dynamics among the third generation and between daughters and mothers" (in press, p. 26). Imparted in their study is the awareness that "Perhaps open, exploratory questions about these issues would be useful here" (Berant & Hever, in press, p. 22).

From a perspective of health, Chaitin (2003) investigated how families contend with and work through their history by exploring the coping styles amongst two or three generations of 20 families of Holocaust survivors. Utilizing and advancing Danieli's (1988) classification of post-war adaptation, Chaitin (2003) identified six distinct coping patterns exhibited by her participants, categorizing them as: "victim families," "fighter families," "those who made it," "numb families," "life goes on," and "split families" (p. 305). Chaitin's (2003) life-story interviews revealed that coping styles, as well, are transmitted to and incorporated by family members across generations. In the realm of psychopathology, Fossion, Rejas, Servais, Pelc, and Hirsch (2003) identified a direct relationship between the trauma experienced by survivors and the psychiatric symptoms developed by their grandchildren two generations later. Specifically, they described the thwarting of the developmental process in an atmosphere of silence, as the grandchildren they encountered in their clinical work lacked a historical root that might provide context for their parents' way of being: "Due to the impossibility of referring to past experience, these families were continually confronted with new situations at each stage of life – particularly when facing issues of separation and independence, thus generating an insurmountable crisis" (Fossion et al, 2003, p. 523).

In the best case scenario, grandchildren of survivors are able to rec-

ognize the intergenerational patterns at play, utilizing words to metabo-
lize their emotional experiences, and integrating their knowledge of
historical traumas with present manifestations of past suffering. When
this does not occur, however, traumas are "paradoxically re-created" generation after generation, with or without conscious awareness (Talby-
Abarbanel, 2011, p. 230). In her case presentation of a third generation
survivor named "Ann," Talby-Abarbanel (2011) captures the incessant
enactments that occur in the face of unspoken and unspeakable grief
and loss. Ann is first described as wrestling with "un-integrated" parts
of herself without a framework for the origin of such disintegration
(Talby-Abarbanel, 2011, p. 219). While confronting her mother about
their tormented relationship, Ann learns of her Holocaust history for the
very first time; she is subsequently able to comprehend the root of her
past obsession with Holocaust books and films, her lifelong creations of
artwork centered on themes of relocation and isolation, and her vivid,
complex dreams of "separateness" and "attachment" (Talby-Abarbanel,
2011, p. 233). Talby-Abarbanel writes:

> Ann added that by avoiding the trauma and by refrain-
> ing from working it through, they [her parents] para-
> doxically re-created the same atmosphere in their own
> family, from which she now needed to distance herself.
> Indigestible non-verbal terror, unbearable pain, and
> apocalyptic fantasies were always in the air (2011, p.
> 230).

Having a place to explore and symbolize their experience (whether
through psychotherapy or through open-ended interviews such as those
conducted in this study) therefore allows third generation survivors to
promote connection and growth within their families, to discover words
that might heal the torment of unexpressed emotions and dynamics,
and to honor their history while re-working its previously debilitating
impact on generation after generation.

Bar-On (2008) relays a personal experience with a student in one of
his workshops, who claimed disbelief about the concept of a "second
generation" of the Holocaust despite her technically belonging within
this group (p. x). Bar-On (2008) recalls the impassioned responses of
this woman's peers, who understandably felt their own experiences con-

tested by her bold, dismissive statement. The disagreements within the field of third generation Holocaust research elicit reactions of parallel intensity, highlighting the personal investment and far-reaching implication of these studies to the individuals conducting them. Bar-On writes: "The ambivalence of researchers in this domain can be understood, as we study a complex phenomenon many years after the original occurrences, effected by several simultaneous processes" (2011, p. xi). Yet, as the grandchildren of survivors are continually motivated to confront their parents' and grandparents' experiences, to articulate multifaceted narratives, and to pursue an intergenerational perspective at once removed from and connected to the Holocaust, it has become increasingly imperative for their traumas to be acknowledged and their voices to be heard.

CHAPTER 2: RESEARCH APPROACH

My life story extends beyond the conscious and the verbal. It has always entailed both the things I said and those that I would not, or could not, articulate. Alongside my family, I reacted to my history for years—whether through unwarranted fear, displaced paranoia, or exaggerated experiences of loss—but struggled to describe the entry of the past in my present life. As I initiated this work, I reflected on the silent communications, unspoken truths, and implicit attitudes that accompany my family identity and continually influence its dynamics. A literature review then provided the long-awaited and desired words to describe the capacities and failures of language in depicting traumatic experience. Upon inviting other third generation survivors to engage in the present interviews, I wondered how spoken and unspoken elements of their accounts, as well, might provide a glimpse into history. Thus, as this "research" got underway and "hypotheses" were set in place, I anticipated that powerful Holocaust themes, emotions, and enactments would direct the course of these interviews. The "data," I assumed, would (for lack of a better term) "speak" for itself.

Ten Jewish women between the ages of 21 and 31 were interviewed in this work; seven identified as "American" and three identified as "half-Israeli, half-American." Clearly in search of mutuality and commonality, I chose to focus solely on women in order to more comprehensively explore the granddaughters' experiences. Participants were recruited from universities and synagogues on the East Coast[1] by word of mouth, having been informed that the interviews would explore the ways in which historical events may have impacted their families and intergenerational developments may relate to their personal identities. Dozens of women promptly and enthusiastically responded to this introductory description of the interviews. The first ten women to express interest and availability were then scheduled for a meeting. A number of the participants later relayed their interview experience to friends, furthering the interest in this work and leading others to contact me in hopes of arranging an

---

1 All names and locations have been changed to maintain the confidentiality of the participants.

interview. Finally, a couple of participants contacted me following our meeting to express their appreciation for the experience and to request a copy of their interview transcript. The urge to share their narratives and reflect on their histories seemed profound, and I was left feeling that these encounters provided a timely, highly desired outlet that many had previously lacked.

Each interview was conducted by me and consisted of one 60- to 120-minute session, depending on the scope of the narrative. All interviews began with my open-ended statement, "Tell me about yourself," as was done by Ewing (2004) in her studies. The conversations then took the form of psychoanalytic interviews, in which I remained as minimalist as possible in my interventions and used my free associations in reaction to the interviewee. Most women spoke fluently and eagerly throughout the interview; however, if a participant remained relatively unresponsive or limited in the depth of her narrative, I posed specific questions in order to stimulate the conversation, keeping the following questions in mind: Who is this person? How does she identify herself? What does she know about her family history? What does she not know and why? Where does she come from? How does that affect her? What is her role within her family? How do the limitations of her knowledge impact her experience? How might she know more? This approach was selected in order to encourage participants to speak openly and freely about their Holocaust history, and to allow me to respond to the content and mood of their stories as well as to my own reactions to the narratives.

Topics of interest that arose in these interviews included the following: In what ways has the Holocaust affected their feminine identities? What are some of their feelings and fantasies related to having a family and being a mother? How do they plan to raise their children similarly to or differently from the ways they were raised? Do they have any recurring dreams or recent nightmares that they recall? Do they have a tendency to avoid talking about certain topics or specific situations? Do they experience any difficulties sleeping or concentrating? How much of an authoritarian figure was present in their family growing up? How much were they permitted to know about their family history? How much were they allowed to feel? Do they report any experiences of fear, helplessness, guilt, shame, humiliation, or expectation of death? Are they frequently agitated, anxious, or angry? While many of these questions were answered throughout the course of the interviews, I posed them directly when I felt there was more to explore on any given topic. At times, my direct questioning was met with hesitation, rejection, or a discreet evasion of the subject matter at hand; in this way, the interviews exposed how the Holocaust has been handled by members of the third generation by tapping into the deep unconscious structures of participants through their use of language, or lack thereof.

Following each interview, I kept a log of my own thoughts, associations, and reactions to the participants' narratives, as well as any feelings or observations that arose during and after the interview. This log served to both keep track of the ideas that were developed throughout the course of the interviews and to engage with my unconscious. The interviews thus became a dynamic event—a process—that explored features of both the transference and countertransference. Furthermore, my exploration was informed by the literature of Packer and Addison (1989) and Josselson, Lieblich, and and McAdams (2003), who maintain that underlying narrative research is the belief that human nature cannot be captured by a single theory, much like text analysis cannot be encapsulated by one person's perspective or interpretation. As Packer and Addison explain, "Interpretive research emphasizes that the researcher must *not* act as if he or she is a value-free researcher who can objectively see things as they 'really' are, or that the 'data' collected is, in some way, independent of the person who collects it" (1989, p. 42). Instead, throughout the interview process, the researcher should bear in mind, "I was the one who was taking notes, asking questions in the interview, and selecting what aspects of documents and literature were significant for my purposes" (Packer & Addison, 1989, p. 41). Thus, these interviews represent the spoken and unspoken elements of communication and understanding between two individual people.

In drawing conclusions from the data, I utilized a thematic analysis to examine the emergent themes, both in the actual interviews and in my own reactions to the narratives, which signified responses to Holocaust trauma. I looked for recurring ideas, for metaphors that evoked particular images, and for words that seemed laden with meaning. I also made a point of focusing on both explicit and implicit information—including pauses, repetitions, slips of the tongue, hesitations, laughter, tears, and tone of voice. Hence, the "data" by definition encompassed both verbal and non-verbal features of the narrative. While this method allowed for layers of meaning to emerge, the complexity of analyzing non-verbal aspects of verbal accounts was also the greatest obstacle inherent in this approach. For example, differentiating between what was purposely left unsaid and what was unconsciously avoided was not always possible. Ultimately, however, within an unencumbered space that welcomed words, silences, and everything in between, these women's life stories began to unfold.

CHAPTER 3: BETHANY

> Recently both of them have been talking about things more, especially my grandfather, because I guess as they get older they want to make sure we remember everything.

In the case of a massive collective trauma like the Holocaust, the transmission of memories and autobiographical information shifts from the individual to the communal. As can be seen in the above quote by a 22-year-old, third generation Holocaust descendant named Bethany[1], individual experience has entirely transformed into collective memory. After all, it is not simply that Bethany was told a story that she is expected to "remember"; it is far beyond a story, and yet it has never been told. One might expect the offspring of survivors to have been infused with rich and detailed accounts of their grandparents' experiences in order for memory to persist. However, in the aftermath of this massive trauma, immense and lasting pain has solicited silence and secrecy over verbal communication. Perhaps not surprisingly, these silences engender the most powerful messages of suffering and an unmistakable cry for help from future generations.

Bethany definitively states, "…they want to make sure we remember everything," as though Bethany and her siblings were present during the Holocaust to create the memory in the first place. Yet, she did not live during the Holocaust, and neither did her siblings. So, how does she continue to "remember"? The post-Holocaust phrase to "never forget" and the Israeli national song "If I forget thee Jerusalem, forget my right hand" immediately come to mind. Like Bethany, Kaplan (1996) speaks to the transmission of memories to future generations:

> When a Holocaust survivor brings a child into the world, she is looking to the child for a second chance at life.

---

1   All names and other identifying details have been changed throughout to maintain the confidentiality of the participants.

She is hoping to shelter her child from the atrocities she suffered. However, in most cases, the shelter of silence becomes a Holocaust monument that casts its shadows over the life of her child (p. 218).

As future generations continue to carry the historical trauma, they serve as memory receptacles for a past they did not experience, and are left to testify as to what happened to their ancestors.

Thus, trauma is transmitted intergenerationally, and can be observed through various life patterns, including dietary, relational, and religious decisions; a general attitude towards the world marked by excessive guilt, fear, and the expectation of death; and a devotion of one's life to an ever-present, unspoken story that must be reconstructed like pieces of a puzzle. That is, amidst debilitating silences and deeply rooted family secrets, third generation Holocaust survivors attempt to construct the foundation of a narrative for their predecessors, and indirectly for themselves. It seems that entire generations are unknowingly devoted to this task; specifics regarding who exactly does the work are secondary. After all, past traumas persist until they have been worked through, and the "unthought known" (Bollas, 1989) drives the life of a third generation survivor until the seeds of awareness are planted and mourning has begun.

Constructing a Narrative in Silence and Absence

"It's just like how you know... you know those are your parents. I've always known my grandparents are Holocaust survivors." Bethany does not recall learning about the Holocaust, nor can she pinpoint a time when she realized that this was her history. The knowledge has simply always been present, like knowing that her parents are her parents. Indirectly, Bethany speaks to the immense work that has gone into uncovering some historical truth within her family's implicit collusion of silence: "I've always known that my grandparents are Holocaust survivors and I don't know how I know that... I don't know. It's just stuff I guess we've gathered or that have come into my head..." The "stuff" she has "gathered" is a jumble of knowledge, made up of concrete information that she has heard, read, and learned, and, more frequently, intangible data that have "come into" her head through associations, feelings, and reactions to silence. Thus, her family secrets exist as an "unthought known":

> B: She had one brother and I've never met him, I've never heard anything about him. They don't speak about him. My grandmother will not like it I think if we ask...
> N: You've asked her?
> B: We've asked her and we've asked my grandpa, who stayed the same... just silent. And for the most part, what we think and what my dad thinks, too... he grew up never knowing his uncle. I think he knew he had an uncle, but that was it. And no one ever spoke of him. And what my dad and mom both tell me is that they think he married someone non-Jewish and went back to France and lives there. I don't even know if he's still alive, but... which is crazy.
> N: How do you think your dad knew that there was an uncle?
> B: I have no idea, I think through pictures... I don't even know if they had anything. But I'm assuming it was just like a picture or something. Because I don't even know... the reason I know... I mean, I feel like I've always known.

Most often, the source of Bethany's knowledge is unclear; thus, a linear, coherent narrative is absent. However, the power of the knowledge remains, like the weight of a silence that cannot be described yet reliably transmits information. Similarly, in attempting to describe her grandparents' nightmares and her father's attempt to communicate this childhood experience, Bethany states:

> I vaguely remember him saying something like, "It was really hard to wake up at night to hear your parents screaming." So, that's obviously something that stuck in my head. But I don't really ever remember him ever telling me that. And I don't know if I read that somewhere... that Holocaust survivors do that... or if that actually did happen. But I think that he's told me that. I just don't

know if he wants to talk about it or... so we just don't.

Bethany's attempt to share an interaction with her father provides a compelling example of the muddle surrounding the transmission of traumatic memory. In a sense, Bethany is asking: Was this memory spoken or read? I think I heard this from my dad, but did the conversation actually happen? How and when and why did it happen? If we spoke, does that mean we can talk about it again? Or maybe the haziness of the memory is a sign that we shouldn't?

Ironically, this jumble of knowledge indicates the beginning of narrative formation. As Bethany attempts to reflect on what she knows, how she knows it, and in what way this relates to the rest of her family's knowledge, there is an increasing desire to know more:

> So the things that I don't say I probably don't know the answers to, but... I don't know, some I might just leave out so you can ask me. But I think because I have never asked him, which I probably should sit down one day and ask him, I just don't know a lot of the things... I just hear.

As Bethany discloses her family's history to a curious interviewer with a curiosity much like her own, the gaps in her knowledge continue to unfold. At points, Bethany's partaking in her family's silence is striking: "But I think because I have never asked him, which I probably should sit down one day and ask him..." Nonetheless, she has succeeded in acquiring a great deal of knowledge, and has become a source of information in her family, particularly for her father. Her willingness to engage with their traumatic past and wonder about both the presence and absence of information allows Bethany to begin working through this past trauma.

Bethany goes on to describe the failure of language in depicting her grandfather's experience:

> My grandfather used to talk about his friends from camp and I thought they were his friends from summer camp... and only like, really, within the past five years did it click in my head... he never went to camp. He was in concentration camp. And I didn't know that growing up. But I

mean I knew he was in a concentration camp, I've known my whole life that my grandfather had numbers on his arm, but it never crossed my mind when he would talk about his friends from camp, you know? He never ever spoke about anything when I was growing up, and my dad knows nothing. And he always says... my dad was in summer camp and I guess a bunch of his friends had parents that were Holocaust survivors and they asked him on *Tisha B'av*[2] to stand up and tell a little bit and he said he just didn't know that much to tell because his parents never spoke about it. Now he's learning a little bit more and he asks me questions because I'm probably the one who knows about it the most in our family.

The above narrative highlights a number of issues. First, Bethany has taken on the role of narrator, and thus of caretaker, in her family. In a sense, her quest for knowledge reassures her father, "It's okay to wonder. We will not kill my grandparents with our curiosity." Thus, Bethany reacts differently to the familial silence. While she abides by the implicit family agreement not to ask, she nevertheless opens the door by what she calls an "interest" in history. Bethany explains her role by stating, "I wanted to know so much more." That is, her ability to become curious simultaneously infuses her with the strength to heal. Ultimately, Bethany's attempt to bridge the gap between the past and the present encourages her ancestors, "It's okay to rejoin the world." Secondly, Bethany's grandfather did not go to summer camp, but Bethany's father did, as did Bethany. In a sense, Bethany's summer camp experiences and associations to summer camp evokes the idea, "I'll go to the right kind of camp that you were supposed to go to as well." That is, Bethany is beginning to work through her grandfather's past trauma partly by compensating for his experiences concretely.

Finally, Bethany's struggle with the word "camp" emphasizes the incomprehensibility of the Holocaust in a post-Holocaust world. In Bethany's attempt to make sense of an unfathomable experience using everyday language, she finds herself hitting a wall time and again; this

---

2   The ninth day of the month of Av in the Hebrew calendar is a day of mourning that is honored by fasting. This day commemorates the destruction of the First and Second Temples in Jerusalem.

reveals the obscenity of attempting to understand or convey the atrocities of the Holocaust. For example, she struggles to describe her late great-uncle's return to his living quarters at the end of the day, stating, "He came home... he came back to the barrack with the yellow band on his uniform." Indeed, there is no way for Bethany or anyone who has never lived in that kind of barrack to comprehend what this experience was like, and how it translates into a world where people come home at the end of their work day. Similarly, when Bethany tries to explain why her grandfather's bar mitzvah took place in Nuremburg, which was not his hometown, she says, "His bar mitzvah he had in Nuremburg, where he had family or friends or something." In Bethany's post-Holocaust world, a bar mitzvah is a time when family and friends are present to partake in the celebration. Of course, Bethany resembles nothing short of the entire post-Holocaust world in her inability to comprehend. That is, Bethany's interview reiterates Dori Laub's (Felman & Laub, 1992) notion of the Holocaust as an event without a witness. As Kaplan states, "Consequently, those who actually did witness the atrocities of the Holocaust are either dead or suffered too much to ever know what actually happened to them." (1996, p. 218). She goes on to explain, "Only the survivors can testify, and since (in order to survive) they could not be fully present during their own massive traumatization, even they cannot truly bear witness" (Kaplan, 1996, p. 218).

Tapping into the "hierarchy of suffering" (Bar-On, 1995) that has evolved regarding Holocaust experiences, Bethany discusses her grandmother's belief that she is not a Holocaust survivor, although she survived the Holocaust:

> My grandfather was in a concentration camp, so... I think that being married to someone [like that] she doesn't really consider herself a Holocaust survivor. And I remember her telling me something: they had gone to a synagogue where everybody is a Holocaust survivor where they're like all old Jewish people, and she said there was an event and they were honoring all the Holocaust survivors and they told all the Holocaust survivors to stand up and come up and like have a, I don't know, an *aliyah*, or something. And she didn't go up and she said, "I'm not a Holocaust survivor," and that really... I

was like, "But you are a Holocaust survivor." She went through hiding, her father got caught in the war, she... you know, she always talks about what she hates the most is that she never went to college and that she never got to go to high school, and she's not stupid but she never got... she stopped going to school when she was 10 years old or something. And she, you know, I think she's saying like she had jury duty and they cut her in the jury as someone who's not bright because she hasn't graduated high school, and she's like, "But I'm not like that." She was never allowed to graduate high school. So like things like that. She's definitely a Holocaust survivor. She's definitely a survivor. But she doesn't even consider herself one. And I think it's just because she didn't get tortured to death, or whatever.

Bethany's grandmother's insistence that she is not a Holocaust survivor likely stems from her sense that others suffered more deeply. Because she "didn't get tortured to death," she feels she cannot serve as a witness to this massive collective trauma. Along this line of thinking, there is no such thing as a witness, as anyone who did "get tortured to death" is no longer alive to provide a testimony. Indeed, Bethany's grandmother is not alone in this belief. In the same way that Bethany's generation will never comprehend the atrocity, and Bethany's grandmother cannot understand the experience of someone who went through a concentration camp, Bethany's grandfather will never know what it was like to die in a gas chamber, as his brother did. Thus, people's construction of hierarchies of suffering speaks to their feelings of alienation from, or closeness to, the event.

The Mechanism of Transmission

Numerous behavioral and emotional patterns emerged in Bethany's interview that linked her grandparents' generation, to her father's, to her own. The first example of this was in discussion of excessive guilt amongst her family members. Recognizing the debilitating impact of such guilt was relatively straightforward when exploring her father's lifestyle.

> My mom always says, "You know he's a Holocaust survivor child because he doesn't enjoy his life ever." That's probably her way of bashing my dad or something, but he doesn't like to go on vacation, he works really, really hard all the time... people always say he's not the normal Jewish doctor because he works so hard and he does everything around the house. Whereas most people hire people to do things, he fixes everything, he makes everything, he has to mow the lawn every week, and we don't ever have a gardener... all those kinds of things. And we always say they resort back to.... I think he probably feels guilty that his parents went through that so he can't enjoy every piece of life because they had to go through that... suffer.

Because Bethany's grandparents suffered through the Holocaust, likely plagued by guilt that they survived while so many others did not, their son unconsciously feels that he does not deserve to live his life to the fullest. He imposes superfluous methods to ensure that he does not "enjoy his life ever," thereby joining with his parents in their past suffering. Logically, of course, this does not make sense; her father's guilt and suffering will not undo her grandparents' experiences, nor will it lessen their pain. Kestenberg's (1972) term "transposition" captures the phenomenon by which a parent's past experiences overwhelm the child's present reality: the past occupies a vast amount of psychological space in the present, and the construct of time is reversed between parent and child. The child's existence unfolds within the parent's past (Kaplan, 1996).

Kaplan (1996) suggests that a child who senses her parent's unspoken shame, guilt and terror is inspired to recreate these circumstances in order to concretize and ultimately cure the parent's trauma. However, she does not address the possibility that a survivor's child might enact a comparable scenario without any insight into his or her actions or subsequent working through, leaving the pattern to be repeated and the work incomplete. Perhaps it is not the survivor's children who can fully testify as to what happened to their parents, but more so their grandchildren, who have the additional perspective of intergenerational dynamics following the traumatic event. Furthermore, while familial silence and secrecy can motivate a child's quest to uncover what happened to the parent, the weight of this journey may be too heavy for a child who witnessed his parents' traumatic symptoms first-hand. For all of these reasons, Bethany has been the first in her family to serve as her grandparents' and father's bridge to life. Her curiosity allows her to begin examining both her grandparents' and father's past trauma, and may lessen the need for future reenactments of past experiences.

Indeed, Bethany recognizes her own battles with guilt and effortlessly links this instinctive reaction to her grandparents' traumatic history and her fantasy that she might have saved them:

> Like, it wasn't what would my parents think, or what would mom say if I brought home a non-Jew, which is usually what most Jewish girls would say. But I was just thinking in my head, oh my God how could I do this to my grandparents? And it would make me feel so guilty because they are these old, nice people who had such terrible lives, and then I'm like how could I do this? So it's a lot of guilt... more than anything. And in my head, my grandparents are these old, they need help, they're so sweet, they're so nice... you just feel bad for your grandparents and then I feel like a hundred times worse, like oh my God what did they have to go through their whole lives, to think that my grandfather lost his entire family and he never had parents and I just feel so *bad* all the time. Anytime that comes into my head, I just want to start crying for him. But to me he's just this little old man that I just want to protect from anything, and I couldn't protect him from that.

Bethany's insight into her guilt surpasses her father's in that she verbalizes feeling "bad all the time" for her grandparents and wanting desperately to protect them from their past. Bethany's guilt therefore arises whenever she imagines they might disapprove of her decisions: "...they are these old, nice people who had such terrible lives and then I'm like how could I do this?" Thus, intergenerational lifestyle patterns in Bethany's family run the gamut from choice of food and romantic partners to religious observances. Following a discussion about her grandfather being forced to eat a dead horse on the death march in Auschwitz, Bethany describes currently knowing her grandfather as a picky eater who "won't try new foods." She reveals, "And when he was finally liberated... I just found this out recently... he was liberated with pasta and he won't eat pasta anymore... he won't eat pizza either but that he says because of the smell, which is beyond me why he doesn't eat pizza." While my first association to Bethany's grandfather not eating pizza related to ovens and a constant smell of something burning, I put these thoughts aside at the time. However, minutes later in the interview, the conversation about ovens and deadness ensued:

> B: My grandmother makes everything. I don't even think he knows how to turn on the oven. Or the stove or anything.
> N: And is your dad a picky eater?
> B: Well he's a vegetarian and he doesn't eat a lot at all. And my mom says that he doesn't love food like a normal person loves food. He eats for necessity for living, not for pleasure. Whereas I definitely eat for pleasure (laughing) and like my brothers who eat tons.
> N: What's his reason for being a vegetarian?
> B: Animal reasons. (Silence.)
> N: How about you?
> B: I don't eat that much meat, I don't really like it...

Bethany's father eats for necessity, not for pleasure, ensuring that he himself could eat a dead horse if forced to. While Bethany does not explicitly verbalize these links between the generations, she leads the conversation in such a way that the transmission of historically-based behaviors and emotions is clear. At times, however, it seems that Bethany's family does not want to acknowledge these links:

> I was really shocked that I never knew that my grandfather's brother's name was Tommy until I started learning about it when I was older. And my first dog that I ever had we named Tommy. And when I found that out I was like, how could we have named our dog after our great-

uncle who had meant so much to my grandfather? Like, what could he have thought? I was like, I feel so terrible. And we ended up giving him away after a couple years, but what did my grandfather think when we said, "We named our dog Tommy"? And I was distraught about this. Tommy had been gone for years, but it was like how could we have named a dog after my grandfather's brother? I was just so upset about it.

Whether Bethany's dog was named Tommy to help her father master feelings towards the name or as an expression of anger towards his father and his life circumstances is unclear. However, towards the end of the interview, Bethany found a way for me to experience her family's dynamic first-hand. About 75 minutes into the interview, Bethany remembered that she had promised to call her father at a certain time in order to be picked up from the interview. She had lost track of time, and called him later than he expected.

> B: [On the phone: Hi, sorry, I'm at Nirit's, I'm sorry... I'm sorry, I'm sorry, I didn't have my phone (laughing). I'm sorry, dad. It's right here but Nirit's been interviewing me so I couldn't answer it. I got here late, I got here late. I'm sorry. I thought you said it was fine. I told you I would be here for an hour but I didn't get here on time. I need like five to 10 more minutes here. I'll be down in five minutes. Sorry.] He thought I died. (Laughing). Oh God. Alright, sorry.
> N: Sorry about that. I didn't think of that.
> B: He's like, I thought you died. Okay.
> N: Did he say that?
> B: He Googled you and everything and he's like wandering the streets.
> N: Oh no...
> B: He was like, "I've been Googling Nirit Gradwohl." I just should have called him and said I may not be done...
> N: He's very protective of you.

As Bethany is in the midst of an interview about the intergenerational transmission of Holocaust trauma, her father circles my block in expectation that Bethany will not come out alive. While fear and expectation of death are understandably common experiences for the children of survivors, there is a sense that the interview's subject matter is increasingly threatening. What might Bethany discover? Will it kill her? Will it destroy her family? Is it possible to talk and cry and feel without complete disintegration? Or must defenses be in place to protect us from the truth of a traumatic world?

In search of her place within a collective narrative, Bethany has begun the work in her family. She asks, she narrates, she comforts, and she heals. In a sense, Bethany recognizes that her life has been and will continue to be dedicated to her ancestors. She will find a way to work through their past traumas regardless of life circumstances:

> I know that whenever I had an opportunity to write a school paper or talk about someone important in my life—every class, every year—that's always what I wrote about. Like, I remember when we learned about pilgrims, I wrote about my grandmother... how she was a pilgrim and came to this country and that she grew up in France where there were pogroms every day. And when they asked "name someone who is your pilgrim," she was my pilgrim. And whenever I had to do "who is your hero," my grandfather was my hero. And "why is he your hero?" Because he was in concentration camp. And I never... not that I don't think that about my other grandparents, but I grew up until 12th grade I had all four grandparents and I never wrote about my other grandparents that way. I mean, maybe I did but I can't remember. But I specifically remember when we learned about pilgrims I wrote about my grandmother. For *every* project I've ever had has been about my grandparents I think...

Bethany turned her school projects into conversations about her Holocaust survivor grandparents. For every topic and for every project, Bethany found a link; this is because for Bethany, nothing else exists as long as Holocaust trauma does. She will write excessively, talk excessively, and cry excessively because she is strong enough to write, talk and cry. She has absorbed an entire history of suffering, and only by doing the work of mourning will she answer her ancestors' cry for help.

> N: And how is it now to talk about it?
>
> B: It's fine to talk about it because I talk about it a lot. I actually spoke to... I worked at a public school in Boston and their eighth grade was learning about the Holocaust so I spoke to every single eighth grade class and it's a huge public school and I told them our story. And all my friends know my grandparents... it's something that comes... that I talk about a lot. So, it's not hard to talk about it, but if I were to... I don't know, sometimes it makes me cry. Every eighth grade class I cried in. Every 25 minutes I was crying. Can't I stop crying already? I know this story, and I know what's gonna happen at the end. I was also really nervous and these kids never met a Jew before in their lives and they knew me and they didn't know I was Jewish.
>
> N: A lot of pressure.
>
> B: Yeah, I wanted to make sure I actually got the point across to them.
>
> N: As if saying it so many times would take the feeling away.
>
> B: Right, I thought it would, but... I was like, I wonder if I'm even going to cry before I went. And then I cried in every single period and I was like oh my God. And I spoke at my synagogue once and I cried there... and I was like, I need to stop crying.

Bethany has dedicated her life to curing her ancestors' Holocaust trauma. She has moved past the phase of acting out situations of guilt, shame, and terror in order to concretize and engage the unfathomable; instead, she allows herself to wallow in their past suffering, thereby mourning the loss and pain that her grandparents and father needed desperately to suppress. In working through her family's collective trauma, the present can exist in its own right, the family can begin to heal, and new narrative possibilities can start to emerge.

CHAPTER 4: LEAH

I'm extremely obsessive-compulsive, not the type of person that diagnoses themselves. Like, in high school, I was seeing somebody for it. I schedule everything and plan everything, so whenever something goes off course, big or small, I have real difficulty dealing with it and that tends to make me feel guilty. And I don't know when I developed that OCD or where that came from. Potentially that's related...

Leah, a 23-year-old, third generation Holocaust descendant, tenuously links her personality and lifestyle to her history as the granddaughter of survivors. "Potentially that's related" she half states and half wonders, having just revealed this personal information three quarters of the way into her hour and a half interview on the topic of intergenerational transmission of trauma. Her insight arrives on the heels of her maternal grandparents' story:

> I know that my grandparents... they had a five-year-old son and he was shot on the street by a Nazi soldier in front of my grandmother. My mom wasn't born yet... this would've been my mom's brother... my mom wasn't born, she never met him... so he was killed when he was five and my grandparents were both taken... they were already married and had a family... they were both taken to Auschwitz, separated, lost each other, and ended up finding each other afterwards.

In the context of her ancestral trauma, Leah's obsessive-compulsive tendencies may serve a number of protective functions: first, she preserves a sense of control in her life by mentally planning every hour of the day, having learned early on that the world is unpredictable and painful. Second, she struggles to master a part of her traumatic history, in that order might undo her family's tragic loss. Along these lines, she unconsciously imagines that by deliberately inspecting every hour of the day, nothing could feel out of control and no one could catch her off guard; thus, her grandparents' son might be saved. Third, Leah engages in thinking to avoid feeling. Perhaps her mind is absorbed by thoughts and lists such that little time or space remains for the emotional burden of past traumas. Finally, Leah's obsessive-compulsive symptoms provide an observable entity, which she can pinpoint as the cause of her pain. Cyrulnik (2005) describes how a person feels relief when she can finally name the source of her inner suffering: "I can join a group and express what I'm feeling. I can consult a doctor and show him a symptom. I'm no longer alone in the world. I now know what I have to deal with and how to get help from people close to me and from my culture" (p. 101).

Leah herself echoes this sentiment: "I just needed somebody to say, like, 'Oh, you have an actual thing with a name, you can blame that, you don't have to blame yourself...'" However, underneath this assertion, like other third generation survivors, Leah does to some extent blame herself: "...whenever something goes off course, big or small, I have real difficulty dealing with it and that tends to make me feel guilty," she says in the opening quote. Indeed, something "big," or more accurately, of massive proportions, has gone "off course." Until her family's trauma is confronted and, as Leah says, "dealt with," she will continue to exist within the shadows of a ghost.

Secrets...

Leah begins her interview by stating, "I actually don't know that much about my father's side of the family. Both of his parents were Holocaust survivors." She explains the absence of knowledge with, "We always just sort of went to my mom's side of the family. We were closer with them anyway and they were more open, and as I'll explain, they have a much more obvious link." She adds, "Even my dad, from what he knows, isn't that good at remembering it or sharing it or as deeply impacted as my mom. She talks about it." The "much more obvious link" Leah is referring to is the ghost of a murdered child who is present every day in the life of this family. In contrast, Leah's father and paternal grandparents were not as "open" and, in Leah's mind, not "as deeply impacted" by their Holocaust experiences. As opposed to her mother, they did not "talk about it." We are left to wonder about Leah's paternal side of the family, who was likely debilitated by internal anguish and unable to give voice to unfathomable experiences. As Judith Herman writes, "The conflict between the will to deny horrible events and the will to proclaim them aloud is the central dialectic of psychological trauma ... But far too often secrecy prevails, and the story of the traumatic event surfaces not as a verbal narrative but as a symptom" (1997, p. 1).

Indeed, the denial of suffering and devastating silences mold a family's way of life, implicitly deemed the only tolerable way of life, and transmitted from generation to generation. When asked about her father's father, Leah recalls:

> He was a very quiet man... he was a very nice man, he absolutely wasn't bitter at all, he was just quiet. He would sit in the chair, we would go to school and come home and he would just be sitting in his chair. He made his own meals. He didn't need anybody to make them for him. He just did his own thing. Even like, he passed away in his sleep, very quietly. You know, he was just this quiet old man.

Leah's assertion that her grandfather "absolutely wasn't bitter at all" and was just "a quiet old man" hints at the possibility of his emotional numbing. Perhaps he did not "need" anything or anyone because he found safety in his isolation from the world, going through the motions of life without any real contact or connection. Likewise, Leah has learned to take what she sees at face value, accepting the dynamics at play: "...he would just be sitting in his chair." Similarly, in speaking about her relationship with her father, Leah states, "I know much less about him. He's just a more introverted person. But that's the sort of relationship we have; when we're together, we're not speaking about world issues or my life, we're just making fun of people that walk by." Leah's descriptions of her father and father's father are matter-of-fact, encouraging the interviewer not to overstep the surface-level descriptions Leah's family has long upheld. Furthermore, her tone indirectly expresses: this is the way it is; there is no need to question myself or my beliefs. Unfortunately, these boundaries reiterate the family's primary struggle, for denial ultimately fortifies trauma. As the subtitle of Davoine and Gaudillière's (2004) book suggests, *Whereof One Cannot*

Speak, Thereof One Cannot Stay Silent.

Alongside silence and secrecy, symptoms persist throughout the generations. Of her father's sister, who lived with her survivor parents until their death, Leah says:

> Oh, I mean like crazy... she hadn't been taking her medications; she had been eating all the wrong things. Like, there was old food thrown around the house. It reeked when my parents first got there. They found something like over $20 in change just in one day strewn about the house. She had bags and bags of, for instance, leather gloves that she had bought, never opened, never worn. She had an entire bag of different pairs of silver earrings... As if you were going out and you wanted a pair of silver hoop earrings so you bought every one you could find and figured you could decide later and return them, and she just never returned them. She never cleaned out the house from her parents' stuff, but after my grandfather passed away she moved out of her bedroom into what was their master bedroom, but she so cluttered her own bedroom that they couldn't even open the door. She would go on like business trips and she wouldn't unpack her suitcase when she came home, so she just went and bought another suitcase and packed it with new clothes. She had dozens of packed suitcases with the tags still on them so my parents could tell where she'd been and where she'd gone.

Clearly, this daughter of Holocaust survivors spent a lifetime mired in the internal devastation of her parents' experience. Never having found a place within language, her family's unmourned suffering flooded her post-Holocaust life. One can only fantasize about the significance of silver hoop earrings and leather gloves; do such accessories represent fragments of knowledge in an existence that unfolds outside of language? What of the numerous packed suitcases, which suggest a preparedness to flee yet an inability to truly escape one's baggage? "...she just never returned them," Leah says of the earrings, speaking volumes about her aunt's incapacity to "return" and rework the original trauma. As Cyrulnik writes,

> This is how emotional restriction constitutes a major sensory privation, an insidious trauma that is all the more damaging because it's hard to become aware of it, to make it into an event, a memory that we could confront and rework. When we don't come face-to-face with a recollection, it haunts us, like a shadow in our inner world, and instead of working on it, it works on us (2005, p. 6).

Consequently, while from Leah's point of view we have not yet broached the noteworthy aspects of her family history, it is impossible to escape the power of a secret, "working... on us."

...Ghosts...

N: I'm really interested in going back to your grandparents' son who was killed. Do you know what his name was?

L: Robert.

N: Robert. Did his name get reused later?

L: My middle name is Rosie; that comes from him. And they had a portrait of him in my grandparents' bedroom... I only saw one apartment, but before I was born they had a few and they always had this picture of him and you can tell—it looks exactly like my brother. My whole family looks alike, like a lot alike. It was my grandfather transferring right into my brother. You can see my mom's face in there; you can see me in there.

N: Wow, what was that like?

L: You know, as much as I have heard about it and I feel like... Not that I understand their experience, but that I'm familiar with their experience... I can't ever imagine it. You know, it's such a horrible loss to not even really get to bury your child because of the circumstances. And I think that their fear of ever losing my mom was so legitimate even though it drove her crazy. You know, he's just this kid that I never met, that I never could have... I definitely can't even imagine as an older child or a man because my mom didn't have any other brothers. There's not like there's somebody that you can see him as. I have no idea what he is to me except that he's just this face in this picture.

N: Right, a face with whom you share similarities. I mean, physically, anyway.

L: Right, like, you can see my brother in there. I mean, I can't think of it as if it was my brother. I can't even imagine that horrible loss. At this point I've lost all of my grandparents so I've experienced death, but not the way you would losing your baby like that.

Leah and her family exist within the subsistence of a five-year-old ghost. In every picture, every mirror, every conversation with her brother, every interaction with a child, and perhaps every encountered "face," hers and that of an "other," the ghost is present. The concrete, visual similarity makes this ghost entirely unavoidable: "It was my grandfather transferring right into my brother. You can see my mom's face in there; you can see me in there." The "much more obvious link" Leah spoke about previously is better understood with this context—what cannot be spoken in this family is tangible and all-consuming, a truth that resurfaces and repeats itself through time. In his *Specters of Marx* (1994), Derrida maintains that a person's life is shaped by attempts to give voice to inner ghosts. He writes:

> Repetition and first time: this is perhaps the question of the event as question of the ghost .... Repetition and first time, but also repetition and last time, since the singularity of any first time makes of it also a last time. Each time it is the event itself, a first time is a last time. Altogether other. Staging for the end of history. Let us call it a hauntology (Derrida, 1994, p. 10).

"Each time it is the event itself," as the haunted and the haunting become one and the same. Leah states, "He's just this kid that I never met," as though "this kid" is an existing person in present time, waiting to be found. Indeed, he is real; alive within her and directing the course of her life.

The metaphor of the "portrait" of a ghost is a powerful one. Derrida's specter, or revenant, invisibly occupies a space that vaguely exists somewhere between the "occupied" and the "occupier" (1994, p. 172). Leah states, "Right, like, you can see my brother in there. I mean, I can't think of it as if it was my brother. I can't even imagine that horrible loss. At this point I've lost all of my grandparents so I've experienced death, but not the way you would losing your baby like that." From brother to baby and baby to brother, the past engulfs the present and the present is the past. "...a first time is a last time. Altogether other," Derrida writes. Thus, the portrait of a ghost manifests both visible and invisible truths, forever a foreign occupier which Leah cannot grasp. She says, "There's not like there's somebody that you can see him as." In other words, he is me but he is not me, he is everything but he is nothing. "I have no idea what he is to me..." she concludes; after all, how well can you really know a ghost?

Within her daily life, and stories about her daily life, the ghost repeatedly shows his face. For example, Leah describes frequent arguments with her mother: "Like, I'll snap at her and she will... I don't want to say she goes off because she doesn't yell, but she gives the cold shoulder like a *five-year-old* might. And it's something I've inherited. So then she and I end up in this cold war..." How does a five-year-old give a cold shoulder? Instantaneously, Leah and her mother are transformed, back into the world of a slaughtered five-year-old brother. Leah's mother turns a "cold shoulder" away from her daughter in the presence of this ghost, and the world turns cold. "So then she and I end up in this cold war," Leah speaks, right back in the original setting, as each time "it is the event itself." Leah continues to show the ways in which the dead remain a part of life:

> N: How do you think it impacted your mom that her parents' first child was a boy and their second child was a girl?
> L: What do you mean?
> N: Any sense of loss of a man?
> L: In terms of loss of a man, I don't think so at all. My

mom and my grandfather were very close, they used to sit and read the newspaper together and watch TV together, so any of those things were like a father wants his son to do those things. I never got the sense that he felt he missed out on any of that. My grandfather *adored* my brother and he would follow him anywhere and whatever my brother said was wonderful, and my grandmother did with me, which is interesting because in my family it's kind of the opposite. I think we were just the idealized versions of what they didn't think they had. Like, I never thought of my grandmother the way she probably feels my mom did, but at the same time she never understood that me and my mom had a similar relationship to what she had. So I think for them it probably spooked them out that my brother looked so much like this kid and maybe that's what made the connection there really strong. But I don't think it's something they would have ever... how can you say someone reminds you of someone that's dead? It's not something like... six of us sit down at the table and say, "Hey, everyone realizes they looked alike, right?"

N: They might not have even realized it...

L: Yeah, but it's like something where my mom and I commented on it, my brother commented on it. It's that obvious.

N: So the two of you were like the idealized siblings, like the two kids they could've had...

L: Yeah, I mean, they, you know, we were their only grandchildren. They fawned over us. We were decent kids—we didn't give our parents any trouble, we get along very well... my grandmother always had this real romantic notion that he would end up marrying one of my friends and I would end up marrying one of his friends because we're so close in age. That's something actually I needed to mention: my mom so much hated being an only child that she had my brother and immediately got pregnant with me, obviously, because she just wanted to start trying immediately so that he would have a sibling, and then she wanted to keep going but my dad was like, "We have two babies, chill." Sort of like the only-child syndrome.

What I fail to realize in my questioning of Leah, but what she quickly reminds me, is that sex and gender are insignificant in the memorialization of her dead. Her mother was created to reinstate her lost brother, and to do all the things "a father wants his son to do." After all, as Kaplan (1996) explains, survivor parents who have lost family members in the Holocaust consciously wish that their post-Holocaust family will replace the family members that were killed; the parent's unconscious wish, however, is that each new child will serve as the return of a dead one. Leah's mother, therefore, was to complete her brother's prematurely interrupted life prior to carrying out her own. We cannot know to what extent she lived a life in her own right; however, Leah clearly states, "My mom so much hated being an only child that she had my brother and immediately got pregnant with me, obviously, because she just wanted to start trying immediately so that he would have a sibling...'" The weight of not having had a sibling was intense, one that her mother was unwilling to repeat for her children. While Leah suggests that her father convinced her mother to "chill" and stop after "two babies," Leah and her brother have in turn been created as the two siblings who might undo the family's past trauma. Leah states, "I think we were just the idealized versions of what they didn't think they had." Indeed, not having two children, a son along with a daughter, was ever-present.

"My mom and my grandfather were very close, they used to sit and read the newspaper together and watch TV together, so any of those things were like a father wants his son to do those things. I never got the sense that he felt he missed out on any of that." Again, a protective screen is in place that limits Leah from fully seeing what she already knows. Because she was not her brother, Leah's mother could never be enough. "My grandfather *adored* my brother" Leah says, though he was "spooked" by the reemergence of his murdered son a generation later. Perhaps, then, my heightened awareness of Leah's mother as a woman, and of Leah as a woman, was related to a sense of gender splitting in this family. "...whatever my brother said was wonderful, and my grandmother did with me, which is interesting because in my family it's kind of the opposite." Earlier in the interview, a similar gender divide arose:

I was in my freshman year of college when my grandmother died and I saw it rip apart my mom and I think
a lot of that was that she felt guilty for the way that she
had treated her. So what my mom did was... she wasn't
necessarily protective of me... she and I also used to butt
heads a bunch... there was a stubborn streak. I was always like a daddy's girl and my brother was really close
with my mom more so than my father. And she always
tried to knock it into me that I had to respect her more.

During the interview, I was left feeling unclear about the details:
Who is close with whom? Which child resembles which parent? Why
does that matter? What is the significance of this sense of preference
for one parent, or one child? Perhaps these gender splits represent the
various fragments within each person, or the more general fragmentation of life during and since the Holocaust. Or maybe these questions
relate to the shame, pride, and envy associated with Leah's knowledge
that she is not a boy, and therefore not like the lost boy so memorial-
ized in her family.

In response to my question about any recent dreams or nightmares,
Leah says:

L: Nothing really specific. I mean, I've had nightmares
about losing people in our family. But they were never
specific, like I don't want to go near water because I had
a dream where my mom drowned. Nothing like that.
N: But it was usually about one of your parents?
L: Usually my brother, actually. You know, we're very
close. I think a part of me always felt like that would be
the hardest person.

The terror of losing her brother overwhelms her dreams. He is both
the special child that the family values and remains worried about, but
also unenviable in his constant closeness to death. Having been born a
girl, Leah both loses and wins.

...And Surrounding Shadows

In explaining how her sense of guilt is related to her obsessive-compulsive tendencies, Leah describes having "dragged out" her brother Friday night, only to result in his losing his coat. "It's not a tragedy," she says, "but I feel horrible about it... I get in my head this is the way things are going to go. I expect everything to be perfect." Similarly, she reveals her need to continuously check certain items and create detailed lists that organize every hour of the day:

> L: I'll go back and check things. I have certain routines. Not in like my apartment now, but my bedroom in New Hampshire, the door has to be closed a certain way. I'll schedule—get ready with the same routine every morning.
> N: Like, shower and then do something?
> L: Yeah, even like put in the mouthwash, while the mouthwash is in, go back to my room and like take out my hair gel, take off the cap, then go back and spit out the mouthwash, then go put in your hair gel... things like that. You know, if my roommate gets up and goes in the bathroom when I need to go back, I'll be like... ugh.
> N: You'll walk yourself through like little things...
> L: Yeah, it's always been manageable, it's not like a crazy thing, but it's a little weird...

Indeed, losing a coat is not a tragedy. Yet, being out of control has led to tragedy in her family history. While Leah worries that her habits might be perceived as crazy, she also reveals a sense of ownership over her compulsions. After my asking whether her brother shares any of these tendencies, Leah responds, "My parents think he's a little compulsive also, but I just think he's bossy." In a sense, Leah insinuates that this is hers and hers is different. Consciously, however, Leah takes herself out of the competition: "I don't feel upstaged nor do I feel the need to upstage someone else and I don't understand why other people do." She is an actress in an old script, constantly upstaged, but long since taken herself out of the running for lead role.

Leah goes on to describe how her grandfather similarly "stuck to his routine." She says, "And my mother always attributed that to his experience where they were just so shell-shocked that they just clung to this routine of normalcy that they created for themselves afterwards. Very old fashioned in that sense." While she does not directly link the "routine of normalcy" to her own life, she indirectly reveals how her daily routine reflects a "shell-shocked" reaction to intergenerationally transmitted experiences. For example, she says, "I fully admit I have no street smarts... oh, I get lost everywhere. If I get myself into some situation, I'm just not smart enough to get myself out of it. You know, I can ride the train all around the city before I figure out where to get off." Understandably, Leah has "no street smarts," because one cannot have street smarts in a world that allows a five-year-old to be shot on the streets. In these ways, she continues to live within the shadow of the Holocaust in a post-Holocaust world.

Nevertheless, Leah's strength and hope persevere. In thinking about her family's suffering, she also reminds herself:

> It seems to me that the thing that I always found most beautiful is that they found each other again. That they clearly instilled in my mother, their only child, a real sense of Judaism. I think of it as like, I know all I need to know to be really proud of them, and to be happy for them, even though it's been hard for them... to think that they succeeded in coming out of it.

While Leah has not come "out of it," she finds herself partaking in an interview, honestly discussing her family history, and entertaining new and conflicting ideas. Exhibiting great courage and resilience, she allows herself to exist fully "inside of it." Similarly, in reflecting on what she might want to do differently as a mother, Leah says:

> My brother and I have always talked about how we want to keep our families close with one another. We didn't have any cousins because my dad had this crazy sister, my mom was an only child, so we're really looking forward to being able to give our kids cousins, which is something that we always talked about. Other than that, I imagine, I'm a lot like my mom who is a lot like her mom, so I imagine I'll be a lot like that.

Like her own mother, Leah wishes to expand the size of her family, thereby welcoming additional players that might bring fresh insight and support. As Leah continues to "butt heads" with history and allows herself to remain fully in it—examining pride but also shame, happiness but also sadness—she evolves from an actress in an old script to a part of something altogether original.

CHAPTER 5: YAEL

N: Did you ever feel there was anything about your family history that you didn't know... like a feeling that a piece was missing?
Y: No.
N: That's amazing.
Y: My family was very open.

As I sat with 23-year-old Yael, a half-Israeli, half-American, third generation Holocaust descendant, I considered her proclamation that secrets and silences were not a part of her family's experience. How *amazing*, I remarked, struck by the simultaneous presence and absence of the unknown in our conversation. Re-reading my personal reaction to Yael's interview, I recall feeling both intrigued and thwarted by elements of the "unsayable" (Rogers, 2006) in Yael's narrative. "No ... My family was very open." Josette Garon (2004), translating and quoting Pontalis (2002) on the motivation for becoming a therapist, states, "'Where do you live? In the vicinity of the unknown'; 'what do you do? I try to guess the presence of secrets'" (p. 85). In contrast to the silence so pervasive in other families of Holocaust survivors, here I encountered a family who valued speeches, founded memorials, and emphasized the communication of their grandfather's story. Nevertheless, I was left wondering about the unknown, or unspoken, elements of Yael's experience. Yael begins:

> Growing up, my grandfather was very vocal. He helped establish various Holocaust museums and always went to go speak, and from a very young age I knew his story, whereas his brother took his name off his arm and never spoke about it. So it's very weird seeing me and my first cousins as opposed to my grandfather's brother's grandchildren... just very different upbringings on knowing about the Holocaust. My grandfather did everything... he survived Birkenau which is the death camp of Aus-

chwitz. He did the death march with his father. He's been to numerous death camps and was very... he was a big speaker and everywhere he went he was never afraid to tell kids, no matter how young they were, what happened and the horrors... he never shed that... he never kept that from us.

What is the nature of the unsayable in a family that is "very vocal" about past traumas? Does it persevere underneath the mask of language, or is it exhumed, deciphered, and even understood? In her opening statements alone, Yael addresses the dichotomy between knowing versus not knowing, speaking versus not speaking, and "shedding" versus "keeping" a memory. As we see in her slip, divergent qualities are distinguished from one another while remaining linked in a mutually defining relationship: "...he never shed that... he never kept that from us." Indeed, he could never "shed" his experiences, but rather "kept" his memories alive, consciously transferring them to his children and grandchildren. Interestingly, synonyms for the signifier "to keep from" include "protect," "shield," "shelter," "save," and "cushion." In transmitting his narrative to his offspring, Yael's grandfather did not protect them from the horrific truths of his experience. Thus, she grew up knowing, in great detail, her family history, and living within its context. At such a point, as Cyrulnik explains, "It is not a question of normal development, since the trauma inscribed in memory is part of the person's history from now on, like a ghost that accompanies him" (2005, p. 2).

Yet, despite a lifetime of "speaking" about the Holocaust, Yael exists within a narrative that she is unable to convey using language. "My grandfather did everything," she says, utilizing the verb "do," a neutral, active word suggesting a conscious decision on her grandfather's part. Furthermore, she states, he experienced "everything." While clearly her grandfather did not undergo "everything," it is impossible to convey to an audience what it means to survive Birkenau, the death march, and numerous other death camps. For her grandfather and an entire population of Holocaust survivors and descendants living after the event itself, nothing and no one can capture this massive trauma, regardless of consistent efforts to impart the experience. He "did everything," and yet we understand nothing of the events. In contrast, remaining silent is associated with a loss of identity: "his brother took his name off his arm and never spoke about it." That is, her grandfather's brother removed the number tattooed on his arm at Auschwitz, "never spoke about it," and, in a sense, removed his name.

Yael proudly states, "...he was never afraid to tell kids, no matter how young they were, what happened and the horrors..." One cannot help but wonder: What is the impact of knowing "the horrors" at such a young age? How do children learn to contain and incorporate historical knowledge into their identities? To what extent are self-blame, guilt, fear, and shame transmitted, leaving these children burdened by the pain and suffering of an entire people? Yael honestly reveals:

> Y: There's a recurring nightmare that I actually still have... I'll have it like once a year, twice a year; it's in my house in Philadelphia growing up. It's just the only dream that I have that's recurring and I'm walking, well not walking... you know the British, the redcoat army? They're like marching after me and I'm running away from them and I always hide in the same bush... and that's the only part of the dream I remember. But I always tell people and they think it's because of the Nazis... because they would just be like, who has an image of like an army marching after you?
> N: And it's just you?
> Y: Yeah, it's just me like running away and I always hide in this bush in front of my house but that's the only part of the dream that I remember when I wake up.
> N: What do you make of it?
> Y: What do you mean?
> N: Well, you said other people related it to the Nazis. Do you think it's connected?
> Y: Probably, (laughing) because the dreams probably started young and I heard some pretty horrible stories when I was young... I don't know if I had nightmares when I was younger but I know that's one nightmare that has always been recurring and it's really scary.

In responding to my question of how old she was when she began hearing her grandfather's stories, Yael stated, "Never a time when I haven't been. I'm sure at some point they started telling it to me, but I don't know an age where they sat me down and were like 'We're going to teach you about the Holocaust.' It was always who we were." Her recurring nightmare is an example of a concrete entrance of her grandfather's history into her present-day experience; after all, the nightmare is now hers. Furthermore, as Davoine and Gaudillière (2004) explain:

> In general, when the world becomes nonsense, children tend to think that they are the cause of the catastrophe, since this is the only way they can make sense of it to themselves ... it is better to assume that one is oneself the cause of an inexplicable event, or to unload it onto the other, than to confront an event without a reason. This is one of the most effective survival strategies in the face of the uncanny, the strange and disturbing field of the Real (p. 72).

Believing that she is, somehow, the source of the catastrophe, Yael undertakes a mission to "avenge" her grandfather for the crimes committed against him. Therefore, the Holocaust becomes not merely a part of Yael's collective and individual identity, but the basic infrastructure through which her world is shaped. What Garon (2004, p. 88) calls a trans-generational "alien transplant" takes root, infiltrating her conscious and unconscious life.

Past Becomes Present...

Yael's sense of ownership regarding her grandfather's pain can be seen in her hierarchical assignment of what survivors "went through":

> Y: And this is gonna sound horrible but it's fine... I never have seen *Schindler's List* or read Holocaust books or watched Holocaust movies... I just can't... not because I think it's horrible, but because I just never... I can't sympathize with other people's stories just because my grandfather's is so horrible. It reminds me of my grandfather and what my grandfather went through. When I hear other people's stories I'm like, "That's nothing

compared to what my grandfather went through." It just angers me that here they are speaking about their stories because it's not even close to, or like what I think is not as close to, what my grandfather went through, and it's just very hard for me to listen to anyone else's story besides my grandfather's.

N: Because in a way it feels like he suffered more...?

Y: Right, it's really ridiculous... I'm always resentful and think that my grandfather had it really, really horribly and went through a lot and... I know other people did too... but, like, when I hear people tell stories, like they hid in a forest and then were okay afterwards... it's really hard for me to come to terms with like... that's almost like cheating for me... so I tend to not...

In the above segment, Yael taps into a frequently mentioned sense of hierarchy regarding the degree to which a person "suffered" through and "survived" the Holocaust. The construction of such hierarchies reflects people's sense of disconnection from, or closeness to, the event. Interestingly, Yael is a third generation descendant of a survivor who maintains a powerful sense of ownership and protectiveness regarding her grandfather's pain. "I can't sympathize with other people's stories just because my grandfather's is so horrible," she says. In a sense, Yael feels that others do not know suffering the way her grandfather does. It seems that Yael has developed a sense of pride through the image of her grandfather as a unique survivor, not one of many but rather different and special. Perhaps she feels this distinctiveness reflects onto the remainder of her family. On a deeper level, however, it sounds as though she is actually describing a personal issue: "It just angers me that here they are speaking about their stories..." Why is she angered by other people's need and desire to speak? Perhaps this anger relates to a sense of envy that they have a story separate from her grandfather's. After all, Yael has spent her lifetime struggling to learn, remember, wrestle with, communicate, and further transmit her family history—an exhausting, all-consuming role. "But, like, when I hear people tell stories, like they hid in a forest and then were okay afterwards... it's really hard for me to come to terms with like... that's almost like cheating for me..." Certainly, a person who hides in a forest for months or years during war does not simply come out "okay afterwards." Her view of such people's experience as dishonest or dishonorable may be a projection of her own sense of guilt: she will always feel like she "cheated" in that she was born generations after the Holocaust and sidestepped the direct experience altogether. Her sense of responsibility for undoing her grandfather's past trauma is immense.

For various reasons, Yael winds up functioning within extremes: her grandfather is described as having experienced "everything," because otherwise he experienced nothing; he had to have suffered most, otherwise he did not suffer at all. Similarly, Yael connects such black and white thinking to her mother's outlook on the world:

> Y: She always brings up my grandfather ... Whenever I'm upset she's like, "You know, if your grandfather could hear you now... it's embarrassing, what would he say?" Like, because he was such a fighter and so strong and built himself up and like didn't give up that that's always my mom's way of... you know, she's always like, "You know what your grandfather went through, how can you be upset about something so trivial?"
> N: Like, "Get over it"?
> Y: Yeah, it's like not that big of a deal, if your grandfather can get over losing his whole family, like, you can get over this.
> N: That sounds so frustrating.
> Y: Yeah, like I'm still upset. I understand it's not that big of a deal, but still upset.

Here we see a short-circuiting of Yael's experience in the face of her family history, as her mother indicates that Yael does not deserve to experience the world in her own right following the historical trauma. Resonating with Yael's view that no one "went through" what her grandfather went through, her mother implies that because others suffered more deeply, Yael's harboring her own sense of loss or disappointment is superfluous. Yael is therefore left wondering: how dare I feel sadness (or fear or anger) unless I am starving, nearing death, and watching my family's murder in a concentration camp? Understandably, she feels "resentful" of other survivors' stories because on some level, she believes no one deserves a story aside from her grandfather—not she, not her mother, not anyone—not even her grandfather's brother who died before the Holocaust:

> My grandfather was 15 when the war started and he actually survived with his father but his father died the day of liberation from typhus, or typhoid, or something with a "typh"... and he lost a sister and his parents in the Holocaust. He also lost a brother but that was pre-Holocaust so it doesn't count.

For Yael, no one else counts the way her grandfather counts. In describing one of her grandfather's experiences in Auschwitz, she further reveals:

> And that's how he survived... in Birkenau, which was the death camp of Auschwitz... they needed a couple people there to take the wheelbarrow from the gas chambers to the crematorium. And so there would be a wheelbarrow where there would be two people in front and two people in back. My grandfather, the first time he did it, he was in the back... and the people in the front were shot... and he realized it was because... sorry, reverse. He was in the front and the people in the back got shot... and he realized that the Nazis were very smart and meticulous and wanted to get things done fast and if they killed the guys in the front it would take time to roll the wheelbarrow over their bodies, whereas if they killed the people in the back they could just keep going. So my grandfather always made sure he was the person in the front, and that was how he survived at Birkenau for a couple of weeks: being the guy in the front...

In order to survive, Yael's grandfather knew he had to be "the guy in the front." His strength and resourcefulness allowed her grandfather to survive even the death camp of Auschwitz. Furthermore, her grandfather not only survived, but built himself up and became what Yael calls, "the main guy in our whole entire family." Thus, "being the guy in the front" was a way of life for him, a necessary way of life for survival to be possible. With their grandfather in the front, Yael and her mother took up positions at "the back" of the wheelbarrow, serving as a buttress or support. Yael recalls, "My mom is—I think because of my grandfather—is like the most neurotic and anal woman you will ever meet in your whole life, like doesn't step away from my grandparents at all, like keeps them close all the time." Supporting her parents seems to have become her mother's full-time assignment.

As Yael reveals, her mother's "over-protectiveness" of her parents became characteristic of the family relationships in general:

> Y: Yeah, I know most people say they have overprotective mothers... mine's to a max, to an extreme. I think I talk to my mom six or seven times a day, minimum. If I'm out I'll be on the phone with my mom, tell her what I had for lunch, literally call my grandma and literally in that time my grandma will be like how was that sandwich? That's how often my family members talk. My mom... I remember Halloween when I was 13... you know when you're old enough to walk around by yourself? Like your Jewish neighborhood? My grandfather would be following me around in the car and my mom was hiding in bushes following me and my friends. They would really be over and beyond. It's remarkable how protective my mom is of everyone in her family, and it's not in a healthy way. People recognize that it's not in a healthy way but she, since my grandfather passed away, I don't know if she's left my grandma's side.
>
> N: Do you feel this gets in the way, or is it endearing and something you guys laugh about?
>
> Y: No, it gets in the way. Like, the type of thing where I know if I don't call her back in a couple hours easily there can be cops outside the apartment looking for me. It's happened. Like, my grandparents lived like a block away, and once when I was 15, we got a new puppy and I went to show my grandparents the new puppy and they weren't home... so I went next door and was there probably for 15 minutes and came out and there were

three cop cars because she didn't know where I was. So she's very neurotic... like, my parents split up and I think it's because she became increasingly more neurotic and more anal about every little thing. I don't know where it stems from...

Yael's family lives with a constant fear that a family member might be taken, killed, or suddenly go missing; these were the circumstances for Jews in Nazi Europe, where each day was potentially a person's last. Therefore, although Yael concludes her thoughts by saying, "I don't know where it stems from," suggesting a desire not to know, she does, of course, on some level know. Her knowledge allows her to link her mother's constant fear and anxiety both to her grandparents' experiences and to patterns in Yael's behavior:

It's very hard for me, the idea to leave my grandma and also my mom... like, my brother is going away, also abroad, and if all three of her kids are out of the country I don't know what she would do with herself—like I really don't. And I couldn't do that to her. There's so many things... like, I know if I see a phone call from her if I'm in the middle of class I have to call her back because she'll just go nuts. She just gets very panicky and like she always says she has an ulcer from worrying about us, but I don't feel bad about that because she brings it on herself the way she worries, and I hope that I'm not going to be like that. But I know with my grandmother, like... I can't tell you how many times when I'm home in Vermont, I call and I know she's home and I call her house and she doesn't answer... like, I'm driving—I immediately get in the car and start driving to her house which is now 20 minutes away. My mom finally moved 20 minutes away which is a huge guilt for my mom but I'll start driving there because, like, I don't know why she didn't answer her phone. Like, most of the time she's taking her dogs outside for a walk but, you know, me and my mom will stay in the same wavelength; one of us will be like, "Okay, we're on our way." It's just, so yeah...

I guess I'm overprotective of my grandma but like not with my mom.

"I hope that I'm not going to be like that," Yael reflects before instantaneously detailing the ways in which she is, in fact, "like that." Her candid narrative reveals the paradoxical dynamic at play. Regardless of a conscious desire to break away from this arrangement, unconsciously she struggles to separate and individuate, as such growth might signify a rejection of her family. Concretely, as well, Yael's lifestyle choices are made "in the name of" her grandfather; for example, she says, "I always did the traditions for my grandfather to make him happy." Furthermore, as she possesses her own fears of abandonment and isolation, Yael finds herself simultaneously seeking safety within her family's enmeshment. A breakup with a boyfriend, safer than a breakup with her family, ultimately brings her into therapy. Thus, the cycle is reiterated and a middle ground is hard to come by; separation and individuation become dangerous developments, ones that could potentially cause someone to "go nuts":

> My brother is in Israel this year. It was a huge deal for my family and my mom letting him go. My brother just wasn't ready for college, like wasn't. He had to take a year off because he was failing high school—he would fail out of college—he needed a break. But it's been very, like my mom, I was in the car with my mom yesterday and my brother is coming home for a week next week and she was just like... literally, this is what she said: "Okay, don't forget, from the 14th to the 23rd, Michael's going to be home." She's like laying out every day and then said (crying voice), "And then January 2nd we're gonna take him back to the airport..." and then she started crying. Like, crying already about taking him back to the airport. That's just ridiculous. Whenever she thinks of him leaving, she cries like every day.

...And Present Becomes Past

Throughout most of her interview, Yael idealizes her grandfather in the present tense; in her sporadic use of the past tense, she seems to suddenly remind herself that he is no longer alive. For example, Yael states, "He has no college education but he's smarter than any human." This present-tense description of her grandfather suggests that he is super-human, still alive and "smarter than" anyone. When she reveals a "rough," angry, and more vulnerable part of his personality, she quickly transforms her comment in an attempt to soften it, seeking to eliminate the possibility that anyone might view him as less than perfect:

> He was kind of the main guy in our whole entire family...
> like, I stayed at my grandparents' for three or four nights
> a week; they just, they were my parents. He was kind of
> a no-nonsense, no-bullshit grandfather; you know, very
> rough around the edges. He would yell. He played cards
> every night with his friends... he would yell and scream
> but everyone loved him for it.

In keeping with the family's tendency to split, there is no room for the seemingly negative to coexist with the seemingly positive, or for one person to exist alongside another: thus, she explains "they were my parents," not "they were *like* my parents." One eliminates the other.

At times, Yael's split causes her true feelings to be distorted or foreclosed:

> Y: ...He ate everything. My grandfather was also very
> anal about what he ate. Like, he had to have his toast
> black, and if it didn't come black, he'd send it back or
> would just get up and leave the restaurant. Like, I can't
> even tell you how many restaurants he's just gotten up
> and left and just like, "I'm not eating here." I thought it
> was endearing, like really endearing.
> N: He would get angry about little things like that?
> Y: Yeah, like he would... like he would be playing cards
> with his friends and one of his friends came over and got
> coy in Hebrew and he would be like, "Shalom." He would
> be like, "Oh, you think you know Hebrew, you big shot?
> How do you say 'give me an apple'?" He was that type of
> personality. Very rough and mean almost. He would yell

a lot all the time... always screaming and yelling but in a
funny way, not a really mean way...

Yael works hard to explain how it is possible that her grandfather was
"mean" but at the same time not mean, screaming and yelling but in an
"endearing" way. She gets stuck in her attempts to idealize *all* of him,
working to present a man worthy of adoration, with no traceable flaw.
Along the lines of this splitting, her grandfather's death represented the
death of "everything": "I remember that for me, when my grandfather
passed away, I lost everything... I lost my grandfather, I lost my father,
I lost my best friend... like, I lost everything." Furthermore, because her
grandfather and her grandfather's history are so much a part of her current existence, Yael struggles to inscribe the past as past.

> It wasn't just losing a grandfather; it was losing our rock
> and our stone and like kind of the person who would
> always tell us what to do. Does that make sense? He was
> just always the organizer of the family. At Passover Sed-
> ers he would obviously be the leader... he wouldn't even
> know people's names and it wouldn't even matter. He
> would just be like, "You, read next." And then he would
> just like stop them, cut them off and be like, "You, next."
> That's how he would lead it—in a very rough way. And
> now, for my family ever since then, Seder is really, really
> hard because it's not as funny anymore.

Indeed, it's not "funny" how lost this family feels without its leader,
its "rock," the man who told them "what to do." It is also not funny to
be left behind with an array of unprocessed, unspoken feelings of rage,
guilt, and shame that is often intertwined with family unity and pride.
By no longer being told "what to do," this family has suddenly become
vulnerable to thinking, feeling, and sprouting from a world of "stone."
Yael's family has spent three generations speaking about the Holocaust and attempting to create a meaningful life in the context of their
collective trauma. The meaning they created was largely based on a con-
tinuance of Holocaust memory, whether through speeches, memorials,
or recounting of stories. Unquestionably, their memories persevere.
However, the work that remains for this family is the "feeling" work,

the more difficult and threatening work that might cause one person to fall off a pedestal or another to individuate from the family. Yael arrives at the interview with a sense of hope, knowing her potential to honestly examine her role within the family, explore her "negative" feelings, and begin to live more fully as a separate individual within the present world. In verbalizing her own narrative, Yael impels herself to reflect on and blend the black and white extremes that can direct her life, and seek a more attainable shade of gray.

CHAPTER 6: REBECCA

Attempts at a "Rational" Life

Well, (sigh) currently there's actually some significant issues going on because my grandfather is senile and has turned against my family. He's come to call my mother a Nazi. He refuses to talk to my mother or me because he sees me as the embodiment of her, talks only to my younger sisters and my father, and to them talks solely about how he hates my mother and how she wanted to lock him up in a nursing home. None of which is true— my mother only has his best interest at heart and if he allowed it she would go up and visit him whenever he wanted.

Davoine and Gaudillière (2004) address the above phenomenon by exploring "The revival of the catastrophes: the old people were sounding the alarm to us; we're in 1938: Munich; we're in 1939: the Blitzkrieg; we're in 1941: Pearl Harbor, and the United States is entering the war. Nothing will ever be the same anymore" (p. xviii). Instantaneously, one trauma embodies every trauma, one frightening situation transforms into every previous experience of fear. More comprehensively, Davoine and Gaudillière's psychological reactions to "traumatic breaks in the social link" include denial ("what happened didn't happen"), survival guilt ("Why them and not us?"), identification with the aggressor ("We had it coming"), perversion of judgment ("the victims were guilty and vice versa"), fascination with mass destruction, the aforementioned "revival of the catastrophes," and, lastly, "trivialization: the proliferation and sophistication of the commentaries going hand in hand with the anesthetizing of feelings" (2004, p. xvii-xviii).

For Rebecca, a 23-year-old, third generation descendant of two Holocaust survivors, some of the above reactions are apparent. While she indicates that her grandfather's stories have been obstructed from her knowledge, historically-relevant dynamics continue to be reenacted and transmitted along the generations of her family. Upon my asking about an event or an experience which may have triggered her grandfather's above accusations, Rebecca attempted to coherently organize the order of events:

> ...My mother made a comment. So he lives by himself in a community center. I don't know what it's like now; I haven't been there in two years. He was fully self-sufficient at the time. My mom said to him that for social reasons he might want to consider assisted living. My family probably knows more about this probably than the normal person because my dad is an elder care lawyer so we understand what these facilities are like; we're not trying to shove him away or anything like that. He took the suggestion in a completely different manner than what it was suggested and just started ranting about how we just wanted to lock him up and never see him again. And how we're not going to put him away, we're not going to lock him up like the Holocaust... and Hitler put him away and... afterwards he struck my mother. That's the story. We don't know where that came from and that was the point where he just started it.

"He just started it," Rebecca concludes, as though she is on trial for her grandfather's provocation. While she neutrally begins the story of that day with "my mother made a comment," this comment quickly evolves into a "suggestion" which he took "in a completely different manner than what it was suggested." Hesitantly, Rebecca reveals that assisted living was proposed, immediately following up this confession with a description of her family knowing "more about this probably than the normal person." She says, "my dad is an elder care lawyer so we understand what these facilities are like; we're not trying to shove him away or anything like that." On a surface level, Rebecca seems to be struggling with the notion that family members of an elder care lawyer know better about these "facilities" and would never "shove" anyone in. However, more deeply at play in this conflict is that Rebecca's family has assumed the role of aggressor in the face of a historically and personally pertinent, victim-perpetrator dynamic. She outwardly rejects, but simultaneously feels a part of, her grandfather's allegation. The discrepancy between conscious, rational logic and unconscious, irrational feelings quickly breaks down. Rebecca's total confusion, "We don't know where that came from," is thus understandable: how did she suddenly transform into a Nazi German? Is she deserving of this accusation? If not, what about this overwhelming sense of guilt that she has in some way brought about his past and present suffering?

Certainly, Rebecca does not need to prove that her mother is not a Nazi, not Hitler, and not in the habit of cruelly maltreating family members as was done to Jews in Nazi Germany. Her grandfather's past and present experiences are incomparable, and the context of person, place, and time has radically changed. Nevertheless, although rationally separate from Nazi imprisonment, Rebecca's grandfather suddenly finds himself in a conversation hinting at relocation, loss of independence, and an altered lifestyle. A world away from, yet at the same time never truly away from, Nazi Germany, Rebecca's grandfather suddenly finds his past and present collide. Instantaneously, he is back in a Holocaust world, and Rebecca's mother (and Rebecca, as her mother's "embodiment") are transformed into Nazis who "want to lock him up and never see him again." Rebecca herself speaks to the clash between the rational and the irrational:

> R: ...so it's actually a very difficult situation because my mother will say she's fine and we know she's not... and she spends a lot more time dwelling on it, much more than she should, because she doesn't work so we know she thinks about it a lot when she shouldn't. We've had a hard time trying to convince her that he is mentally not there. She doesn't seem to accept it.
> N: What does she think is going on?
> R: She tries to reason with him. Like, try to respond to his accusations with a rational answer, whereas he's not a rational person so it doesn't matter what you say back...

Similarly, Rebecca later recognizes that "being rational with someone who is mentally insane is just not going to get you anywhere." Yet what happens when an entire narrative, the overarching context for a person's past and present, is "mentally insane"? That is, in Rebecca's and her family's post-Holocaust life, nothing can ever again be simply sane. Therefore, by focusing on the fact that her senile grandfather cannot be reasoned with, Rebecca also stops short of exploring her own "insane" reactions to her grandfather and his story. As Danieli (1981, 1984) discusses in her work with Holocaust survivor patients, countertransferential issues with these individuals can take on terrifyingly powerful dimensions. Similarly, Rebecca's reactions to this cut-off, yet all-pervading moment in time with her grandfather are likely overwhelming: perhaps she feels immense guilt for his past experiences, for not having lived through the Holocaust herself, or for wanting to lock him up, like the Nazis did; she may be undergoing murderous rage at her grandfather for calling her a Nazi, for mobilizing her guilt, or for not rising above hostility and resentment himself; finally, Rebecca could be experiencing a combination of dread and horror, shame, grief and mourning—all countertransference themes described by clinicians working closely with descendants of Holocaust survivors (Danieli, 1981, 1984). Instead of exploring these possible feelings, however, Rebecca suggests that her family "shouldn't" dwell on the irrational but rather neglect or avoid them in what could become a "conspiracy of silence" (Danieli, 1984). She therefore forecloses an array of experiences, grasping at a more orderly sense of self. Ironically though not surprisingly, Rebecca's mother has a more difficult time chalking up the experience of being called a Nazi to her father's mental insanity; thus, Rebecca finds herself having "a hard time trying to convince her that he is mentally not there."

Feeling as though I was treading lightly so as not to overstep my boundaries and elicit anger or shame, I cautiously inquired about Rebecca's feelings surrounding her grandfather's attack:

> N: And has this been upsetting for you or have you been able to keep a distance from it and serve as a kind of rational voice for your mom?
> R: (Laughing) It's a weird question I guess because subconsciously... my sisters asked me a lot over the years. So, I completely understand that he's mentally insane and I understand that what's going on now is not normal, is not how a normal person would react because he's mentally not there. And my sister doesn't accept it;

like, she'll talk to him and she'll just start hysterically crying and it will impact her whole day... happens like once a month when she talks to him, and my mother also will get incredibly upset about it. My father and I are fine. And I'm not sure if I'm just sub-consciously upset that I'm not consciously realizing it, or if I really am just really okay with the situation. Cause I feel fine with it. I'm not sure why. I'm just really fine with it. Like, I understand he's insane. It's a sad situation, but this is what happens. I'm not really sure. I think I'm okay with it ... I'm fine.

The "anesthetizing of feelings" referred to by Davoine and Gaudillière (2004) allows Rebecca to be "consciously" okay with the idea of her mother and her being called Nazis. The eldest daughter of three, and most apparently her mother's daughter, Rebecca wonders whether perhaps she is "sub-consciously upset," or if she is "just really okay with the situation." While she struggles out loud with the question of whether or not she is "fine," it becomes increasingly clear that she is, in fact, anything but fine: "My father and I are fine ... Cause I feel fine with it. I'm not sure why. I'm just really fine with it ... I'm not really sure. I think I'm okay with it ... I'm fine." This repetitive assertion that she is "fine," one that encouraged the interviewer not to question the declaration, established a barrier, tenuous but respected, between narrator and listener. Throughout this discussion, Rebecca's eloquence and refined mannerisms further enhanced her sane self-presentation. Nevertheless, Rebecca's previous declaration "my mother will say she's fine and we know she's not" reverberated throughout the interview, suggesting that Rebecca's externalized "we know she's not fine" may be a reflection of her own internal reality.

Day-to-Day Amidst the Irrational

In attempting to share his traumatic Holocaust experiences with his family, Rebecca's grandfather encountered an audience unable to serve as an audience. Rebecca reveals:

Growing up, my mother said my grandparents... especially my grandfather... wanted to talk a lot about his stories, which she didn't listen to, and her brother, Thomas, really refused to listen to. Her brother, Thomas, had an extremely bad relationship with his parents to the extent that he left home. They've had absolutely no contact with him over the years; he really cut them off when he was 18, and that was because my grandparents are very difficult to deal with, particularly my grandmother. But part of that was he just didn't want to deal with the stories and my grandparents always tried to press it on him.

The struggle of survivors attempting but failing to communicate their anguish has been commonly discussed in the Shoah literature, as have the various responses to such attempts. Danieli (1984) writes, "This conspiracy of silence is not confined to psychotherapists but is part of the conspiracy of silence that has characterized the interaction between survivors and society at large since the end of World War II" (p. 24). Interestingly, Rebecca's depiction of her family's unwillingness or inability to listen sheds light on her grandfather's "insane" explosion later in life, as the shut-out and buried experiences ultimately press for ex-press-ion. At the same time, it is likely that Rebecca's mother and uncle did a great deal of listening and containing growing up, engaging with the traumatic and traumatizing topic to such an extent that Holocaust history overwhelmed and overshadowed their present lives. Perhaps boundaries and separation were implemented as a final, concrete attempt at an existence somewhat liberated from the Holocaust. Maybe physical separation from their survivor parents served as their only hope for a life increasingly removed from the trauma.

The inability to communicate reappears throughout Rebecca's interview:

Yeah, so my grandmother, she was really hard to communicate with... you couldn't have a conversation with her... I don't think she knew anything about me at all actually, you know in terms of what I was doing in school, who my friends were, what I liked doing... they would just sit and talk about like general stuff... they would

talk a lot about the weather, stuff like that, and we would
play games with them but it was all very forced.

Rebecca expresses frustration regarding her inability to communicate with her grandmother and grandfather, whom she feels were
generally limited to superficial topics, like the weather. Nevertheless,
she wishes to be known by them, as an individual with friends, likes
and dislikes, etc. The resulting communal experience in this family is
therefore a sense of not being asked, not being heard, and ultimately,
not being known; while her grandfather cannot impart his life story,
Rebecca likewise encounters restrictions on what she can convey. Thus,
although these family members share similar hopes and desires, they
seem to exist within two separate worlds. Rebecca accounts for some of
this disconnect by describing her grandparents' Holocaust community:

> R: There were a lot of Holocaust survivors in their com-
> munity, so socially it became relatively isolated. Like, my
> grandfather worked; my grandmother was a fantastic
> real estate broker mainly because she was the pushiest
> thing you've ever met. She did pretty well there because
> of that. Socially, they just hung out with other Holocaust
> survivors who I think had similar mentalities. So, I think
> it was a reflection of adjusting and there just wasn't a big
> need to adjust.
> N: But they were trusting enough to maintain those
> relationships?
> R: Yes, within the Holocaust community. There's a very
> big difference between survivors and non-survivors
> there. Very big. All their friends were. All their friends
> were.

Rebecca emphasizes, "There's a very big difference between survivors
and non-survivors." Indeed, the differences transcend age, language,
and life experiences. Rebecca's grandparents cannot talk about their
grandchild's friends, likes and dislikes, because they themselves were
stripped of these benign childhood experiences. In her work, "I Was
a Shoah Child," Yolanda Gampel writes of children in the Holocaust,
"Through the creation of a 'false self' these children were able to func-

tion as adults, in the bodies of children, thereby enabling their survival. Inordinate capacities to struggle and to manage without the comfort of tears and teddy bears were evidenced by these child-adults" (1992, p. 391). While her "child-adult" grandparents attempt to cling to their superficial knowledge of a benevolent worldview, their treatment of every human encounter, every morsel of food, and every hug reflects an unadjusted mentality unfitting for the present time. Indeed, Rebecca's grandparents are in need of assistance in living in a post-Holocaust world. The "suggestion" made by Rebecca's mother was likely one of many attempts at reconnecting her disconnected father to humankind.

The void and hollow existence of a Holocaust survivor following this massive trauma could not be transmitted to Rebecca's mother or to Rebecca in a verbal capacity. While this is generally the case given that language is a superimposed phenomenon that serves as a distant substitute for the actual experience, the rejection of language was maximized in this family. Therefore, the dynamics of her grandparents' past experiences were acted out with family members instead, revealing themselves through familial interactions and relationships. For example, Rebecca's mother, who did not herself live as a Jew during Nazi Germany, nevertheless understands what it means to be assaulted and charged with an ambiguous crime; Rebecca's uncle, regardless of attempts to flee his history, knows first-hand what it means to be disjointed and isolated, somewhat like an orphan; finally, Rebecca can easily identify the experience of not being treated like a human. She recalls this type of environment:

> So, growing up, going there was just like... we hated it. We would go once every two or three months, and they live like two hours away from us in Maine and they always treated us like dolls; you know, they would just hug you and kiss you regardless of what you said or wanted, you had no actual opinion or no actual being, you were just a cute grandkid...

"You had no actual opinion or no actual being," Rebecca explains, an insignificant, lifeless "doll," outwardly appearing like a human but inwardly not alive. As Gampel (1992) writes, "In the face of the terrifying and traumatic reality of the Shoah, the ego of the Shoah child was forced to function automatically and without expression of feeling" (p. 391). Indeed, a "doll" appears and performs in whatever manner desired by the holder of the doll, moving mechanically and without emotional expression. Similarly, Rebecca describes her grandmother's treatment of her mother by stating, "She always dressed my mother in skirts. My mother came home from college one day with a pair of jeans and my grandmother tore them up and threw them away." Again, we have a glimpse into the life of Rebecca's mother as a doll, dressed by her mother in skirts and unacknowledged as an individual with desires, feelings, and abilities. The boundary-less, intrusive treatment of people in this manner arose again in the context of food:

> We always went there and we always had a huge feast in front of us regardless of what time it was of the day and we were required to eat another huge feast like four hours later. There was a ridiculous amount of food around all the time and if we didn't absolutely stuff ourselves and then eat again four hours later and do the same thing we were just ridiculed. When I was younger, in elementary school, I was a small kid and my grandmother was worried to the extent that she called the nurse at my elementary school, pretended to be a social worker, and said to the nurse, "I'm calling as a social worker of the state. There's a student there, Rebecca. She is being abused— she's not being fed." And the nurse was a friend of my mother's and she understood that it was my mother's mom. So right away she called my mom and said, "I think your mother just called." So my mother was pretty upset about that, because she did some stuff like that.

Rebecca was "required to eat" whenever her grandparents played mealtime; however, the experience was anything but a game. She found herself forced to "absolutely stuff" herself, creating a physically visceral image of the human body as a plastic, manufactured entity. The connections to Rebecca's previous depiction of her grandmother as "the pushiest thing you've ever met" comes to mind, both because of the word "pushiest" and because of the description of a person as a "thing." Along these lines, in response to my question about her mother's ability to protect her in these situations, Rebecca replied:

> My mother would, but... I guess there wasn't a need for a barrier because all that really happened was we would go there and they would tell us how cute we were for a few hours. And then there'd be the whole food issue if we didn't eat like five helpings or fill our seven-year-old bodies.

Rebecca's grandmother, having survived Bergen-Belsen, is convinced that her granddaughter's thinness relates to "being abused" and "not being fed." She intervenes on her granddaughter's behalf, as if traveling back in time and saving herself from the starvation of the death camp. Through this muddled repetition and concretization of history, her grandmother acts out a chaotic attempt to undo her own past suffering. Yet in re-writing history such that someone could save her, her grandmother simultaneously winds up exploiting Rebecca and her mother. Understandably, as Rebecca says, her mother was "pretty upset about that."

The reserved, nonchalant description of anger as "pretty upset" is congruent with Rebecca's later ambivalent depiction of her mother's "harshness":

> R: I know she was brought up kind of under the stick more than the carrot strategy. I know she got into a lot of fights with her parents... she never specifically talked about their outbursts... she also only talks about what she wants to, which is just an issue with her in general, so there's a very big possibility that she decided that that's just something she's not going to talk about again, which I wouldn't be surprised about. She is definitely more strict with us than she's needed to be over the years, which has been tempered by my father because they balance each other out very well in that regard. And that's something that's been talked about between my father and myself and my sisters. My mother has a certain way of doing and if things aren't done that way she

gets very annoyed.

N: Like what?

R: Nothing serious, she just has a much harsher tone of voice, and much more condescending than she needs to be... both to my sisters, myself, and my father. Generally given the circumstances surrounding whatever vent there is, there's absolutely no reason for it. I think that it is significantly less than what she faced growing up...

In Rebecca's use of the phrase "the stick more than the carrot strategy," she refers to her grandparents' utilization of punishment rather than reward. A number of interesting topics arise in this narrative, including a return to food; a tendency for her mother to "decide" what she wants to talk about and refrain from discussing other topics; and finally, her mother's "unnecessary" harsh and condescending tone with her immediate family. While Rebecca protectively suggests that this pattern is "nothing serious," she also reveals that it is serious enough to have been discussed by her father, her sisters, and herself. Furthermore, while she reminds herself that her mother's harshness is "significantly less than what she faced growing up," she nevertheless seems to be grappling with the fact that her mother has upsetting outbursts of anger that should be taken "serious." Rebecca continues to struggle with whether or not her mother's anger is a "big deal" in the subsequent exchange:

R: A lot of my tendencies which I find naturally coming out are more towards my mother... my mother got annoyed when it wasn't a big deal and she got annoyed a lot...

N: Little things?

R: Not little things but... yeah, I guess. Things that she shouldn't have gotten annoyed about she would, and she would be much harsher in certain respects than she should have.

N: Would she get angry?

R: Not angry but basically like one harsh sentence and that would be it. It wasn't like a continual thing at all. She wouldn't yell or scream; it would just be like a much harsher tone of voice than was needed. Growing up, it was something I got used to. My youngest sister is significantly younger than me, she's 14, so when I go home and see that every time it happens, I'm just shocked to realize that's how things are done... which we're trying to work on as well with her.

N: So it's out in the open?

R: We're trying to make it that way. Yeah, she's definitely harsher than she should be.

Rebecca states "it wasn't a big deal," but understandably feels uncomfortable with my labeling the triggers for her mother's anger as "little things." By explaining that her mother "shouldn't" have been annoyed or was harsher than she "should" have been, there is a sense that Rebecca maintains a certain impression of how a mother "should" or "should not" behave. That is, she *should* not be "angry," she *should* not "yell or scream," and in the case that she does, it *shouldn't* be a "continual thing." It seems that Rebecca's primary struggle surrounds her own feelings of anger and aggression, further shedding light on her discomfort in the role of the Nazi aggressor with her grandfather. She concludes, "we're trying to work on that as well with her" and "we're trying to make it that way," clearly indicating her recognition that something has to change. This attempt to open up a dialogue about her mother's impact on the family may ultimately be personally constructive for Rebecca as well; after all, she notices that many of her tendencies "naturally coming out" are similar to her mother's. It seems that Rebecca has been able to broach the long-avoided, frightening conversation of family dynamics, acknowledge the sometimes uncomfortable patterns, and initiate a potential for change.

CHAPTER 7: SAMANTHA

Holocaust Trauma: One, Two, Three Generations

S: So he, um, was born in Poland in Bialystok and he had a mom and a dad and I believe two sisters, and all of them were killed in the war. And my grandfather himself was in the concentration camp; he was in Auschwitz. He might have also been in other ones but I'm not sure. And he... when America liberated the concentration camps, he came to America. Anyway, they ended up in New York, and he met my grandmother and... um... let's see... actually, that's like a whole other story because my grandmother was never diagnosed but I think she was Bipolar amongst God knows what other mental illnesses she had. So, my grandfather himself was obviously very affected by the war and the combination of the two of them was not good and they just made each other sicker and my mom's childhood was really difficult and I think that the war had a huge impact on my mom and on me...

N: In what way?

S: In her house, it was.... (long silence). I guess I've just been told bits and pieces but I know something that could have come from the war or that I could relate to it in my head is that they used to make my mom eat and drink milk when she was full and she didn't want anymore. And they like forced her... so she would hide food that she didn't want to eat in her closet. Now that I'm even talking about it, not only is it probably relevant but it's like the opposite of that happened for my grandfather because you know, they didn't have food.

N: You say now that you talk about it, have you thought about it before, for example, the food?

S: I've thought about the food and the fact that because my grandfather probably was starving... and the com-

bination of that with my grandmother's weird issues
with food... and then they were weird with food with my
mom. But I never thought about the fact that it was so
like, the fact that she was hiding food in her closet when
she was a little girl was literally like the opposite of my
grandfather probably like starving.

Samantha, the 31-year-old granddaughter of a Holocaust survivor,
delves into a number of issues often tentatively mentioned by Holocaust
descendants only moments into her interview. She touches on mental
illnesses, the emergence of patterns through the generations, the "huge"
impact of the war on all three generations, and the ongoing struggle
surrounding food. "...he had a mom and a dad and I believe two sisters,"
she says, individually listing each murdered family member rather than
clumping them into the category "family," or more specifically, "parents
and siblings." In this way, each family member is separately acknowledged. She goes on to relate her mother's relationship with food to
that of her grandfather, stating, "...the fact that she was hiding food
in her closet when she was a little girl was literally like the opposite of
my grandfather probably like starving." Samantha elucidates the link
between starvation and not having food on the one hand, with hoarding
and ensuring an ongoing supply of food on the other. Indeed, having
versus not having to some extent represent opposites: opposites so intimately connected through this family's past experiences that they begin
to coalesce into one mutually-defining entity. After all, hunger alone de-
lineates the experience of being full, and hoarding implies a fear of not
having in the future. As her mother hid the food that she did not want
to eat in the closet—instead of throwing it out or giving it away—she
behaved the way her father might have behaved in Auschwitz had he
stumbled upon a supply food: eat some now and save the rest for later.

Annie Rogers writes in the opening personal anecdote of her novel,
The Unsayable: The Hidden Language of Trauma:

I had always been attracted to heights—tall rocks, fire
escapes, trees, and precipices. As I teetered at the edge
of the school roof, I did not know that my father had
actually committed suicide. He'd jumped and fallen five
stories to his death ... My mother finally told me this af-

ter the art teacher called and informed her of my sojourn
on the school roof (2007, p. 14).

Similarly, Samantha's mother likely understood her hiding of food
as an attempt to avoid excessive, forced eating; in Samantha's words,
"And they like forced her... so she would hide food that she didn't want
to eat in her closet." However, in the midst of discussing this behavior,
Samantha is able to arrive at an intergenerational viewpoint, an outlook
which gives further meaning to her mother's tendencies and anchors it
in history. The mutually defining "opposites" are thereby linked as counterparts, exposed over two generations, in two different worlds, offering
a here and now observation of what happened *there*. That is, Samantha's
openness and insight allow her to recognize her mother's reenactment of
her grandfather's concentration camp experiences. Samantha continues:

> Um, my grandparents, both of them had multiple sui-
> cide attempts. They were always taking pills and going
> into hospitals. My grandfather I think somatized a lot
> of his mental anguish and um... he was physically sick
> but I think a good percentage of his physical illness was
> really mental because he would go to the hospital and
> they would say there was nothing wrong. But he was
> sick and when I really think about it... he had this thing
> called scleroderma, and I'm not sure exactly what that is
> but I know he had it his whole life. And as he got older,
> he kind of looked like 20 years older than he was, and
> towards the end of his life he looked like he was 90 but
> I think he was 70. And there were a few years where he
> could only whisper. I don't know if that was like... now
> that I think about it now, it probably was mental. But
> at the time it seemed like some sort of a physical thing.
> For years he only whispered when he spoke. And what
> else did he do... he could only eat mushy food... he had a
> lot of digestive, a lot of digestive issues. Um... and he...
> when I got a little bit older he would try to talk to me
> about the war but he would always end up crying. And I
> think I was too young to understand so I didn't really ap-
> preciate what he was telling me, and also it would bother

me. I would be like, "I don't want to go visit him, he's just gonna cry and then I'm gonna cry and I don't wanna do that." But now that I'm older, I understand what he was trying to talk to me about.

As the descriptions of her grandfather's life pour out of Samantha, overwhelming us with stories of suicide attempts, hospitals, and illnesses, we begin to have a sense of the engulfing and overpowering nature of these experiences on her upbringing. Nevertheless, she speaks honestly about these incidents, exploring her grandfather's limitations as well as her own inability to bear witness to his past trauma. "My grandfather I think somatized a lot of his mental anguish ... I think a good percentage of his physical illness was really mental because he would go to the hospital and they would say there was nothing wrong." The need to somatize his mental anguish expresses her grandfather's inability to *do* something with his grief; to verbalize it or sublimate it or work through it in some way. As Cyrulnik (2005) writes,

> The most common emergency defense mechanism is the symptom, an observable phenomenon expressing a part of the invisible inner world. As soon as the symptom illustrates the pulverization of the internal world, the person can pinpoint an image for his own unhappiness and hence feels better. He knows where the pain comes from and can finally give a name to it (p. 101).

It seems Samantha's grandfather's pain took the form of many names—whether scleroderma, digestive issues, or literally an inability to speak—all elements of something terrible and inarticulate.

Faced with the medical opinion that "there was nothing wrong" with him, Samantha's grandfather descended deeper and deeper into his tortured internal world. Samantha's recollection that "For years he only whispered when he spoke" provides a concretized example of an existence hanging somewhere in-between attempts at language and the inevitable, "unsayable" nature of his experiences. Unfortunately, though understandably, the murmurs of memory are often met with a refusal to take in—a reluctance to join in the suffering: "...I didn't really appreciate what he was telling me, and also it would bother me. I would be like, 'I don't want to go visit him, he's just gonna cry and then I'm gonna cry and I don't wanna do that.'" Unable to verbally share his war experiences with his family, her grandfather's tears poured out of him, flailing for release. Ultimately, barely comprehensible through whispers and tears, his memories were forced underground and registered physically instead.

The physicality of her grandfather's suffering reappears in Samantha's later discussion of her grandmother's physical abuse of him:

> N: So was he ever diagnosed? Was he hospitalized psychiatrically?
>
> S: I don't really know, in my family a lot of things were hidden, especially when we were younger. So I know he was in the hospital a lot of times and I'm assuming some of it was psychiatric. There was abuse between my grandmother... my grandmother I think used to physically abuse him.
>
> N: Oh, wow.
>
> S: So, I don't know really the extent of that, but I was told at one point that towards the end of their life... my mom said something like that she hit—my grandmother hit him with a menorah, and um, something about him falling out of bed or she pushed him out of bed or something. And he was so sick at the end, he had cancer, he had bone cancer in his stomach and bones, and then um... I was gonna say something else about the abuse but I forget what it was.
>
> N: Did your mom ever get abused?
>
> S: I don't know. She always says there were always things flying in the house. So I think things that my grandmother was probably throwing. She might have been hit, I don't know. Um, I was gonna say something else about... *oh*, what I was gonna say was that my mother told me when I was older after my grandfather had died that he, that my grandmother had abused him for years but that he never told anyone and never told my mother because he was so ashamed. Um (silence)... this is really depressing.

In contemplating and organizing facts that she "knows" from those she "assumes," we get a sense that Samantha is constructing a narrative for herself for the first time. While she first suggests she does not "know really the extent of that," she later recalls, "*oh*, what I was gonna say was that my mother told me... that he, that my grandmother had abused him for years but that he never told anyone and never told my mother because he was so ashamed." As soon as she "remembers" having been told this information by her mother, Samantha falls silent, then truthfully discloses, "this is really depressing." It is no wonder that knowledge of her grandfather's abuse and silent shame are momentarily "forgotten," as blocking them out serves to protect Samantha, and the remainder of the family, from experiencing the ensuing "depressing" feelings. Thus, for a moment, she chooses not to "know really" and reaches for a concealing safety net with the statement "in my family a lot of things were hidden." Moments later, Samantha discloses much more than expected: she reflects on her experience in the moment, sits with the weight of the pain, and then reassures the interviewer, "I think it's good to talk about it, but it's just like *ugh*..." In a sense, Samantha communicates, "This is hard work, but I am able and willing to do it."

Interestingly, Samantha's mother began to divulge information about her own father only after his passing. Perhaps with his death, the search for truth was ignited. More likely, however, Samantha's mother could no longer contain the family secrets on her own, and spilled onto her daughter to help carry the load. That is, while family dynamics and historical memory had been transmitted nonverbally to Samantha throughout her life, she was additionally elected as the conscious, verbal beneficiary of family narrative. It is unsurprising that Samantha struggles to organize the lines between fantasy and reality, certainty and uncertainty; after all, her mother's attempts to reveal and conceal information overlapped throughout her childhood, creating a hazy, muddled grasp on what could be counted as true. Samantha goes on to describe seemingly contradictory but nevertheless coexisting experiences of withholding secrecy and a violation of boundaries that characterized the chaotic atmosphere of her childhood home:

> S: ...I think "oh, it's just because I was a child," or "you don't tell your children that," or "we had things when we were children..." But I definitely think that in my family,

with my parents, we were never told when the grandparents were sick or when something bad happened, or we were told a few weeks later. I even remember that once my dad passed out and he went to the hospital and my parents didn't tell me until the next day. And I was so mad, like I just feel like that's not fair. And at that point I was an adult.

N: So they thought you couldn't handle hearing it?

S: Yeah, they didn't want to burden me with it... which I guess I do understand if you're a child. So I feel like I was never told all these things and then when I became older it started. My mom started to tell me all these crazy things about her family...

"...and then when I became older it started," says Samantha, recalling a turning point in her life in which silence and secrecy were replaced by boundary-less spilling of personal anecdotes and feelings. It is unclear when and why the transition occurred. However, it seems that Samantha was confronted with both excessive secrecy and excessive disclosure in adulthood, creating an erratic and unpredictable environment for her. In either scenario, Samantha's lack of control and stability is palpable: she remains blindly uninformed when her father spends a night in the hospital, yet is asked to contain all the "crazy" details about her extended family. She is left bewildered, feeling she never "had things" when she was a child; after all, "having" implies retaining something at least relatively consistent. The chaotic atmosphere of her childhood is further revealed through Samantha's discussion of the intergenerational transmission of trauma through three generations of her family:

N: So how do you think the way your mother was raised impacted her as a mother? Do you see that in her?

S: Yeah. She could have used like 20 years of therapy. But I think she's afraid to really touch on anything. So she never, she always was afraid. She didn't tell me she was afraid, but I think she was afraid. I think it impacted us a lot—we used to fight a lot. Also, it really affected me when I was a child because... my mom was a young mother; she was 24 when she had me. And she was taking care of her parents because they always depended on her. So she was always getting calls about what's wrong, just complaining about all these different health issues, and um... I think it was more than I was saying. I think they would call her and say things about their bowel movements and there were enemas... just like, weird, weird things going on. And they would always get sick and have to go to the hospital or they were swallowing pills, so she was kind of raising me and my sister but she was also running around taking care of them. And I don't think that she... I think there was a way that she could have addressed that and lived with that if she could have gotten help that would have prevented it from taking over her life. But instead, she totally allowed it to take over. Plus, whatever issues she and my dad were having... obviously, her upbringing affected her choice in relationship with my dad and my dad wasn't always the most supportive husband, or I should say the most active husband. Like, he went to work and that was his job. According to what my mom says he was never very active in child rearing and household things and other things like that. So I think in a lot of ways he was missing emotionally and physically. So she was taking care of us and she was taking care of her parents, and I think she was pissed, and I think she took a lot of it out on me.

N: So you had to deal with her anger a lot.

S: Yeah.

N: And did she hit you? Was there abuse in your house?

S: Not chronically, but there were a few instances that I do recall with her hitting me. She definitely didn't hit me all the time, but she did scream at me all the time. And I definitely think there was some form of emotional... like, I definitely feel that I did not look to her as a support, I was more fearful of her when I was growing up. I think a lot has changed since then, but still, you carry that with you forever...

N: Is your grandmother still alive?

S: No, she committed suicide closely after my grandfather died. She went bonkers and took a bunch of pills.

Samantha's ability to reflect on her chaotic childhood experiences and early relationships is remarkable. She suggests, "I think there was a way that she could have addressed that and lived with that if she could have gotten help that would have prevented it from taking over her life. But instead, she totally allowed it to take over." Indeed, Samantha is simultaneously acknowledging her own journey to "address" it and prevent it from "taking over" her life. In what might have been an overwhelming presentation of a family narrative for a one-hour interview, Samantha's insight and awareness instead provided a certain sense of hope and growth during and following the hour. While her mother's raw, unprocessed, and consuming emotions encouraged her not to "really touch on anything" throughout her life, Samantha sought to achieve the opposite. She begins by emphasizing her mother's debilitating fear: "She didn't tell me she was afraid but I think she was afraid"; as well as her mother's escalating anger that mounted into explosive rage: "So she was taking care of us and she was taking care of her parents, and I think she was pissed, and I think she took a lot of it out on me." Furthermore, Samantha is not limited by shame or humiliation when discussing boundary-less revelations in her family: "I think it was more than I was saying. I think they would call her and say things about their bowel movements and there were enemas... just like, weird, weird things going on." That is, she is able to recognize and discuss the most difficult and the most "weird, weird things," thereby eliminating the power of silence and creating space for introspection.

Perhaps it is no coincidence that Samantha's grandfather married a woman who abused him, or that her mother chose a non-supportive, passive husband. Given their traumatic histories and the workings of family dynamics, aspects related to partner choice, food-related issues, and the foreclosure of feelings trickled down through the generations. Furthermore, silence surrounding their histories debilitated their chance of working through the past and establishing a place within the present. Thus, the first and second generations of Holocaust survivors found themselves enacting past traumas, adopting roles previously despised, and finding release around aggression but never understanding why. In discussing her own physical and emotional abuse by her mother, Samantha acknowledges the incessant power of early experiences, stating, "I was more fearful of her when I was growing up. I think a lot has changed since then, but still, you carry that with you forever..." We are therefore left with a number of questions: How many generations will receive this traumatic history? Does examining her history, her early relationships, and her inherent predispositions alter Samantha's course, splitting her path from that of her ancestors? Or will Samantha forever remain on the same course, working instead to recognize where she came from, where she is going, and how to more fully live her life along the way?

First Glimpses into Generation Number Four

> N: Going back a little, you mentioned your mom being really angry as a result of how she grew up. I'm wondering how that plays out for you in terms of anger.
> S: Yeah, well her anger was never really expressed in a modulated form. It was either explosive or covered over by anxiety, and God knows what else it's covered over by. And one of my issues in my therapy was working on expressing my anger, because before I was in therapy I did not allow myself to get angry because when I did it felt like... deadly or something. Because of the way I experienced it when I was younger. So I had to learn that anger is okay. You can be angry without killing someone (laughing).

While she laughs at the seemingly obvious statement that a person can be angry without killing someone, this realization has clearly been a major accomplishment for Samantha. Having experienced anger and aggression that was never "modulated" throughout her childhood, anger that was either "explosive or covered over by anxiety," Samantha's own expression of anger felt loaded and "deadly" for a long time. Through what she calls "life changing" therapy, she discovered that "anger is okay," clearly opening up her world to the possibility of tolerating this emotion and surviving its intensity. Learning to deal with anger, however, was only one of many battles for Samantha, who regularly fears engaging in some of her predecessors' family patterns. For example, she recalls the onset of panic attacks surrounding major events in her life, such as the engagement to her husband and the birth of her baby boy:

> And then... we were engaged and we were gonna get married and I was having a lot of anxiety, like trouble breathing. And I think it had a lot to do with getting married and not re-doing my parents' relationship... I was like, okay, I have to go to therapy. And I stayed in that therapy for two and a half years and that was I think the most impactful therapy. And then, when I had Taylor and I was having panic attacks, I went back for a brief time. That was pretty brief. I think I was more sleep deprived than anything.

The fear of "re-doing" her parents' relationship, of becoming a wife or a mother like her mother, is consistently on her mind. Samantha later describes her panic attacks as, "It would feel like I couldn't get a full breath. It wasn't a full-fledged panic attack. I was breathing but it felt like the air wasn't satisfying me." Understandably, her unremitting attempts to not recreate the past, and the ongoing awareness and determination to do things differently in the present, can be altogether exhausting. As Samantha begins to describe never getting "a full breath," feeling that the "air wasn't satisfying" her, it seems that the struggle to break away from historically entrenched family patterns requires a "full-fledged" attempt: every last breath is devoted to this cause, and every new breath is assessed for intergenerational meaning. As I asked Samantha about whether or not she reflects on herself as a mother, she responded emphatically, "Every... day":

> N: So do you think sometimes about yourself as a mother and how you want to be with your children and what you would want to differently?
> S: Every... day I think about that. I mean, I definitely try to take the good stuff that my parents gave me and do the bad stuff differently. I'm very conscious of not

losing my cool, not yelling, not taking out my anger on him. If I'm angry at something, at Jacob my husband, or whatever, just putting it off till later. Not being so impulsive and just really recognizing the importance... recognizing the importance of being a full support for him and taking care of him and not ever being a scary... I used to be scared when I would hear my mom's footsteps down the hall and I don't ever want him to feel like that. I want him to come snuggle with me and to know that I love him unconditionally. I know logically that my mom loves me unconditionally and has, but the way that I was growing up it felt like her love was not unconditional. When she got angry, it felt like I was totally abandoned.

N: How was it giving birth to your son and becoming a mother and that whole transition?

S: That was probably the hardest thing that I have ever done. I mean, after I had him, I had panic attacks. I don't know how much of it was hormones and how much of it was mental, probably some combination of both. But I was so scared. I did not know what to do with him. I mean, I've never been like a baby person. And then on top of everything, I think I was just so scared of re-doing everything... But I think I was so aware of it that I'm fine. And it's gotten so much better, like I'm fine now. But I think the beginning of being a mom was super, super hard. And I think probably has a lot to do with my own growing up.

N: Was there anything specific that was hard?

S: Feeding was hard because he was kind of colic-y and I think he had acid reflux and I had to switch his formula like five times and he was constipated so we had to have prune juice and he was spitting up a lot. But he always ate, so that was okay. (Silence.) It is just interesting thinking about when you're feeding your newborn baby, you want them to eat. But I think I am very aware of... because of everything that happened with my mom and forcing, he eats what he wants to eat and if he stops eating I just assume that he's not hungry...

In her attempts to do things differently from her parents and grandparents, Samantha to a large extent succeeds. She works hard not to become a "scary" figure to her husband and child, and to provide them with the unconditional love she felt she lacked growing up. She suggests that recognizing her fears, hopes, and desires has been the key: "But I was so scared. I did not know what to do with him... And then on top of everything I think I was just so scared of re-doing everything... But I think I was so aware of it that I'm fine," she says, and indeed there is a sense that her self-reflection allows her to pinpoint her weaknesses and reach out for help when necessary. Of course, each decision she makes, whether in parenting or in her marriage, is linked to an entire history of decisions—ones she might circumvent, and ones she might not. For example, Samantha describes consciously struggling with her baby's eating habits: on the one hand, she says, "you want them to eat," but on the other, "because of everything that happened with my mom and forcing, he eats what he wants to eat and if he stops eating I just assume that he's not hungry..." Each decision and behavior is consciously (and unconsciously) linked to her history, thereby allowing her to feel she "addressed that and lived with that." Similarly, in describing her choice in partner, Samantha reveals the changes through the generations:

> He's like a super-involved husband and father. And it's very equal in our relationship, like we both do everything. Like, he cooks, and he totally spends so much time with Taylor and takes care of him. On the weekends, I have to do homework pretty much all day and it's just like him and Taylor.

Despite, or perhaps because of, the numerous transformations she has willfully sought and achieved in her life, Samantha's day-to-day existence and moment-to-moment decisions inevitably summon her history. Whether she is feeding the baby, driving her car, or crossing the street, she experiences a combination of fear and gratitude:

> S: I definitely have had thoughts... I was thinking about it this morning as I was getting ready... it has to do with

everything that's going on in the world today, but it probably also has to do with the Holocaust... just like the fear. I would have these fears after I had the baby... well, I think about how lucky I am a lot. How lucky I am to live in America and how lucky I am that I have food and a house and a car and I go to school. And yet I just feel like I couldn't really be any luckier in terms of those things. And then I just think, like I've had a couple of thoughts, like fears... oh, maybe it was the World Trade Center that made me think about it. But just like, at any moment, what if somebody came and took away Taylor? And, again, I think I had these thoughts when he was a baby and I was feeding him his bottles... and what if something ever happened where there was some kind of thing that happened like a war or some kind of attack, and I couldn't get out of the house and get food for him? Like he would be starving. Or something about having my freedom and my power taken away, or having him taken away from me or something happening to him, or him being hungry or just how horrible that would be. That would be like the worst thing.

N: A lot of third generations talk about fear of death and loss.

S: Yeah, I think a lot of moments sometimes during the day I just think about that everything could really just end. A bus could hit me, lightning could strike me, war could break out—anything could happen. Usually, like 99% of the time, that gives me a good feeling... a feeling like I have to appreciate this moment, and I have to appreciate all the moments I've had up until now. You just never know. And we're all gonna die someday anyway, so just appreciating my freedom and everything I have. Kind of like an every day gift.

Alongside a historically-pertinent recognition that life cannot be taken for granted, Samantha describes the fears that accompany each day, causing her to "appreciate this moment" and "appreciate all the moments I've had up until now." She engages with some the most frightening questions and scenarios: "something about having my freedom and my power taken away, or having him taken away from me or something happening to him, or him being hungry or just how horrible that would be." In facing these fears rather then leaving them untouched and unexamined, Samantha also attains gratitude and the sense of "an every day gift." It is *through* her link with history that she more fully lives in the present.

CHAPTER 8: RUTH

Shame... or Pride

R: When I was in Madrid... I spent a semester in Madrid my junior year of college... I lived with this very, very old woman for like two days. She was like 90. Then I moved in with another family... it was a young mother and two daughters. I was gonna move again, so whatever, it's fine. But I noticed on the table after being there for a few weeks... it had different tiles on it... and one of the tiles in the center was a swastika. I was 20 years old and in a foreign country and I basically... I don't want to say that I hid the fact that I was Jewish, but I really tried to avoid the conversation. To me even, and that's not, look... that's nine or eight years ago. *I can't believe that I did that.* It's embarrassing to me that I didn't say something to someone at the time. And I remember asking her about it much later, right before I was leaving to come back to D.C., because I felt like I didn't know what was going to happen to me. She told me it was some like witch symbol or something and it wasn't what I thought it was. I guess it doesn't really matter, but that, like, we're talking about 2000.

N: I guess she didn't want to talk about it.

R: I know, it's crazy.

N: So you lived there.

R: I lived there. I lived there for five months (laughing).

N: You ate on that table.

R: Yeah. (Silence.) If that was me today I can't imagine being there for more than five minutes without saying something or leaving or doing something else.

N: I think it speaks to how hard it is to approach that topic.

R: It's very hard. Look, there's certain times when you feel it's easier to not say something than to say something, and the fact that that goes on only proves the point that there are people who are anti-Semitic and people don't feel like they're thought of equally. To be ashamed or to hide the fact that you're Jewish from someone, the fact that that goes on today, is terrifying to me.

The 28-year-old granddaughter of two Holocaust survivors, Ruth reveals feeling ashamed for having been silenced in the face of a swastika. "I can't believe that I did that," she emphasizes, "It's embarrassing to me that I didn't say something to someone at the time." What might Ruth have said or done to alter the event or subsequent feelings about the event? Should she have engaged in a dialogue about anti-Semitism, the meaning of the swastika, or the injustice of history? Could she have tackled the reality of racism in the modern world, demanding an explanation for this woman's anti-Semitic beliefs, or even more ambitious: attempted to change this woman's opinion? Had Ruth revealed the fact that she was Jewish, might she have served as an example of a "normal" Jew, merely a young woman like any other, not at all someone to be feared or hated? Or might she have felt some relief in revealing her Jewish identity, even if this meant she was not "thought of equally," because she served as a living, breathing memorial for her murdered ancestors? How much of history can one person take on?

If history cannot be undone and sometimes "it's easier to not say something than to say something," why not remain silent? What is the value of broaching "that topic"? In Ruth's case, her past silence continues to plague her: "If that was me today I can't imagine being there for more than five minutes without saying something or leaving or doing something else." In essence, she is saying, "If that was me today I would not have been silenced by shame." She struggles to rationalize her silence with the fact that she considered making a change: "I was gonna move again, so whatever, it's fine"; and attempts to expunge the intensity of the topic altogether: "I guess it doesn't really matter." However, she is horrified and embarrassed by her experience of shame, as the feeling implies the presence of something to be ashamed *of*. She concludes, "To be ashamed or to hide the fact that you're Jewish from someone, the fact that that goes on today, is terrifying to me." That is, silence and humiliation about her background are "terrifying," given that millions

were tortured and murdered for what was considered a "shameful" identity, while others stood silently by.

Although she regrets it, keeping her background a secret seemed to
protect Ruth from experiencing an extensive sense of loss and anguish
in a setting that might have undermined her painful history. She says,
"I remember asking her about it much later, right before I was leaving
to come back to D.C., because I felt like I didn't know what was going to
happen to me," implying a two-sided fear: of an internal breakdown in
defenses and of an external attack. Indeed, there is always the question
of choosing to speak versus remaining silent. At the same time, however,
speech that is driven by the pressure to prove oneself and the need to
represent an entire history of a people might similarly (though perhaps
successfully) divert attention from a person's underlying shame. Thus,
while silence may appear to be the weaker, dishonorable counterpart of
language, shame can exist in both speech and silence.

How Ruth might react in a similar situation eight or nine years later
we cannot know. However, reflections on her past silence have driven
her adult identity. She has attempted to transform her shame into pride,
standing tall and strong, becoming self-sufficient and accomplished,
and proving to the world that there is nothing to hide:

> R: ...the strength of a person, you know... there's noth-
> ing that I would want anybody to do for me because I feel
> like I can do it for myself. The same way my grandmother
> is, the same way my mothers is, sort of taking ownership
> and...
> N: Do for you... what kinds of things?
> R: Anything at all. The idea that you have to be not just
> independent but able to really survive on your own
> from, you know, emotionally, physically, financially, and
> maybe especially as a female... that may be a little bit of
> a different mentality but it's not... I'm not sure how to
> even describe it... my grandmother is probably, I mean,
> she's stubborn to no end but one of the most strongest
> human being I've ever encountered, and my mom's the
> same way; I mean, almost difficult to a point, right? My
> dad's biggest challenge is trying to do anything for her
> because she does everything by herself. My mother had

more of a sense of guilt that she always felt she always had to do for her mother because of what they went though. I don't think I have that at all. I feel more of a responsibility to carry on being... having a Jewish family than anything, which I feel like for my mother was just a given. You know, that generation, obviously they were gonna marry somebody Jewish. For us it's now kind of more in the air. So that's something that to me is very important.

"I feel more of a responsibility to carry on being..." she trails off, clearly referring to a responsibility to carry on being a Jew. Given the struggle between shame and pride, silence and language, perceived weakness and strength, carrying on her Jewish identity is understandably a complex and loaded responsibility. She depicts the "strength of a person ... the same way my grandmother is, the same way my mothers is, sort of taking ownership and..." "Ownership," she suggests, implying the act of possessing and acknowledging her characteristics. For example, in "taking ownership" of who she is, Ruth might say, "This is mine" or "This is me." Thus, her confident depiction involving the "strength of a person" stands in contrast to her previous remark, "I don't want to say that I hid the fact that I was Jewish, but I really tried to avoid the conversation." Has Ruth worked through her past shame—examining, questioning, and exploring it—such that she now carries a sense of pride and ownership in its place? Or has shame been camouflaged by pride, as the two coexist on a continuum that is influenced by person, time, and place? Having been shaken by the discovery of a debilitating sense of shame, it seems that Ruth acquired a determination to rework this emotion and modify its role in her present identity.

Ruth attempts to explain the meaning of the "strength of a person," stating, "there's nothing that I would want anybody to do for me because I feel like I can do it for myself." Interestingly, in later describing her grandmother's concentration camp survival, Ruth divulges having written a school paper about the notion of "camp sisters": "It was about how people survived through a safety of having a sister. It wasn't typically a sister—could've been the most random person. Just that yin-yang kind of balance of pulling each other through... creating that kind of family..." While Ruth recognizes her grandmother's need for the support of another person in order to survive the camps, Ruth herself has worked to consciously eliminate the need for support from anyone. It seems Ruth's "strength of a person" relates to her past shame; in not wanting anyone to do anything for her and feeling like she can do it herself, she hopes to prove that the frightened, humiliated girl of eight years ago is gone. Her internal sense of self, therefore, continues to be driven by her individual and collective history, by her naturally arising shame, and by her disapproval of this emotion. In response to shameful affects, and her ongoing embarrassment about previous inaction, Ruth demands of herself unwavering pride and "strength": never again will she be the silent, frightened, 20-year-old student in a foreign country; never again will she feel anything but proud of her Jewish heritage; never again will she be the timid granddaughter of Holocaust survivors who is understandably stifled by the horrific truths of history. Never again.

But Ever-Present... Fear

Towards the conclusion of the interview, Ruth reveals that she no longer tears up during interviews like this one, while in the past she likely would have cried. The following conversation arose from this recognition:

> N: So how is it to sit here and talk about it and notice that you're not crying?
> R: I don't know. Maybe in some ways after being... you know, you get yourself to a certain point and I've always been someone who can create distance. You know, you've sort of got that emotional guard, like, I keep this here and compartmentalize it a little bit. So, I'm sure there's some of that. And I was also just... I don't even want to call it an acceptance, but it's kind of like you see this reality of what it is and it's kind of like there's nothing you can do about it but to move forward with the knowledge and the strength of what has happened and make sure the people around me don't forget. And maybe the next generation everyone will see each other as equal, but I don't know.
> N: So have you always had the ability to compartmentalize, or has that developed more recently?

R: No, that's old news.

N: You just kind of realized you were able to put distance between things?

R: Daughter of a psychologist.

N: Were you in therapy?

R: 24 hours a day (laughing). No, never.

Establishing a distance and compartmentalizing various aspects of her life have allowed Ruth to maintain what she calls an "emotional guard." She says, "I don't even want to call it an acceptance, but it's kind of like you see this reality of what it is and it's kind of like there's nothing you can do about it but to move forward with the knowledge and the strength of what has happened and make sure the people around me don't forget." Ruth attains a sense of strength in her "acceptance" of the past, feeling there is nothing she can "do" about it except make a place for history and ensure that historical realities are transmitted to future generations. However, reaching a level of acceptance required developing an emotional guard and an ability to compartmentalize her feelings; again, a reference to Ruth limiting certain experiences in order to maintain "strength." Furthermore, her use of humor allows Ruth to find relief in the intensity of her experiences. Yet, her feelings of fear, shame, and pride become less compartmentalized and increasingly hazy in the face of a 13-year-old boy's questioning of historical facts:

> To me, at this point more than anything, I see it... because I see so many people, especially like dating/ marrying people who are not Jewish... and to me, most importantly, I feel like that would be disrespectful and not continuing the importance and the strength of how I identify, and how much of my family was killed, and so many of those issues that to me create a really strong force and desire to have a Jewish family and Jewish children and to teach them. And it scares me because I think there is a lot of forgetting that is about to go on. I have a 13-year-old cousin in L.A., who I saw a couple weeks ago, and he told me a kid in his school got punched in the face because he said the Holocaust never happened. And my guess is that that is like the tip of the iceberg in that you

know my children's generation, our children's generation, will have a real uphill battle in terms of identifying themselves as Jews in many ways. And I think that
the way I see myself as the granddaughter of Holocaust
survivors... I don't see if that... I don't know if my children will feel as I felt. I think a lot of that generation will
never know or touch a survivor the way a lot of us have.

While she hesitantly suggests the possibility that in "the next generation, everyone will see each other as equal," Ruth's ongoing fear and
vulnerability continue to influence her day-to-day life. She says, "I see
so many people, especially like dating/marrying people who are not
Jewish... and to me, most importantly, I feel like that would be disrespectful and not continuing the importance and the strength of how I
identify..." Ruth speaks to the commonly-held view of intermarriage as
the greatest threat to the survival of Judaism—a modern-day form of
annihilation anxiety. Furthermore, she struggles to depict "the importance and the strength" of her identity in contrast to her brothers, who
"live under a different set of rules: one of them is married to someone
who isn't Jewish, one of them probably will marry someone who's not
Jewish, and I think two of us will." When asked why she thinks this
sense of responsibility largely falls on her shoulders, Ruth suggests:

> I think that the responsibility that my mother felt has
> been ingrained in me, not so much my brother. You
> know, boys grow up to be like their fathers, girls grow
> up to be like their mothers. I think that I have a lot of
> that. It's just something I've always taken more seri-
> ously than my siblings for whatever reason.

Whether or not the split between the genders fully explains the role
that Ruth plays in her family, undertaking the battle to "never forget"
has become her lifelong journey. Alongside this responsibility, the issues of respect, the "strength" of her present Jewish identity, the past
murder of her family members, and the desire to raise Jewish children
in the future all blend into one: "I feel like that would be disrespectful
and not continuing the importance and the strength of how I identify,
and how much of my family was killed, and so many of those issues that

to me create a really strong force and desire to have a Jewish family." One sentence summarizes one ongoing, collective narrative.

Understandably, Ruth fears that "there is a lot of forgetting that is about to go on," feeling that history, like pride, is a fragile, vulnerable entity. What will happen when her children can no longer "touch" a survivor (or be touched by one)? Will they continue to "know" their collective trauma, to feel the complicated combination of shame, pride, and fear that she experiences? Is grappling with a constant threat of annihilation synonymous with maintaining a Jewish identity? Or can her children identify themselves as Jews without the torment of regular confrontations with the past? In attempting to describe her grandfather's Holocaust stories, Ruth reveals:

> I mean, I lost track of some of them, I was so young... it's like, what do you know when you're like five years old? I remember him sitting me down on his lap and trying to tell me these things and I had a) no interest, and b) no patience. I wanted to go run around and do whatever... so I felt very cheated later after he died because so many things that he wanted to share that aren't there anymore.

Ruth's words illustrate that the obstruction of history is a very real and omnipresent fear, one that Ruth has tackled head on, but that began first and foremost in her own personal experience. Having had "a) no interest, and b) no patience," a five-year-old Ruth turned away from her grandfather's lap, causing the details of his stories to disappear from her conscious memory. On some level, it seems Ruth hopes that her efforts to "never forget" will not only ensure the survival of Holocaust history at large, but might also reinstate her grandfather's lost tales, resurfacing and reestablishing the truths of his-story. Concretely, Ruth goes a step further in her efforts to transmit a disappearing history; below she describes a murdered relative, a ghost, who has accompanied the family narrative from past to present, and will be carried into the future:

> R: My grandfather's sister, who I obviously never met, but whenever I think about her... I guess probably because I identify... she was 12 and she was killed right away and that breaks my heart.

N: Why do you think it's her?

R: I think because she's someone specific; she was a young female. I've heard him talk about her. She was his baby sister. And his mother, who he described as the best woman ever... and I'm sure his sister was her little angel.

N: What was her name?

R: Toni.

N: Do you think you'll name children after...?

R: Yeah.

Ruth feels personally and intimately connected to her grandfather's murdered sister, clinging to a fantasy of the person and maintaining a relationship to her name. The Holocaust therefore attains a present-day feel, and the murder of Toni carries the weight of someone Ruth knew well in present time. Thus, every anti-Semitic individual, every questioning 13-year-old, every ignorant or fearful or hateful person produces a threat; however, this is not a threat that history *might* at any moment reappear, but rather a realization that history *does* at every moment reappear. After all, a sense of safety, acceptance, and equality (all internal and external experiences) have not yet been achieved. Furthermore, Ruth describes one of her recent conversations about whether or not she should "hate all Germans," who themselves believed, "we hate these Jews; we want to kill them":

> I don't feel hopeless. I do feel that there is a lot of anti-Semitism still. Actually, I had a conversation last week about "Do I hate all Germans? Should we hate all Germans?" Well, I mean, the obvious answer is kind of like, not all Germans did this and that's a little bit of a ridiculous stance to take, but I was in Germany when I was abroad for a weekend and I will tell you I felt very uncomfortable. Even hearing the language made me uncomfortable. I can't imagine what it would do to my grandparents. And I think even within the United States... even within D.C., or wherever it is, and... we live in a largely Jewish... at least a largely Jewishly-aware city, and I still think there's a level there that people don't even talk about... the same that there's racism against

blacks that people don't talk about. Maybe they talk about it more, I don't know. When I had this conversation about "Should we hate all Germans?" with someone, what I said was, "Look at those people's grandparents, right? Cause it's the same third generation. So they grew up like, 'We hate these Jews; we want to kill them.' Those are their grandparents. Maybe they really disagree, but a lot of them... that's kind of what they grew up with, and that's scary." And to say that these people are so far different from their grandparents I think is a leap of faith that I don't know if I'm personally comfortable taking. I think that that's like a jump... that's a big jump... Putting a lot of faith in people that I don't know if I have.

Ruth speaks to an ongoing sense of fear and insecurity that she carries, as the Germans of Nazi Germany and contemporary Germany blend into inseparable entities; after all, she likewise reveals the ways in which third-generation Holocaust survivors, deeply impacted by their traumatic history, are intertwined with their ancestors' experiences. She wonders to what extent "faith in people" will allow her to consider "that these people are so far different from their grandparents," ultimately deciding that "that's a big jump." When past and present collide, therefore, the leap towards something "so far different" is immense. Ruth's question about hating "all" Germans is provoked by Nazi Germany, although it is asked within the context of a "Jewishly-aware" city. As she tackles some difficult questions related to projection and introjection—they hate us so we should hate them—her collective, historically-laden fear, shame, and pride are tangible. Towards the end of her interview, I asked Ruth about her mother's choice of the mental health profession:

No, I never asked her how she really got interested. I think she probably needed a way to kind of figure out what was going on with them and how that related to her, because it's a real big burden to bear even if you understand it. She still gets upset with her mother all the time, with someone who you can honestly understand what's going on, but understanding and feeling are two different things.

"...but understanding and feeling are two different things," Ruth suggests, shedding light on her own separation between what she knows and what she experiences. While she knows that Jewish pride is a fundamental element of her self-esteem, she cannot help but feel occasional fear, shame, and embarrassment about her history. Although she understands that she was born generations after the Holocaust, she oftentimes experiences historical dynamics unfolding in the present. Finally, while she knows that nothing can undo her painful past, she feels that grappling with it might lessen the blow of the traumatic event. Thus, Ruth concludes, "...it's a real big burden to bear even if you understand it," highlighting the ultimate, unavoidable meeting between knowledge and emotion.

CHAPTER 9: MIRIAM

M: I also have kind of a rebellious side. I've gotten a lot of emotional satisfaction out of feeling... sort of rebuffing what I'm supposed to be. Another interesting piece... my first love was this Slovak guy from Eastern Europe who was Christian... wore a cross around his neck... and it was like years of devastating... I didn't date him for years, but... not Jewish, he was from Eastern Europe, from Slovakia. I went to visit him once with his grandmother and like, they had, like, chicken soup with matzo balls but they were long and not round, and there were like, donuts with jelly on the side and... I was very, very pulled to him... like, oh my God, his grandmother was a collaborator with the Germans. And he'd tell me stuff and anyway... I played out a lot of stuff around a lot of rebelliousness. Also, I think I felt close to him. In some ways there was a lot of cultural difference... but I think I also felt really comfortable with him. There was something comforting for me with him. He was from Eastern Europe and anyways there was a lot of kind of intrigue...
N: How was that for you, the religious differences, background differences... all the things that came to mind?
M: It felt really wrenching. I think for a while he didn't tell his family that I was Jewish. He had an uncle who was a priest, and thought he would be disapproving... like, took me to see the area that used to be the Jewish part of town... it was clearly abandoned. Told me the Germans had taken over his grandfather's house and the backyard and stuff and I really had this sense of like... it was awful, I felt like I was in bed with a collaborator and it was killing my grandmother, and my mom was extremely opposed to it; said it wasn't going to be good for me, that I would have... you know, there was a lot of deterrence. I felt really fragmented. I didn't know how

my Jewish self was going to be. It was also really interesting and intriguing to be like in a church in Slovakia and Kristallnacht was there. It was also exciting... I definitely played it out like constantly.

"I've gotten a lot of emotional satisfaction out of feeling... sort of rebuffing what I'm supposed to be," says 29-year-old Miriam, a half-Israeli, half-American, third generation descendant of the Holocaust. Her tale of her "first love" powerfully captures how history comes alive in her present-day existence. "I was very, very pulled to him," she reflects, and the meeting of a Jewish descendant of a Holocaust survivor and a Christian descendant of Slovak "collaborators" is saturated with images linked to past and present. Miriam conveys the "comforting" but also "wrenching" effects of this bond; after all, the connection they shared was established three-quarters of a century ago, under circumstances diametrically opposed to the present. Through her "rebellious" nature, Miriam blurs the boundaries between love and hate, rebelliousness and allegiance, owned and disowned identity. While she feels she is "rebuffing" who she is "supposed to be"—referring to herself as divided from her ancestors—it is precisely in this "rebuffing" that Miriam summons her roots. In a sense, she "plays out" an existence entrenched in repetition and reenactment: finding herself in a "comforting," yet "wrenching" dynamic, struggling to grasp and loosen the tie of history. To do so, she reenters her ancestors' world, "in bed with a collaborator," "killing" her grandmother, feeling "fragmented," "intrigued," and fused with the experience of the Holocaust.

Miriam goes on to verbalize feeling "tortured" and "haunted" by this experience years later:

> M: He was basically... I had come back and he was finishing up another year and I was graduating from college and trying to figure out what to do with myself. And he was really ready to move out to Chicago. I was totally tortured and I just thought, well, what kind of job is he gonna get and am I going to have to move out to Slovakia? What do I do? And the religion thing was huge, and I didn't know what to do, and so I broke up with him... but then I really felt haunted by it for like

years later. We still write each other cards in the mail. He's been with the same woman for... I don't feel like it's processed... often when I talk about it I'll start crying. I felt like he was this ghost that was like haunting me for years and I really regretted breaking up with him.

N: Yeah, in a way he represented so much more... he was himself, but he was also...

M: Right. He was this whole different world, he was also... I was playing out everything—relationships, power... it was extremely exciting for me.

By "playing out everything—relationships, power..." Miriam and her "first love" engaged in an enactment of their shared history, both attempting to master something unknowable and inexplicable. As she took on the more powerful role and ended the relationship, Miriam instantaneously challenged the course of history in the present (in her exertion of power), but also left history untouched (in that history can be forever replayed but not reversed). Furthermore, the impact of terminating this connection was devastating for her, as Miriam experienced a sense of loss and distance from this man, and from the history that bound them together. She states, "I felt like he was this ghost that was like haunting me for years..." That is, with the termination of the concrete, the bond evolved into an elusive, ever-present awareness of all that was lost. While this man seems to have entered a new relationship, Miriam is left feeling that the entire experience remains unprocessed, and that she might "start crying" whenever she speaks of it. Therefore, her statement "it was extremely exciting for me" speaks to the exhilarating revival of history and all of its accompanying emotions and dynamics. In the ensuing discussion of Miriam's subsequent decision to date only Jews, Miriam reveals:

M: I think it felt better to me. I think for a long time it really felt like... maybe as I've gotten older and I've gotten closer to sort of feeling like wanting to get married or something like that it just felt better... but I think for a long time I think "Jewish" meant being married with a white picket fence and stuck and boring and suburbia...

acquiescing and not being an individual... which makes
sense in my family... I tend to be attracted to people that
have some good amount of push and pull with religion.
N: Do you envision raising your kids Jewish?
M: Yeah, although when I think about what kind of sto-
ries I'm going to tell them, I don't know very many...
N: Well, you have your own stories.
M: Right, I have my own stories.

In Miriam's depiction, "Jewish" seems to stand for "free of conflict,"
lacking a "push and pull with religion" and also with history. She explains,
"...'Jewish' meant being married with a white picket fence and stuck and
boring and suburbia... acquiescing and not being an individual..." That
is, Miriam's definition of the word "Jewish" means to escape "being an
individual," and falling into a preformed mold that might prevent her
from asserting control, expressing her individuality, and developing a
unique sense of self. Interestingly, the image of the "white picket fence"
serves as an American symbol of the ideal middle-class suburban life,
with a family, 2.5 children, sizeable house, and serene existence. Unsurprisingly, Miriam feels impelled to escape this standard, as it does
not capture her individual or collective identity. As she explicitly states
in the opening of her interview, "My grandparents had accents and I
was very convinced that was the normal course of things, although it
also made me feel different than my American Jewish peers. I just didn't
quite identify with American Judaism." In her rebellion from "American
Judaism," Miriam simultaneously searches for her roots. In retrospect,
my comment "Well, you have your own stories" seems to address the
fact that whether or not she knows her ancestor's specific tales, she
quite evidently and concretely merges with her history, discovering
parts of herself along the way. Ironically though perhaps not surprisingly, Miriam later discusses her grandmother's "secretive" nature, and
reveals a striking parallel between her grandmother and herself, stating
in passing, "She was in love with a non-Jew and you know there was all
this... she's just very, very secretive." This intergenerational repetition
of patterns reveals Miriam's ever-present connection with history, even
in her disconnect from the details.

Binging on History

Miriam contextualizes the fact that she does not "know" very many stories through a description of her mother's lifelong accumulation of "all" the stories:

> I think she feels it's her responsibility of the second generation to like have all the information. She must have sensed a lot of the sadness of her parents having lost that old world, and their approach, I think, was try to forget it, and hers was to try to recover it and contain it. I'm sure she and I in very different ways have tried to find ways to master and try to make sense of a lot of pain and disruption, and that was her way of doing it.

Miriam's insight regarding her attempts to "master" and "make sense of a lot of pain and disruption" is compelling; while her grandparents attempted to "forget" their sadness and her mother worked hard to "recover it and contain it," Miriam is left with a determination to not "acquiesce" to either pattern. Thus, she chooses not to take in the stories, yet to maintain connection to her history in her own way. Miriam continues:

> M: I feel like I... I think it's probably typical... my mother like wants to be... sees herself as the memory receptacle. She's constantly asking extremely detailed questions to my grandmother and my great aunts and uncle about, like, before the war and during the war. She wants the details and the history and you know... at this point she has more of it than my grandmother does because my grandmother kind of gets confused... or she'll remind my grandmother what was in her house, or you know... or she'll like trace... she's obsessed. The first thing she does is finds out a last name and tries to trace like family lineage in Eastern Europe and she... like, she can be diagnosed with PTSD. She's extremely fearful. There's always impending disaster. She's very good in crisis.
> N: Can you give an example of that fear... how that impacts her?

M: My father has commuted to Chicago for the last five years and she won't sleep in bed without him, she sleeps on the couch, and has like a scissor under her cushion and the alarm is on and she will often... whenever I go out somewhere she'll tell me to take my ID with me and I'll ask her why, and she's like, "In case you die they can identify the body." She's just overprotective throughout and just has issues... she's definitely gotten better. You can just see she has the worst-case scenario... she's highly anxious, she's really reactive... she probably has survivor skills. She's obese, she has diabetes; she cannot take care of herself. She spends a lot of time obsessing about my grandmother. I guess that's another reason why my grandmother is alive... with the case of survivors, they can't let themselves go because they're worried that if they do die it will destroy their children. And my mother's like really concerned about keeping her alive even though she's in a wheelchair and catheterized and quite unhappy a lot of the time.

Miriam's mother serves as the "memory receptacle" for her family, growing increasingly obese with all that she takes in. That is, in order to "master" her history, she is impelled to "recover and contain" all of the historical pain, literally and figuratively stuffing herself full. As Miriam describes, "she's like a *repository* for all this terrible stuff." On the one hand, therefore, her mother's obesity symbolizes her ancestors' starvation; on the other hand, Miriam's mother is literally overextended by the burden of the past. She cannot possibly "take care of herself," because she is far too busy "obsessing" about Miriam's grandmother, spending an entire lifetime "keeping her alive." The transmission of anxiety, distrust, and fear are evident in Miriam's concrete examples of her mother sleeping with scissors under her cushion and demanding that Miriam carry an ID so that her dead body might be identified. Furthermore, as Miriam states, "she can be diagnosed with PTSD. She's extremely fearful. There's always impending disaster. She's very good in crisis." That is, traumatized by her ancestors' experiences, Miriam's mother "can be diagnosed with PTSD," as though she survived the experience herself.

Attempting to Restrict the Past

Miriam describes the ways in which she disconnects from her mother's stories, and more generally establishes boundaries between her mother and herself:

> M: I mean, she usually doesn't get totally through a story. I mean, she'll start to tell me something and I'll kind of try to listen because like she's trying to tell me something and part of me thinks I'd want to know some this stuff in the future. And about two or three sentences later I haven't heard a word she's saying. We're somewhere in the middle of like Poland or Russia, and she'll talk for a while and I'm not listening but I'm kind of nodding, and then at some point I'm just like, I can't hear anymore. Thanks, I'm done.
>
> N: Is that generally kind of your reaction to her? Or mostly just on that topic?
>
> M: No, she and I also clash and I find her overwhelming in general, and I think that's a good classification of things. But, no, I often find her kind of boundary-bending or there's stuff kind of spilling over into our world or... I think when I was younger for a long time I felt like... or you know, the beginning stages of therapy... that I had no idea who, or what, were my emotions and what were anyone else's... I think my father also had a traumatic childhood and I was depressed and I didn't really have a sense of what it was. I didn't think it was mine, I think... I mean it was mine, you know, carrying around a lot of their stuff. So I think I got... I tried to create boundaries.

As the boundaries are blurred and her mother's experience begins "spilling over" into Miriam's world, Miriam successfully blocks out the stimuli. "I'll kind of try to listen because like she's trying to tell me something and part of me thinks I'd want to know some this stuff in the future. And about two or three sentences later I haven't heard a word she's saying," she explains. Ultimately, she is left with the feeling, "I can't hear anymore. Thanks, I'm done." Having been completely overwhelmed by her grandmother's past experience as well as her mother's reaction to history, Miriam understands that much of what she is filled with is "a lot of their stuff." She perceptively states, "I had no idea who, or what, were my emotions and what were anyone else's." That is, she had no idea whose emotions she was carrying or who she suddenly embodied. She did, however, sense, "I didn't think it was mine," and protectively attempted to set boundaries in place.

In separating herself from her mother and from historical narrative, Miriam does not become emotionless or unaware. Instead, her distance from the familial enmeshment and chaos allows her to more fully explore and understand her experience. The importance of her successfully doing so can be seen in her discussion of "crazy-making" experiences with her mother. That is, Miriam seems to be fighting not only for individuality, but also for her sanity:

> Something just happened to me the other day and it's... oh, I got home and she was cooking and I said, "Is dinner going to be soon? I'm hungry and I'm wondering if I should have a snack or not." And she said, "No, it won't be for a while," which to me means hours. So I had a larger snack. Fifteen minutes later my dad is home and she said, "Whenever you guys want to eat" and my dad said, "I'm hungry" and I said, "Didn't you say dinner would be in a while?" and she denied the two of us having had that exchange. Later I said, "You know, if you forgot or changed your mind or made a mistake, it's not a big deal. But when you deny the exchange happened, it makes me so confused about reality. It makes me feel like I'm crazy." She just can't... she's like, "Why do you get so angry?" You know. There's just no way of talking to her most of the time. We often get into a clash which will be about something and then we just let it drop and come back together and we're fine... instead of talking it out. I don't know.

Miriam attempts to explain "...when you deny the exchange happened, it makes me so confused about reality. It makes me feel like I'm crazy." That is, in addition to not knowing which thought or emotion belongs to her, Miriam also cannot trust the events that unfold in her everyday life. She winds up feeling "so confused" about reality, as she cannot distinguish true from false, hers from theirs, reality from fantasy. While she confronts her mother about the impact of altogether denying a real exchange, it seems that there is often "no way of talking," no true communication, between mother and daughter. The lack of a shared language, therefore, sheds further light on Miriam's desire not to know her family's stories, or to actively seek out past trauma; after all, the present is already brimming with the trauma of the past, and is in and of itself overwhelming. Along these lines, Miriam explains her conscious effort not to engulf herself in Holocaust-related films or books:

> I feel like there is this place in me that can just be totally bottomed out and I know where it is and have done enough of it and I'm just not interested... I feel like it floods me or I get flooded. Like, I don't understand what purpose it has for me. Like, as an educational tool... the same questions as my mother's stories. Like, do I need any more details? Like, I certainly don't know very much about it... Like, I feel like the acquisition of that information just feels like an emotional overload. I don't know what purpose it has for me. I don't know how to translate the "Never forget" message... do I think it's important? Do I identify with the AJWF global social justice movement approach? But no, I... I don't know... I don't want to be inundated with it. I want it to be useful to me. I'm not using it in a generative way. I don't know... maybe it'll change...

In an effort to not be "totally bottomed out" but rather make it "useful" for herself, Miriam attempts to acquire historical information in moderation. She adds, "I find my way of dealing with it is to download articles or something." That is, "articles" related to her Holocaust history seem to provide an accessible amount of information, which serve a "purpose" and remain a "generative" tool. Indeed, it seems Miriam's established boundaries between herself and her history are firm. However, in a brief discussion about her father's lineage, Miriam reveals a much more extensive curiosity and connection to his experiences of loss and grief. When asked what might have drawn her more to her paternal history, Miriam suggests, "Maybe I was trying to piece together my dad more. He could be very calm but then some sort of invisible wire will trip him. You know, it was really very clear what was going on with my mom..." Despite her clashes with her mother, Miriam innately understands and identifies with her mother's experiences. Furthermore, regardless of her established boundaries or desire for distance, Miriam maintains an instinctive closeness to, and knowledge of, her Holocaust history. With or without the details, the past is inescapably a part of her.

Maintaining Weight and Substance

M: I went to a nutritionist senior year of high school and I got myself to a therapist my sophomore year of college and I think I constantly negotiated issues around like having a very loving family, it's very enmeshed, it's very sad in some ways—being a part of the family means sort of being sad and depressed and having my mother in particular sort of make these clinical, global statements about the family.

N: "Everyone's depressed? Everyone's sad?"

M: Right, and if my sister's not... it's strange, how did that kind of emerge? I mean, my sister also has her own anxieties. The apple doesn't fall far from the tree. So, I think it's individuating and being not severely depressed, but all those things that come with fears of being abandoned.

N: How did you get yourself to a nutritionist?

M: I had some kind of weird eating habits in high school. It wasn't awful but it was uncomfortable and I think I instinctively have like, "something's wrong and I'm gonna take care of it" approach.

N: So you were eating a lot or you were constricting?

M: Both. I sort of remember I wasn't eating until I got home from school, and I was binge eating and tried to make myself throw up a few times and I just couldn't. I was really eating a ton of food. It felt awful.

Describing how she found her way to a nutritionist and a therapist—and later, into the mental health profession—Miriam reveals some of the insights she acquired along the way. For example, "Being a part of the family means sort of being sad and depressed and having my mother in particular sort of make these clinical, global statements about the family." A number of questions arise from this exploration: how much of herself does Miriam have to sacrifice in order to remain an accepted member of the family? Will she be able to balance "individuating and not being severely depressed" with her "fears of being abandoned"? Or will she continue to contain other people's emotions and experiences, regardless of her attempts to establish distance and boundaries? Miriam reveals the difficulty of truly separating, as fears of being "alone" ultimately carry her back to her family:

> There was some point in grad school where it felt very clear to me I was done being depressed, and all of a sudden I was extremely anxious and kind of panic attack-y. And occasionally, in the last five years, there have been times when I'm really afraid I'm gonna get really, really depressed and that just hasn't happened. I think I'm now less anxious than I was in the first sort of kind of flip. I don't think it's uncommon that those mix together. Not recently but I certainly like... when I was in graduate school in the middle of the night there was this sudden like, "I'm alone" and worried about my parents dying and constantly visualizing...

In acknowledging that she was "done being depressed" and finding herself feeling "less anxious" than before, Miriam separates herself from her family. Moments later, however, she reveals an arising fear of her "parents dying." On some level, it seems that separating and finding herself to not be anxious, or to not be depressed, is a dangerous pursuit; one that might even kill off her parents. It is no wonder, therefore, that statements like "Everyone's depressed" and "Everyone's sad" provide a sense of safety for Miriam and her mother. After all, "clinical, global statements about the family" are by definition "global," such that Miriam will not have to carry them on her own. Thus, Miriam responds to a question about depression with, "No... I don't feel depressed. I think my baseline might be a little lower..." Her "baseline" is indeed "lower," because if it were higher she might find herself "alone."

Miriam concludes her interview by questioning her choice of social work as her profession and doubting her ability to feel "empathetic" towards others:

> Part of me also wonders what kind of... do I want to hear about other people's problems, or is this about my own stories? Like, this doesn't have to be my role... I can do something else, I can think about the world. I can think about social structures. I don't have to exist in this murky, complicated vortex of feelings with superposed structures that make your life complicated. People ... They're interesting... I think sometimes the experience of having patients is... they can be different enough from me that it doesn't really trigger feelings of being haunted by someone else's stuff. Sometimes I feel like my empathetic response has been turned off too much. I don't think it has... I just was like way too sensitive... I just really had to kind of control it.

While Miriam hopes to achieve some "mastery" and "control" over her feelings, believing she was "way too sensitive" in the past, she has thus far been unable to separate from the "murky, complicated vortex of feelings" that dominates her day-to-day life. Hopefully, she will never completely separate from this type of "existence." After all, while she claims, "this doesn't have to be my role," she finds herself pulled towards helping "people" and more fully understanding herself. Thus, the question, "do I want to hear about other people's problems, or is this about my own stories?" seems superfluous. It is through her own stories and experiences that she will better understand, tolerate, and feel empathy for "other people's problems."

CHAPTER 10: MALKA

There's something about women being the carriers of the stories. Women are the carriers of history. I think there are some things she told me that she would never even tell my dad. I think even my maternal grandmother tells me things that she doesn't tell anybody else either. There's something about being a granddaughter... there's something about being a woman. One woman will tell... I think men... I don't think my grandfather would have ever told me anything. He was a very quiet and sweet man. I don't know if that was ever something that was even talked about at all. According to my dad, it was simply not talked about at home. It was just known and it was not spoken of, but I think she thought it was something that was important for me to know her story. You know, I think my brothers got snippets, again, packaged in my presence, you know like, "And this is why you should do things, because these things can happen." But, I think there was something different about telling me versus telling them. There's something very maternal about having that. It's like an emotional burden that women carry and I don't know if men can carry it or if men would share that. I think that she knew that in telling me it would be passed on; and telling me, it's something that's kept sacred.

"Women are the carriers of history," says 29-year-old Malka, understanding that "there's something about being a granddaughter" that unites her with a lineage of stories and storytellers. She is a link in an ongoing chain of women who serve as imparters of all that was lost, and all that remains, of the Holocaust. The image of women bonding in Anita Diamant's (1997) fictional novel *The Red Tent*, sharing tales and experiences within a community of women, hovers nearby throughout our discussion. "It was just known and it was not spoken of," she says, with resolve to do things differently. Malka recounts her grandparents' escape and survival of the Holocaust: while her 18-year-old grandfather chose to separate from his family and trek from Poland to Russia by foot, her 14-year-old grandmother was ordered by her parents "don't come home" from summer camp, and was likewise the family's sole survivor. Herself half-Israeli, half-American, and living in the U.S., Malka's identity comprises various splits: Israeli versus American, survivor versus escaper, the bearer of knowledge and language within a family of silence and disownment. Malka believes, "There's something very maternal about having that. It's like an emotional burden that women carry and I don't know if men can carry it or if men would share that." Throughout her interview, Malka quite clearly depicts the ways in which she holds, nourishes, and fosters the "emotional burden" that is her history, much like a mother sustains her baby. "I think that she knew that in telling me it would be passed on; and telling me, it's something that's kept sacred." Malka, the third generation keeper of her "sacred" family record, is at once the inheritor, possessor, and imparter of history. Malka goes on:

> So it's passed on through the women. I don't think that men necessarily share these things in the same way. I don't think they have the hearts to hearts; they don't have the conversation; it's simply not in their ... it's not how they're socialized. They bury their feelings, they bury their traumas; they deal with it, they suck it up and they move on... despite the emotional ramifications that come thereafter, but they don't deal with it. They don't talk about it... whereas women, we do—we talk, we cope, we rely on each other, we talk about things with our family. My dad, you know, not so much. Only again, later in life and only to me... doesn't talk to my brothers about these things either... doesn't talk to my brothers about how hard it was to lose his mom... doesn't talk to my brothers about how hard it is for him to be alone now and how it ... You know, the loss of his mom, the loss of his whole family, and what that means to him.

"I don't think they have the hearts to hearts" says Malka, knowing men to turn away from emotional connection and exploration, choosing instead to "deal" with their traumas by curbing them and focusing elsewhere: "They bury their feelings, they bury their traumas," she says, "...despite the emotional ramifications that come thereafter." Her word choice referring to the way men "suck it up" is interesting, given that the slang expression suggests a tendency to deal with something difficult or unpleasant by shutting it out; in another sense, however, to "suck it up" means to take in, and absorb, the material. Thus, even in burying their feelings, or perhaps especially in burying their feelings, the emotions are sucked in, and soaked up. Whether or not this gender split—women "cope" and men "bury" their traumas—is a clear-cut differentiation beyond Malka's experience, she speaks to the division between those who sustain curiosity about themselves and their history, and those who choose not to know. In a later discussion of her mother, Malka reveals, "My mom didn't really talk about it. To her, she was Israeli, and that was all there is to know." In other words, her mother's sense of self was entirely fabricated by the fragments of identity she selected for herself. After all, as Malka explains, her maternal, "Israeli" lineage is intimately intertwined with the Holocaust and survivors:

> ...My mom's family is sixth generation Israeli. They've been there for a very long time, and my grandmother actually grew up on the beaches of Tel Aviv, like where all the hotels are now—that's where she lives. Her family was helping smuggle in survivors. Her family was bringing them in and housing them and hiding them because they lived right on the beach.

Whether female or male, resistance to talking about "what that means" is widespread, and carries "emotional ramifications that come thereafter"—way after, for generations to come.

"There's Simply No One"

M: Yeah, I don't know. My dad, he never talked to me about it... snippets here and there, but it was never something that was... the fact that I only learned about a lot of these things when I was in my mid-20s, I mean, kind of tells about how little I knew growing up. I knew where they were from. I knew that they had lost their family. I knew basics... they went to Russia... I didn't even know the real story of how she got there. I didn't know... she didn't even tell me like, how did she even deal with being there? Her family was not that far and she had no idea where they were. You know, how do you even deal with that as a teenager? I can't even fathom. I can't fathom losing my parents now, how do you deal with that at 14? I didn't even get the story from my grandfather because he passed away when I was young. How do you make a decision when you're 18 years old to just pack up and leave? Like, how do you do that? How do you say, "I'm going to save myself"? I don't know.

N: It is completely unfathomable.

M: It is unfathomable. You know, like God forbid we ever know something like that, but like, how do you make those decisions? How do you say like: "I don't care if you don't believe me anymore, I'm not sticking around to see how this ends?" I don't know. And there's something that saddens me so much about the fact that I don't know, that that part of us is lost, and because there's no other family it's never going to be known.

Malka's questions wrestle with *how* her grandparents were able to survive their past experiences: "... how did she even deal with being there? ... how do you even deal with that as a teenager? ... How do you make a decision when you're 18 years old to just pack up and leave? ... how do you do that? How do you say 'I'm going to save myself'?" Indeed, the decisions they made, the lifesaving determination that impelled them, and their capacity to persevere is unfathomable. Within the established boundaries of language and silence, Malka never found the opportunity to verbalize these questions to her grandparents. Perhaps she formulated her questions in depth, considered posing them at some point, or even approached them with curiosity. However, the time was never right because the message was clear: listen to what I choose to tell you and do not press for further information. Alongside her history, therefore, Malka's unanswered questions remain. Her sense of not knowing the full truth about her family, and herself, is ever-present: "And there's something that saddens me so much about the fact that I don't know, that that part of us is lost, and because there's no other family it's never going to be known."

Malka continues to dwell on the concrete fact that "There's no one" alive anymore to shed light on the past:

> It's not like there are secret cousins that could be living somewhere that like, "Oh, maybe they know." It's just gone. That whole generation, even my grandmother's aunt, didn't have any children. I mean, there's nobody. There's nobody at all. There's not someone random, like a descendant of someone that can figure out how to piecemeal it together. There's no one. That to me is... the kind of sadness and grief and trauma that's carried on is that there's simply no one. There's no one to carry on the legacy. There's no one to even know it happened. And I think the past year or so is what my dad's really been trying to deal with and struggle with is this... lack. It's just gone.

Malka reiterates, "It's just gone ... there's nobody. There's nobody at all. There's not someone random, like a descendant of someone that can figure out how to piecemeal it together. There's no one." She repeats this thought time and again, emphasizing and simultaneously contemplating the meaning of her words. How can there be no one? What happens if not a single person can explain or at least assemble some missing pieces of her history? Will she forever feel confused by and futilely compelled to understand—like "pieces" of a "meal" that will never fully satisfy her? As she insightfully explains, it is precisely in not knowing, in the utter "lack" of her history, that trauma is transmitted: "...the kind of sadness and grief and trauma that's carried on is that there's simply no one." In this way, Malka continues to carry the "emotional burden" of her history because there is "no one" to fill the emptiness within her. Furthermore, Malka's comment that "God forbid we ever know something like that" suggests that knowledge of the event occurs only through the experience itself. That is, even answers and stories will fail to clarify the unknowable. As Malka later states in conversation about her grandmother:

"I only started getting these little snippets of stories as she was kind of preparing for her departure from this world. Like, 'There are things I need to tell you. I didn't tell you these things before; this is what you need to know.'" These "snippets," however, cannot fill the void of history.

Thus, Malka is left with endless questions, wondering how her grandparents were able to persevere. What impelled them to maintain strength? How did they go on? What was it like? Where did they turn? How did they feel? Malka believes she will be unable to fully understand herself, and her place within the context of her ancestors, as long as she remains cut off from the details of her past. Deep down, however, it seems that Malka holds the answers to some of her questions, without having ever heard them from another family member. That is, the answers lie within herself:

> But there were no stories. There was no talk about it at all, and that part of our history was very much lost in our family, I think. We don't even have a proper telling of what happened because they were so traumatized and so alone that they just wanted to move on. They in many ways gave up their Judaism, they in many ways... they had ham in the house... and were not very observant, and I mean, they never really were, but it was something that was so... I mean, my last name is now Dan. My last name wasn't Dan; my last name was Davidson. My dad changed it. You know, very much don't want to deal with your Jewish identity. That was something only bad things came from. While they were clearly Zionists and believed in the state of Israel, there was something that separated being Israeli and being a *shtetl*[1] Jew, and those two things are different and they would be different and we will make it different. So that kind of cutoff between the past and what is the future, and how we are going to make that future, was very evident because that was just not spoken about.

---

1   The Yiddish word "shtetl" is derived from the German word "Stadt," town. "Shtetl" often refers to a town with a large Jewish population in pre-Holocaust Europe.

The apparent disconnect between the truths of the past and desire for the future is a powerful one. Speaking to the well-recognized, post-Holocaust contradiction between the strong, independent Israeli Jew, and the weak, powerless *shtetl* Jew of Eastern Europe, Malka reveals her family's belief that "...those two things are different and they would be different and we will make it different." In a sense, her family, along with an entire (young) nation of Israelis sculpting an identity immediately following the Holocaust, maintains that the past is not the past if one chooses to avoid it. Thus, she says, our future "would be different" because "we will make it different." The word *Sabra*, meaning an Israeli-born Jew, is derived from the Hebrew name for the prickly pear cactus "tzabar." The reference is to a resilient, thorny plant with a thick external coat and a softer interior; that is, rough on the outside, but sensitive on the inside. The stereotypical distinction between masculine and feminine once again arises in this label, as does the split between one's external and internal self. However, the modern, post-Holocaust Israeli Jew might in many ways be a new type of Jew, but simultaneously remains the same old Jew with a new shell: hardened over time. Furthermore, while the image of the strong and forceful Israeli Jew seeks to eliminate the weak, fragile, and passive representation of the European *shtetl* Jew, the two remain intimately intertwined. Malka therefore says "we will make it different" instead of "it is different," because Davidson turned into Dan only after a deliberate attempt to cut out the middle. One name clearly defines the other, just like "strong" elucidates the meaning of "weak," "masculine" relates to "feminine," and "there were no stories" gives greater meaning to an hour and a half interview.

"Such a Big Deal"

Feeling cut off from her history, Malka goes on to reveal the tangible roots of this disconnect:

> M: My mom didn't really talk about it. To her, she was Is-raeli and that was all there is to know. And again, I think it's a part of that "We're Israeli and that's who we are." Everything that came before us before that was before that; this is our new identity.
>
> N: It's so interesting, trying to start anew and believing

that the past won't be carried on within...

M: So many of our family friends who are Israeli changed their last names. It's all kind of shortened; it's easier to say; no longer Jewish sounding. Davidson to Dan—I mean, could you be any shorter? You could've just said "D." Very much breaking away from that past, breaking away from that part of their identity. And while it's so important for them to have us to be Jewish, it's to be Jewish in a certain way.

In her mother's assigning a single, new label for her identity—"Israeli"—or her father's shortening his name from "Davidson" to "Dan," the history of Malka's family is literally abridged. Past attempts to wipe the slate clean, however, leave Malka with a sense of lack and ignite her quest for something more. Her sense of personal responsibility to carry the past, present, and future, for herself and for her entire family, is evident. "There's something very maternal about having that," she says, because for Malka, her history has become like her baby: she cannot go back in time, undo, or escape the connection to her past; and on most days, she would not want to. Instead, she will forever uphold it, feed it, and convey its meaning to future generations, doing everything in her power to keep it alive. After all, who else would care for this child? "There's simply no one" that is willing to help carry the load. Not surprisingly, in discussing potential baby names for her future children, Malka states, "Mind you, my ovaries are totally not ready for any of the babies at all, but if one more person tells me they're pregnant, I'm gonna lose my mind." Her envy of others' pregnancies is understandable, given that there is no room for "any of the babies" in her life so long as baby history is at the forefront, demanding attention and consideration.

Along similar lines, Malka's father struggles to incorporate his children in his definition of the word "family" and in his sense of place in the world. How can others exist when history and all of its figures overpower the present? What is the place of his descendants, if connection to his ancestors has been disavowed? Malka describes her father's mentality following the death of his mother:

But I think it was not just loss of a mother; it was loss of the family. Like, "I'm an orphan. I have no one. I have no family. There's no one to help me with this. There's no one to help me take care of anything. I'm by myself." And I was like, "Dad, you have us." He was like, "It's just not the same. Of course, I have you. Of course you're my... but it's just different."

Sadly, Malka's father feels that "I have no one. I have no family," even in the midst of a conversation with his daughter. Indeed, as he explains, "It's just not the same"; after all, in his mind, his offspring are detached from their predecessors, precisely because he had wanted it so. Yet, as he finds himself alone, seemingly the last survivor of a vanishing history, he feels "There's no one to help me take care of anything. I'm by myself." Thus, his attempts to wipe out his past seem to have frozen his grief in time. Malka insightfully captures this phenomenon:

> I was sensitive enough to know she'll share with me what she wants when she wants to because otherwise it wouldn't be such a big deal. It was just this unspoken-of thing that hung over my dad and his parents... it was just this like unspoken-of, constant grief that was there. And so I would never... I would ask once in a while but like... it's interesting. I actually look like my grandmother's mother... like, frighteningly so. And so she has this one picture of her parents—that's the only picture she has— and we now have it. She doesn't have any pictures of her little brother. There was just so much that was lost that she couldn't ... you know, snippets here and there.

Malka explains, "It was just this unspoken-of thing that hung over my dad and his parents... it was just this like unspoken-of, constant grief that was there." The grief "hung over" them in silence, a tenacious, intensifying silence, like thunderclouds gathering before a storm. Filled with electricity, the pressure ultimately struggles for release. Malka further reveals, "I was sensitive enough to know she'll share with me what she wants when she wants to because otherwise it wouldn't be such a big deal." Without her grandmother or father speaking a word, Malka understands the request to leave the past untouched and unspoken. It must be "such a big deal," Malka winds up thinking to herself, and history is transmitted through the authority of silence. As Kaplan (1996) writes of the second generation survivor: "At first the child knows only that one or both parents are hiding some terrible secret. And the child wonders, 'What is the meaning of the absence, the silence? What is the truth that must never be spoken?'" (p. 219). Malka, the third generation recipient of this knowledge, is the first to explore her "double life" existence, recognizing how events that occur in the present are filled with reverberations of things that happened in the past (Kaplan, 1996, p. 231). Along these lines, Malka questions her family's ability to remain silent even in the face of the "frightening" physical similarity between Malka and her great grandmother. Similarly, she reveals her father's ongoing fear of loss:

> My dad has dreams about losing us, his children, all the time. Like, all the time. Even now, dreams about losing us. I don't know if that's a common paranoid parent thing, but my dad throughout my childhood would come running into my room in the middle of the night to make sure I was still there. Even now, as an adult, when I'll randomly sleep over at my parents' place, he'll come in the middle of the night and make sure I'm still there.

Closed off from his awareness of history within the present, the historical trauma perseveres with force. Malka understands of her father, "Like, he clearly has dealt with his own trauma growing up. You know, there are classic signs of children who are Holocaust survivors and the shit that they deal with, and like he just is completely emotionally distant, but completely emotional at the same time." Interestingly, Malka discusses the "classic signs of children who are Holocaust survivors," pegging her father as a survivor of the Holocaust, not a descendant of survivors. Even as a second generation survivor, her father is felt to be a child survivor of the Holocaust. This terminology depicting future generations as "survivors" or "not survivors" reappears in a later discussion of Malka's own sense of fear:

> M: I think I'm a lot more aware of anti-Semitism. My husband's not even a Holocaust survivor, but grew up with a strong Zionist family, but left Russia when the government got bad and just like... this fear that we

don't... people can turn against you... you can think
you're nice and cozy in the place where you live and then
you're not so nice and cozy anymore.
N: Do you see that affecting the way you live, like the
day-to-day type of things?
M: In a way, it does. I'm hyper aware of it. I'm hyper
aware of the bias in the media. I'm hyper aware of how
much we're hated. I just am, and I find it so ridiculous
when people don't see that. It's like, yeah, we're Jews.
We're hated.

Malka finds herself to be "hyper aware of how much we're hated,"
making up for generations of family members who chose not to be
aware. For Malka, therefore, the bias, the fear, and the hate seem omnipresent. Malka's allocation of second and third generation survivors
as "children who are Holocaust survivors" therefore speaks to her sense
of closeness to the event. After all, although it occurred in the past, its
impact and presence is tangible in the present. Throughout her interview, Malka questions and explores her family's detachment from the
trauma, wondering how and why they repressed their histories. At the
same time, however, Malka describes her family's inherent distance
from the Holocaust during and immediately following the event itself.
Because they were not themselves prisoners in the camps, and did not
die during the event, her family by definition did not suffer in "the same
way" as others:

M: It's just weird... because it's not talked about. It was...
you know, in a way, they weren't in the camps, so it was
this kind of transient trauma because they didn't have
to... they lost their families so they couldn't have suffered the same way that their family did so it was this
like, even more passed on. It was just so weird. You
know, because they survived it but they didn't really.
They weren't there.
N: They themselves probably felt very disconnected.
M: Yeah, they lost their family but they never knew
what their family went through, so it's not like they can
even fathom, and yet they have no one. You know what

I mean? So that kind of disconnect is a kind of survivor guilt, too. Like, I lost my whole family and I managed to... my family talked about that a little bit... how like why wasn't... like, her brother was eight and he was too young to go to sleep-away camp, and so he missed the boat. You know, like, "Why did I make it?" Because they were safe. They were very blessed that they didn't have to go through any of that.

N: Do you feel you have that kind of guilt that carries on, in terms of what you choose to do in the name of your family?

M: Well, yeah, of course. Like, where are we going to live, and how come we're not living in Israel, and like, why aren't we living the Zionist dream that our grandparents fought so hard for? You know. Why aren't we there when we should be there? But oh yeah, there's a total guilt of: are we being good Jews? Are we being good enough Jews? Are we giving the right things? Are we making all the sacrifices that all of our grandparents went through? Like, both sides of our family our grandparents ate shit, you know. They just did. They had a shitty, shitty, shitty life. You know. Our parents had a crappy life, too. They did. My mom had a happy childhood, but, like, they had nothing. You know. They had nothing. And for a lot of my childhood I felt very guilty. You know, she was like suck it up and deal with it. Learn to deal with it...

N: Like forever paying back something that you don't owe.

M: Yeah... Like, look at how much they suffered so they could be there and we're not there. Of course, I think it's something we'll always struggle with. Like, how do we live there? I mean, it's hard to live there. But in many ways it's just as hard not living there.

Malka says, "...they lost their families so they couldn't have suffered the same way that their family did, so it was this like, even more passed on. It was just so weird. You know, because they survived it but they didn't really." In this way, Malka links her grandparents' escape to their experience that they did not "really" survive, and to the ensuing "survival guilt" that remains. As Malka explains, "transient" trauma seems to be "even more passed on" because of its vague, indescribable nature. "...so it's not like they can even fathom, and yet they have no one," she says, meaning they did not witness the horrors of the Holocaust, yet they have also seen the horrors of the Holocaust quite directly. A sense of connection and disconnection to the traumatic event therefore co-exist, regardless of a survivor's specific circumstances. While Dori Laub (1992) explains that "there is no such thing as a witness" of the Holocaust because anyone with a true understanding of the event was killed, every survivor, escapee, and descendant of the Holocaust is simultaneously a carrier of the trauma in his or her own way. Malka describes the impact of her history on her present-day decisions; from where she lives and being a "good enough Jew," to maintaining a sense of Zionism and compensating for all those who "ate shit." In the same way, Malka captures the importance of transmitting the knowledge and the "utter loss" to her future children:

> ...everybody was killed in the Holocaust. It still gets to me. Of course it does. And I wonder how my children will feel about that; I wonder how they're gonna know about it; I wonder how much connected they're going to be to that notion of utter loss. I can only fathom it to a certain extent because I know what my grandmother went through. They won't know my grandparents. They won't know what it's like to have lost... you know, that whole concept is going to be lost to them, and how do you pass that on? Not that you want to savor it, but there's something that's so important about our history as people, you know, and I think maybe that's why I have such... maybe that's why we've always been such Zionists, too. No matter what, what does my father-in-law say? Like, "Israel's like your child with special needs... you love it, it has problems, but you've got to keep it." Like, there's something... you need to have that country because things happen and people hate Jews. And that was something that was just known. It was something that was just passed on... it was like, people will hate you

and people will kill you and you can lose everything you have in a second—don't ever think it can't happen. And that was why you need this country to exist. You don't need to live there, but it has to exist. And it has to be there and it has to be safe, because at the end of the day that's really the only place you can go when the shit hits the fan.

"Not that you want to savor it, but there's something that's so important about our history as people," Malka perceptively states, comprehending the importance of memory and the intergenerational transmission of history. The fear that her children "won't know what it's like to have lost," however, is a needless one, as they will undoubtedly receive this knowledge from their mother on some level. "Savoring" the existence of memories and willingly exploring their knowledge is less of a certainty. Alongside her history "as people," Malka simultaneously hopes to transmit a sense of safety and belonging that she attained through Zionism and a love of Israel. As she quotes, "Israel's like your child with special needs… you love it, it has problems, but you've got to keep it." Thus, alongside her past, Malka passes on the potential for a rewarding present and future.

CHAPTER 11: JESSICA

Without Memory or Desire

The act of acknowledging, exploring, and expressing her own experiences allows a granddaughter of survivor(s) to more fully comprehend her history. That is, she must not have sorted through historical tales in order to construct a family narrative; the ability to recognize her past depends entirely upon her willingness to engage with her self in the present. What occurs when a young woman finds value in blocking her feelings and experiences? What of the individual and collective memories? Jessica, the 23-year-old granddaughter of a Holocaust survivor and the sister of another interviewee, explains:

> J: It's weird... I feel like I'm really bad at remembering my childhood. Like, some people remember all of the details. I'm really like, vague on it, but I feel like what sticks out is just her... like, she would yell a lot—like, *scary* yelling. Like, I feel like people are like, "Oh, yeah, my mom yells," like, whatever... but it's like the combination of the look in her eyes and the tone and like, how she would yell, was, like, scary. And I was like... I guess that when it started, like, I would block it out. Like, my sister, when my mom would yell at her she would cry... which is, like, normal, but I would just stare at her.
> N: You wouldn't cry?
> J: Yeah.
> N: So you kind of survived it by not focusing on it?
> J: Yeah, exactly. And I don't even know what she was screaming about. Like, when I think about it now, I'm like, what could I have done to evoke such anger?

Whether or not Jessica recognizes that she is not herself the root of such rage, she contemplates ways she might have "evoked such anger."

After all, a child will first and foremost blame herself for events she cannot understand. In explaining how anger impacts her today, Jessica reveals, "Like, when these other things happen, I get upset because it's me... like it's my fault... like I caused this to happen..." Her mother's "*scary* yelling," therefore, speaks to the severity of her mother's anger as well as Jessica's belief that she is single-handedly powerful and destructive enough to cause this eruption. In all its intensity, the experience is incomprehensible and staggering to Jessica within the present-day context; after all, the extent of her mother's fury relates to years of pent-up anger and frustration, having served as a caretaker for two traumatized, volatile, suicidal parents. Thus, its immensity could not be taken in, but rather needed to be blocked out. "I would just stare at her," Jessica says, creating in me the image of a hollow, plastic replica of Jessica sitting dispassionately before her shouting mother, untouched by her blows. The ability to dissociate was a powerful and valuable tool throughout Jessica's childhood, one that protected her from her mother's emotional flood, the ever-present traumatic past, and Jessica's own sense of helplessness and destructiveness. At the same time, it seems that alongside her dissociations, Jessica simultaneously lost track of her life experiences. This hazy and elusive sense of the world continues in her day-to-day life: "I feel like it's hard to hold onto things. Things that, like, my friends remember. Like, today they were giving the pre-nursing exam and I'm just like, 'What was on that?' It wasn't that long ago and I can barely remember?"

In sharp contrast to her self-depiction as a non-crying, detached little girl, Jessica opens her interview with the statement "Okay, I'm probably going to cry." Within moments she is in tears, sharing freshly acquired insights regarding her mother's denial of emotions (except for, as it turns out, anger), and her own attempts to foreclose feelings:

> J: I recently started going to therapy. I talk about my mom a lot. I feel like she doesn't show her emotions a lot and she equates that with being strong. And I talked to her also recently for one of my psych classes about... I just like interviewed her and we ended up talking about her dad and like the Holocaust and stuff like that and... I think she equates not showing emotions with being strong... like he had to be strong to get through that.

And that's what she thinks being strong is: like, not showing any emotions. I never realized before, but when I started therapy I realized that my whole life I've been like holding back my emotions, like, bottling everything up inside... so I think that in that way that's how it's affected me.

N: So how has it been in therapy?

J: It's really hard because now I feel like I'm overflowing with emotions... like, I need to find like a balance. Like, every time I go to therapy I cry the entire time. So, eventually, I am hoping I can find a happy medium. Like, not bottling everything up and not crying all of the time.

"...he had to be strong to get through that," Jessica states, revealing an entrance-point of the past in the present, manifesting itself in this family's sense of the word "strong": "I feel like she doesn't show her emotions a lot and she equates that with being strong." The emotionless mother is reminiscent of Jessica's dissociative childhood self, as this self-protective quality was transmitted through the generations. However, the meaning of the word "strong" is certainly altered depending on scale and context; maintaining strength during the Holocaust in a concentration camp is incomparable to exhibiting strength in a post-Holocaust world. With the help of therapy, Jessica successfully begins to break out of incongruous classifications and beliefs.

"It's really hard because now I feel like I'm overflowing with emotions," she says, regaining access to an abundance of feelings denied for generations by preceding, "strong" family members. Having been barred release for so long, the expression of feelings understandably erupts without "balance," pouring out in excess. Most certainly, these feelings belong to Jessica: after "bottling everything up" throughout her life, she courageously discovers how to express herself. At the same time, however, these feelings belong to her mother, her father, her grandparents, and every family member unable to communicate his or her emotions. For the first time, Jessica breaks down the emotional barriers that previously prevented her from seeking an authentic expression of her self.

Jessica describes the measures taken by her mother to not display the slightest trace of sadness: "...sometimes you can see her getting upset, but she'll never admit she's upset or just let it out. Like, she'll just be like, 'Oh, my allergies...' like if her eyes are getting watery." In describing her mother as "not showing emotions" or unable to "admit she's upset," Jessica sheds light on her mother's incessant anger, often an enactment of the avoided underlying feelings. In other words, her mother's lack of emotional expression helped generate her later explosions. Unsurprisingly, with anger running rampant throughout her life, Jessica continuously struggles to escape its force:

> J: Yeah, I feel like that's how I am now. Like, I put everything on me. Like, the way people act towards me affects me so much. Even though rationally I know like they're having a bad day and that's like their stuff... but it affects me so much, which is really hard right now because one of my instructors is kind of not so nice and it's really hard for me to not take it personally.
> N: So someone else gets angry and you feel like it's your doing?
> J: Yeah, and I can't handle people being angry. Like, I can handle it, but not well. Just even, like, strangers... a bus driver once yelled at me but like... he was letting people on without paying and I didn't realize it and paid, and he like kind of yelled at me. And something like that just like ruins my entire day. I feel like other people can just like brush it off.

Jessica cannot simply "brush it off" because anger is a heavily loaded emotion in her history. Therefore, seemingly minor expressions of anger, like a bus driver yelling at her for paying the fare, has the power to ruin Jessica's entire day. After all, any anger directed at Jessica serves as a reenactment of her early childhood experience; the bus driver becomes like her mother, and in seconds Jessica is transformed into a frightened, destructive, and guilty little girl. Jessica struggles to explain why she tends to "put everything" on herself, speaking not only about her relationship with her mother and others around her, but also about a sense of responsibility for her family's traumatic history. In later describing her "issues with people not liking" her, Jessica once again addresses her own mistreatment while alluding to her family's past persecution:

I feel like that's one thing I'm working on more in therapy because I feel like I never realized it before (crying)... but when I think about it, it's like obvious that I have issues with people not liking me... like, I want everyone to like me, so I won't say anything cause I don't want them to be mad at me. Well, I'm bad with people being mad at me. So I just feel like maybe they won't like me anymore. And, like, in therapy we brought that back to my mom getting angry, and another aspect of her getting angry is that when she gets mad about something she holds onto it forever and ever and ever. And it'll be like months and months later and she'll bring it up.

Jessica's description reveals that not only was she the recipient of anger in the heat of an angry moment, but her mother clung to every transgression "forever and ever and ever." Thus, Jessica was never free from the firm grasp of her mother's fury, awaiting a recurrence of the situation "months and months later," unable to find comfort at the conclusion of an eruption, always living in the presence of dis-ease. Understandably, Jessica's anxiety level was heightened. Yet, even in her constant state of anxiety, Jessica worked hard to suppress her discomfort:

I feel like I've been dealing with anxiety by like not feeling it kind of. I just like push it down. Because now I realize I'm a very anxious person. Like, anxious about exams and about clinical... and, like, now that I think about it, I always had nerves about doing new things, even if they're not new, like going to camp every summer. Like, I love camp, but just like the change of it was like I always get an upset stomach. So nerves like, yeah, that's how my anxiety always comes up... with an upset stomach instead of like... it came out physically, my anxiety.

As she describes "not feeling" her anxiety and finding ways to "push it down" served to eliminate Jessica's conscious awareness of her anxiety for some time. Unconsciously, her anxiety was intense and unwavering, finding expression in various forms, sometimes physically, as Jessica says, and other times through her dreams:

N: Do you have nightmares?

J: Well, occasionally, but not, like, Holocaust related.

N: Any that stand out or any recurring ones?

J: One that stands out is I feel like I had a dream where there was this overarching like voice—kind of maybe like the voice of God, but not God, because it was evil and kind of like trying to kill me. And there was like a wall and it kept getting closer.

N: So then what happened?

J: I always wake up before I either escape or get squished.

N: So you've had that dream more than once.

J: Maybe more than once, or someone trying to kill me. Not often though...

N: Maybe with the wall closing in, feeling a little stuck...?

J: I have like, anxiety dreams all the time. Like where I'm supposed to be in a million places at once.

N: And you can't get there?

J: Like in once place and then I realize I'm supposed to be someplace else *and* someplace else. And the dreams where you're like late for school and stuff like that.

Jessica's "anxiety dreams" allow some of her tension to be released during sleep, whether she is "supposed to be in a million places at once," the "voice of God" is trying to kill her, or a wall keeps "getting closer" until she gets "squished." While releasing tension in her sleep in no way eliminates her waking anxiety, the dreams allow some of her "not felt" feelings to be expressed. Furthermore, her recollection of these dreams reveals her ability to hold onto some feelings and bring them into consciousness. Finally, her verbal recounting of her dream life plants the dreams in her waking narrative. Thus, the dreams provide an opportunity for Jessica to reflect on the arising feelings—if she chooses to do so—without having to recognize and acknowledge them in her daily life. However, Jessica's proclamation that her nightmares are not "Holocaust related" reiterates her tendency to not fully want to know. After all, moments earlier, Jessica described her mother and grandfather's Holocaust-related nightmares:

J: My mom said he would scream in the middle of the night from nightmares about it.

N: What about your mom? Did she have nightmares?

J: Not that I know of. Like, I asked her during our conversation if she could tell me things that he would tell her, but she wouldn't tell me because she said, "You'll have nightmares."

Jessica finds herself "stuck" somewhere between past and present, between knowing and not knowing. While she may not *want* to know the full meaning of her mother's nightmares or her own, it seems that she *does* on some level know, evoking the notion of the "unthought known" (Bollas, 1989). "Well, occasionally, but not like Holocaust related" she tells me, reassuring herself that she has escaped the family pattern of Holocaust-related nightmares, and that her struggles are separate from this history. Yet, without hearing her grandfather's Holocaust stories or tracing his experiences on a historical timeline, Jessica's family narrative and collective identity inevitably revolve around this historical, traumatic event. At the core of her nightmares, her "bad" memory, and her search for answers, the Holocaust is ever-present.

Reconstructing Memory

The enormous amount of not-knowing Jessica utilized in order to survive her childhood was likely a useful tool within an unknowable, unreachable family. Jessica describes fragments of memories within a memory-less past:

J: ...I think her and my dad went to therapy together when I was younger, when I was like nine. Like, I feel like I remember them leaving the house once a week at night and I feel like they weren't going out to dinner... and they were like yelling a lot during a certain period of time.

N: So no one ever told you that? You pieced it together?

J: Yeah, no one told me they were going to therapy.

N: Do you feel like you had to do that a lot? Sort of like fragments... putting the fragments together, figuring things out?

J: I feel like that's the only thing I had to put together because everything else was so well hidden from me that I wouldn't know if like someone told me. But even when my mom told me she was always running off to like put my grandmother in the hospital or get her out of the hospital... even when she told me, it wasn't like, "Oh, that makes sense, you were running around." It wasn't like that. It was like, "Really?" I just had no idea. Like, I don't remember her running around. Like, she tells me that she would leave me with like her best friend, who I used to think I was related to, but like I don't remember. I feel like the first time I went to therapy I said that I'm really bad at remembering things and she implied that that's a defense mechanism to just not remember it.

N: And what do you think about that?

J: I think that that makes sense to me. Like, to me it doesn't feel like something I'm doing intentionally.

Instead of feeling abandoned, terrified, and in the dark about her parents' whereabouts, Jessica blocked out the experience of her missing parents altogether. By the time her mother explained that her absence was caused by "running off" to take care of her grandmother, Jessica had completely erased the experience, allowing her to state, "I don't remember her running around." Her mother's best friend, whom Jessica saw frequently enough to believe that this woman was a relative, has been completely blocked from Jessica's recollections. Time spent with this woman throughout Jessica's childhood has been altogether erased. Indeed, the defense mechanism of "not remembering" is not an "intentional" response to her upbringing; after all, intentionality suggests active, purposeful doing or thinking. Instead, Jessica's experience has been characterized by avoidance, denial, and dissociation from her surroundings, as she resiliently learned to enclose herself in the safety of not-knowing.

As discussed above, Jessica is by no means the first in her family to utilize the tool of not-knowing. For example, Jessica introduces the word "oblivious" in the following story:

My mom said like that my grandma would stay in bed all

day and not do anything. And my grandpa would come home from work and he would think that she just had gone to bed... like she had gotten up and done whatever. So she said he was oblivious to her in general, like, her sickness.

In remaining oblivious, unaware, and unconscious of his wife's illness, her grandfather was able to never truly know his wife's experience. What might he have found, had he chosen to see? What might Jessica discover in removing her shield of oblivion? Would she unearth the impact of having been abandoned by her mother on most days of her childhood? Might she expose the role of the Holocaust on her individual and family narrative? Could she tolerate the accompanying feelings?

While many generations of Jessica's family engaged in ongoing enactments and repetitions without further curiosity or exploration, Jessica courageously found her way into therapy. She explains her ability to do so with the following:

> J: Something happened and basically I felt like I was being overly emotional about it. Like, I didn't know why I was that upset about it... so that's when I started going to therapy. Basically it was just emotions from everything that had built up and was coming out now.
> N: It's really amazing you could get yourself into therapy.
> J: Like, I thought about it for a while but then kept not actually doing it because I thought I could survive without it. I think I will benefit from it. That's another reason why I didn't go to therapy: I didn't want to think that I needed help. Like, I could handle it myself, which is like, from my mom, I think.

Once again, the past is alive within the present, encouraging Jessica's mother, and later Jessica, to learn to "survive" without help. While they could clearly "survive without it," as her mother proved throughout her life, "survival" is most simply defined as a "continued existence" (and the antonym of "survival" is "death"). Thus, this terminology implies a basic, physical survival, one reminiscent of Jessica's grandfather's survival in the concentration camps. Furthermore, the words "overly emotional" reveal Jessica's belief that within a specific scenario, she responded with an excess of feeling beyond the scope of that situation. Jessica explains, "Basically it was just emotions from everything that had built up and was coming out now." Indeed, Jessica is "overly emotional," carrying three generations' worth of unexpressed feelings "that had built up" over time. When she concludes the interview by comparing the interview experience to therapy, Jessica reveals: "Like, every time I go to therapy... I'm just gonna cry. Like, I should be prepared to cry. Cause I used to go and like, 'I feel good, this week was good, like, I don't think I'm gonna cry.' But I would anyway." That is, Jessica's tears have nothing to do with the present—with whether or not "this week was good"— and everything to do with working through generations of past trauma.

In addition to the incessant flow of tears, talk therapy is an experience altogether deviating from Jessica's lifetime of silence:

> J: My dad is like super mellow. My mom's the one screaming her head off and my dad just sits there, like I would just sit there.
> N: So you're more like him?
> J: Yeah, I feel like we're both really quiet. My therapist suggested calling him more, but it's kind of weird because we're both quiet and we'll just sit there in silence.
> N: So what is your silence about?
> J: To me, it just feels like I don't have anything to say. Like, other people have asked me, "Why are you so quiet?" And I'm just like, "Why do you talk so much?"

Jessica describes how her father "just sits there," similarly attempting to block his wife's shrieks. Not surprisingly, in the face of a mother "screaming her head off" and a father retreating into silence, Jessica feels, "I don't have anything to say." Organizing or even recognizing her thoughts and feelings seems exhausting, if not impossible, within this chaos, and Jessica consequently assumes "silent" and "shy" as safe descriptions of her personality. In exploring the role of silence, her family's foreclosure of feelings, and her own trouble with memory, Jessica uncovers her individual identity as well as a historically-insightful family narrative.

In addition to therapy, Jessica has discovered alternative ways to examine, question, and make sense of her childhood. Most significant is her experience of babysitting:

> N: And doing things differently as a mom... do you ever think about how you would want to be as a mom, or is there anything you would do differently from your mom with your kids?
> J: Yeah, I thought about that a little and especially I feel like in therapy... I've talked about how the moms I baby-sit for are with their kids also. Like, one of them sometimes reminds me of my mom and the other one never... I think is the best mom ever and I would never... like, I've been babysitting for them for a while and I've spent a lot of time when the mom is there—like if they don't go out right away—and I just realized that I admire how she is with her child. Like, she's just so patient and just, like, so calm and I hope I can be like that.
> N: It must be so strange to see a mom like that.
> J: It's like, wow.

Through babysitting, Jessica hopes to better understand what it means to be a mother in general, and her own mother specifically. She encounters fragments of her mother in other mothers, and is able to analyze them from a safe distance. Furthermore, in witnessing other mother-daughter dynamics, Jessica hopes to more fully know herself. For example, she reveals, "I talked about it in therapy—like the mom of the two girls, she'll yell about something if the little one spills food at the table... like the tone of her voice is familiar. And in my head I'm like, all she did was an accident and she's like five." Thus, within the context of "babysitting," Jessica is able to examine her upbringing, her mother's misplaced rage, and the prospect of herself as an innocent child undeserving of blame or reprimand. Like therapy, babysitting provides Jessica with an opportunity to engage in new relational possibilities in an unencumbered space. Of course, Jessica will continue to contend with her earliest relationships throughout her life; yet, having mentioned "therapy" over a dozen times in her interview and sought out therapeutic activities, it seems Jessica has begun the meaningful work of self-exploration.

CHAPTER 12: BRIANA

It's Not You, It's Me

Briana, a 22-year-old granddaughter of Holocaust survivors, articulately captures the evolution of emotional blunting within her family:

> My grandparents on my dad's side were both Holocaust survivors and the first result I think I saw, or was conscious of, was probably depression throughout the family in the second generation, and people not wanting to share their feelings or expressing feelings or expressing love verbally, and hearing stories about how my grandparents never said, like, "Good job," or "You're good enough." It was more like, "You're not good enough," because they didn't feel good enough because they felt like they shouldn't have survived. They felt a lot of guilt for surviving. So it trickles down to the third generation, I think, through the parents, the second generation—having to deal with how they grew up and not knowing how to change it.

Through the use of projection and introjection, Briana's father and grandparents demonstrate the conscious and unconscious transmission of trauma intergenerationally. As Briana insightfully explains, her grandparents communicated the message "'You're not good enough,' because they didn't feel good enough because they felt like they shouldn't have survived." In this way, survival guilt was passed on to Briana's father—also not "good enough"—resulting in "depression throughout the family" and "people not wanting to share their feelings or expressing feelings or expressing love verbally." Later on, Briana adds, "I think anger is also heavily present, not just like depression... like, anger with my dad, anger with my aunt, and my uncle also..." That is, various family members utilized anger, often an enactment of undigested, avoided emotion. As Briana describes growing up with a father who struggled to verbalize his love for her, she recalls her attempts to understand his lacking emotional displays, as well as to repair the injury of his own withholding parents.

> I think we saw my dad as being emotionally aloof, like we noticed he wouldn't say the same things my mom was capable of saying, like verbalizing or showing... we were always told by our mom that it's not about us, it's about how he grew up and his parents... and we would talk to my grandparents about it as little kids, like, "Why don't you tell Abba[1] you love him more?" And whatever, stuff like that.

The image of "little" Briana innocently attempting to mend the divide between her father and his parents is a compelling one. "Why don't you tell Abba you love him more?" she questions, capturing the essence of the void. Yet, how can expressions of "love" possibly survive the chaotic upheaval of emotions following massive psychic trauma? As Briana's mother emphasizes in an attempt to explain her husband's "aloof" nature, "it's not about us, it's about how he grew up and his parents..." In other words, history steers the present, such that "love" in the present remains intimately coupled with "love" for all who were lost. As Briana describes her father's household growing up: "... they say it was like dark and it was sad and like all they heard about was all the family members they didn't have anymore... like, who was missing, who wasn't there, and what a struggle it was... how lucky they were to be alive." Thus, "not knowing how to change it," Briana's father continues to exist within a "dark" and "sad" world, forever joined with those who are missing. In this consuming relationship with absence, he becomes himself an "absent" and "aloof" father, therefore deeming Briana a part of this cycle as well.

In an attempt to better understand this powerful *thing* which dominates her father's life and represents competition for fatherly attention, Briana recalls turning to her grandparents: "We asked them questions all the time when they came over. We asked them detailed questions. I think the second generation didn't do that apparently. Like, my dad wouldn't ask them questions, but like, all the grandchildren felt com-

---

1   This is the Hebrew word for "father."

fortable." In struggling to comprehend her father and her family history through "detailed questions," Briana distinguishes herself from the second generation by feeling "comfortable"; that is, she eliminates the silence and attempts to understand, and maybe, one day, undo this *thing*. Furthermore, Briana recalls, "I remember talking to my grandparents about it a few times just because I was so upset about it, but I think we've ultimately accepted that, like, they did the best he could, he did the best they could." In Briana's confusion of pronouns, "... they did the best he could, he did the best they could," she seemingly concedes to the merger between her father, her grandparents, and their shared history. Later in her interview, Briana recounts the ways in which she "was so upset about it":

> I think it took a while to realize where I was coming from, like really realize, but it had to do with having a father who was absent and making it seem like you're not good enough all the time. I guess my siblings didn't internalize it as much as I did... just because I was very emotional and whatever, but I think as time went on it had to do more with my dad and not so much with the rest of my family. Like, it's difficult because I know it came from my grandparents who didn't really have a choice in how they dealt with their problems, and he didn't have a choice in how he had his childhood, but it definitely trickles down to the third generation.

Briana's self-image as "very emotional"—in contrast to her siblings, whom she believes "didn't internalize" their "absent" father as much as she did—is common amongst third generation survivors. In a sense, the collective, third generation identity revolves around an "overly emotional" self, whether owned or disowned. After all, as Briana reminds herself, her grandparents "didn't really have a choice in how they dealt with their problems" and her father "didn't have a choice in how he had his childhood." Therefore, because others suffered more deeply, harboring her own sense of loss or grief is regarded as exaggerated, often considered "too much" or labeled "overly" sensitive. Alongside her predecessors, however, Briana likewise "didn't really have a choice"; in later describing the various ways her siblings have dealt with their shared history, it seems Briana served as the "emotional" one for her ancestors, her siblings, and future generations alike:

> B: I think being an artist makes me overly expressive sometimes, but I definitely am not afraid to express what I'm feeling with my family or friends.
>
> N: Yeah, you've said that you are "overly expressive" and "overly emotional." Is that what people call you or do you just feel very expressive?
>
> B: I think my older sister was very protective when we were little... with bad relationships going on with my brother and my dad... and so she kind of put up this stronghold on the family and didn't show how it was affecting her. But I on the other hand was really little and so I cried about it all the time and was very expressive, particularly of what I was expressing. But then as time went by, I went to therapy and realized what the problems were... like, eventually, after a long time, I decided I needed to open up to the family and think about, like, why I had issues and maybe was dealing with them but not in a very direct way. And so I talked to my brother and my sister and my mom about what went on in my family for me in terms of my dad. I never really talked to my dad about it.
>
> N: I'm amazed. How did that go?
>
> B: Well, my mom always wanted to be let in throughout the therapy process, but I, like, refused to and it took me a long time to be able to open up to her about it, which was difficult for her. And then my older sister was away from home the whole time and she wanted to know more about it but I didn't open up that much to her about it... and then, in like the middle of college, my brother finally said that he wanted to know about what had gone on because he also had not been home, so I finally opened up to him about all of it. I think it was a shock for him to realize about how much my dad had affected me or how much the family had affected me, but I also thought he needed to know about it because God forbid one of his

kids had some sort of problem and he had some knowledge because he had a sister with the same problem.
N: They couldn't see how it was affecting you or how it
might be affecting them...
B: I think to some degree it was foreign to them. I think
they have their guard up and I don't. They're able to be
much more closed and I'm not.
N: What do you think it is about you?
B: I think it's the artist thing. I'm really emotional, like
I don't really know how to keep a guard up—it just kind
of all comes in. I don't know how to filter out the emotions. I'm very sensitive. I think my siblings are sensitive
too, but they are really able to like not talk about their
feelings and be okay, and I'm just kind of not like that.

As the "overly expressive" member of her family, Briana depicts letting each family member in on "what went on" for her growing up in
their family. Playing the role of the "sensitive," "artist" sister who does
not "really know how to keep a guard up" or "how to filter out emotions," it is clear that Briana serves as the unguarded, open, and honest
communicator of their shared experiences. While Briana believes of her
brother "it was a shock for him to realize about how much my dad had
affected me or how much the family had affected me," she alludes to
knowledge that there may have been more at play for her siblings than
they let on: of her sister, she recalls "... she kind of put up this stronghold on the family and didn't show how it was affecting her..." That is, a
"stronghold" allowed her sister to maintain a sense of order and control.
Along these lines, Briana later reveals her sister's own attempts to engage with her history:

B: We've all been back to Poland... like my three siblings...
not my parents. But we definitely saw the concentration
camps. My sister even went back to my grandma's house
that she grew up in. We've definitely all been back there
to see it.
N: How was that?
B: Very hard. I actually didn't cry the whole trip... the
only time in my life I haven't cried... just because I think

it's too much. My sister is actually going into Holocaust studies... she's getting a masters in Israel. She's working at a Holocaust museum.

N: So it sounds like she and your brother are figuring things out without the emotional piece...

B: Yeah. She gets connected to it differently... I don't even think she's recognized it's affected her personality or her relationships with other people. Any issues she's had with boys, I don't think she's connected that with how my dad treated her.

As Briana insightfully explains, her sister "gets connected to it differently," enveloping herself in Holocaust studies and working with Holocaust material, as if separate from her personality. Thus, while her siblings seemed to "not talk about their feelings and be okay," they found alternate, intellectualized outlets for their experience. Briana therefore serves as the elected emotional expresser, the bearer of feelings and disarray, for her family. Furthermore, although Briana maintains conflicting feelings about having "cried about it all the time," she also captures the strength of her ability in her statement, "I definitely am not afraid to express what I'm feeling with my family or friends." In other words, her courage allows her to do the emotional work that others feared before her, and continue to fear alongside her. Perhaps her brother's "shock," therefore, also relates to his amazement with Briana's candidness and strength; the same amazement I felt as I listened to the role she plays and the work she has done in her family.

Briana understands that the transmission of history will not end with her generation. Regarding sharing her experiences with her brother, she states, "I also thought he needed to know about it because God forbid one of his kids had some sort of problem and he had some knowledge because he had a sister with the same problem." That is, Briana predicts that the current patterns and "problems" will persevere. At the same time, however, it seems that Briana has successfully opened the door to honest dialogue between her siblings. She reveals, "Yeah, we all talk about it a lot. We make promises not to do certain things he does... we analyze his siblings... we want to just get along and stuff like that." Hoping to do "certain things" differently from her father, and from his family altogether, Briana and her siblings promise one another to "just get along." This hope for the future is further actualized within a foundation of open conversation and awareness. As Briana emphasizes, "But I definitely want to think about a lot of the things like my dad did when I was growing up, and like change how I interact with my kids, and be very different than that."

It's Not Me, It's You

To what extent will Briana "be very different" as a parent than her father, if the patterns have been initiated and the dynamics persevere? How many more generations will receive the message "it's not about us, it's about how he grew up"? Or worse, how many will not make the historical connection in the first place? In a sense, the vague but ever-present place of history can be better understood through Briana's depiction of her father's roundabout insults: "It's probably from their parents always saying bad things instead of positive, but like they're very conscious of, 'It wasn't an insult, I'm just saying...' or like, 'Don't take it personally, but...'" The experience of passive yet aggressive, "mean" insults is like the back-handed subsistence of history within the present: indirect but personal, subtle but strong, seemingly shallow but deeply impacting.

Briana reveals how contending with her history remains an ongoing, inescapable challenge, for example through her grappling with anorexia: "So, I struggled with it for three years of high school. And my parents were really supportive in getting help and my dad... it was really hard for him to see. I think he knew he had something to do with it. I think my mom also felt guilt about it which didn't help with the guilty situation..." Briana openly links her eating disorder to her father, his upbringing, and the historically-relevant, ongoing "guilty situation." Briana goes on to share her parents' attempts not to "see" her disease:

> B: I definitely had to tell them. I think it's also... now it's more common knowledge—if you see someone who's underweight, you kind of freak out about it. But then, my mom... just thought I wanted to be better looking or whatever it was. But after like a good seven months, I was so frustrated that she didn't see it that I shouted at her that I needed help and convinced her that I needed

help... and my friends had to convince her I needed help...

N: So she really didn't want to see it.

B: Yeah. Then we had to approach my dad. He wanted to talk about it... not really talk about it... but he wanted to make me eat. Like, "You're not allowed to talk about it with me, you're not allowed to discuss it," and it put a halt on our relationship for a while. He didn't want to discuss the problem underlying it; he just wanted to fix it on the surface.

N: Make you eat.

B: Yeah.

N: So how bad did it get?

B: It wasn't like dire but... by the time the pediatrician found out, she was like, "She needs to eat immediately and take care of this." I think they were scared, well, I don't think my parents ever understood what... but it was a scary situation because it was so new to everyone. But I opened up about it pretty fast because I think I wanted to get better because I didn't want to continue this forever and the therapist was really good...

"I was so frustrated that she didn't see it that I shouted at her that I needed help and convinced her that I needed help... and my friends had to convince her I needed help..." Briana recalls, shedding light on the extent to which her family was unable and unwilling to see Briana and her experience. Furthermore, her father's inability to tolerate an honest verbal exchange is apparent in his complete rejection of his daughter and their relationship: "...but he wanted to make me eat. Like, 'You're not allowed to talk about it with me, you're not allowed to discuss it,' and it put a halt on our relationship for a while." Her father's immense sense of guilt and fear is tangible, as he was unable to tolerate the situation but rather wanted to be rid of it: through his demand "you're not *allowed*," her father clearly begs, "don't say it *aloud*." Briana's own sense of guilt for creating another "scary situation" emerges in her comment, "I didn't want to continue this forever." Her word choice—to "want to continue this forever"—suggests a deliberate maintenance, as though she developed the eating disorder on purpose. Perhaps this intentionality speaks to Briana's sense of competition with history, which regularly absorbs her father's attention, and which will undoubtedly last "forever."

Another example of history continuously presenting itself in Briana's life can be seen in her frightening dreams about the Holocaust:

> B: For as long as I can remember, I always had dreams about the Holocaust—usually like hiding and being terrified of being found, not really like fighting back or anything... I think my siblings have also struggled with dreams of the Holocaust.
> N: So you were hiding?
> B: Yeah. With like people we know.
> N: And you've had them since you were a little girl?
> B: Yeah, I remember being like eight or nine. I was with another friend and we talked about how we all had dreams like that and we were so terrified. It was such a central part of my childhood. I was so scared of it.
> N: So how is it now?
> B: It's still scary but it's so commonplace now it's not like a jolt anymore.
> N: Would it be on random nights or do you think something specific happened...?
> B: Sometimes random nights... sometimes something will be bothering me and it will come out in terms of the Holocaust. I remember last year, I was feeling really guilty about something or I thought I should feel guilty about it, and it came out in the way of the Holocaust and Nazis being around and being buried alive... it's like the imagery I use of the scariest thing I can think of.

Briana's awareness that things "come out in terms of the Holocaust" allows her to more fully explore and understand her experiences. While she describes how "the Holocaust and Nazis being around and being buried alive" serve as "imagery" to convey her feelings, she also captures the way in which these images impact and intensify her emotions. Her comments "It was such a central part of my childhood" and "I was so scared of it" depict the extent to which the past can come alive within the present. Feeling "terrified" and "jolt"-ed, she ultimately discusses her dreams with siblings and friends, such that the historical trauma grows yet another root in her conscious day-to-day life. Along similar lines, Briana traces the meaning of "goodbye" within the "Holocaust mentality" of her post-Holocaust world:

> ...like when we say goodbye to people or when things end, we're extremely upset about it. It's like the whole Holocaust mentality. Whenever we said goodbye to our grandparents, they got very emotional because they thought of goodbye as, "That could be the end." So it was embedded in us that goodbye was the biggest deal in the world; if one of our friends go away we get very tense.

Briana's ability to link her eating disorder, nightmares, and "good-byes" to her history allows her to maintain a more comprehensive understanding of her past, and to live more fully in the present. In her romantic relationships, for example, Briana describes discovering her desire for "emotionally available and open-hearted" men:

> I think I try to go the opposite of my dad, and there are times where I consciously went for the exact same kind of person as my dad, realized it pretty fast... he showed a lot of the same characteristics and I kind of ran away to some degree. But I definitely analyze like every guy that comes into the picture... with my mom, also. Like, "Do you see any characteristics that are the same? If so, what are they?" Like if they're similar, I shouldn't be with him...

Ultimately, Briana's self-exploration and historical curiosity facilitate her differentiation between the characteristics and desires that belong to her, and those that belong to her ancestors. Instead of continuously hearing "It's not you, it's me" and struggling to understand the meaning of this distinction, Briana is able to take on the assertion herself: "It's not me, it's you." After all, she alone can confirm or dispute the deepest parts of herself. In her final depiction of what is most distinctly hers—her name—Briana describes the "strong willed" woman she is named for:

B: We talk a lot about who we're named after, what their characteristics were, why we were named after them... we realized that's how we want the same thing for our kids...

N: Who are you named after?

B: I'm named for my mom's side—her grandmother.

N: And what were her characteristics?

B: She was like an immigrant from Russia; she was apparently very strong-willed. And her husband had come here first but then never sent for her. And she already had like four kids, so she just got on the boat by herself and came over here—no money and nowhere to go—but she somehow found him, had three more kids with him, and then they got divorced and she had all the seven kids alone. She raised them all herself; never got remarried. But she was very charitable, giving, also kind of a harsh mother, I think, but definitely strong willed.

As she continues to "raise" her family by doing their emotional work as well as her own, Briana quite powerfully exhibits the strength of will, vigor, and generosity of her namesake.

CHAPTER 13: DISCUSSION

Reworking Trauma Trails: Possibilities for Resilience

Working on meaning is the most private of activities.
Anything that has been imprinted with a trauma will
always fuel representations of the memories that constitute our inner identity. That meaning lives on inside
us and provides our life with its themes (Cyrulnik, 2007,
p. 18).

Through psychoanalytic interviews with the granddaughters of Holocaust survivors, I uncovered in this work the themes which organize
the lives of ten women. While the particulars of each woman's narrative
and viewpoint are unique given the circumstances of her individual and
family history, one constant truth persists throughout the narratives:
that trauma trails exist within third generation survivors—whether
conscious or unconscious—and are embodied in their day-to-day lives.
Thus, the imprints of trauma which "constitute our inner identity"
prevail; with or without conscious awareness, with or without our predecessors' attempts at reintegration into the world, with or without our
rummaging into history in search of answers. Yet, this is not to say that
granddaughters of the Holocaust are necessarily debilitated by their
links to history. Instead, trauma trails must be welcomed, explored,
even fostered, for growth to be achieved. The case of Leah, for example,
reveals how a strong, open, and hopeful young woman can maintain a
protective screen that limits her from fully engaging with and reworking her traumatic history. Consequently, Leah relies upon obsessive-
compulsive tendencies to provide her with a sense of order and control.
Samantha, on the other hand, delves into her historically-rooted fears,
hopes, and desires, arriving at an intergenerational viewpoint that anchors her identity within history and unfastens the grip of a previously
unexamined past. As a result, Samantha nurtures growth, attains emotional insight, and initiates new life possibilities. As long as the offspring
of survivors attempt to cut off their connection to intergenerationally

transmitted trauma, they will undoubtedly *be owned by* residues of the past. Conversely, the study of meaning, the acknowledgment, exploration, and working through of trauma, will allow the granddaughters and future descendants of the Holocaust to *own* their histories and further integrate their identities.

Each of the ten interviewees exposed both the ongoing shadow of the Holocaust, and the strength and resilience she developed alongside her inherited traumatic history. After all, the act of narrating an evolving narrative is in and of itself a demonstration of progress: the intimate disclosures of individual feelings, memories, and beliefs cultivate the narrator's sense of self and simultaneously integrate the past, present, and future. Such developments signify the potential for growth and change, and speak to the hope inherent in each one's search for insight. As Cyrulnik (2007) explains,

> Narration becomes a way of working on meaning ... Sometimes the witness exists only in the imagination of the injured subject, who is talking to a virtual listener as he tells himself his story ... Memories of images pass through their minds, and they are framed by words that comment on them, explain them, hesitate and then begin to describe the scene by using other expressions. Thanks to this work, the narrative can slowly extract the event from the self (p. 37-38).

As the narrator begins "working on meaning," resilience is born. It is through verbalizing, sharing, and grappling with her own representations that the narrator discovers such activities to be increasingly bearable, and increasingly necessary. In this way, these ten interviewees courageously engaged with new narrative possibilities in an unencumbered space—some for the first time, others for the 100th time—revealing their wounds to themselves and reworking their identities.

Unfortunately, a common misperception regarding change in a post-Holocaust world suggests that resilience is measured by the extent to which survivors and their families are able to reintegrate into society following this massive traumatic event. I often encounter women interested in my work who ask about my "findings," only to then half-frantically suggest why their particular family situation is different from the participants of my interviews. One woman assured me that *her* survivor grandparents did not seem troubled by their past; another revealed that *her* parents successfully made a place for themselves in society; a third explained why *her* family did not truly suffer through the Holocaust the way her neighbor's family did; and yet another woman maintained that *her* family was not impacted by the event generations later. Indeed, the thought that one cannot escape such an overwhelmingly traumatic history can be frightening, infuriating, and numbing all at once. To some extent, however, each of these women is right: some of their families appear to have made a 180-degree turn and begun a seemingly transformed, "successful" life. However, it is important to note that social achievements and change of circumstances do not necessarily indicate a reworking of trauma or a healing of internal suffering:

> When we draw up a balance for the last fifty years, we find that most Holocaust survivors did, despite everything, have families and become part of society once more ... Having had to fight so as not to go under helped them to succeed in life because they could dissociate their success from what was still a painful inner world ... All these examples of morbid courage explain why social success can go hand in hand with personal difficulties (Cyrulnik, 2007, p. 172).

As Cyrulnik explains, the distinction between one's "adaptation" to a post-Holocaust world and one's development of emotional "resilience" must not be overlooked:

> This form of adaptation may lead to success at school or in society, but it cannot be called resilience. Before we can speak of "resilience", the subject must begin to rework his idea of his wound in emotional terms. Now, the paradoxical success stories that exploit a psychotrauma by adapting to it do not rework any representations. This is not resilience and, what is more, this type of defence allows the psychotrauma to re-emerge at a later date; the subject thought it had been forgotten, but it had simply been avoided or buried (2007, p. 172-173).

Misinterpretations and misrepresentations of healing are widespread. Avi Sagi-Schwartz, a prominent Holocaust researcher who has conducted quantitative studies and meta-analyses on the subject of intergenerational ties, repeatedly concludes from his researches that Holocaust trauma has not been transmitted to second or third generation offspring of survivors. One such study, for example, reports that:

> Holocaust survivors (now grandmothers) showed more signs of traumatic stress and more often lack of resolution of trauma than comparison subjects, but they were not impaired in general adaptation. Also, the traumatic effects did not appear to transmit across generations. Holocaust survivors may have been able to protect their daughters from their war experiences... (Sagi-Schwartz et al., 2003, p. 1086).

The notion that Holocaust survivors "successfully protected" their children from the influence of their traumatic past is contradicted by the findings of this work. The repetitive and evocative depictions of trauma trails amongst the third generation are very evident in the narratives of the current participants. On a more basic level, it seems unhelpful and dismissive to categorize a survivor who displays signs of traumatic stress as "not impaired in general adaptation." Sagi-Schwartz's understanding of "general adaptation" is limiting, and does not include the kind of complex understanding of "resilience" and "health" in a post-Holocaust world that my participants' interviews suggest.

Cyrulnik's (2007) perspective, on the other hand, is resonant with my own. Responding to Sagi-Schwartz's assertion that "the difficulties were definitely not passed on to their children," Cyrulnik is very clear on the limitations of a detached or apparently objective perspective:

> What does this mean? It means that personal interviews are more coherent than the findings of scientific research. Everyone was surprised to find that these young survivors were so successful. But if we talk to them about their subjective lives, we quickly discover that their emotional lives are disordered and that the schematic clarity

of social adventurism was the only thing that put them at their ease. In their heart of hearts, they experienced great sorrow. In order to stop themselves thinking that no one could love the living corpses they had become, that they exuded unhappiness and that they would communicate their unhappiness to those who deigned to love them, they took refuge in the only activity that prevented them from suffering. When they could do that, the rules of life were clear, and all they had to do was get up early, go to bed late and think of nothing but work. All they needed to follow the narrow path that led to social success was their courage. They ceased to suffer, and even found a certain peace, but the pain was never far away. They were saddened by their own emotional incompetence... (2007, p. 238).

Indeed, the emotional work of resilience is an immensely difficult venture. The challenge for members of the third generation of the Holocaust is heightened by the denial and dissociation of two preceding generations. Thus, the groundbreaking journey into one's history, filled with untouched, unexplored, seemingly "dangerous" emotions, can be a lonely and isolating endeavor. It is no surprise, therefore, that "3G" (third generation) groups have been launched, and within just a few years, have multiplied in popularity. This development reflects the continued coalescing of the third generation as an identifiable group, and the desire to unite in dialogue and reflection of what it means to identify as a third generation survivor. As the 3G NY website declares: "The mission of 3GNY is to serve as a living link between the history of the Holocaust and today" ("3GNY," n.d.). This "living link" is rooted in the community's pursuit of communication, education, and reflection. A "message from the group's steering committee" elaborates:

> We, the grandchildren of Holocaust survivors, come from diverse backgrounds and work in various fields, but we all share a unique family history. We are also the last living link to Holocaust survivors. It is only through us that future generations will know the actual stories of

our grandparents' survival and the unimaginable losses of that generation.

What will we tell them? How do we ensure that our grandparents' stories of loss, survival and hope are remembered? What is our legacy and how do we articulate it?

By forming 3GNY, we sought to create a forum—a community—for grandchildren of Holocaust survivors where together we could answer these questions ...

Ultimately, our coming together is about more than socializing. It is to decide the best ways of shaping and passing on the legacies of our grandparents and parents. As grandchildren of Holocaust survivors, it is vital we use our personal connection to bring to consciousness the realities and lessons of the Holocaust ("3GNY," n.d.).

Certainly, the lives of third generation survivors continue to be "steered" by their grandparents' past experiences. The ongoing questions—"What will we tell them? How do we ensure that our grandparents' stories of loss, survival and hope are remembered? What is our legacy and how do we articulate it?"—will undoubtedly persevere, both as individual and communal struggles. As long as the "realities and lessons" of the Holocaust are continuously brought to "consciousness," the case for resilience is hopeful. After all, it is only through such attempts that the most frightening parts of oneself and one's history are acknowledged and worked through. Likewise, while conducting these interviews, the compelling need for these women to impart their stories was palpable; by wrestling with history, they advanced on the route to self-knowledge and acceptance. As Kaplan reminds us, "The failure to mourn, to weep for the dead and for the unborn, guarantees a return of the repressed, until—one day—there is nothing but absence and silence, and no one to testify" (Kaplan, 1996, p. 237). This inquiry attempted to delve into the work of mourning, to battle absences with presences, and to resist the verdict of silence by creating a space for language. If it succeeded, the voices of these women will serve as an ongoing invitation to engage in open dialogue and self-reflection.

* * *

On the day I designated for printing the initial draft of my dissertation, which would later form the basis of this book, I found myself catching a northbound train to complete the final preparations at my parents' home. Both my mother and father would be available, I knew, eager to lend a helping hand, possibly lessening my sense of isolation that had developed over the previous days. Upon my arrival, they heart-warmingly displayed their approval: of the conclusion of my research, of the significance of the subject matter, and of the tangible presence it aroused of my late grandmother. It had been approximately two months since her passing, with her death preceding the completion of my work by a mere eight weeks. The weight of her physical absence was colossal. I slumped down in the backward-facing bench of the train, knowing I was moving forward to my destination, yet willing the world to travel backwards in time to allow me to face my grandmother once more—with a copy of the manuscript in hand.

"Do you think she would have read this?" I asked my father, as we nervously watched the printer churn out page after page of my work in his upstairs office. "Oh, absolutely," he answered emphatically, and I felt momentarily at ease. I am not sure what sort of conclusion I had imagined for my research—perhaps a sense of organization or finaliza-tion or even validation—someone or something that could clarify the burdensome and conflicting feelings I bore throughout the process. In retrospect, I am aware of the ways in which this experience served as an essential step along my path of self-discovery, a path which transported me closer to my grandmother than ever before. My desire to pass the manuscript back to her, through the generations, stemmed from the hope that such a retroactive gesture might heal the wounds of trauma and silence. Nevertheless, the transformations of our shared history have undoubtedly begun. As I continuously cope with the knowledge I gather as well as the questions and absences that remain, I hope to inter-weave my trauma trails with an ongoing journey toward self-awareness and resilience.

EPILOGUE

Life Before This Study

> In order to become whole we must try, in a long process, to discover our own personal truth, a truth that may cause pain before giving us a new sphere of freedom. If we choose instead to content ourselves with "wisdom," we will remain in the sphere of illusion and self-deception (Alice Miller, 1997, p. 1).

As far back as I can remember, a yellow Star of David outlined in black with the words "Jude" sewn across its center hung in my grandparents' Jerusalem apartment. It was a small, cloth piece—small enough to walk past without noticing, particularly amidst the floor to ceiling bookshelves and distinct collection of artwork that lined the apartment.

Then again, it had always been framed.

As a young girl, I understood the glass covering as a statement about the unfairness of childhood and the plethora of adult decisions that I did not understand. There it hung, protected, calling out to me: "This bright, pretty star is not to be touched." It might have served as a soft doll blanket, I had thought—or a bold, taped-on addition to a crayon drawing of the evening sky. My parents would applaud my creativity, I imagined. Yet, the message was clear, and the last thing I wanted was to become a daring, questioning, potentially displeasing granddaughter. Someone else could bring it up.

Years passed, and the conversation never came. We continued our lives around that piece of memorabilia—eating meals at the table across from it, playing pick-up-sticks on the carpet beside it, admiring 1970's photographs my grandfather captured of Israeli soldiers praying at the Western Wall that hung alongside it. And, as I grew older, I no longer inspected the Star; I walked past it without awareness or desire, never questioning what it meant to live amidst this item, a symbol originally intended as a badge of shame associated with being a Jew.

Oh, I'm sure the Star was acknowledged on certain occasions—maybe on Holocaust Remembrance Day, or perhaps during Shabbat meals for which my grandparents' old friends had been invited to join. But the details surrounding the Star remained a mystery. Whose Star was it? Did one person wear it, or were Stars interchangeable amongst family members? What were the circumstances surrounding the receiving, wearing, and saving of that Star, and what was the journey that led it to its current home?

I did not ask these questions aloud and I never reflected on them in silence. It was as if the Star was not even there.

One Wednesday afternoon during my graduate school years, I sat in the office of my mentor, Dr. Michael O'Loughlin, discussing potential dissertation topics while seizing the opportunity to share childhood experiences and speak without boundaries. I did not think of the Star at the time, nor did I have words to explain my disjointed narrative. Yet I began to speak, and what surfaced was a reflection on familial silence, a subtle but powerful recognition of all that was and all that remained unsaid. And, somehow, without knowing it at the time, I spoke out of a deeply rooted longing—a hunger for truth and a hunger for pain—phenomena that were clearly intertwined in my mind, encouraging me for years to walk on by, to avoid a closer look, and to remain silent.

As I embarked on the "research" which ultimately led me to a doctoral dissertation and the present book, trauma and my vague understanding of "bearing witness" hovered nearby from the start; these were ambiguous concepts at first, ones that became increasingly defined through the process of a literature review, but which remained in the realm of "intellectual wisdom" until I began my interviews. While reviewing the Holocaust literature, I immersed myself in the material but also made certain to remain immensely busy with other tasks. I recall preparing to view a segment of the film *Shoah*, setting aside a couple of hours on a Sunday afternoon, knowing that I would subsequently clean my apartment and grocery shop prior to meeting my friends for dinner. I was aware of my need for structure in these moments: throwing myself into the material and the process, then throwing myself right back out of it. This was my approach at the time, seemingly satisfying my need to consume myself with the subject matter but also maintain my "separate" life.

Nevertheless, I felt nervous prior to beginning the interviews, as if I was asking participants to unload an entire history of a people and sit with the resulting discomfort. I fantasized about the potential outrage and disapproval that would surge out of participants who felt pressured or pushed or provoked by my questions, and viewed myself as an intrusive, unfeeling, demanding interviewer. I was instantaneously a young girl once more, fearing my family's response to my asking unspeakable questions and broaching forbidden themes. In these worried moments, it did not matter that my participants were willing individuals who had heard of my study and were interested in conversing on the subject matter.

As a way of sidestepping my anxieties, I busied myself with the concrete details surrounding the preparation of interviews. Would I welcome participants into my apartment, enter their home or office, or meet them at a third, neutral place? Should we sit down at a table, enhancing a sense of structure to the interview dynamic, or should we lounge comfortably (or semi-comfortably) on couches? Would I place a box of tissues nearby, taking care of participants and honoring the potential emotionality that accompanies this work, or was I assuming a certain emotiveness that might ultimately not arrive? What of the unused tissues?

And so, the interviews began.

Fully Inside It

Throughout the weeks of interviews that followed, I listened, with much eagerness and curiosity, and felt an immediate, overwhelming sense of relief. My relief stemmed in part from the realization that these women would not stand up mid-interview and storm out of the room; but beyond that, relief reflected my understanding that there were others like me—women who lived generations following the Holocaust, remained acutely entwined with their traumatic past, and yearned to explore this further. Most compelling of all was that words existed for these women's narratives—even the most disorganized or defensive narratives—and that, through language, each woman summoned her history, confronted painful realities, and reached towards creating a unique version of "truth." Yet the greatest common denominator amongst us was apparent: it was our willingness to show up in the first place, bearing our Stars for all to see.

The truth of the matter was that shame accompanied our Stars; this I knew inherently but became increasingly attuned to as the interviews progressed. What began as an external, deliberate attempt to "mark" and shame the Jews evolved into an internalized shame, incorporated into my identity and those of the women before me. Alongside that shame was a strong sense of guilt—how guilty we felt that a degree of shame about our history, culture, or religion existed in the first place. It was a difficult history, but one that we had survived and were *supposed* to consistently feel proud of; otherwise, the message was, "we" (no less than the entire Jewish people) had "lost."

At the same time, we clung to our pride—a deeply-rooted though somehow more fragile feeling surrounding our Stars. Pride was held high and paraded around, in a sort of exhibition, yet the exhibit occurred behind protective glass. Throughout the interviews, I sought to know more about this pride, and came to appreciate the strength and resilience that developed alongside our traumatic history. I thought of my family's Star and longed to be near it, to touch it, and to join in the act of fastening it to its framed place on the wall.

As the interviews progressed, I tapped into sadness about the unspoken truths surrounding our Stars, anger about the need to keep pages of our family autobiographies blank, and fear of what might be uncovered if these pages were filled. Last of all, I experienced eagerness and hope, aware of the mourning process that was taking place before me and sensing the development of community through our coming together to speak.

Nevertheless, our commonalities unfolded alongside our differences. While certain interviews conjured up associations to my own experiences, others did not. I noticed myself grow protective of some women, wanting to bolster them up and soothe their insecurities; yet I felt more challenging with others, pressing them to complete a thought or urging them to tackle a visibly challenging conflict. I took note of these discrepancies, wondering about individual differences amongst the interviewees and my own level of comfort in confronting certain experiences over others. Undoubtedly, my reactions and interventions varied from woman to woman, unfolding somewhat within and somewhat outside my awareness.

I consciously anticipated playing a number of roles in these interviews: that of a confidant, a sounding board, a bystander, or even a demanding interviewer. Yet the most difficult position to embody was that of the aggressor; at times, I perceived myself in this light following the slightest questioning of an interviewee. For example, at one point during a participant's depiction of her grandfather's experience in Eastern Europe, I asked a clarifying question about the manner in which her grandfather learned that his parents had been killed. The interviewee became frustrated by my question, informing me that she knows this story only as her grandfather had previously told it, and that whatever information she omits is likely unknown information to her. However, she then corrected herself and stated that she may accidentally forget to highlight adjacent stories, and that it would be okay for me to follow up with questions. Despite her permission, I found myself limiting my speech throughout the remainder of the interview.

Similarly, my own frustration arose when I sensed that ambiguity was unwelcome in the interview and therefore prematurely foreclosed. For example, a number of the interviewees spoke in a firm, sure voice that indirectly expressed, "I am confident of what I'm saying and I do not want that contested." At least one of the interviews felt like a power struggle from the start; her superimposed, intellectualized language and lack of affect pointed to the discomfort with the subject matter and the importance of boundaries in the room. I felt distanced in these moments and unable to make a connection, proceeding with caution so as not to cause pain. Yet, in curtailing a conversation that could potentially incite anger or shame, I felt my own frustration escalate; I treaded lightly with questions as I grew increasingly quiet, became increasingly blank, and, ultimately, was left increasingly drained.

These were difficult moments to tolerate and comprehend. How could I feel frustrated with an interviewee who was clearly struggling to convey her experience and simultaneously maintain her sense of self? How could I have anything but positive regard for someone who had been through so much and was willing to partake in this journey in the first place? What did it mean if I desired to push further, despite a clear communication that someone did not want to proceed? Indeed, the interviews tapped into my earliest childhood insecurities and replayed my own intergenerational dynamic: I was either the daring, questioning, potentially displeasing granddaughter, or the fearful, passive, compliant granddaughter who was left in an illusory state, with unanswered questions, a profound void of meaning, and a yearning for more.

At the same time, attempts to satisfy my own needs often led to the mobilization of guilt. For example, during one of the interviews,

I was aware of my desire for the interviewee to become increasingly emotive, thereby enhancing the intimacy between us. I longed for this contact—which stemmed from my own wish for kinship and connectedness—sustaining me in my search for a community that appreciates intergenerational Holocaust dynamics. Yet, I felt guilty for experiencing this desire, and as I walked her to the door and inquired about friends who might also be interested in sharing their stories, I felt like a needy, pushy, selfish interviewer who was inconsiderate of the participant's feelings or her time. Following her departure, as I reflected on this feeling, I wondered about the balancing of needs that took place in these interviews. Moreover, I came to reflect on the delicate weighing of needs that persisted throughout generations of my family. I wondered: could there be enough space for us all? How does one individual come to seek her own personal truth, particularly within a system that is fearful of pain? Do one woman's present-day needs and desires undermine the experiences of those who struggled before her? Who is entitled to speak of trauma, and what of all those bearing witness along the way?

Coming Out of the Experience, Or Not

Following the conclusion of my study, I unexpectedly found myself in a state of depression. This starkly conflicted with the encouragement and congratulations I received from friends and family around me, who lovingly emphasized that the completion of a dissertation should be a time of joy, pride, and relaxation. Yet, to their disbelief and perhaps a bit to my own, I was left feeling entirely isolated and overcome with grief. While my past experiences had demonstrated that endings are generally accompanied by loss and mourning, the loss surrounding this work was far more intense than I could have anticipated. The process had been an all-consuming, life-altering experience of extremes: it was at once draining and nourishing, disheartening but inspiring, startling while at the same time deeply familiar. I was fully inside it, without recognizing the existence of an "outside." And suddenly, it all came to an end.

The relationships I built throughout the course of this work undoubtedly shaped the void that was left behind. I developed and strengthened countless connections as I progressed through the experience, both interpersonal (with the ten interviewees, with my family, with my mentor, etc.) and intrapersonal (with my deepest fears, wishes, and needs, with my voice as expressed through writing, with the act of narration itself). My relationship with my grandmother spanned both realms: while we remained intimately connected in real life (though generally not through direct communication about this work), she was also an internalized figment of my mind throughout this process. Prior to but particularly following her passing, I turned to the image of my grandmother time and again, allowing me to encounter her world, learn from her thoughts, feelings and behaviors, and bump up against her way of being. With the summation of my study, this active and vigorous link seemed, somehow, to grow more passive and dimmed. Holding onto my sorrow soon became a conflictual experience in and of itself; while on the one hand I felt that I could never adequately mourn the multifaceted losses surrounding this work, I also questioned whether I retained my grief as a way of maintaining a connection to her.

Further adding to that void was the shocking realization that having invested so much of myself into this work did not necessarily mean that the people in my life would read it. This ranged from certain family members to friends and even to my therapist, most of whom read the "personal parts" related to my individual experience but could not muster their time or energy for the interviewees' narratives. Members of my dissertation committee themselves admitted on the day of my dissertation defense that they read the first few narratives and then set the work aside. I felt shocked, hurt, and misunderstood, confused about the impact of the stories and of my interpretations. Was the work entirely too much? Too long? Too dense? Should I have imparted these narratives in a more digestible form? Was it the content of the interviews, the reactions it elicited, or the act of bearing witness that turned people away? While I recognized the committee members' resistance to personal history, suffering, and memory, my own intergenerational dynamics surfaced once more—perhaps this material should not have been touched, or maybe I did not have a right to circulate, let alone verbalize, these thoughts. I feared the interviewees' reactions as well, and experienced a great deal of guilt while contemplating publishing my work. Nevertheless, while I continued to struggle with the question of whether my own needs and desires were warranted, I came to recognize and understand this pattern within a multi-generational perspective.

As time and the immediacy of the experience passed, others' reactions grew faint and the personal significance of my work began to shift.

I reflected on "trauma," which originates from the Greek word "a wound," and came to regard the completed manuscript as my "trauma baby": its traumatic nature contained generations of knowledge and spoke of truths that were difficult to bear. I had given birth to something entirely unique to me, containing those parts of myself that I would hope to transmit to future generations, those parts that I had long kept hidden, as well as those parts that I did not know to exist. And, with its birth, it bestowed an incredible gift—it held up a mirror before me, pointing to invaluable insights about my reality and about my sense of self, as a granddaughter, as a psychologist, and, a few years later, as a mother in this world.

Looking back, while I had attempted to prepare myself for the experience that I thought lay before me, there was no way to anticipate the journey ahead. I had told myself, "By initiating this quest, I will have to confront generations of silence and my own ambivalence surrounding my search for truth." But how could I have known what this really meant? How could I have envisioned so fully enveloping myself in this work, living and breathing a world of trauma? It is amusing to recall a time when I sought to maintain distance between myself and this experience; in the end, it was the impossibility of distance and the breakdown of silence that led "to a new sphere of freedom." And as my grandparents' belongings continue to be divvied up amongst family members, one item will travel across the world to me: that little yellow Star, waiting to be hung in my apartment, inviting questions that I hope will no longer go unasked. Who knows—one day, I may even remove the Star from its protective encasing of glass.

REFERENCES

3GNY: A NYC-Based Group for Grandchildren of Holocaust Survivors. (n.d.) Retrieved August 1, 2009, from http://www.3g-ny.org/.

Améry, J. (1998). *At the mind's limit: Contemplations by a survivor on Auschwitz and its realities.* (S. and S.P. Rosenfeld, Trans.) Bloomington: Indiana University Press.

Appelfeld, A. (1995, April 20). Fifty years after the Great War. *Yediot Aharonot,* p. 28.

Arad, G.N. (2003). Israel and the Shoah: A tale of multifarious taboos. *New German Critique, 90,* 5-26.

Atkinson, J. (2002). *Trauma trails—recreating song lines: The transgenerational effects of trauma in indigenous Australia.* North Melbourne: Spinifex Press.

Auerhahn, N.C., & Laub, D. (1998). Intergenerational memory of the Holocaust. In Y. Danieli (Ed.), *International Handbook of Multigenerational Legacies of Trauma* (p. 21-41). New York: Plenum Press.

Auerhahn, N.C., & Prelinger, E. (1983). Repetition in the concentration camp survivor and her child. *International Review of Psychoanalysis, 10,* 31-46.

Bachar, E., Cale, M., Eisenberg, J., & Dasberg, H. (1994). Aggression expression in grandchildren of Holocaust survivors: A comparative study. *Israeli Journal of Psychiatry and Related Disciplines, 31* (1), 41–47.

Balint, E. (1963). On being empty of oneself. *International Journal of Psychoanalysis, 44,* 470-480.

Bar-On, D. (1995) *Fear and hope: Three generations of the Holocaust.* Cambridge: Harvard University Press.

Bar-On, D. (2008). Forward. In H. Wiseman & J. P. Barber, *Echoes of the trauma: Relational themes and emotions in children of Holocaust survivors* (p. ix-xiii). New York: Cambridge University press.

Bar-Tal, D. (2001). Why does fear override hope in societies engulfed by intractable conflict, as it does in the Israeli society? *Political Psychology, 22*(3), 601-627.

Berant, E., & Hever, H. (in press). The granddaughters of female Holocaust survivors on their maternal side. In M. Rieck (Ed.), *The Holocaust: Its traumatic and intergenerational effects in comparison to other persecution, and its reflection in the arts.* Berlin: Verlag Irene Regener.

Berger, A.L. (1990). Bearing witness: Second generation literature of the "Shoah." *Modern Judaism, 10*(1), 43-63.

Bergmann, M.S., & Jucovy, M.E. (Eds.). (1990). *Generations of the Holocaust.* New York: Columbia University Press, reprint. (Originally published by Basic Books, 1982).

Berman, E. (1985). *From war to war: Cumulative trauma.* Paper presented at a meeting of the Israel Association of Psychotherapists.

Bion, W.R. (1959). Attacks on linking. *International Journal of Psychoanalysis, 40,* 308-315.

Bollas, C. (1989). *The shadow of the object: Psychoanalysis of the unthought known.* New York: Columbia University Press.

Borowski, T. (1976). *This way for the gas, ladies and gentlemen* (B. Vedder, Trans.). England: Penguin Books.

Boulanger, G. (2005). From voyeur to witness: Recapturing symbolic function after massive psychic trauma. *Psychoanalytic Psychology, 22,* 21-31.

Caruth, C. (Ed.). (1995). *Trauma: Explorations in memory.* Baltimore: The Johns Hopkins University Press.

Celan, P. (1958). Speech on the Occasion of Receiving the Literature Prize of the Free Hanseatic City of Bremen, as quoted in *Selected Poems and Prose of Paul Celan* (J. Felstiner, Trans.). New York: W.W. Norton & Company, 2001, 395.

Chaitin, J. (2003). "Living with" the past: Coping and patterns in families of Holocaust survivors. *Family Process 42*(2), 305-322.

Charles, M. (2003). The intergenerational transmission of unresolved mourning: Personal, familial, and cultural factors. *Samiksa: Journal of the Indian Psychoanalytic Society, 54,* 65-80.

Cole, T. (2002). Representing the Holocaust in America: Mixed motives or abuse? *The Public Historian, 24* (4), 127-131.

Coleridge, S.T. (1798). "The Rime of the Ancient Mariner." In E. H. Coleridge (Ed.), *The complete poetical works of Samuel Taylor Coleridge* (p. 186-209). Retrieved from http://www.gutenberg.org/files/29090/29090-h/29090-h.htm

Coser, L.A. (1992). Introduction. In M. Halbwachs, *On collective memory* (p. 1-34). Chicago: The University of Chicago Press.

Cyrulnik, B. (2005). *The whispering of ghosts: Trauma and resilience* (S. Fairfield, Trans.). New York: Other Press (Original work published 2003).

Cyrulnik, B. (2007). *Talking of Love: How to overcome trauma and remake your life story.* (D. Macey, Trans.) New York: Penguin Books. (Original work published 2005).

Danieli, Y. (1981). Countertransference in the treatment and study of Nazi Holocaust survivors and their children. *Victimology, 5,* 45-53.

Danieli, Y. (1984). Psychotherapists' participation in the conspiracy of silence about the Holocaust. *Psychoanalytic Psychology, 1,* 23-42.

Danieli, Y. (1988). The heterogeneity of post-war adaptation in families of Holocaust survivors. In R.L. Braham (Ed.), *The Psychological perspectives of the Holocaust and of its aftermath* (p. 109-127). Holocaust Studies Series. Boulder, CO: Social Science Monographs.

Davoine, F., & Gaudillière, J.M. (2004). *History beyond trauma: Whereof one cannot speak, thereof one cannot stay silent.* New York: Other Press.

Derrida, J. (1994) *Specters of Marx: The state of the debt, the work of mourning, and the new international.* (P. Kamuf, Trans.) Great Britain: Routledge. (Original work published 1993).

Diamant, A. (1997). *The Red Tent.* New York: St. Martin's Press.

Doneson, J.E. (1996). Holocaust revisited: A catalyst for memory or trivialization? *The Annals of the American Academy of Political and Social Science, 548* (1), 70-77.

Eizenstat, S.E. (1990). Loving Israel—Warts and all. *Foreign Policy, 81,* 87-105.

Elbedour, S., Bastien, D.T., & Center, B.A. (1997). Identity formation in the shadow of conflict: Projective drawings by Palestinian and Israeli Arab children from the West Bank and Gaza. *Journal of Peace Research, 34*(2), 217-231.

Epstein, H. (1979). *Children of the Holocaust: Conversations with sons and daughters of survivors.* New York: G.P. Putnam's Sons.

Ewing, K.P. (2004). Anthony Molino in conversation with Katherine Ewing. In A. Molino (Ed.), *Culture, subject, psyche: Dialogues in psychoanalysis and anthropology* (p. 80-97). Connecticut: Wesleyan University Press.

Felman, S., & Laub, D. (1992). *Testimony: Crises of witnessing in literature, psychoanalysis, and history.* Great Britain: Routledge, Chapman and Hall, Inc.

Felsen, I. (1998).Transgenerational transmission of effects of the Holocaust: The North American research perspective. In Y. Danieli (Ed.), *International Handbook of Multigenerational Legacies of Trauma* (p. 43-68). New York: Plenum Press.

Fink, R. (1999). *A clinical introduction to Lacanian psychoanalysis: Theory and technique.* Cambridge: Harvard University Press.

Fonagy, P. (2001). *Attachment theory and psychoanalysis.* New York: Other Press.

Fossion, P., Rejas, M., Servais, L., Pelc, I., & Hirsch, S. (2003). Family approach with grandchildren of Holocaust survivors. *American Journal of Psychotherapy, 57*(4), 519-527.

Fraiberg, S., Adelson, E., & Shapiro, V. (1975). Ghosts in the nursery: A psychoanalytic approach to the problems of impaired infant-mother relationships. *Journal of the American Academy of Child Psychiatry, 14* (3), 387-421.

Frankl, V. (2006). *Man's search for meaning.* Boston, MA: Beacon Press.

Freud, S. (1924). The loss of reality in neurosis and psychosis. *The Standard Edition of the Complete Psychological Works of Sigmund Freud, Volume XIX* (1923-1925): *The Ego and the Id and Other Works,* 181-188.

Gampel, Y. (1992). I was a Shoah child. *British Journal of Psychotherapy, 8*(4), 391-400.

Garber, Z., & Zuckerman, B. (1989). Why do we call the Holocaust "The Holocaust?" An inquiry into the psychology of labels. *Modern Judaism 9*(2), 197-211.

Garon, J. (2004). Skeletons in the Closet. *International Forum of Psychoanalysis, 13,* 84-92.

Grotstein, J.S. (1990a). The "black hole" as the basic psychotic experience: Some newer psychoanalytic and neuroscience perspectives on psychosis. *Journal of American Academy of Psychoanalysis, 18,* 29-46.

Grotstein, J.S. (1990b). Nothingness, meaninglessness, chaos, and the "black hole" I—The importance of nothingness, meaninglessness and chaos in psychoanalysis. *Contemporary Psychoanalysis, 26* (2), 257-290.

Halbwachs, M. (1992). *On collective memory* (L. Coser, Trans.). Chicago: The University of Chicago Press (Original work published 1941).

Herman, J. (1992). *Trauma and recovery: The aftermath of violence—from domestic abuse to political terror.* New York: Basic Books.

Hutton, P. (1994). Sigmund Freud and Maurice Halbwachs: The problem of memory in historical psychology. *The History Teacher, 27*(2), 145-158.

Jacobson, D.C. (1988). "Kill your ordinary common sense and maybe you'll begin to understand": Aharon Appelfeld and the Holocaust. *AJS Review, 13*(1), 129-152.

Jacobson, D.C. (1994). The Holocaust and the Bible in Israeli poetry. *Modern Language Studies, 24*(4), 63-77.

Josselson, R., Lieblich, A., & McAdams, D. P. (Eds.). (2003). *Up close and personal: The teaching and learning of narrative research.* Washington, DC: American Psychological Association.

Kaplan, L.J. (1996). *No voice is ever wholly lost: An exploration of the everlasting attachment between parent and child.* New York: Simon & Schuster.

Kestenberg, J.S. (1972). Psychoanalytic contributions to the problem of children of survivors from Nazi persecution. *Israel Annals of Psychiatry and Related Disciplines, 10,* 249-265.

Kestenberg, J.S. (1989). Coping with losses and survival. In D.R. Dietrich and P.C. Shabad (Eds.), *The Problem of Loss and Mourning: Psychoanalytic Perspectives* (p. 381-403). Madison, WI: International University Press, 381-403.

Kestenberg, J.S., & Brenner, I. (1996). *Last witness: The child survivor of the Holocaust.* Washington, DC: American Psychiatric Press.

Klein, M. (1948). A contribution to the theory of anxiety and guilt. *International Journal of Psychoanalysis, 29,* 114-123.

Koenig, S. (1952). Israeli culture and society. *The American Journal of Sociology, 58*(2), 160-166.

Lacan, J. (1968). *The language of the self: The function of language in psychoanalysis.* (A. Wilden, Trans.). Baltimore, MD: Johns Hopkins University Press.

Langer, L.L. (1991). *Holocaust testimonies: The ruins of memory.* New Haven: Yale University Press.

Lanzmann, C. (Director and producer). (1985). *Shoah* [Motion picture]. France: Les Films Aleph, Historia Films, 566 min.

Laub, D., & Auerhahn, N.C. (1985). Prologue. *Psychoanalytic Inquiry, 5,* 1-8.

Levi, P. (1989). *The drowned and the saved.* (R. Rosenthal, Trans.). New York: Vintage International (Original work published 1986).

Litvak-Hirsch, T., & Bar-On, D. (2006). To rebuild lives: A longitudinal study of the influences of the Holocaust on relationships among three generations of women in one family. *Family Process, 45*(4), 465-483.

Matte Blanco, I. (1988). *Thinking, feeling, and being: Clinical reflections on the fundamental antinomy of human beings and world.* London: Routledge.

Midgley, N. (2006). Psychoanalysis and qualitative psychology: Complementary or contradictory paradigms? *Qualitative Research in Psychology, 3* (3), 213-232.

Miller, A. (1997). *The drama of the gifted child* (3rd ed.) (R. Ward, Trans.). New York: Basic Books (Original work published 1979).

Mintz, A. (2001). *Popular culture and the shaping of Holocaust memory in America.* Seattle: University of Washington Press.

Mork, G. (1980). Teaching the Hitler period: History and morality. *The History Teacher, 13*(4), 509-522.

Neusner, J. (1973). The implications of the Holocaust. *The Journal of Religion, 53*(3), 293-308.

Novick, P. (1999). *The Holocaust in American life.* New York: Houghton Mifflin Company.

Novick, P. (2003). The American national narrative of the Holocaust: There isn't any. *New German Critique, 90,* 27-35.

Ogden, T. (2001). *Conversations at the frontier of dreaming.* Northvale, NJ: Jason Aronson.

Ogden, T. (2004). The art of psychoanalysis: Dreaming undreamt dreams and interrupted cries. *International Journal of Psychoanalysis, 85,* 857-877.

O'Loughlin, M. (2006). On knowing and desiring children: The significance of the unthought known. In G. Boldt & P. Salvio (Eds.), *Love's return: Psychoanalytic essays on childhood teaching and learning.* New York: Routledge.

O'Loughlin, M. (2007). Bearing witness to troubled memory. *Psychoanalytic Review, 94*(2), 191-212.

O'Loughlin, M. (2008). Radical hope, or death by a thousand cuts? The future for indigenous Australians. *Arena Journal, 29/30,* 175-201.

Packer, M.J., & Addison, R.B. (1989). *Entering the circle: Hermeneutic investigation in psychology.* Albany, New York: State University of New York Press.

Pontalis, J-B. (2002). *En marge des jours* (In the margins of the days). Paris: Gallimard. [Translated by and cited in Garon, 2004.]

Rebhun, U. (2004). Jewish identity in America: Structural analyses of attitudes and behaviors. *Review of Religious Research, 46* (1), 43-63.

Reilly, J. (1986, Winter). Maus: A survivor's tale [Review of the book *Maus: A survivor's tale,* A. Spiegelman]. *The Journal of Historical Review, 7*(4), 478. Available from Institute of Historical Review website: http://www.ihr.org/jhr/v07/v07p478_Reilly.html

Rogers, A.G. (2006). *The unsayable: The hidden language of trauma.* New York: Random House.

Rubenstein, I., Cutter, F., & Templer, D.I. (1989–1990). Multigenerational occurrence of survivor syndrome symptoms in families of Holocaust survivors. *Omega: Journal of Death and Dying, 20* (3), 239–244.

Sagi-Schwartz, A., van IJzendoorn, M.H., Grossmann, K., Joels, T., Grossmann, K., Scharf, M., Koren-Karie, N., & Alkalay, S. (2003). Attachment and traumatic stress in female Holocaust child survivors and their daughters. *American Journal of Psychiatry, 160* (6), 1086-1092.

Sagi-Schwartz, A., van IJzendoorn, M.H., & Bakermans-Kranenburg, M.J. (2008). Does intergenerational transmission of trauma skip a generation? No meta-analytic evidence for tertiary traumatization with third generation of Holocaust survivors. *Attachment & Human Development, 10*(2), 105-121.

Scharf, M. (2007). Long-term effects of trauma: Psychosocial functioning of the second and third generation of Holocaust survivors. *Development and Psychopathology, 19* (2), 603-622.

Segev, T. (1991). *The seventh million: The Israelis and the Holocaust.* New York: Owl Books.

Sigal, J.J. (1998). Long-term effects of the Holocaust: Empirical evidence for resilience in the first, second, and third generation. *Psychoanalytic Review, 85*(4), 579-585.

Sigal, J. J., DiNicola, V. F., & Buonvino, M. (1988). Grandchildren of survivors: Can negative effects of prolonged exposure to excessive stress be observed two generations later? *Canadian Journal of Psychiatry, 33* (3), 207-212.

Solomon, Z. (1993). *Combat Stress Reaction: The enduring toll of war.* New York: Plenum Press.

Solomon, Z. (1998). Transgenerational effects of the Holocaust: The Israeli research perspective. In Y. Danieli (Ed.), *International Handbook of Multigenerational Legacies of Trauma* (p. 69-83). New York: Plenum Press.

Spiegelman, A. (1986). *Maus I: A survivor's tale: My father bleeds history.* New York: Pantheon Books.

Spiegelman, A. (1991). *Maus II: A survivor's tale: And here my troubles began.* New York: Pantheon Books.

Sullivan, H.S. (1968). *The interpersonal theory of psychiatry.* New York: W,W. Norton.

Talby-Abarbanel, M. (2011). "Secretly attached, secretly separate" Art, dreams, and transference-countertransference in the analysis of a third generation Holocaust survivor. In A.B. Druck, C. Ellman, N. Freedman, & A. Thaler, (Eds.) *A new Freudian synthesis: Clinical process in the next generation* (p. 219-237). London: Karnac Books Ltd.

Tarantelli, C.B. (2003). Life within death: Towards a metapsychology of catastrophic psychic trauma. *International Journal of Psychoanalysis, 84*, 915-928.

Taub, M. (1997). The challenge to popular myth and conventions in recent Israeli drama. *Modern Judaism, 17*(2), 133-162.

Weiss, M. (1997). Bereavement, commemoration, and collective identity in contemporary Israeli society. *Anthropological Quarterly, 70*(2), 91-101.

Wiesel, E. (1961). *Night.* New York: Hill & Wang.

Wiseman, H., & Barber, J. P. (2008). *Echoes of the trauma: Relational themes and emotions in children of Holocaust survivors.* New York: Cambridge University Press.

INDEX

CPSIA information can be obtained at www.ICGtesting.com
Printed in the USA
LVOW121356030812

292736LV00003B/1/P

GLOBE EARTH S

Bryan Bunch
Senior Author and Editor, Globe Science Series

•

Barbara A. Branca

GLOBE FEARON
Pearson Learning Group

ABOUT THE AUTHORS

Bryan Bunch, a former high school teacher and editor of school science materials, currently teaches mathematics at Pace University in Pleasantville, New York. Mr. Bunch is president of Scientific Publishing, Inc., and the author of handbooks on current science and medicine, and the co-author of *The Timetables of Science* and *The Timetables of Technology.* He is an editor/author of many other science reference books and teaching materials.

Barbara Branca, a former junior high school earth science teacher, is the author of several science workbooks and a contributing writer to science textbooks and reference books. She is currently an editor and publishing consultant and is also active in environmental education in New York state.

Executive Editor: Barbara Levadi
Project Editor: Laura Baselice
Production Director: Penny Gibson
Production Editor: Nicole Cypher
Marketing Manager: Sandra Hutchison
Photo Research: Jenifer Hixson
Cover Design: Nicole Cypher
Cover Photo: European Space Agency/ Cover Photo Researchers

ISBN 0-8359-1174-8

Printed in the United States of America

7 8 9 10   06 05 04 03

1-800-321-3106
www.pearsonlearning.com

Table of Contents

UNIT 4 ROCKS AND MINERALS

UNIT 5 EROSION AND WEATHERING

UNIT 6 THE OCEANS

UNIT 7 THE EARTH'S HISTORY

UNIT 8 CLIMATE AND THE ENVIRONMENT

UNIT 9 WEATHER

UNIT 10 THE SOLAR SYSTEM, STARS, AND THE UNIVERSE

To the Student

Welcome to *Globe Earth Science*

Globe Earth Science is different from other science books you have used. Each lesson starts with a question that will be answered in the lesson. The question is followed with **Exploring Science,** a story of one of the many interesting or exciting parts of earth science.

After that, you start the lesson itself. Here is where you will learn about the ideas of earth science. We stick to the ideas that are most important. You will not need to learn a lot of dull details. Here also there are activities called **To Do Yourself.** They provide a way to see how earth science works first hand. There is also a **Review** that will help you remember what you have learned. Both **To Do Yourself** and **Review** provide places where you may write answers in the book.

There are also reviews at the end of each unit. **Summing Up** sections in some units review everything you have studied in the book so far. Other units feature **Careers in Earth Science,** short descriptions of how people work using the ideas of earth science. You can also find out what is needed to get into these careers.

Those are the parts of *Globe Earth Science*. The whole book was put together with you in mind. Try it. You'll like it.

Barbara A. Branca
Bryan Bunch

UNIT

1

INTRODUCING THE EARTH

Lesson One

What Is the Earth Like?

Exploring Science

Is There Life on the Planet? One December day a space traveler from Earth passed close to a small planet. Automatic sensors on the craft studied the atmosphere, weighed the planet, and checked for signs of life. It measured the atmosphere above a continent, finding large amounts of the gas oxygen and other gases produced by living things. It also detected strange radio signals. There was life on the planet! It was the only planet in the universe known from space measurements to contain living creatures. The space vehicle was moving so fast that it took two years to turn back for a second look.

The space traveler was *Galileo,* a robot built for long voyages through space. It had also passed by another planet, Venus, where there was no life. Unlike the planet with life, Venus showed no oxygen in the air. Instead, Venus was covered with clouds of poisonous acid.

There were many other differences between Venus and the other planet, although both planets were almost exactly the same size—both planets were 12,000 kilometers across.

After the *Galileo* visit, humans also studied the planet with life from space. They could see large circular storms form and die down. They saw the air as a thin layer of "dark blue light," following the curve of the planet. From a distance the planet was blue and white: blue from the great oceans that covered it; white from the clouds of water in the air. Closer to the planet, the humans saw large land regions. Great chains of mountains ran along these continents. Although *Galileo* told them there was life on the planet, the humans in space could not see buildings or signs of civilization.

● What planet do you think *Galileo* was studying? Why?

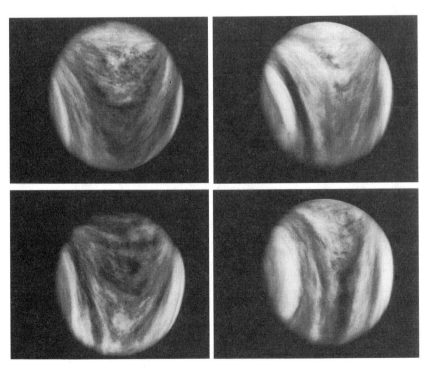

Four different views of the planet Venus.

Introducing the Earth

Galileo recognized life on Earth. People in spacecraft can see much from space. Imagine flying over the United States in a spacecraft. You could see the kinds of **features** that cover the earth. Some of the features are mountains, rivers, islands, and oceans.

Use the map as your flight path. You will be flying from west to east. Draw an arrow to show your direction. Your lift-off is from the Hawaiian Islands in the Pacific Ocean. Oceans cover about 70 percent of the earth's surface.

As you fly east from Hawaii, you come to the west coast of North America. North America is one of seven large land masses, or **continents** (KON-tuh-nunts). Continents make up most of the land on earth. Which state in the United States is not on a continent?

Look along the west coast of North America. Notice all the **mountains.** Mountains rise high above the surrounding land. A group of mountains forms a **range.** What are the low places between mountains called? The mountains and **valleys** along the west coast form the Pacific Mountain region.

Flying past the mountains you see high, flat areas called **plateaus** (plah-TOHS). Find the Columbia Plateau and circle it. The Columbia Plateau is cut by two deep **canyons.** Canyons are deep grooves worn into a plateau by swift **rivers.** Now take a detour south of the Columbia Plateau. This area is the Basin and Range region. This region has no outlet to the ocean. It contains a large **lake** with very salty water. What is the name of the lake?

Continue traveling east until you reach the

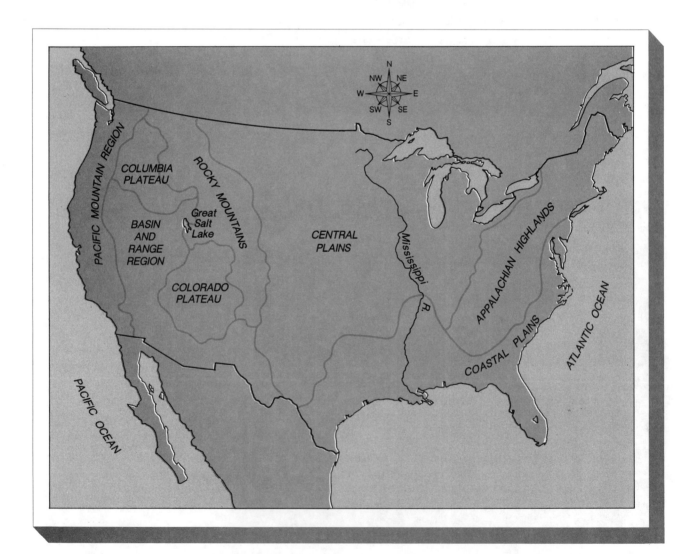

Rocky Mountains. Some of these mountains are five kilometers high. Just beyond the mountains is a large, flat **plain.** The Central Plains is the largest region of the United States. Farther east, you see the long path of the Mississippi River. Next, on the eastern edge of the plains, is another range of mountains called the Appalachian (ap-uh-LAY-chee-un) Highlands. These mountains are not nearly as high as the Rockies. Cross over these mountains and go on to the east coast. Along the east coast of North America the continent meets the Atlantic Ocean. Your ocean-to-ocean trip has taken only 20 minutes. How close did you come to the place where you live?

Another kind of map is often used to show the Earth's features. On a **topographic map** all the places that have a given height are connected by a line. The top of a tall mountain might show as small ring labeled "1500 meters." The bottom of a long valley might show as a line labled "100 meters." Using a topographic map you could tell that you would have to climb 1400 meters to reach the top of the mountain. Other features on topographic maps are shown by special symbols.

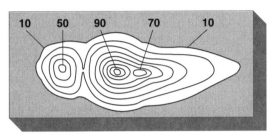

A topographic map shows the elevation of features on the earth.

Review

I. Fill in each blank with the word that fits best. Choose from the words below.

mountains   lakes   oceans   plain   islands   plateau

Regions of steep land are called _____ . Somewhat lower,

flatter land is called a(n) _____ . The central part of the

United States is a very flat _____ . Both the east and west

coasts are bounded by _____ .

II. Circle the underlined word that makes each statement true.

    A. A body of land surrounded by water is a(n) (island/lake).
    B. A low area between mountains is a (canyon/valley).
    C. The place where a continent and ocean meet is a (coast/range).

III. Look at the map on page 2. Mark where you live with an **X** if it is on the map. Name four of the features in the area.

_____

_____

_____

Lesson Two

How Do Scientists Learn About the Earth?

Exploring Science

The Mystery of the Scratched Rocks. All over Europe there are large rocks, or boulders, that do not look like most of the other rocks nearby. Many of them are covered with deep scratches. Where did the boulders come from? What made the scratches?

Some scientists were curious about these large rocks. They examined the scratches carefully. The scratches did not seem to be made by people or animals. Perhaps the rocks were scratched during a great flood. Fast moving rivers can carry small rocks a long way. But the boulders seemed too large to have been moved by water. Also, the scratches did not match those in rocks that had been tossed about by moving water.

Many of the mysterious boulders are found in Switzerland. Switzerland is a land of very high mountains and deep valleys. Some of the valleys hold thick masses of ice called **glaciers** (GLAY-shurs). In 1821, a scientist found that the old scratches on the boulders looked like new marks found on rocks near a glacier. Could a glacier, a frozen river, move boulders and produce the strange marks?

These questions interested a Swiss scientist named Louis Agassiz (AG-uh-see). Agassiz visited a cabin built on a glacier. There he heard a strange story. The cabin had been moving downhill since it had been built. It had traveled 2 kilometers in 13 years!

Near the cabin, Agassiz drove a straight line of stakes deep into the glacier. Two years later, the stakes were no longer in a straight line. The ones near the sides of the glacier were in the same place. But the ones near the middle had moved. Agassiz had shown that a glacier could move!

Now it all made sense. As glaciers moved, they dragged boulders from one place to another. Along the way, the boulders were scratched by other rocks.

Agassiz knew there were similar boulders all over northern Europe. He reasoned that at one time glaciers must have covered all of Europe. Later Agassiz showed that, in the past, glaciers had also covered Canada and the northern United States.

● Why are glaciers formed in areas where there are very high mountains?

This "river of ice" in the Swiss Alps is the longest glacier in Switzerland.

The Ways of the Scientist

A scientific idea goes through many stages. One scientist may build on the ideas of others. Many times, a better idea replaces an older one. For example, Agassiz borrowed the idea that glaciers caused scratches on rocks. But he didn't believe that glaciers could move until he set up a test to prove it. Testing is an important part of any scientist's work. Although not all scientific ideas develop in the same way, there is a general pattern that scientists follow.

OBSERVING. Scientists watch closely or observe things around them. Scientific **observation** (ob-zur-VAY-shun) is more than just seeing. It can be hearing the sounds made by an earthquake. It can be smelling the odor near a volcano. Scientists use such tools as telescopes to help them see and amplifiers to help them hear. Scientists use all their senses to gain information that they record carefully.

An observation that is basic to science is **measurement.** A measurement tells *how many* or *how much.* For example, Agassiz may have counted the rock layers near the glacier or measured the distance the glacier moved. When an observation is stated as a number, it can be compared with other numbers. Agassiz may not have been able to observe the glacier moving. But by using measurements, he could be sure that it had moved.

COLLECTING INFORMATION. Reading is one way in which scientists collect information. Scientists can read about, or research, the observations and ideas of other scientists.

Scientists also observe how things are alike and how they are different. For example, noticing that the scratches on the mysterious boulders were like the scratches on rocks found near glaciers was an important clue to solving the mystery of the boulders.

RECOGNIZING A PROBLEM. Most people did not notice that the large boulders were different from the other rocks nearby, but scientists noticed. They asked the question, "Why are these rocks scratched?" Scientists state a problem in the form of a question. Then they try to find the answer.

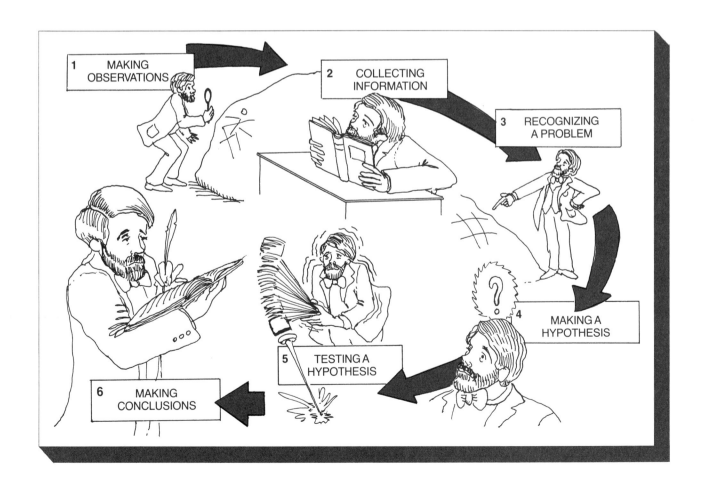

MAKING HYPOTHESES. At first, some scientists thought that the rocks were scratched in a flood. Later, others thought that the rocks were scratched by glaciers. If glaciers could move, that would help explain the scratched rocks.

An explanation of what you observe is called a **hypothesis** (hy-POTH-ih-sis). The hypothesis helps you make **predictions,** to say beforehand what will happen. If the predictions are correct, the hypothesis becomes a **theory.** The theory may still be wrong. If other observations or tests do not fit the theory, the theory must be changed or replaced.

TESTING HYPOTHESES. You must be able to test a hypothesis. Sometimes the test is another observation. At other times, you may want to carry out an **experiment.** An experiment is a kind of trial that tests a hypothesis. Placing the stakes in the glacier was the experiment Agassiz used to find out if glaciers really moved.

MAKING CONCLUSIONS. Only after testing the hypothesis does a scientist conclude that something is true. Agassiz made the **conclusion** that glaciers move. What are the steps he took to get to his conclusion? Use the diagram to trace his steps.

To Do Yourself How Do Different Materials Settle into Layers?

You will need:

Large peanut butter or mayonnaise jar with lid, pebbles, small stones, sand, soil, large glass or pitcher, and water

1. To the jar add equal amounts of pebbles, small stones, sand, and soil until the jar is ⅓ full.
2. Using the glass or pitcher, fill the jar with water. Cover and shake thoroughly.
3. Allow the contents to settle completely.

When different-sized particles are mixed with water, the heaviest material settles fastest. It forms the bottom layer. The lightest material forms the top layer.

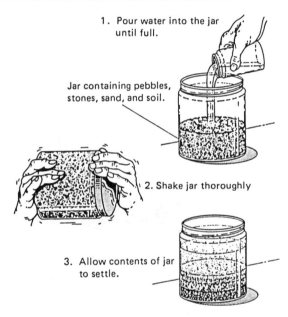

1. Pour water into the jar until full.

Jar containing pebbles, stones, sand, and soil.

2. Shake jar thoroughly

3. Allow contents of jar to settle.

Questions

1. What is the problem? _____
2. What is your hypothesis? (What do you think is the answer to the problem?)

_____

_____

3. What was your experiment? (What did you do to test the hypothesis?)

_____

_____

4. What did you observe? _____

_____

5. What is your conclusion? _____

_____

Review

I. Fill in each blank with the word that fits best. Choose from the words below.

experiment   hypothesis   measurement   conclusion   predictions   test

A scientist wants to explain something she has observed. First, she states a(n)

_____ . The statement becomes a theory if the

_____ the scientist makes are correct. She must be able to

_____ her theory. She may plan an experiment. If the

experiment supports her theory, then she can make a _____ .

II. Number the statements (1, 2, 3, and 4) to show how a scientific theory is developed.

A. _____ Making a prediction.

B. _____ Making observations.

C. _____ Performing an experiment.

D. _____ Stating a hypothesis.

III. Decide which term best fits each statement.

observation   measurement   hypothesis   theory   experiment

A. Someone noticed that rocks near glaciers had scratches on them like the

scratches on boulders found in the valleys. _____

B. Agassiz said that northern Europe had once been covered by ice.

_____

C. The cabin on the glacier had moved 2 kilometers in 13 years.

_____

D. A lot of ice on the northern part of the earth might change the movement

of the earth through space. _____

E. The kind of scratches made on rocks could be checked. Specially marked rocks are placed in a river. When these rocks are removed from the river,

their scratches are examined. _____

What Is the Ocean Like?

Exploring Science

Why the Sea Is Salty. Have you ever swallowed a mouthful of ocean water? If so, you know that ocean water is quite salty. Did you ever wonder why ocean water is salty but river water is fresh?

"Fresh" water in rivers and streams does have some salt in it. The salt is dissolved from rocks as the water passes over them. But because there is very little salt, the water tastes fresh. Streams flow into rivers. Rivers eventually flow to the ocean. The rivers bring some salt to the ocean everyday.

While salt is being carried to the ocean, something else is taking place. The sun heats the ocean. Some water evaporates and leaves salt behind. This process has been going on for the last billion years. It has made the ocean salty. Some salt also leaves the ocean. This salt settles to the ocean floor as solid particles. Some salt becomes part of the animals and plants that live in the ocean. All this gaining and losing of salt balances out. The result is that the ocean is about 3.5 percent salt by mass. In 1000 grams of ocean water, you would find about 35 grams of salt.

● Suppose the temperature all over the earth became warmer. What would happen to the saltiness of the ocean? Explain your answer.

Salt can be "mined" from the ocean by evaporating sea water.

The World Ocean

The earth is sometimes called the "blue planet." The blue comes mostly from water, and over 70 percent of earth's surface is covered with water. Nearly all of that is in the ocean.

No doubt you can point out the Pacific Ocean and the Atlantic Ocean on a globe map of earth. These oceans are the shores of most of the United States. One part of the United States, the northern coast of Alaska, touches a different ocean, the Arctic. The other great ocean on the planet is the Indian Ocean.

The oceans of Earth have no boundaries. They run into each other. There is only one world ocean. Each of the four named oceans is a part of the world ocean. Even so, the oceans are not alike. The Pacific Ocean is by far the largest and deepest. The Arctic Ocean is cold and shallow, and is often covered with ice. The Atlantic seems to be younger than the others. Different oceans also have different plant and animal life.

The ocean waters cover features that might surprise you. Under the oceans there are very high mountains, steep trenches, great canyons, and vast plains.

Until recently we knew more about space and other planets than we did about the oceans of our own planet. Today, however, some of the mysteries of the oceans have been solved. We know where the oceans come from. We know what the sea floor looks like. We know why the oceans have not filled up with soil or sand washed from the continents.

The World Ocean

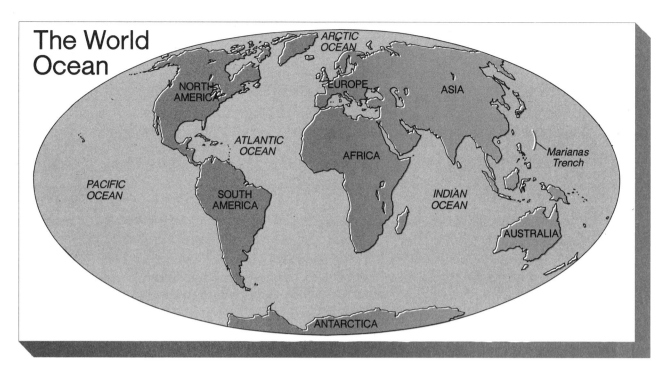

To Do Yourself   How Can We Separate Sand, Salt, and Water?

You will need:

2 glasses, small funnel, teaspoon, paper filter (such as coffee filter), sand, salt, and water

1. Add 1 teaspoonful each of salt and sand to half a glass of water. Stir thoroughly.
2. Fold the filter to fit in the funnel. Place the funnel over the other glass and pour the mixture through it.
3. Allow the liquid to evaporate.

Salt dissolves in water but sand does not. You can use a filter to separate sand and water, but not salt and water. You separate the salt from the water by letting the water evaporate.

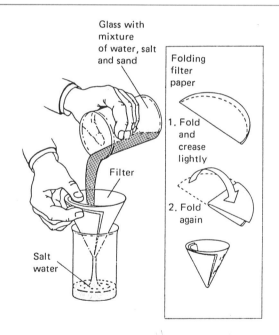

Questions

1. What observation shows that sand does not dissolve in water? _____

_____

2. What do you observe after the liquid has evaporated? _____

_____

3. List ways of removing sand and salt from water. _____

_____

Review

I. Fill in each blank with the word that fits best. Choose from the words below.

separated   **rain**   ~~water~~   **rivers**   **oceans**   **land**   **salt**   **connected**

More than 70 percent of the earth is covered with _water_ .

Most of the water on earth is found in the _oceans_ . Ocean water contains more _salt_ than river water.

Because all the oceans are _ran_ , they form one world ocean.

II. Circle the underlined word that makes each statement true.

A. The earth is sometimes called the (water/dry) planet.
B. The ocean floor has (larger/smaller) features than those on the land.
C. The deepest part of the ocean is found in the (Atlantic/Pacific).
D. Salt in river water comes from (rocks and soil/oceans).

III. Answer in sentences.
Scientists do not consider the "Antarctic Ocean" to be a separate ocean. Where would an "Antarctic Ocean" be? Why is it not a separate ocean?

_____

_____

_____

Lesson Four

How Does the Earth Change?

Exploring Science

Is Iowa Going Out to Sea? The eastern part of the Central Plains in the United States is one of the best farming regions on earth. One reason is the topsoil. Topsoil is rich, black soil that is formed by the decay of dead plants and animals. Topsoil is formed best by the decay of tall grasses. Such tall grasses have grown in the eastern Central Plains for most of the past 65 million years.

Another reason why this part of the nation is good farmland is this region gets plenty of rain. Farther west, in the Central Plains, there is just not enough rain for tall grasses or for most crops to grow.

Because it has deep topsoil and the right amount of rain, Iowa grows the best corn in the world. Much of the corn is used to feed cattle and other farm animals. Iowa's topsoil is one of the great resources of the United States. There is a problem, however. The tall grasses that once covered Iowa are no longer there. The land is now covered with cornfields. The roots of the grasses once held the soil in place all year. But corn is grown only in the summer. Even when corn is growing, much of the topsoil remains bare. Iowa loses topsoil as it produces corn. In fact, five tons of topsoil are lost every second in Iowa.

Where does the topsoil go? Iowa gets a lot of rain. Where the ground is bare, rain can wash away the topsoil. The soil is carried to streams. The streams flow into the Mississippi River. The Mississippi flows into the world ocean. Iowa is being washed out to sea.

What can be done to stop the topsoil from being washed away? Look at the picture. Better farming methods can be used to help protect the topsoil.

● Which is more likely to be true?

A. If Iowa had less rainfall, it would lose more topsoil.

B. If Iowa had less rainfall, its corn crop would not be as good.

This farmer is using a no-till system of soil conservation. The wastes from the preceding crop are left on the ground. These wastes (mulch) prevent soil erosion and keep moisture in the soil.

The Changing Earth

Has the earth always looked the way it does today? If you had traveled across the country over 100 years ago, you would have crossed the same mountains and plains you would cross today. People have made some changes. In the last 100 years, forests have been cut down. Cornfields have taken the place of grasslands. But the earth's features—the oceans, mountains, plains, and plateaus—still look the same as they did 100 years ago.

To a person, 100 years seems like a long time. But it is a very short time in earth's history. Scientists think that the earth is 4.5 billion years old. During that great length of time, there have been changes in the earth's features.

Think of a mountain. Every time it rains, the water washes a little of the mountain's soil down the slope. Streams on the mountain, swollen by rain, carry away small rocks. The water also dissolves salt in the rocks. The dissolved salt is also carried away.

Winds blowing across the mountain also carry away soil. Wind and water carry away only small amounts of the mountain each day. But after millions of years, the entire mountain is gone.

If water and wind can break down a mountain, why are there still mountains? Why did they not wear down long ago? The answer is that new mountains are always being formed. Some mountains, like those in the Appalachian Highlands, are worn smooth. They are old mountains. Others, like the Rocky Mountains, have tall, jagged peaks. They are young mountains. Which picture below shows a young mountain?

To Do Yourself   How Does Water Wear Away the Earth?

You will need:

A new bar of soap, a sink with running water

1. Hold the soap directly under the faucet.
2. Allow the faucet to drip cold water, one drop at a time, onto the soap. Observe for several minutes.
3. Gently increase the water flow and record what happens.
4. Hold the soap at an even greater tilt and observe what happens.

   Running water wears away rock as it does soap. Soap is soft and dissolves in just minutes. It takes years and years to wear away rock.

Questions

1. What happened to the soap under running water? _____

2. How did the results change when you increased the flow? _____

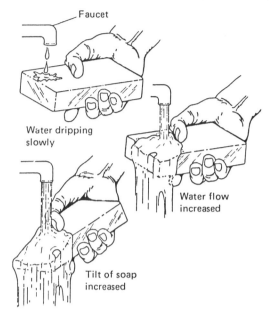

Faucet

Water dripping slowly

Water flow increased

Tilt of soap increased

Review

I. Fill in each blank with the word that fits best. Choose from the words below.

billions   rough   water   mountains   smooth   oceans   several

While forests have changed in the past 100 years, _____ and

valleys still look the same. But every day, _____ and wind

wear away rock and carry soil to the _____ . However,

because the earth is _____ of years old, some tall, jagged

mountains have become _____ .

II. Answer in sentences.
The Alps in Switzerland have large valleys carved into the mountains. What forces helped to shape these valleys?

_____

_____

_____

What Is Inside the Earth?

Exploring Science

A Trip Into the Earth. In southern Africa there is a plains region called the Witwatersrand (wit-WAW-turz-rand). The surface of the plain is marked by gray rocks. In 1886, George Walker and George Harrison noticed small, shiny specks in the rocks. The specks were gold. Other people found out and a gold rush was on. Many people dug mines.

Today, the East Rand Proprietary Mine is the deepest mine of any kind on earth. Suppose you could go down into the mine. What would it be like?

On the surface, there is a giant steel tower. The tower is used to raise and lower elevators into the mine. The top of the mine is covered because the mine is air conditioned.

Air conditioning is not a luxury here. It's a necessity. The walls of the mine can become quite hot. Near the surface, rocks and soil have the average temperature of the air temperature at the surface. But as you go down, it gets hotter. How much hotter depends on the kind of rock. In limestone or granite, the temperature goes up about 20° C for every kilometer you go down. In shale, the temperature goes up at a rate of 47° C per kilometer.

The Rand mine is 3428 meters deep. That's more than 3 kilometers. At the deepest level of the mine, the rock temperature is 52°C. Death Valley reaches that temperature on really hot days. The elevator stops short of the deepest level. At 3288 meters, the temperature of the rock is 51° C. This is the hottest temperature that the air conditioners at the top of the mine can handle.

● The rock temperature at the surface of a mine is 20° C. One kilometer below, the rock temperature is 67° C. What kind of rock is in the mine?

The structures shown here contain elevators and air conditioners for a gold mine in Africa.

Making an X-Ray of the Earth

Have you ever seen an X-ray? In an X-ray photograph, a person's bones and some other body parts can be seen. What would an X-ray of the earth show?

You really cannot make an X-ray photograph of the earth. X-rays cannot go very far into the earth. However, vibrations called **shock waves** or **seismic** (SYZ-muk) **waves** can travel long distances in the earth. Some of those waves can travel from one side of the earth to the other. Such waves are created by earthquakes. By studying and measuring shock waves, scientists can learn a lot about the inside of the earth. They can tell when a shock wave travels through a solid or a liquid.

The part of the earth that we live on is the **crust.** Look at the crust in the diagram. The thickness of the crust changes from place to place. At what parts of the earth is the crust the thinnest? Under the oceans, the average thickness is 10 kilometers. Under the continents, it is 35 kilometers. Even the thinnest part of the crust is too thick for us to explore fully. No well has ever been drilled all the way through the crust. The deepest well is only 20 kilometers deep.

Scientists know from studying seismic waves that the layer of the earth below the crust is different from the crust. The crust is made up of familiar kinds of rocks. In the layer below the crust, the rock is different. This layer is the **mantle** (MAN-tul). Over 80 percent of the earth consists of mantle rock.

The mantle is about 2900 kilometers thick. This layer does not seem to be the same all the way through. The top part of the mantle and the bottom part of the crust is like a very thick liquid. Like all liquids, it can flow. Farther down, the mantle becomes solid.

Seismic waves show that another change takes place below the mantle. This portion of the earth is the **core**. The core is about 6800 kilometers across. The upper part of the core is called the **outer core**. Like the upper part of the mantle, the outer core seems to act like a liquid.

The Earth's Crust

The average thickness of the crust is 35 kilometers. Beneath mountains, however, its thickness can be 70 kilometers thick.

No one knows for sure what this liquid is. It is probably molten iron and nickel combined with oxygen. Toward the center of the core, the material acts like a solid again. This **inner core** is probably iron and nickel too.

You have just learned about three different layers that make up the earth—crust, mantle, and core. The rocks of each layer are shaped by two things—heat and pressure. As you get deeper into the earth, both the heat and the pressure become greater. At some levels, like the upper mantle, heat has a greater effect than pressure on the state of rocks. Heat causes the rock of the upper mantle to flow like a very thick liquid. At other levels, such as the lower mantle or inner core, pressure has a greater effect. The materials at these levels are solid.

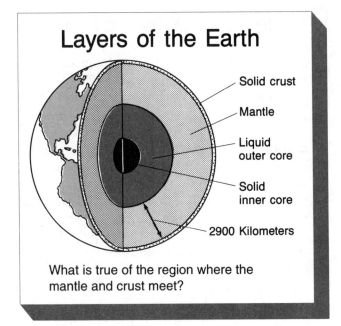

Layers of the Earth

- Solid crust
- Mantle
- Liquid outer core
- Solid inner core
- 2900 Kilometers

What is true of the region where the mantle and crust meet?

To Do Yourself   How Can We Make a Model of the Earth?

You will need:

4 different colors of modeling clay

1. Use one color clay to form a ball about 2 cm across. Add a layer of another color evenly all over the ball until the ball grows to about 5 cm across.
2. Build a layer in a third color until the ball becomes 10 cm across.
3. Use the fourth color to apply a very thin layer to the ball.
4. Have your teacher slice the ball in two with a knife.

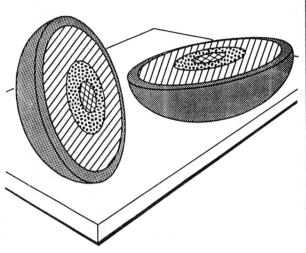

Scientists often use scale models to represent much larger objects or objects they cannot really see.

Questions

1. Starting from the outside of your model, name the layers of the earth represented.

_____

2. Name the thickest and thinnest layers. How are the rocks which make them up

   different? _____

3. How are scale models useful? _____

_____

Review

I. Fill in each blank with the word that fits best. Choose from the words below.

core   crust   liquid   melt   mantle   hot   seismic waves

The part of the earth that we can explore with mines or wells is the top part of

the _____. Scientists use _____ to find out what the inside
of the earth is like. The region where the crust and mantle meet behaves like a

_____. As you move toward the center of the earth, heat sometimes

causes solids to _____. Increased pressure makes them solid. Near

the center of the earth, the _____ is probably made of metal combined with oxygen.

II. Match the part of the earth from column A with its description in column B.

A	B
1. _____ crust	**a.** liquid iron and nickel
2. _____ upper mantle	**b.** solid rock under great pressure
3. _____ lower mantle	**c.** ordinary solid rock
4. _____ outer core	**d.** solid iron and nickel
5. _____ inner core	**e.** very thick liquid rock

III. Answer in sentences.
How is the study of the earth's interior an example of *indirect* observation?

_____

_____

_____

Review What You Know

A. Hidden in the puzzle below are the names of features of the earth. Use the clues in the statements below to help you find the names. Circle each name in the puzzle. Then write each name on the line next to its clue.

```
R C R A N G E C O N T I N E N T P
A O Q E T U I P B I E S Z C V E H
L A T H E O R Y S T P L A T E A U
E S T I V A L L E Y L A K E X R C
X T B U L D C O R E X N P L I M A
P C R U S T A L V O T D L O M A Q
I H O M O U N T A I N D A T R N U
R O M E M V O I T E S T I N G T A
H Y P O T H E S I S R O N E O L P
P E R C A X R A O C E A N P N E I
E M E A S U R I N G C L O E D R K
```

1. The layer of the earth we live on. _____

2. The place where the sea meets the land. _____

3. A group of mountains. _____

4. A body of fresh water surrounded by land. _____

5. A body of land surrounded by water. _____

6. A broad, flat part of the earth that is not much higher than the region around it. _____

7. A flat part of the earth that is higher than the region around it.

   _____

8. One of the seven land masses into which the earth is divided.

   _____

9. One of the large bodies of water of earth. _____

10. A low place between two mountains. _____

B. Write the word (or words) that best complete each statement.

1. _____ A river wears a deep groove into a plateau. The feature that results is called **a.** plain **b.** canyon **c.** valley

2. _____ An earth scientist finds rock layers exposed where a road is being built. His explanation of why the layers are tilted is called a **a.** hypothesis **b.** measurement **c.** conclusion

3. _____ About 30 percent of the earth is covered by **a.** glaciers **b.** continents **c.** oceans

4. _____ Every day, soil and rock is carried to the oceans by **a.** movements in the mantle **b.** plants and animals **c.** wind and water

5. _____ The interior of the earth is **a.** all liquid **b.** all solid **c.** partly liquid

6. _____ Most of the land on earth is on the **a.** islands **b.** continents **c.** plains

7. _____ A trial to test a hypothesis is a(n) **a.** theory **b.** experiment **c.** observation

8. _____ Salt in the ocean comes from **a.** glaciers **b.** seacoasts **c.** rocks and soil

9. _____ The crust of the earth is thinnest under the **a.** plains **b.** mountains **c.** oceans

10. _____ The thickest layer of the earth is the **a.** crust **b.** mantle **c.** core

C. Apply What You Know

Answer each question with a word or phrase.

a. What name is given to a region that has few hills or highlands?

_____

b. A certain hypothesis makes correct scientific predictions. What does the

hypothesis become? _____

c. How did we learn about the interior of the earth? _____

d. Over what period of time would you expect to see large changes in mountains, canyons, and similar features of the earth?

_____

e. What two factors determine the state of rocks and metals inside the

earth? _____

D. Find Out More

1. Make a map of the area around where you live or around the school. If you live in a large city, make a map of a city park. Label features such as rivers, lakes, mountains, and so forth. If the feature has a name (for example, Mount Thomas or Long Pond) use the name on the map.

2. Set up an experiment to detect changes caused by wind and water. In a shallow box or tub, make a small "mountain" about 50 centimeters high out of mud and small rocks. Make sure there is a hole in the box so water can drain out. Place the "mountain" outside and, if possible, photograph it. Carefully measure its height. Look at the mountain one month later. Compare it to the photograph. Measure its height. Write a report on what you learned.

3. Make a poster showing the different layers of the earth. Include an enlarged version of the crust and show the deepest mine and deepest well. Display the poster in your classroom.

UNIT

2

VOLCANOES, MOUNTAINS, AND EARTHQUAKES

Lesson One

What Causes Volcanoes to Erupt?

Exploring Science

Mount St. Helens Blows Its Top. At 8:32 A.M. on May 18, 1980, Dr. David Johnstone shouted into his radio. "Vancouver, Vancouver! This is it!" He was never heard from again.

Less than two months before, Mount St. Helens in the state of Washington had started smoking. The ground around it had begun to shake. People were warned to keep away. But on May 18, Dr. Johnstone was studying the mountain from eight kilometers away. Mike and Lu Moore were hiking at a "safe" distance from the volcano. Closer to the eruption than anyone (except Dr. Johnstone) was 84-year-old Harry Truman. He refused to leave his home.

Mike and Lu Moore described that fateful Sunday morning: "Suddenly the sky turned black." They raced across the steaming countryside. As hot rocks fell around them, they ran into a shack. That shack saved their lives.

Sixty-one people were killed. Harry Truman was among them. He was buried under mud that slid down the mountainside. The destruction and loss of life that occurred that day will be remembered for years to come.

● Which seems more likely to be true?

A. The heat energy that caused Mount St. Helens to erupt came from the inner core of the earth.

B. The heat energy that caused Mount St. Helens to erupt came from the mantle of the earth.

Mount St. Helens erupting on May 18, 1980.

Volcanic Eruptions

Mount St. Helens is a **volcano** (vol-KAY-noh). A volcano is an opening in the earth's crust where hot, melted rock from inside the earth comes to the surface. Many volcanoes look like ordinary mountains. Once in a while, though, the top of a volcano begins to "smoke."

The smoke from a volcano is made of steam, hot gases, dust and ash. Many volcanoes also produce rivers of red-hot melted rock, called **lava.**

When these materials rush to the surface, a volcanic **eruption** (ih-RUP-shun) takes place. Such an eruption can cause great damage. Many of the gases from a volcano are poisonous. Large pieces of hot rock, called volcanic bombs, may fall on people or buildings. Volcanic dust and ash can settle over a wide area. The flow of the lava cannot be stopped. The red-hot rock burns or buries just about everything in its path.

The lava that flows from a volcano comes from underground pools of melted rock, called **magma.** Magma is so hot that it melts other rocks around it. These heated rocks—and any water they may contain—begin to expand. That is, they start to take up more space. But expansion is stopped at first by solid rock all around

the melting rocks. The pressure inside the earth increases. Finally, a hole breaks open at the surface of the earth.

When the surface breaks, pressure is released. Water turns to steam. The steam and other gases in the rock expand quickly. If there is a lot of gas in the rock, the volcano erupts, or "blows its top." A **crater**, a deep hole in the surface, is formed when rock and ash are flung from the top of the volcano. When Mount St. Helens erupted, a huge chunk of the mountain blew away.

When there is less gas, magma rises to the surface more slowly. It flows out of the volcano as lava. Both explosions and lava flow reduce the pressure caused by the heated rocks. When the pressure eases, the eruption is over. The mountain continues to smoke and rumble. If there is more magma below the surface, a volcano can erupt again. Perhaps the new eruption will come in a few days or in a thousand years.

Volcanoes that have erupted recently are called **active** volcanoes. Those that have not erupted since people have kept records are called **extinct**. Volcanoes that have not erupted for many years are said to be **dormant**, which means "sleeping."

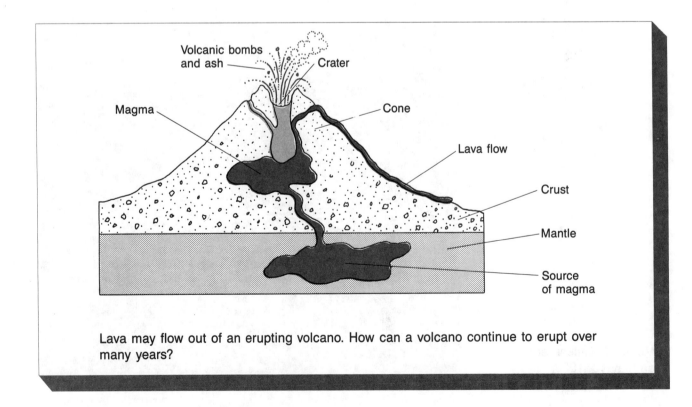

Lava may flow out of an erupting volcano. How can a volcano continue to erupt over many years?

To Do Yourself Why Do Heated Liquids Stay Hot?

You will need:

Two identical canning jars, hot water, 2 thermometers, modeling clay.

1. Fill both jars with the same amounts of hot water (about 50° C).
2. Wrap the sides of one jar with clay. Flatten a piece of clay wide enough to cover the top of the jar. Use a pencil to make a hole in the flattened clay for a thermometer. Place the clay on top of the clay-sided jar.
3. Place a thermometer in each jar. **Caution: Thermometers break easily!** Work very carefully when pushing the thermometer through the clay "cap."
4. Measure the temperature of the water in each jar every 5 minutes for 30 minutes. Record the temperatures in the table.

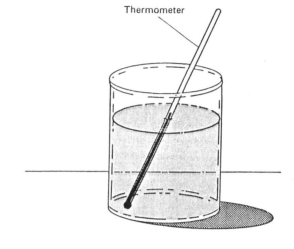

Thermometer

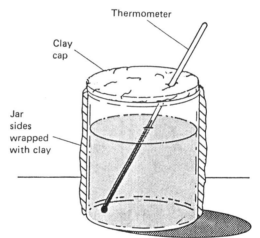

Thermometer

Clay cap

Jar sides wrapped with clay

Data Table

Time	Temperature	
	Open jar	*Covered jar*
Start		
5 minutes		
10 minutes		
15 minutes		
20 minutes		
25 minutes		
30 minutes		

Questions

1. Predict which of the jars will be hotter after 30 minutes. _____
2. Do your results agree with your prediction? How can you explain your results?

_____

_____

3. Why does magma stay hot for thousands of years? _____

_____

Review

I. Fill in each blank with the word that fits best. Choose from the words below.

eruption   **gases**   **lava**   **magma**   **ash**   **crater**

Inside a volcano, _____ melts rocks, causing them
to expand. The pressure makes a hole in the surface where steam, other

_____ and volcanic _____ can escape.

Often, red-hot melted rock, or _____ , flows out of a
volcano.

II. Circle the underlined word that makes each statement true.

A. Large pieces of hot rock from an eruption are called (ash/bombs).
B. Mount St. Helens is an example of an (extinct/active) volcano.
C. Melted rock underground is called (lava/magma).
D. A hole produced by a volcanic eruption is a (crater/pool).

III. Answer in sentences.

A volcano is about to erupt. Inside it are rocks that contain a lot of water.
Describe what will come out of the volcano. Describe what the volcano will
look like after the eruption.

_____

_____

_____

How Do Volcanoes Differ?

Exploring Science

A Problem That Grew Overnight. In 1943, a man named Pulido was farming in Mexico. He had a problem with his cornfield. Part of the field had sunken down, leaving a big hole. Each time Pulido filled in the hole, the hole would open up again.

One day Pulido went to the cornfield to plow. Not only was the hole still there, but there was a big crack in the field as well.

Suddenly, the field seemed to come alive. The ground around the hole rose higher than Pulido's head. Smoke and ashes poured from the hole.

By the next day, there was a volcano about 10 meters high in Pulido's field. A week later it was 150 meters high. The new volcano was called Paricutín (pah-ree-koo-TEEN). Soon the volcano erupted, burying part of the nearby town with lava and ash. Today, Paricutín is a small mountain. It no longer erupts. It is dormant.

● What materials probably built up the volcano in Pulido's field?

This photo shows the gullies that formed on the south side of Paricutín.

Three Kinds of Volcanoes

Paricutín is an example of an explosive volcano. The hill, or mountain, formed by this eruption is a **cinder cone**. The ash and hot rocks from this type of volcano land close to the crater. They collect in a pile shaped like a cone with steep sides. The more ash and rocks produced, the bigger the cone.

The dramatic growth of Paricutín shows how fast a volcano can form. Not all volcanoes form in the same way.

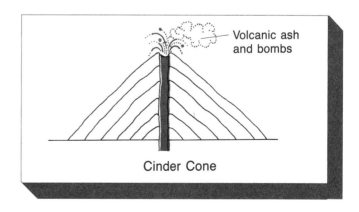

Volcanic ash and bombs

Cinder Cone

A **shield** (SHEELD) **volcano** looks like a broad, low hill. It does not have a steep cone. Shield volcanoes form when lava spreads out over a wide region. The lava flows away from the volcano as it slowly cools. Shield volcanoes can cover a large area. The Hawaiian Islands are shield volcanoes.

In a shield volcano, gases escape easily from the hot lava. There are few explosions caused by trapped gas. Shield volcanoes are "quiet" compared with explosive cinder cones. Few explosions mean little ash is shot up. There is not enough ash to build a cone.

The third type of volcano is known as a **composite** (kuhm-PAHZ-it) **cone**. These "mixed" volcanoes have layers of built-up lava and layers of volcanic ash and rock. Composite volcanoes are the most common type. Mount St. Helens is a composite volcano.

There are over 600 active volcanoes around the world. Studying them has helped scientists learn a great deal about the earth's crust.

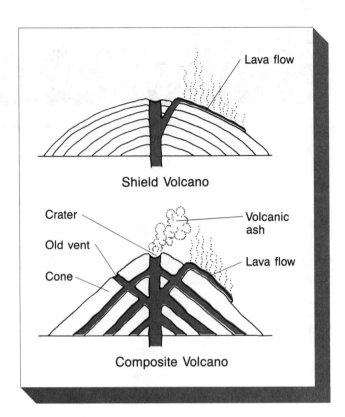

Shield Volcano

Composite Volcano

To Do Yourself
How Can We Demonstrate the Force of a Volcano?

You will need:

Modeling clay, empty frozen juice container, baking soda, vinegar, measuring cup, tablespoon, knife, wide dish

1. Carefully cut the container in half. **Caution: Always handle sharp objects with great care!** Mold clay around the container to make a model volcano.
2. Place 2 heaping tablespoons of baking soda into the volcano.
3. Pour 1/4 cup of vinegar into the volcano. **Stand back** and watch what happens.

A volcano forms when magma rises to the surface of the earth. An erupting volcano may release steam, gases, ash, and lava.

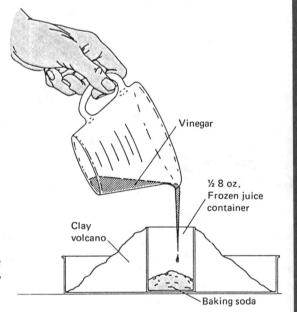

Questions

1. Describe what happened in your model volcano. _____

_____

2. Compare your model with an actual volcano. How are they alike? How are they

different? _____

Review

I. Fill in each blank with the word that fits best. Choose from the words below.

lava   composite   magma   shield   ash   cinder cones

The shape of a volcano is determined by whether it is formed mostly from

flowing _____ or from tall piles of _____.

Volcanoes called _____ are formed from a mixture of lava flow

and ash. All volcanoes get their energy from hot _____.

II. Write *cinder cone, composite cone,* or *shield volcano* for each phrase or example. Answers will be used more than once.

A. _____ Broad, flat, covering a wide area

B. _____ Generally small with steep sides

C. _____ Layers of lava and ash

D. _____ Hawaiian Islands

E. _____ Mount St. Helens

F. _____ Paricutín

III. Answer in sentences.

Mount St. Helens is part of the Cascade Mountain Range. Do you think there are other volcanic mountains in this range? What do you think is beneath these mountains?

_____

_____

_____

How Can Rocks Fold?

Exploring Science

When the Sea Covered the Mountains. What would you see if you went hiking in the Swiss Alps? You would find a picture-postcard scene of snow-capped mountains and wildflower fields. But would you expect to see the remains of animals that once lived in the ocean?

About 500 years ago, Felix Hemerli hiked in the Alps and came home with some strange treasures. At the tops of mountains, Hemerli collected rocks that contained fossils. Fossils are preserved remains of once-living things. Finding fossils was not strange in itself. But the fossils Hemerli found were from sea animals. Remember, the Alps are very high and Switzerland is far from the ocean. How, then, did fossils of sea animals get to a mountain top?

Some people thought that the sea had once been very deep, covering even the mountains. Hemerli had a different idea. He noticed that there were huge curves in the rocks of the mountains. Hemerli suggested that the land had once been flat. The sea had covered it. Animals lived and died in the sea and were buried in the muddy sea bottom. This mud gradually hardened into layers of rock. Millions of years later, some force pushed the edges of the rock. The pressure made the middle of the rock layer buckle like a folded piece of paper. The top of the fold became the top of a mountain. The fossils were carried to the mountain top along with the rock.

Hemerli's idea was ignored for centuries. In 1905, a tunnel was built through the Alps. In the sides of the tunnel the folds in the rocks could be seen clearly. Hemerli was right. The Alps were formed by great folds in rock.

● Rocks are very hard, solid objects. Under what conditions could rocks be soft enough to fold?

These rocks in Glacier National Park, Montana, show dramatic evidence of folded layers.

How Rocks Fold

You have probably held a rock in your hand. A piece of rock seems quite solid. Yet, there are places where a rock layer looks as if it has been bent. That is exactly what has happened. Strong forces in the earth's crust have bent the rock up or down. You can notice this most easily where one kind of rock is on top of another kind of rock.

The layers of rock may have been bent so much that they curve upward in the middle. Scientists call these upward folds **anticlines** (AN-tih-klyns). Very large anticlines can become mountains. Where a fold bends down in the middle, a **syncline** (SING-klyn) is formed. Such a fold often forms a valley. You can remember the difference by thinking of a capital A for anti-

cline. The top of the A points upward like the fold does.

Folds in rocks are caused by forces deep within the earth. You have learned that the layer beneath the crust, the mantle, has greater heat and pressure than the earth's crust. Sometimes this heat and pressure affects rock layers deep in the crust, causing them to bend. Also, many

To Do Yourself   How Do Rock Layers Change?

You will need:

Four sheets of paper (two white, two black), ruler, pencil, scissors

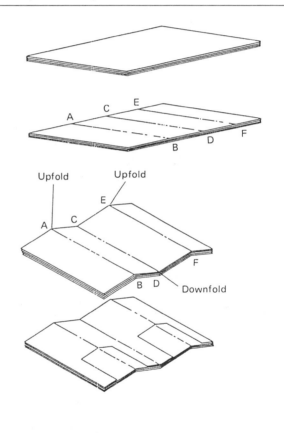

1. Stack the four sheets with a white sheet on top followed by black, white, and black.
2. Use the ruler to draw the fold lines shown. Bring the edges of the paper up and fold at line CD. Then make "peaks" at AB and EF.
3. Place the paper on a flat surface. How many anticlines and synclines have you made?
4. Use the scissors to cut out the area of the top sheet of paper as shown. **Caution: Always handle sharp objects with great care!**

The sheets of paper represent layers of rock. The folds are anticlines and synclines. Removing part of the top sheet represents the wearing away of part of the top rock layer.

Questions

1. Which folds show the "wearing away"? _____

2. Why would these folds wear away first? _____

_____

3. What color "rock" would cover your hills and valleys? _____

4. Does your model explain why hills and valleys often show different kinds of rocks?

   How? _____

_____

rock layers beneath the surface of the crust have a lot of water in them. The water in the rock helps them bend more easily. This process of bending rock takes place over millions of years.

The diagram below shows several anticlines and synclines. The folds are not always straight up or down. Many times the folds are tilted. Sometimes wind and water wear away the tops of the anticlines. When layers are tilted or worn away, it is more difficult to explain how the rock folded.

You have probably heard of the Appalachian Mountains. They are anticlines of rock layers that were folded. Many of the rock layers have since been worn down.

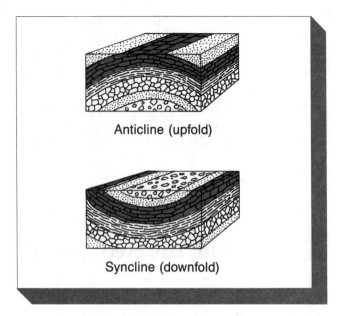

Anticline (upfold)

Syncline (downfold)

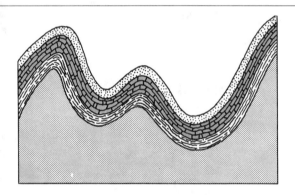 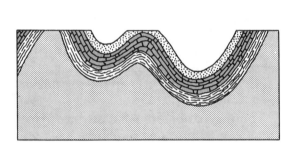

The two diagrams show the same rock layers at two different times. What has happened to most of the anticlines in the diagram at the right?

The upward folding of these rock layers forms an anticline.

Review

I. Fill in each blank with the word that fits best. Choose from the words below.

worn   rocks   heat   anticlines   synclines   tilted   pressure

Deep within the earth, _____ and _____ cause rock layers to fold. Where the folds are upward, structures called

_____ form. Where the folds are downward,

_____ form. The upward folds can be _____ away by wind and water.

II. Mark with an X the events that cause rocks to fold.

A. _____ Heat in the mantle

B. _____ Water in the rocks of the crust

C. _____ Wearing away of rock layers

D. _____ Pressure in the mantle

III. Draw a pattern to show one syncline between two anticlines. Answer in sentences. Why are synclines usually found where there is more than one anticline?

_____

_____

How Can the Earth's Crust Break?

Exploring Science

Discovering the Perfect Mountains. The year was 1807. The American West was still wild. The dusty plains seemed endless. Rugged mountains rose up against a backdrop of deep blue sky. Adventurers and cowboys rode the trails seeking their fortunes. They found this new land to be filled with surprises.

John Colter was certainly surprised when he rode through a part of Wyoming. What this "mountain man" saw before him was a stream of hot water shooting straight into the air. It shot up higher than the tallest pine trees! As he continued his trip, he was in for another surprising sight. Out of the flat plain rose the most perfect, pointed mountains he had ever seen.

What surprised and amazed Colter almost 200 years ago can still be seen today. Each year millions of visitors watch "Old Faithful" shoot its stream of hot water in Yellowstone National Park. Beyond Yellowstone, other visitors hike through the majestic Grand Teton Mountains. Because of their beauty, both of these areas are now national parks. Their beauty will be preserved for future generations.

● Which seems more likely to be true?

A. The Grand Tetons were caused by the action of wind and water.

B. The Grand Tetons were caused by changes in Earth's crust.

The Grand Teton Mountains have been described as "perfect" mountains. Can you see why?

Cracks in the Earth's Crust

Scientists believe that Yellowstone Park was dotted with active volcanoes 60,000 years ago. Lava flowed from the volcanoes many times and formed layers. Eventually, the layers made a smooth, flat plain. But the Grand Teton Mountains are nearby. How did they form?

The layers of lava were very heavy. The tremendous weight caused the crust to break. Instead of a straight line, the break formed a zigzag pattern. On one side of the break, the ground rose. The jagged edges of the break became the peaks of the Grand Tetons.

Rocks deep in the crust bend with the great heat and pressure. Closer to the surface, there is less heat. When rocks close to the surface are under pressure, then, they may break rather than bend. A break in the earth's crust is called a **fault.** There is usually movement along a fault. Often this movement is vertical, or up and down. When the ground on one side of a fault sinks, this is known as a **normal fault.** When one side of a fault rises, it is called a **reverse fault.** (Remember the *r*'s. In a reverse fault, one side rises.) Along a third type of fault, a **strike-slip fault,** the movement of the ground is horizontal or sideways. The San Andreas fault in California is an example of a strike-slip fault.

When the vertical movement along a fault is repeated enough, a mountain range will be formed. The Grand Tetons were formed by a big reverse fault. Mountains that are formed along a fault are called **fault-block** mountains.

Faults and cracks also form in crustal rock beneath the earth's surface. These spaces sometimes become filled with magma. The magma fills the spaces and then cools and hardens. This hardened rock will have the same shape as the space it filled. If the magma oozes between horizontal layers of rock, the magma forms a horizontal shape, called a **sill.** When

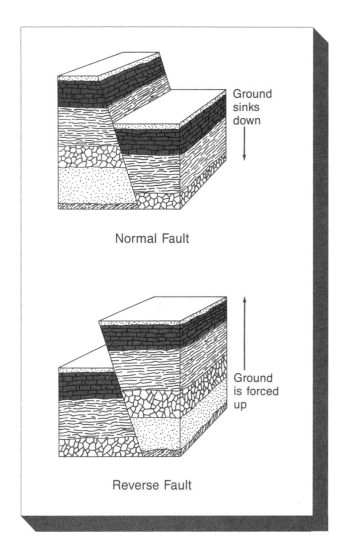

Normal Fault

Ground sinks down

Reverse Fault

Ground is forced up

magma oozes into cracks across rock layers, a wall of rock, known as a **dike,** is formed. The diagram on page 34 shows dikes and sills.

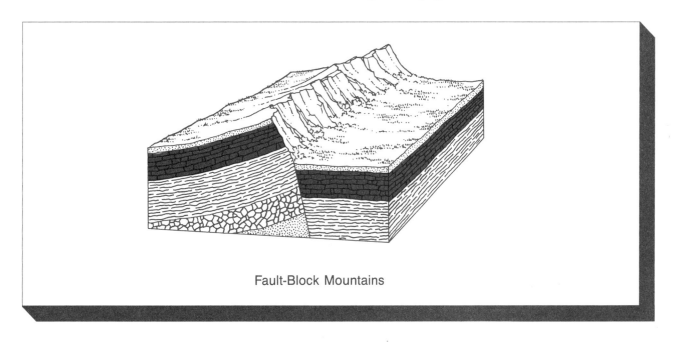

Fault-Block Mountains

Sometimes a huge pool of magma will cool and harden below the surface. A huge mass of rock called a **batholith** (BATH-uh-lith) forms. The batholith may be so large and so heavy that it creates pressure on the rock around it. Cracks created in the rock fill with magma and form sills and dikes. If there is movement at the surface along these cracks, mountains may form. The core, or roots, of the mountains will be the batholith.

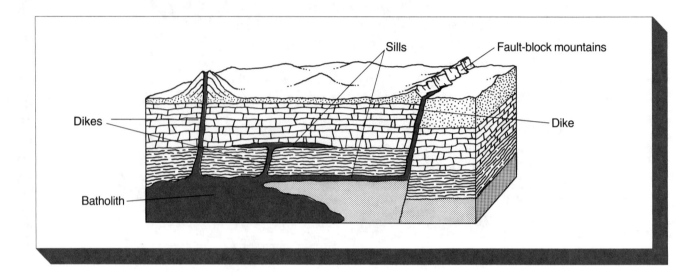

Review

I. Fill in each blank with the word that fits best. Choose from the words below.

**sill   normal   anticlines   fault-block   dike   reverse   faults
magma**

Breaks in the earth's crust are known as _____ . When one

side rises, a _____ fault forms. This process produced the

Grand Tetons, a range of _____ mountains. Faults are

sometimes filled by _____ . Rock formed in a horizontal

fault is called a _____ .

II. Write *T* if the statement is true. If the statement is false, change the underlined word to make it true.

A. _____ Mountains may form when part of the crust rises along a <u>fault</u>.

B. _____ Mountains may form when rocks in the crust <u>bend</u>.

C. _____ A large pool of magma that cools underground is a <u>dike</u>.

D. _____ The core of a mountain may be a <u>batholith</u>.

III. Answer in sentences.

Imagine that you have discovered a new mountain range and named it after yourself. Describe one of the several ways in which it could have formed. Then draw a picture to go along with your explanation.

What Are Earthquakes?

Exploring Science

Earthquake in Los Angeles. Just before dawn on January 17, 1994, disaster struck Los Angeles, California. Buildings and freeways collapsed. A motorcycle police officer on a highway overpass found the highway dropping below him. Mountains rose a foot or higher in an instant.

The first earthquake lasted only 10 seconds. But 57 people were killed, 8000 were injured, and 92,000 buildings were damaged. Gas pipes broke and the gas started fires. Water pipes broke, so there often was no water to put out the fires. Dozens of small quakes continued in the Northridge area of Los Angeles for days.

Other problems developed later. A month after the earthquake, dust from the shaking earth caused people in Los Angeles to catch a disease known as valley fever. A year after the quake, scientists reported that a hundred or so steel-framed buildings had been greatly weakened. Some buildings had to be abandoned.

● During an earthquake, the crust seems to move along a line. What is that line likely to be?

A parking garage shows the effects of the 1994 earthquake.

Earthquakes

The city of Los Angeles is located near a very famous fault line—the San Andreas (SAN an-DRAY-uhs) fault. Most earthquakes take place along faults. Before a quake, pressure begins to build on both sides of a fault. The pressure would be released if the crust could move. But the rocks on each side of a fault tend to be locked together. They do not move easily. When the pressure is great enough, however, one side of the fault slips down or slides rapidly along the fault.

This movement releases the stored energy. This energy causes vibrations in the earth. Have you ever heard the dishes rattle as a large truck passed your house? The vibrations caused by the movement of the crust are similar. They are, however, much stronger.

Vibrations travel in different patterns, or waves. In one pattern, particles of the earth through which the wave is traveling push together and pull apart. This pattern is known as a **P** wave, or **primary wave**. It is similar to the movement of the coils along a slinky spring.

Earthquakes also touch off **S waves,** or **secondary waves.** These waves are similar to the snakelike pattern you can make if you flick one end of a rope.

P waves and **S** waves start at the **focus** of the earthquake. The focus is the place where the movement of the crust begins. It may be close to the surface or hundreds of kilometers below. The earthquake is strongest at the spot on the surface right above the focus. This point is the **epicenter** (EP-uh-sen-tuhr) of the earthquake. Places near the epicenter usually suffer the most earthquake damage.

A third type of earthquake wave is formed when **P** and **S** waves reach the earth's surface. These *surface* waves travel along the earth's surface.

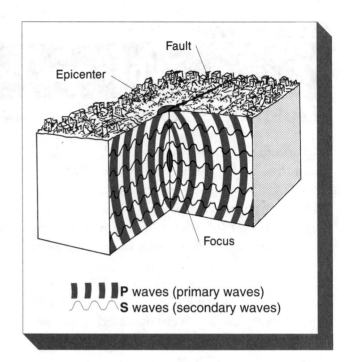

I I I I **P waves (primary waves)**
~~~~ **S waves (secondary waves)**

To Do Yourself How Do Vibrations Cause Objects to Move?

You will need:

A tuning fork, a shallow pan, a small piece of wood or cork, water

Tuning fork

1. Fill the pan with water and float a small piece of wood or cork in the water.
2. Hit the tuning fork on the heel of your hand. While the tuning fork is vibrating, dip its prongs into the water.
3. Describe what happens to the floating object.

The spot where the fork hits the water is similar to the focus of an earthquake.

Questions

1. What happens when the tuning fork hits the water? _____
   _____

2. What do you call the patterns made by the vibrations in the water? Where are they
   strongest?_____

3. In which directions do the patterns travel? _____

Review

I. Fill in each blank with the word that fits best. Choose from the words below.

epicenter   focus   primary   secondary   earthquake   crust

A rapid movement of the crust along a fault causes a(n) _____. The movement sets off waves. Waves in which particles push together and pull apart

are known as _____ waves. The waves start underground at the

_____ of the earthquake. On the crust, the places nearest the

_____ usually receive the most damage.

II. Circle the word that makes each statement true.
  A. The place where an earthquake starts is the (epicenter/focus).
  B. Waves in the crust travel (in all directions/upward only).
  C. An earthquake occurs along (a fault/the mantle).
  D. (Primary/Secondary) earthquake waves are similar to waves in a rope.

III. Answer in sentences.

If the focus and the epicenter of an earthquake were in the exact same spot, where would that spot have to be?

_____

_____

_____

How Are Earthquakes Measured?

Exploring Science

Using Numbers, Not Words. Imagine that you are a newspaper reporter who must describe an earthquake. Would you be able to do it?

In 1927, reporters pestered a physics student named Charles E. Richter (RIK-tuhr) who was working with earthquake research in California. He gave some thought to the problem of answering their most common question: "How big was it?" Richter reasoned that if every earthquake was given a number, it could be compared to other quakes.

The set of numbers Richter developed is called the Richter Scale. The number that is assigned to each earthquake is called its **magnitude** (MAG-nuh-tood). Today when there is an earthquake, scientists and newspaper reporters alike ask: "What was its magnitude?"

Measurements are made with a **seismograph** (SYZ-muh-graf). This tool is made from a heavy weight, a pen, and a moving roll of paper. The weight is not connected with the earth. Thus, it does not move as the earth shakes. The pen,

attached to the weight, draws a continuous line on the rolling paper. When the earth shakes, the roll of paper shakes with it, but the pen stays still. As the paper moves up and down or back and forth, the line on the paper becomes wavy.

Each magnitude is a measurement of the size of the wave. The waves can be very small or very large. Each whole number on the scale measures a wave that is 10 times the height of the number before it. The energy of the earthquake varies more than wave height. An earthquake of magnitude 5 does not cause much damage. But an earthquake of magnitude 6 is from 30 to 60 times as energetic. It can cause great damage.

● Circle the correct word.

The waves from one earthquake measure 1 centimeter high on a seismograph. Those from a second quake are 2 centimeters high. The first earthquake was (stronger/weaker) than the second earthquake.

What We Learn from Earthquake Measurements

Scientists have learned much about the inside of the earth by measuring earthquake waves. A seismograph shows three kinds of earthquake waves that travel through the earth. **P** waves and **S** waves, remember, are sent out at the focus. The **P** waves are caused when parts of the earth move back and forth. **S** waves are caused by up-and-down vibrations.

P waves travel faster than **S** waves. **P** waves always arrive at the seismograph first. (Think: Secondary waves, second.) The difference in the

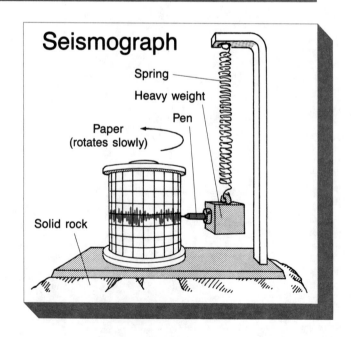

Seismograph

Spring

Heavy weight

Pen

Paper (rotates slowly)

Solid rock

time it takes for **P** waves and **S** waves to arrive at a station tells how far away an earthquake is.

When **P** and **S** waves reach the earth's surface, surface waves are formed. These waves are longitudinal, or **L** waves. Surface waves travel along the surface and reach the seismograph last. These waves cause the most damage during an earthquake.

To Do Yourself   How Can Earthquakes Be Located?

You will need:

Pencil

1. Look at the table. It shows the time it takes **P** waves and **S** waves to travel given distances. This is called travel time.
2. On the grid, plot the information from the table. The plots for 500 km and 1000 km are done for you.
3. Connect the **P**-wave dots with a solid line Connect the **S**-wave dots with a dotted line.

Data Table

Distance (km)	Travel Time (min)	
	P waves	S waves
500	1.0	2.0
1000	2.0	4.0
1500	3.0	6.0
2000	4.0	7.5
2500	5.0	9.0
3000	6.0	10.0
3500	7.0	12.0
4000	7.5	13.0

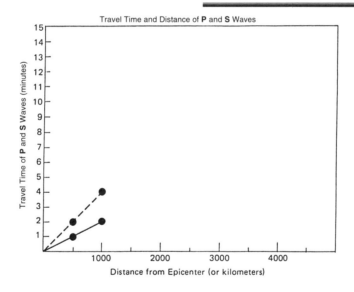

Travel Time and Distance of **P** and **S** Waves

Questions

1. What is the difference between the arrival time of **P** waves and **S** waves after traveling 1000 kilometers? _____ After traveling 3000 kilometers?

   _____

2. How does the difference between arrival time change as distance from the epicenter increases? _____

3. Using your graph, find out what distance **P** waves and **S** waves have traveled when the difference between their travel times is 4.0 seconds. _____

Review

I. Fill in each blank with the word that fits best. Choose from the words below.

**magnitude   S waves   seismograph   rotates   P waves   L waves
Richter Scale   weight**

A(n) _____ is an instrument used to measure earthquakes. It has a
steady pen and a drum of paper that _____. The waves that arrive first
are _____. Up-and-down vibrations below the surface of the earth are
called _____. The surface waves that cause the most damage during an
earthquake are _____. The Richter Scale measures the
_____ of the quake.

II. Circle the word or number that makes each statement true.

    A. Most earthquake damage is done by (primary/longitudinal) waves.
    B. An earthquake of magnitude 6 produces seismograph waves (2/1000) times as
       high as one of magnitude 3.
    C. The magnitude is a measure of the (length/energy) of an earthquake.

III. Answer in sentences.

A large earthquake occurs in Alaska. Its shock waves are detected in San Francisco
and in New York City. Compare the differences in travel times of the **P** waves and
S waves in these cities.

_____

_____

_____

What Causes Tsunamis?

Exploring Science

The Monster That Shook the Bay. Along the coast of Alaska there are many bays. Several are long and narrow and have steep cliffs along the water's edge. One particular bay is different from the others. Beneath its water lives a monster.

The people who live near the bay know about the monster. In their stories, they picture it to be a giant frog. When it is unhappy, the frog tosses water from the bay and destroys the land.

Scientists know about the monster, too. It is really a giant fault that runs across the front of the bay. When the crust along the fault moves, it causes an earthquake. Then the area erupts in violence. The bay floor rises. Parts of the cliffs that line the bay are hurled into the water. An enormous wave rolls down the bay.

On July 9, 1959, the frog must have been very unhappy. It produced an ocean wave more than 500 meters high—higher than the Empire State Building. It was the largest ocean wave that has ever been recorded.

● Which seems more likely to be true?

A. The giant wave in the bay was caused by strong winds created by the earthquake.

B. The giant wave in the bay was caused by huge chunks of rock falling into the bay from the cliffs along the shore.

Tsunamis and Harbor Waves

In Anchorage, Alaska, the "Good Friday Earthquake" of 1964 measured over 8 on the Richter scale. More than 100 people were killed. Damage was in the millions of dollars. On that same day, several people drowned in California. They were swept into the ocean by a **tsunami** (tsoo-NAH-mee). A tsunami is a huge ocean wave started by an underwater earthquake.

During the Alaska earthquake, the crust on one side of the fault slipped down several meters. This change in the level of the ocean floor caused several tsunamis to form. One of these mammoth waves reached Japan, 6500 kilometers from the epicenter.

A tsunami has a great deal of energy. As it travels across the deep ocean, its energy is spread out between the ocean surface and ocean bottom. Therefore, the wave is not very high. However, when the tsunami approaches land, its energy becomes concentrated. As the ocean becomes shallow, the wave rises well

This school in Anchorage, Alaska, was wrecked by an earthquake in 1964.

above the normal level of the ocean. On reaching shore, this great wall of water crashes over the land. Such a wave causes destruction greater than that caused by the original earthquake.

While tsunamis hit the coast, another type of wave may be causing damage in bays and harbors. During the earthquake, sections of the shoreline surrounding a harbor may come crashing down into the water. This landslide can cause huge **harbor waves** to form. When the Good Friday Earthquake struck Alaska, landslides caused harbor waves up to 30 meters high. A harbor wave can be as destructive as a tsunami, but it does not travel as far.

Tsunamis produced by the 1964 earthquake washed many ships into the center of Kodiak, Alaska.

To Do Yourself   Why Are Tsunamis Dangerous?

You will need:

Large plastic tub, small plate, masking tape, pencil, water-color marker

1. Place the plate upside down in one corner of the tub. Tape one edge of the plate to the bottom of the tub so the plate can move like a hinge.
2. Tape the eraser end of the pencil to the opposite edge of the plate.
3. Draw a "city" about halfway up the tub on the inside wall. Use the water-color marker.
4. Fill the tub with water up to the city.
5. Create a tsunami by lifting the plate with the pencil several times.

A tsunami can be dangerous. It can travel hundreds of kilometers per hour. This giant wave has tremendous amounts of energy.

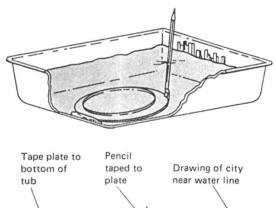

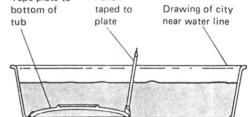

Tape plate to bottom of tub   Pencil taped to plate   Drawing of city near water line

Questions

1. Does your model show what happens during a tsunami? Describe what you observed. _____

_____

2. What are some causes of tsunamis? _____

_____

Review

I. Fill in each blank with the word that fits best. Choose from the words below.

harbor wave   earthquake   shallow water   open ocean   fault   tsunami

During a(n) _____, a part of the ocean floor may slip down or rise

up, starting a wave called a(n) _____. The wave becomes more

concentrated when it reaches _____. Another kind of wave,

a(n)_____, is caused by landslides.

II. Next to each description, write the correct term.

A. _____   May travel thousands of kilometers across the ocean

B. _____   Are caused by rock and earth falling into a bay during
an earthquake

C. _____   Movement of the crust along a fault

III. Answer in sentences.
Sometimes island volcanoes collapse into the ocean. There is no earthquake
detected on land, but a tsunami starts. How could this be?

_____

_____

_____

What Do Earthquakes Tell Us?

Exploring Science

Coming Apart in California. Would you like to plan a vacation trip to Mexico? Which Mexico will you visit? Part of Mexico, called Baja (BAH-hah) California, is separated from the rest of that country.

Further north, in the United States, the state of California is famous for its oranges. In the Imperial Valley there is a peculiar orange grove. The trees were planted in perfectly straight rows. Today the rows are broken about two-thirds of the way across the grove. There is a shift of about three meters. Then the rows of trees continue in a straight line.

In Holister, California, a warehouse is coming apart. It was built soundly and it is not very old. Yet cracks have opened in the concrete floors. Gaps appear in the walls.

How are these events connected? The connection is the **San Andreas fault.** The fault is a giant crack in the crust that runs through southern California. Baja California is separated from the rest of Mexico by the fault. The rows of orange trees were planted across the fault and the warehouse was built on it.

● Circle the correct word.

Based on the evidence described in this section, movement along the San Andreas fault is mainly (vertical/horizontal).

These rows of lettuce show how the land moved during an earthquake along the San Andreas fault.

Learning From Earthquakes

Did you know that southern California has about 200 to 300 earthquakes each year? Fortunately, most of them are small. Most California earthquakes occur along the San Andreas fault. Look at the map on page 45. The Great San Francisco Earthquake occurred in 1906. Almost ninety years later, a powerful earthquake struck Los Angeles. When will the next big California quake strike?

Scientists cannot answer this question for certain. But they are working on ways to make predictions about earthquakes. By studying activity around a fault in China, scientists correctly predicted an earthquake in 1976. Because people were told to leave the area in time, many lives were saved. Even so, thousands perished in that powerful quake.

Shock waves from earthquakes have helped scientists learn two important things about the inside of the earth. They have learned what the different layers of the earth are and what they are made of. By using explosives, scientists can even produce waves similar to those in earthquakes. By following the paths of the waves, they learn more about the interior of the earth.

Earthquake waves travel faster in some materials than in others. When it was discovered that earthquake waves speed up at a certain distance below the surface, scientists concluded that the earth must have a mantle under the crust.

Waves also show what the earth's layers are made of. Recall that earthquakes send out **P** waves and **S** waves. **P** waves travel through liquids and solids. **S** waves travel only through solids. **S** waves do not travel through the outer core of the earth. This information helped scientists conclude that the outer core must be like a liquid.

Scientists record earthquake data from all over the world. There are over 1000 seismograph stations that "listen" to the movements of the crust. The locations of earthquake activity seem to produce a pattern. Could there be a reason why earthquakes and faults occur in certain places? Perhaps this pattern could explain why California is "coming apart." Scientists think that they have an explanation. You will learn more in the next lesson.

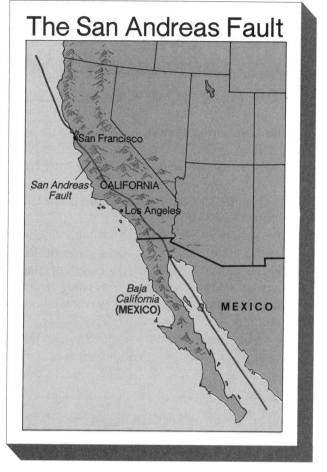

The San Andreas Fault

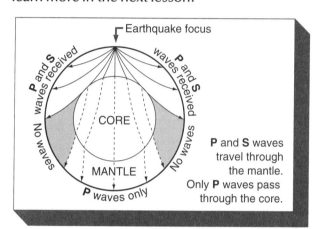

P and S waves travel through the mantle. Only **P** waves pass through the core.

Review

I. Fill in each blank with the word that fits best. Choose from the words below.

mantle   P waves   S waves   inner core   outer core   layers

Earthquake waves tell us about the different _____ of the earth. Because waves change speed under the crust, the earth must have

another layer, the _____ . The waves that cannot go

through liquids are the _____ . These waves stop when

they reach the _____ .

II. Circle the underlined word or number that makes each statement true.

A. Waves in the mantle travel (faster/slower) than in the earth's crust.
B. In some cases, scientists have been able to (prevent/predict) an earthquake.
C. There are about (200/1000) seismograph stations in the world.

III. Answer in sentences.
Scientists are working on ways to *prevent* earthquakes. They make holes in the crust so some of the pressure near faults will be released. Should scientists try to change nature? In what other ways could earthquake disasters be prevented?

What Causes Earthquakes and Volcanoes?

Exploring Science

The Lost Civilization. Almost 4000 years ago there was a great civilization on the islands in the Mediterranean Sea. Mysteriously, the island civilization vanished. Except for the legends passed on by the early Greeks, the civilization was forgotten. What happened?

The answer can be found in a small, crescent-shaped island called Santorini (san-do-REE-nee). It is all that remains of a once-larger island known as Thera. Thera had a thriving civilization. Some people think that it was the legendary Atlantis. Thera was north of Crete—a much larger island that had an advanced civilization.

Thera was formed by a volcano. In about 1650 B.C., the volcano began to erupt. Although there are no records, most of Thera must have been destroyed. Great clouds of ash rained down on nearby Crete, burying parts of it. At that time, the volcano on Thera sank into the sea during a great earthquake. In Crete, oil lamps tipped over, setting fire to most of the towns. The civilization on Crete did not recover.

● Which seems more likely to be true?

A. Thera was a quiet volcano.

B. Thera was an explosive volcano.

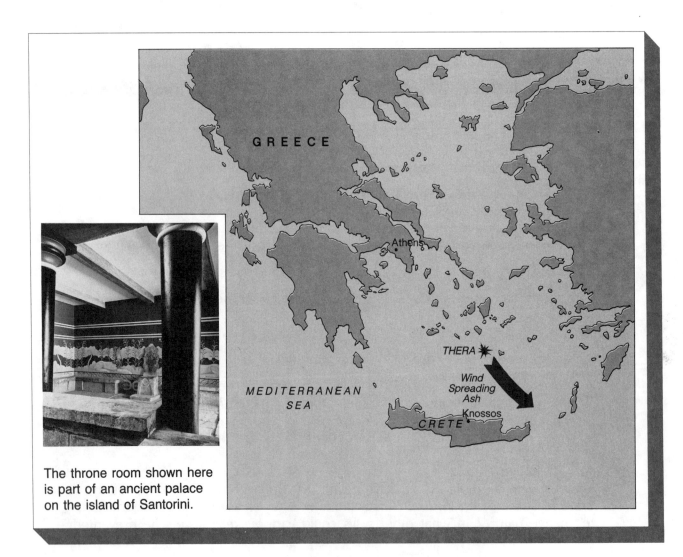

The throne room shown here is part of an ancient palace on the island of Santorini.

Plate Theory Explains Earthquakes and Volcanoes

The volcano and earthquake that destroyed ancient Thera were twin disasters of great size. These events show the earth's crust at its most powerful and active. Why did they happen?

To discover the answer to this question, let us review what happens when the crust moves. The crust shifts around faults, causing earthquakes and tsunamis. Sometimes mountains are thrust up along faults. In some places magma rises to the surface and forms volcanoes. Other times, magma cools underground and forms mountains above it. Each of these processes changes the "face" of the earth.

For years, scientists looked for a common thread that could tie all of these dynamic events together. After many observations and hypotheses, scientists have come up with a workable theory.

Recall that the earth's crust is just a thin layer of rock resting on the much thicker mantle. If the earth were compared to a hard-boiled egg, the earth's crust would be the eggshell. In their theory, scientists picture the earth's crust broken into several pieces. Each piece is called a **plate.**

Each of these crustal plates rests on the upper part of the mantle. All of the surface features of the earth—continents and oceans—are carried by the plates. One plate may carry all or part of a continent. Another may carry an entire ocean with its rocky bottom. Yet another plate might carry part of a continent and part of an ocean.

The earth has 6 to 8 major plates and several smaller ones. These plates move very, very slowly. You may wonder how huge areas of solid rock can move at all. The crustal plates move because they are "floating" on the mantle. Scientists think that the lower part of the crust and the upper part of the mantle is a solid that sometimes acts like a liquid. Like rubber or soft plastic that can be pushed and shaped, this layer has some "give" to it.

As they float, some plates move toward one another. Where they bump into each other, the force may cause faults to form. In such areas, earthquakes and volcanoes are likely to occur. Most of the "action" on the crust occurs at the places where plates meet.

The plate theory can be used to explain what happened to Thera. Thera was on the boundary of two plates that have been pushing into one another for millions of years. One result of this activity has been the formation of a chain of volcanoes. Thera was one volcano that really blew its top.

Plate collisions have also built mountains and valleys. In other parts of the earth, plates are moving away from each other. You will learn more about these events in Unit 3.

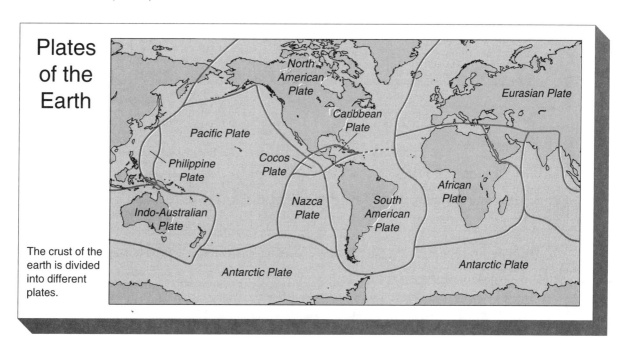

Plates of the Earth

North American Plate

Caribbean Plate

Eurasian Plate

Pacific Plate

Philippine Plate

Cocos Plate

Nazca Plate

South American Plate

African Plate

Indo-Australian Plate

Antarctic Plate

Antarctic Plate

The crust of the earth is divided into different plates.

To Do Yourself   Where Is the "Ring of Fire"?

You will need:

A red pen or pencil

1. The map shows the Pacific Ocean and the continents that border it. Notice that the map has a grid marked by numbers and letters.
2. The table on page 49 lists some of the volcanoes that you have learned about in this unit. Using the grid numbers, find where each is located. Mark the spot with a dot and label it with the name of the volcano.

3. Draw lines to connect the volcanoes.
4. Locate each of the earthquakes that are listed. Mark each with an X. Add the names of the earthquakes.

   The line that you have drawn around the Pacific Ocean is sometimes referred to as the Ring of Fire.

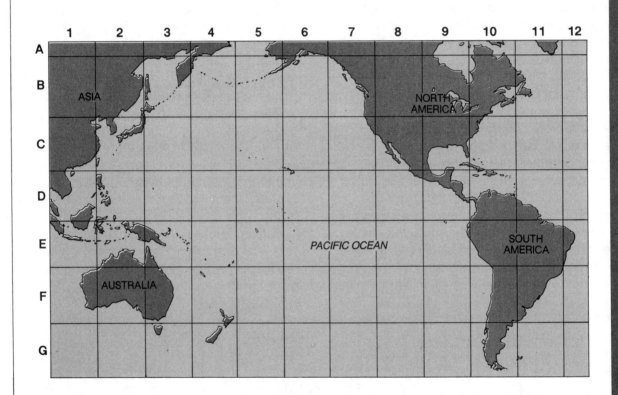

Questions

1. Why do you think this line is called the Ring of Fire? _____

2. Are the earthquakes found near the Ring of Fire? Why? _____

_____

3. The Pacific Ocean is on the Pacific plate. What do you think is happening around

   the edges of that plate? _____

Some Well-Known Volcanoes and Earthquakes

Volcano	Description	Grid Location
Mount St. Helens, Washington	Worst U.S. volcano disaster in recent history	B-7
Krakatoa, Pacific Ocean	Eruption in 1883 could be heard as far away as Africa	E-1
Paricutín, Mexico	The cinder cone that grew overnight	C8
Cotopaxi, Ecuador	The world's highest volcano	D-9
Aleutian Islands	Volcanic island chain between the U.S. and Russia	A-5–B-3
Pinatubo Philippine Islands	Eruption in 1991 causes cooler weather worldwide	D-2
Mount Fuji, Japan	Famous snow-covered mountain of Japan	C-2
Earthquake	**Description**	**Grid Location**
San Francisco, California	Great Earthquake of 1906	C-7
Anchorage, Alaska	"Good Friday Earthquake" of 1964	A-6
Tokyo, Japan	Killed thousands in 1923	C-2–C-3
Yungay, Peru	Completely buried the town in 1970	E-10

Review

I. Fill in each blank with the word that fits best. Choose from the words below.

plates   oceans   crust   core   meet   mantle   erupt

The earth's crust is separated into several _____. The plates float on the lower part of the earth's _____ and the upper part of the _____. The earth's continents and _____ are carried by the plates. There are often volcanoes and earthquakes where two plates _____.

II. Mark the statements that are true with *T*. Mark the statements that are false with *F*.

A. ____The plates are made of rock and never move.
B. ____Earthquakes often occur in the same area as volcanoes.
C. ____Most activity in the earth's crust occurs away from plate boundaries.

III. Answer in sentences.
Ancient Thera is not in the Ring of Fire. It is part of a group of volcanoes that dot the Mediterranean Sea. What is probably true of this area? _____

_____

A. Use the clues below to complete the crossword.

Across

  1. A crack in the earth's crust
  4. Mountain where magma comes to the surface
  5. Fine particles from volcanoes
  7. Broad, quiet volcano
  9. Opposite of a reverse fault
  10. Primary or secondary _____
  11. Movement of crust near a fault

Down

  1. Where an earthquake starts
  2. Melted rock above ground
  3. Blown out top of a volcano
  6. A _____ wave causes damage in bays
  7. Magma that hardens in a horizontal fault
  8. Magma that hardens in a vertical fault
  10. Opposite of strong

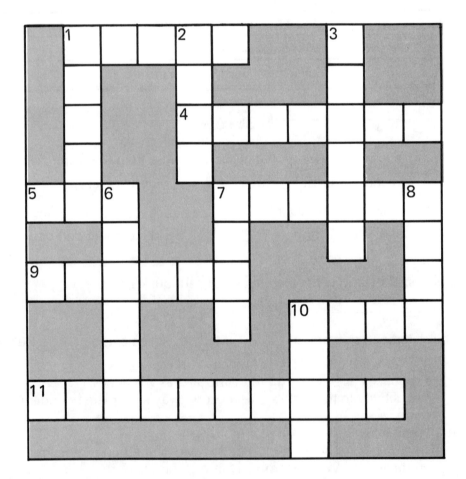

B. Write the letter and word that best complete each statement.

  1. _____ Melted rock released from an erupting volcano is **a.** magma **b.** lava **c.** ash

2. _____ The hole that remains when the top of a volcano has blown away is a(n) **a.** shield **b.** anticline **c.** crater

3. _____ A volcano with a cone and lava flow is a **a.** cinder cone **b.** shield **c.** composite

4. _____ The upward fold in layers of rock is called a(n) **a.** syncline **b.** anticline **c.** reverse fault

5. _____ Faults, anticlines, and volcanoes may all form **a.** mountains **b.** dikes **c.** plates

6. _____ Movement at a fault *does not* produce a(n) **a.** earthquake **b.** tsunami **c.** crustal plate

7. _____ The greatest amount of earthquake damage is done by **a.** P waves **b.** S waves **c.** L waves

8. _____ The spot on the crust above the start of an earthquake is its **a.** focus **b.** epicenter **c.** mantle

9. _____ The Richter Scale measures an earthquake's **a.** distance **b.** L waves **c.** magnitude

10. _____ Much volcanic and earthquake activity happens along the edges of **a.** crustal plates **b.** batholiths **c.** continents

11. _____ A feature *not* made of cooled magma is a **a.** sill **b.** dike **c.** fault

12. _____ You are more likely to walk in the crater of a volcano that is **a.** active **b.** extinct **c.** erupting

13. _____ Scientists learned about the layers of the earth by studying **a.** earthquake waves **b.** differences in volcanoes **c.** plate boundaries

14. _____ The crust of the earth is formed from **a.** one solid piece **b.** two separate pieces **c.** many separate pieces

15. _____ In which pair of terms can the first cause the second? **a.** earthquake/tsunami **b.** cinder cones/shield volcanoes **c.** longitudinal waves/primary waves

16. _____ Under pressure, unheated rock may **a.** break **b.** expand **c.** flow

17. _____ At the core of some mountains are large masses of cooled rock called **a.** dikes **b.** batholiths **c.** sills

18. _____ The volcanoes around the Pacific Ocean form the **a.** Richter Scale **b.** Ring of Fire **c.** epicenter

19. _____ The earthquake waves that arrive at a seismograph first are **a.** P waves **b.** S waves **c.** L waves

20. _____ The plates of the crust are floating in the **a.** ocean **b.** mantle **c.** core

C. Apply What You Know

1. The diagram shows a composite volcano. Label its parts. Use the terms below.

   lava   **crater**   **cone**   **volcanic ash**   **magma**

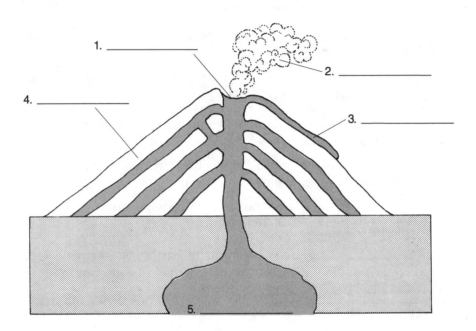

1. _____
2. _____
3. _____
4. _____
5. _____

2. Name two other types of volcano. _____
3. What is the difference between active and extinct volcanoes?

   _____

4. Earthquakes sometimes take place near volcanoes. Where do both

   volcanoes and earthquakes occur? _____
5. Volcanoes may form mountains. List two other ways in which mountains

   may form. _____

D. Find Out More

1. Use an almanac to find a list of the most powerful earthquakes and volcanic eruptions. Mark each one on a map of the world. Add a label to show the name of the volcano and the date of its eruption or the place and date where the earthquake occurred. Display the map in the classroom.
2. Find some current books on earthquakes in the school or local library. You may also want to try to find articles on earthquakes in science magazines. Find out what scientists are doing to predict earthquakes. Make a report for the class.
3. Visit a road cut or quarry in your area. Look for anticlines and synclines in the exposed layers of rock. Make a model of what you see.
4. What mountains are nearest to where you live? Are they old or new mountains? Try to find out how these mountains were formed.

Careers in Earth Science

Listening to the Earth. Earthquakes send powerful shock waves through the earth. By "listening" to the way these waves travel, scientists have learned about the layers of earth. But these waves can also cause death and destruction. So scientists would like to predict when earthquakes will occur.

Geophysicist. One of the jobs of a geophysicist is listening to the earth. Geophysicists usually specialize in studying the solid earth, the liquid earth, or the atmosphere. They use complex instruments to measure the magnetic field of the earth. They carry out tests from satellites in space. Using computers, they analyze data found in the field.

Geophysicists study earth science, physics, and mathematics in college. Many have advanced degrees. They may work for private industry or the government.

Instrument Technician. When geophysicists are making observations they are often helped by instrumentation technicians. These technicians install, test, and service the instruments used in field tests. Technicians may have a specialty, such as installing seismographs or repairing underground cables that connect to computers. The experience for this position comes from attending a technical school or on-the-job training.

This technician is checking the circuits of an instrument panel.

These geophysicists are using X-ray equipment to study rock samples.

UNIT

3

MOVING PLATES

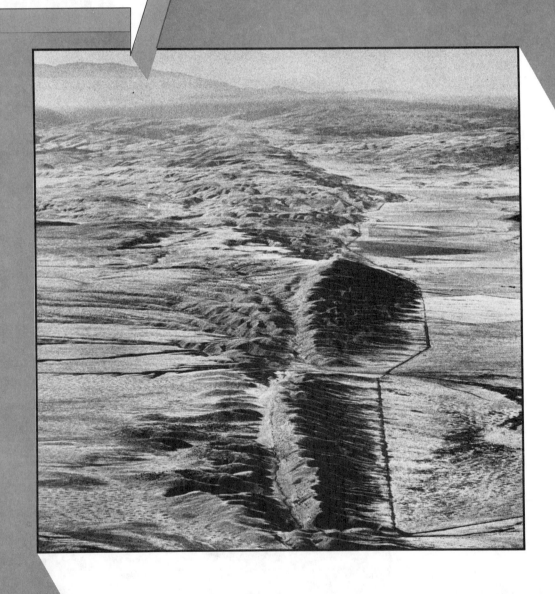

What Is Plate Tectonics?

Exploring Science

The Puzzle of the Continents. What kind of person would ride in a hot air balloon or go sledding near the North Pole? A person like Alfred Wegener (VAY-guh-nur) would do these things. Wegener had been trained to study the weather. But his curiosity and keen observations led him to study many other subjects.

Wegener often used maps of the earth. He noticed that the continents were like pieces of a jigsaw puzzle. For example, if Africa were pushed over to South America, the edges of the two continents would fit together snugly.

Wegener had a hypothesis to explain this fit. He thought that all the continents had once been part of one large continent. He called the huge land mass **Pangaea** (PANG-gay-uh). Wegener said that Pangaea had broken up hundreds of millions of years ago. Its broken pieces had then drifted apart, forming the continents as we now know them.

Wegener suggested this idea in 1912. Soon after, war broke out in Europe. Wegener fought and was wounded. While he was recovering from his wounds, he wrote a book that described some proof for his theory. But scientists did not accept his idea. They felt that Wegener was not really trained as a **geologist**—a scientist who studies the earth.

Wegener continued his work anyway. He made several research trips to the island of Greenland, in the Arctic Ocean. On his last trip in 1930, the weather turned bitterly cold. Supplies were short. Wegener did not survive. It

Alfred Wegener first proposed the idea of continental drift.

was not until many years after his death that Wegener's ideas were once again considered by scientists.

● Which of the following could be evidence that a single landmass broke up to form the continents we know today?

A. People on different continents speak different languages.
B. Fossil remains of the same plants and animals are found on both sides of the Atlantic Ocean.

Plate Tectonics and Continental Drift

Wegener's idea came to be known as the theory of **continental drift.** At the time Wegener stated his theory, scientists believed that the continents and ocean floors were one continuous mass of solid rock. They couldn't imagine how the continents could go plowing through the ocean floor. Wegener didn't really know *how* it happened either. But he believed he could show that Greenland was moving a tiny distance away from Europe each year.

Wegener also had other evidence that the continents were moving. This evidence came from the remains of a small dinosaur. Millions of years ago, dinosaurs roamed the earth. One dinosaur, called *Mesosaurus* (MEZ-uh-sor-us), was about the size of a dog. It had long jaws and teeth. Fossil remains of Mesosaurus have been found in only two places, eastern South America and western Africa. Mesosaurus was small. It couldn't swim across the Atlantic Ocean. How, then, could its fossils appear in both Africa and South America?

Wegener believed that the two continents had been next to each other in Pangaea. Mesosaurus had lived in the combined area. When Pangaea split, the remains of Mesosaurus were left on two different continents.

Wegener's "proof" was not enough. His ideas were ignored until the 1960s. By that time, scientists had new evidence that the crust of the earth was moving. They had developed a theory to explain the crustal movements. That theory was **plate tectonics** (tek-TON-iks). *Tectonics* means "construction." The theory states that the crust consists of several plates. The plates move slightly as they "float" on the earth's mantle. The continents and oceans are part of the moving plates, and move with them.

Scientists now think that Wegener was right. The continents did drift apart. But they did not plow through the oceans. Instead, moving plates carried the continents and parts of the ocean floor. As the continents separated, new ocean floor was formed.

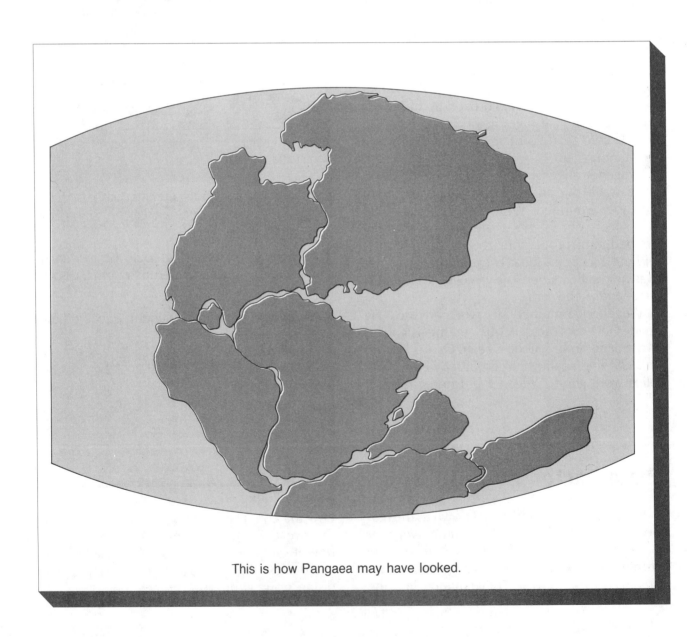

This is how Pangaea may have looked.

To Do Yourself   How Can You Reconstruct Pangaea?

You will need:

Tracing paper, pencil, scissors, paste, cardboard or construction paper

1. Trace the continents shown on the map.
2. Carefully cut them out. **Caution: Always handle sharp objects with great care!**

3. Arrange the pieces to form Pangaea. Paste them onto cardboard or construction paper.

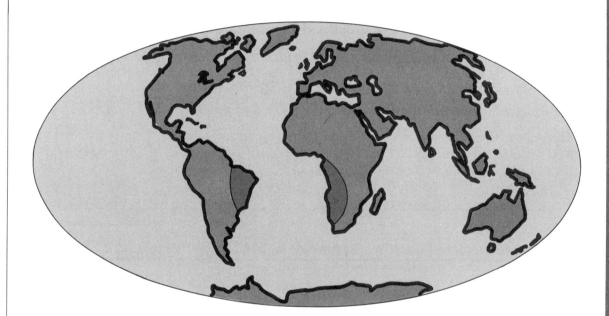

Wegener proposed that all the continents had been one large continent which he named Pangaea. He matched the fossil records to prove his hypothesis.

Questions

1. Which continents seem to fit together? _____

_____

_____

2. Do you think that Pangaea ever existed? _____

Give facts to support your answer. _____

_____

_____

Review

I. Fill in each blank with the word that fits best. Choose from the words below.

continental drift   **plates**   **continents**   **plate tectonics**   **Pangaea**
Mesosaurus

In 1912, Alfred Wegener proposed that all of the _____ had

once been one land mass which he named _____ . His

theory of _____ was not accepted then. Years later,
scientists "rediscovered" Wegener's idea when they developed the theory of

_____ .

II. Mark with an *X* the ideas that supported Wegener's theory.

A. _____ The continents fit together like pieces of a jigsaw puzzle.

B. _____ Similar fossils are found on different continents.

C. _____ The ocean floor is solid rock.

D. _____ Greenland is moving away from Europe.

III. The chart below compares two theories. Fill in the missing parts.

Continental _____	The continents of today were once _____ . They slowly _____ .
Plate _____	The crust is made of several _____ that float on the _____ . The plates move carrying the _____ .

How Do Moving Plates Cause Mountains to Form?

Exploring Science

When the Continents Separated. Did you ever see a film shown at high speed? An event that takes a long time can be shown to happen very fast. For example, a flower can be seen to bloom in seconds.

The story of the moving continents really takes place over millions of years. Imagine a movie shown at very high speed. The movie starts 250 million years ago, but time is sped up so that a million years goes by each minute. Even at that rate, the movie is over four hours long. Bring lots of popcorn.

The story opens with one large land mass on earth, Pangaea. Nearly an hour into the film, Pangaea starts to split up. Over the second hour Europe separates first. Then the mass that will form North and South America and Africa.

An important actor in the third hour is a large continent near the South Pole. Soon a piece of the southern continent starts to move north. This piece of land is India. Ten minutes later, the rest of the continent breaks in two. Part moves away to become Australia, while part stays behind as Antarctica.

In the last hour and a half, India slams into the continent of Asia, the largest part of the former Pangaea. Where India meets Asia, the world's highest mountains, the Himalayas, are shoved up by the collision.

● Circle the correct word or words.

Most likely, the continents (are/are not) still moving.

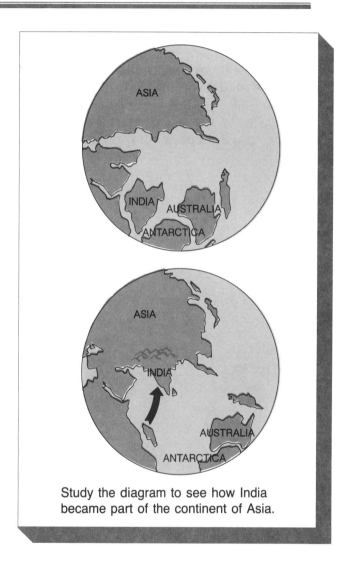

Study the diagram to see how India became part of the continent of Asia.

Mountains Form and Change

The plates carry continents and ocean floor. They drift slowly on the mantle. Some plates are moving apart. Some are moving toward each other. The motion of the plates brought the continents to their present positions. It also produced many of the features on earth today.

In some places, plates moving toward each other collide. When plates collide, the edge of one plate may be forced up over the edge of the other plate. The rock of the upper plate is broken and crumpled. This crumpled area of rock becomes a mountain range. The Himalayas were formed when the plate carrying India collided with the Asian plate. In Europe, the Alps were formed in the same way.

The Himalayas are quite young. They are "only" about 50 million years old. Their peaks are sharp and jagged. Mountains change over time. They wear away. They get rounder. Think of mountains you have seen. Are they pointed or rounded?

As the tops of mountains wear away, a change takes place in the earth's crust. The crust moves up to balance the loss of material from the mountain top. Look at the diagram. The block of wood floating in water stands for a mountain. As the block wears away, it gets lighter. Its weight does not push down on the water as much. Therefore, the block floats higher in the water. As much of the block remains above water after it has worn away as it did before.

Like the block of wood, the crust that holds the mountain floats in the heavier rock of the earth's mantle. As a mountain wears away, it does not weigh as much. So the crust floats higher in the mantle. As the crust rises, the mountain rises with it. The force of the mountain's weight pushing down is balanced by the crust pushing up.

The processes that build mountains and wear them away are very slow ones. They take millions of years. As one part of the crust is building up, another part is wearing away.

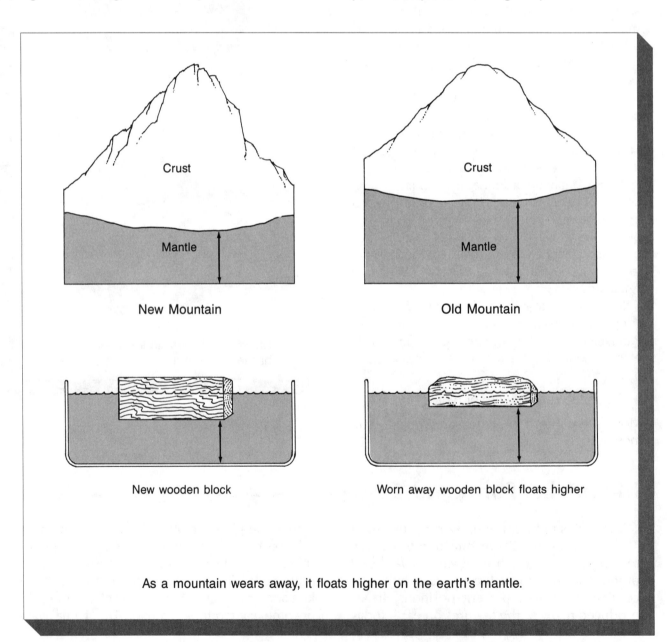

New Mountain

Old Mountain

New wooden block

Worn away wooden block floats higher

As a mountain wears away, it floats higher on the earth's mantle.

To Do Yourself What Keeps Mountains Tall?

You will need:

A double pan balance, 2 small bowls, water, sand, spoon

1. Place a bowl on each pan of the balance.
2. Make a "mountain" of sand in one bowl. Add water to the other bowl until the pans balance.
3. Remove some of the sand from the "mountain" and place it in the water.

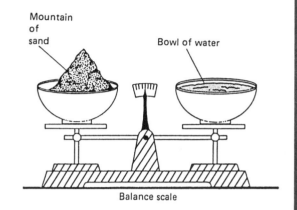

Mountain of sand

Bowl of water

Balance scale

Mountains are floating in the earth's mantle. As a mountain wears away, sand and soil are washed away. The mountain becomes lighter and floats higher in the mantle.

Questions

1. What happened to the model mountain as you removed sand? _____
_____

2. As a mountain wears away, where do its particles go? _____
_____

3. What happens to the height of a mountain as it ages? _____

Review

I. Fill in each blank with the word that fits best. Choose from the words below.

plates   upward   downward   built up   pointed   mountains   rounded

When two _____ collide, the rock of the continents is forced

_____. The collision usually forms _____. Over

time, mountains become _____.

II. Circle the underlined word that makes each statement true.

  A. The ocean floor and the continents are carried on (mountains/plates).
  B. Mountains may form when plates (collide/sink).
  C. The movement of the continents took (billions/millions) of years.

III. On a separate sheet of paper, answer in complete sentences.

  What happens to the crust as mountains are worn down?

What Causes Ocean Trenches?

Exploring Science

A Voyage to the Bottom of the Sea. It is January 23, 1960 in the clear, blue, South Pacific. Don Walsh and Jacques Piccard have entered a ship called the *Trieste* (tree-EST). The *Trieste* is not an ordinary vessel. It will take its passengers to the deepest part of the world ocean, the Challenger Deep.

Slowly, silently, the *Trieste* descends. It will be hours before it reaches the bottom, 11 kilometers below. Only 300 meters down, the sea around the ship is black. No sunlight can reach this depth. Floodlights on the *Trieste* show a few sea creatures through the small window. Some odd-looking fish even produce their own light.

At the bottom, the pressure exerted by the water is enormous. It is more than one ton on an area the size of your thumbnail. The floor is covered with material that has washed down the steep walls of the Challenger Deep. Incredibly, there are animals living on the ocean floor. This record-breaking dive made scientists more curious. What causes such depths to form in the ocean floor?

● Circle the correct word.

The deeper you go into the ocean, the (warmer/colder) the water temperature gets.

TRIESTE

The *Trieste* exploring the ocean bottom.

Trenches

You have learned that when plates carrying continents collide, mountain ranges are formed. What happens when a plate carrying a continent collides with a plate carrying ocean floor?

Plates are composed of two kinds of rock. The rock that makes up the ocean floor is heavier than continental rock. When the plates collide, the heavier rock of the oceanic plate slides below the plate carrying the continent. Part of the ocean floor is pulled along. This part of the lowered ocean floor forms a deep **trench** where the plates meet.

The floor of the western Pacific Ocean is mov-

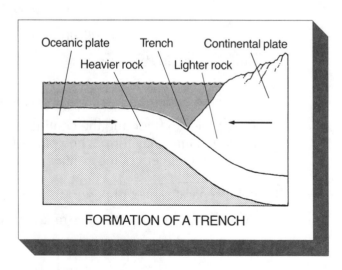

Oceanic plate · · · Trench · · · Continental plate

Heavier rock · · · Lighter rock

FORMATION OF A TRENCH

ing below the Australian and Asian plates. As a result, the world's deepest ocean trenches have formed in the western Pacific.

One plate does not slide smoothly under the other, however. The edges of the light plate crumple, forming high mountains. In the ocean, the tops of these mountains become chains of islands known as **island arcs.** The Marianas islands are the island arc behind the Marianas Trench.

The diagram compares the highest and lowest places in the world. Both of these features were formed by colliding plates.

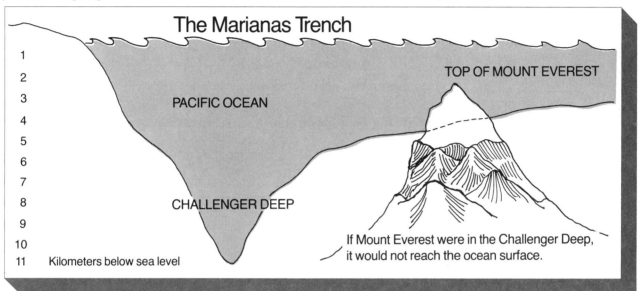

The Marianas Trench

1
2
3
4
5
6
7
8
9
10
11 Kilometers below sea level

PACIFIC OCEAN

CHALLENGER DEEP

TOP OF MOUNT EVEREST

If Mount Everest were in the Challenger Deep, it would not reach the ocean surface.

To Do Yourself   **What Happens When Light and Heavy Plates Collide?**

You will need:

1 sheet of writing paper, 1 sheet of construction paper, a smooth, flat surface

Writing paper

Construction paper

1. Lay the sheets of paper, edge to edge on a smooth, flat surface.
2. Make sure the edges of the paper are touching. Then push the papers together as shown in the diagram.
3. Repeat the procedure several times and record your results.

Questions

1. When the two sheets slide past each other so that they overlap, how many times is the writing paper on top? _____ on the bottom? _____

2. Describe what happens when the two sheets refuse to slide together easily. _____
_____

3. Explain why the oceanic plates slip under the continental plates. _____
_____

4. Use this model to explain how an ocean trench forms. _____
_____

Review

I. Fill in each blank with the word that fits best. Choose from the words below.

lighter   heavier   plates   ocean floor   island arcs   trenches

The rock of the continents is _____ than ocean rock. When plates

carrying _____ collide with continental plates, the heavier rock

slides below the other plate. This situation causes ocean _____.

_____ may form when lighter rock is pushed up.

II. Identify each of the following as a *mountain, trench,* or *neither.*

A. _____ Himalayas   D. _____ Marianas

B. _____ Mt. Everest   E. _____ Pangaea

C. _____ Alps   F. _____ Challenger

III. Answer in sentences.

In Unit 2 you learned about the Ring of Fire around the Pacific Ocean where many volcanoes occur. Do you think that the ocean trenches are near the Ring of Fire? Why?

_____

_____

_____

Lesson Four

What Are Hot Spots?

Exploring Science

Hawaii's Ninth Island. How would you like to swim off the beaches of the Hawaiian island of Loihi? You may have to wait a few thousand years. This ninth Hawaiian "island" is still far below the surface of the Pacific Ocean.

Like the Hawaiian islands, Loihi has been formed by volcanic activity. Most of the volcanoes that formed the Hawaiian islands are no longer active. But on the big island of Hawaii, two volcanoes, Kilauea (kee-lou-AY-ah) and Mauna Loa (MOU-nuhLOH-ah) erupt frequently. The area around the volcanoes is a national park. When the lava is flowing, millions of visitors are treated to a spectacular show.

Loihi is not far from the big island of Hawaii. The volcano that is making Loihi grow is fed by the same magma source that feeds Kilaeua and Mauna Loa.

When will Loihi rise above the surface of the water and become a real island? No one knows. Scientists think that we may not see Loihi for thousands of years.

● Circle the correct word.

Most of the Hawaiian islands are probably (younger/older) than the mainland of the United States.

Volcanoes in the Middle of a Plate

Most of the "action" on the earth's crust takes place where two plates meet. That is where many volcanoes are found. Loihi and the other volcanoes of Hawaii, however, are in the middle of the Pacific plate. How did these volcanoes form?

The age of the volcanoes gives us a clue. Find the big island of Hawaii on the map. Mauna Loa and Kilauea are still active. Now trace a path toward the northwest. You come across Diamond Head on the island of Oahu. This is the well-known peak of an extinct volcano. Continue northwest beyond the last island. Beneath the surface are other extinct volcanoes, called **seamounts.** Why does Hawaii have so many volcanoes of different ages?

Imagine holding a board over a candle. The candle makes a burn mark on the wood. If you move the board slightly every few minutes, the candle will produce a chain of burn marks. The board and the candle are a model of how Hawaii's volcanoes formed. Under the Pacific Ocean, hot magma from the mantle rises to the surface as a **hot spot.** A volcano gradually forms over the hot spot. The ocean floor, however, is

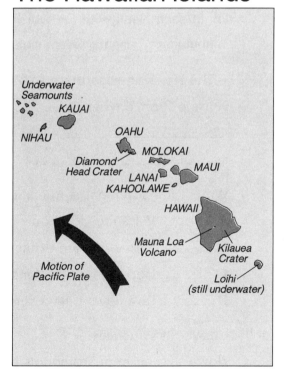

The Hawaiian Islands

Underwater Seamounts

KAUAI

NIHAU

OAHU

MOLOKAI

Diamond Head Crater

LANAI

KAHOOLAWE

MAUI

HAWAII

Mauna Loa Volcano

Kilauea Crater

Loihi (still underwater)

Motion of Pacific Plate

on the Pacific plate. The plate is moving while the hot spot stays in the same place. Thus, volcanoes form in different places on the plate.

The extinct volcanoes and seamounts were formed long ago when they were over the hot spot. Mauna Loa and Kilauea formed more recently. Loihi is on the hot spot now.

Hawaiian volcanoes are shield volcanoes. They have been formed by many "quiet" flows of lava. The lava pours out of the volcano and spreads out for a great distance before cooling.

The Pacific plate has several chains of volcanic islands and seamounts. Scientists read these chains like a detective reads fingerprints. They show that the Pacific plate is moving west. As it moves it collides with other continental plates. Deep trenches form where these plates meet.

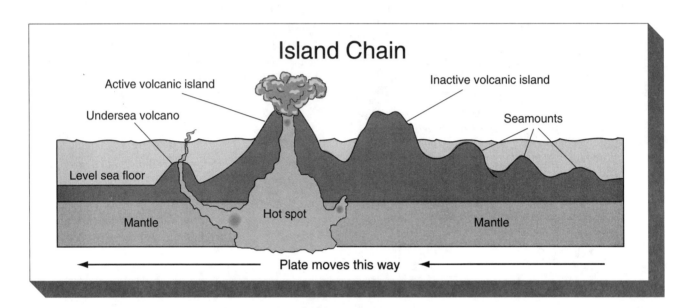

Island Chain

Review

I. Fill in each blank with the word that fits best. Choose from the words below.

mountains   magma   seamounts   shield volcanoes   crust   hot spot

The Hawaiian islands are a chain of _____ . Each volcano formed when _____ came to the surface at a _____ . The extinct volcanoes underwater are known as _____ .

II. Write **T** if a statement is true and **F** if it is false.

A. _____ Volcanoes form only on the edges of plates.

B. _____ Seamounts are extinct volcanoes that are underwater.

C. _____ Hot spots move along with the Pacific plate.

D. _____ Lava flows from a shield volcano.

III. Answer in sentences.

How can a chain of seamounts be used to tell which way the Pacific plate is moving?

Lesson Five

What Is a Mid-Ocean Ridge?

Exploring Science

The Birth of an Island. November 14, 1963, was not just another day for the crew of a fishing boat near Iceland, in the North Atlantic. With surprise and some fear, they watched as steam shot up from an icy sea.

A huge explosion shook the area. Dust, ash, and light rock were thrown into the air. A few days later, the surface of the ocean was broken by a new volcanic island. The island was named Surtsey (CERT-see) after a giant in Icelandic legend.

Soon a crack opened up on Surtsey. Lava poured out, covering the dust and ash. The lava hardened, protecting the island from the strong ocean waves. Today, Surtsey is on the map. It is about 1 kilometer across and rises 150 meters above the sea.

● What do you think happened in the water around Surtsey while the island was being formed?

Surtsey. A new volcanic island comes into the world with a "bang," showering steam and ash in all directions.

Continental Shelves and Mid-Ocean Ridges

What would the Atlantic Ocean look like if you could "pull the plug" and let out the water? The drawing of the ocean floor shows that the continents do not stop at their coastlines. They continue a short distance beneath the shallow waters beyond the coastlines. These areas are **continental shelves.** They are part of the continents rather than the ocean floor. At one time, the continental shelves were above the level of the sea. The same forces that shape the land formed the features of the shelves.

Try fitting the continents together as you did earlier. This time include the continental shelves. The shelves are really the edges of the continents. You will find that the continents fit better when you use the shelves as the outline of your puzzle.

Now look at the middle of the floor of the Atlantic Ocean. The giant mountain range is called the Mid-Atlantic Ridge. This mountain range is an example of a **mid-ocean ridge.** Follow the Mid-Atlantic Ridge north to south. It rises above the surface at Iceland and a few other small islands.

With a pencil, trace the shape of the Mid-Atlantic Ridge. Notice that it has the same shape as the coasts of the Americas, Europe, and Africa. It looks like a huge line dividing the ocean in half.

You have been learning about what happens when two plates collide. The mid-ocean ridge shows what happens when two plates separate. When plates separate, magma rises and fills the gap between them. Rising magma formed the island of Surtsey. In fact, magma at the Mid-Atlantic Ridge formed the floor of the Atlantic Ocean.

Mid-ocean ridges form wherever plates are moving apart. They are found on the floor of every ocean around the world. You will learn more about activity at the ridges in the next lesson.

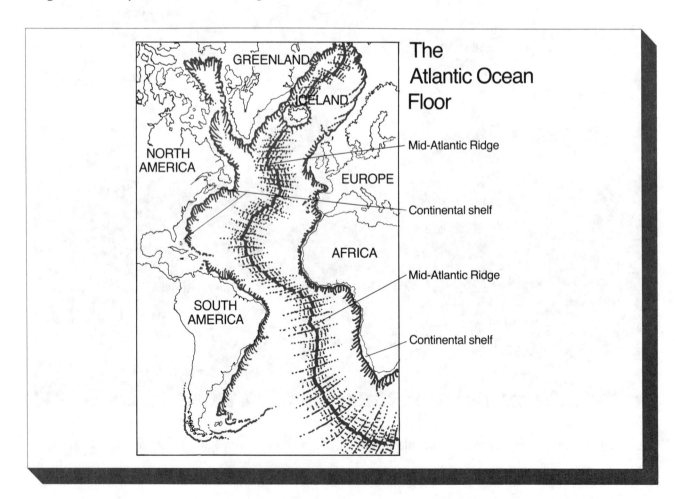

The Atlantic Ocean Floor

GREENLAND

ICELAND

NORTH AMERICA

EUROPE

Mid-Atlantic Ridge

Continental shelf

AFRICA

Mid-Atlantic Ridge

SOUTH AMERICA

Continental shelf

Formation of a Mid-ocean Ridge

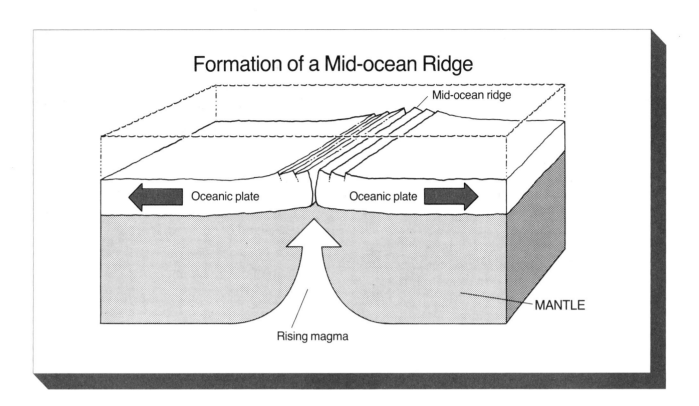

Review

I. Fill in each blank with the word that fits best. Choose from the words below.

> **mountains   mid-ocean ridge   plates   hot spot   magma   separate
> collide   continental shelf**

If you travel beyond the coast of a continent, you first reach the

_____ . Continue out over the ocean floor until you reach

a range of mountains called a _____ . At this point, plates

_____ and _____ comes to the surface.

II. Mark a statement **T** if it is true and **F** if it is false.

A. _____ Magma rises at the continental shelves.

B. _____ The Atlantic is the only ocean where a mid-ocean ridge is found.

C. _____ The continental shelves are really part of the continents.

III. Answer in sentences.

Describe what happens when two plates separate.

_____

_____

_____

How Does the Ocean Get Wider?

Exploring Science

An Island Dividing. In Iceland there is a place where the island is being pulled apart. A mid-ocean ridge runs through the middle of Iceland. At the center of the ridge, magma rises to the surface and forms new crust. The new rock spreads out to each side and hardens. The western part of the ridge moves farther west. The eastern part of the ridge moves farther east.

Not only is Iceland growing but it is also getting free hot water. The magma heats some of the underground water. In some places, the heated water breaks through to the surface and forms hot springs. The steam from these springs can be used to make electricity. The water is used for cooking, bathing, and home heating. So while the weather in Iceland may be cold, heat from the earth keeps the Icelanders warm. You can see why Iceland is sometimes called the land of "fire and ice."

● Which of the following is most likely true?

A. The island of Iceland is slowly disappearing into the sea.

B. The island of Iceland is slowly growing wider.

Some parts of Iceland have their own natural steam-heating systems.

Sea Floor Spreading

Iceland is part of the Mid-Atlantic Ridge that is above the sea. What is happening in Iceland is also happening at the bottom of the Atlantic.

Down the middle of the Mid-Atlantic Ridge there is a **rift valley.** Rift means separation. Many places along the rift valley have flows of melted rock. The rock is rising where the earth's plates are separating. When the rock reaches the floor of the ocean, it cools and becomes solid. Then, as the two parts of the crust on each side move apart, more melted rock rises. In this way the Atlantic Ocean is growing wider as the sea floor spreads. This widening is called **sea-floor spreading.**

Sea-floor spreading solves two mysteries about the ocean. The first mystery is why the ocean floor is not more deeply covered with deposits of soil and the remains of animals that have died in the sea. Over millions of years, thick layers should have formed on the ocean floor. Instead, there is just a thin layer of such materials. The reason for this lack of solid deposits on the ocean floor is that new sea floor is always forming.

The second mystery is why crustal rock beneath the ocean is much younger than that beneath the continents. The crustal rock under the continents was formed when the continents formed over two billion years ago. The rock of the ocean floor has formed from melted rock at the mid-ocean ridges. This new rock is pushed across the floor of the ocean as even newer rock forms. The crustal rock closest to a mid-ocean ridge is always the youngest.

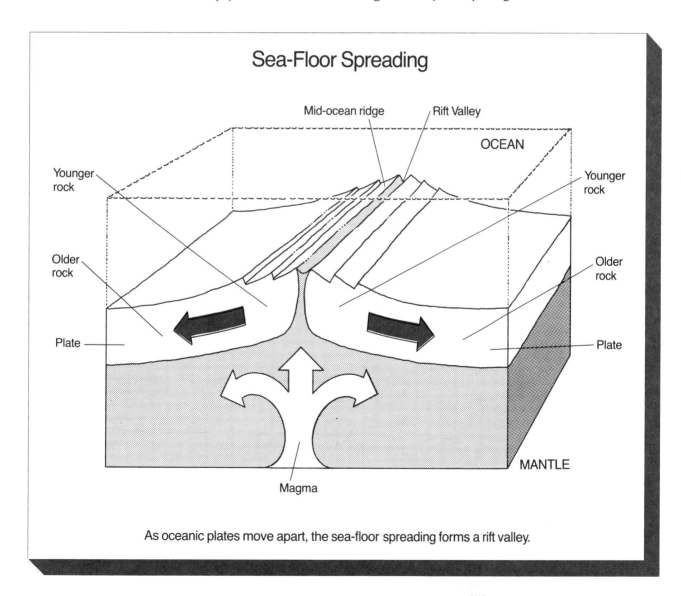

Sea-Floor Spreading

Mid-ocean ridge   Rift Valley

OCEAN

Younger rock

Younger rock

Older rock

Older rock

Plate

Plate

MANTLE

Magma

As oceanic plates move apart, the sea-floor spreading forms a rift valley.

Crustal rock of the ocean floor is different from continental rock in several ways. Because it was formed beneath the sea, rock from lava that flows at mid-ocean ridges cools more quickly than lava from volcanoes on land. Rapid cooling of lava produces smaller crystals on the ocean floor, while continental rocks often have large crystals. The rock, called **basalt**, that is commonly found on the ocean floor is denser than most rocks that make up the continents. Basalt is often very dark as well. While less-dense continental rock forms in thick piles, the oceanic crust is very thin, sometimes only five to ten kilometers thick.

To Do Yourself What Do Crystals Tell Us About the Ocean Floor?

You will need:

A heat source, graduated cylinder, water, salt, 2 small Pyrex beakers, stirring rod, heat-resistant pad and gloves

Caution: Use great care when heating anything! ALWAYS wear heat-resistant gloves when handling hot objects. Place hot objects on a heat-resistant pad, NOT on a desk or table top.

1. Add 20 mL of water to one beaker. Boil the water.
2. Stir salt into the water. Stop adding salt when no more will dissolve.
3. Carefully pour half of the salt water into the second beaker.
4. Heat the first beaker without boiling until the water evaporates and crystals appear. Let the other beaker cool until all the water evaporates.

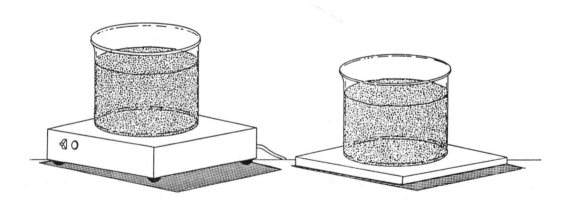

When materials cool quickly, small crystals form. When they cool slowly, large crystals form. The ocean floor is made of rock with small crystals.

Questions

1. In which beaker did small crystals form? Why? _____

_____

2. How do you know that the rock of the ocean floor cooled rapidly?

_____

_____

I. Fill in each blank with the word that fits best. Choose from the words below.

sea-floor spreading   rift valley   thicker   younger   ridge   ocean floor

In the center of the Mid-Atlantic Ridge is a _____ . At
many places, magma rises forming new _____ .
_____ explains the age of the sediment thickness on the
ocean floor. They are _____ than those of the continents.

II. If the statement is true write *T*. If it is false, change the underlined word to
make it true.

A. _____ There is a <u>rift valley</u> in Iceland.

B. _____ The patterns of <u>sediment thickness</u> are evidence that the sea floor
is spreading.

C. _____ The rock of the ocean floor cooled <u>slowly</u>.

III. Do you agree with this statement? If Christopher Columbus set off for America
today, he would have a longer trip than he had almost 500 years ago. Give a
reason for your answer.

_____

_____

_____

What Force Moves the Plates?

Exploring Science

Plumes in Rock. When you hear the word *plume*, you probably think of feathers. But there are other meanings of the word *plume*. Long ago people thought that the trail of smoke rising from a small fire looked like a very long feather.

Smoke rises because it is hotter than the air around it. The hot fluid is pushed up by the cool air forcing itself below the smoke. Any partly hot, partly cold mixture of fluids develops movements like smoke, movements that are called **convection** (kuhn-VEK-shuhn) **currents**. The hot smoke rises as part of a convection current. As it cools, it begins to level out or even to sink. This pattern of rising, leveling, cooling forms the curl of a plume of smoke.

Very hot rock behaves as a fluid. Hot magma rises through cooler rock the way a plume of smoke rises in the air. So geologists call such rising blobs of hot rock plumes, just like plumes of smoke.

A superplume is a single giant blob of hot rock. When it reaches the surface, it flows over everything. About 15 million years ago, a superplume covered most of Washington and Oregon states with a thick layer of lava.

● Explain how the energy from a plume of rising magma could push the plate above it in a particular direction.

Heat Moves the Plates

In this unit, you have learned about the movement of the earth's plates. It takes great amounts of energy to move these huge pieces of the crust. This energy comes from the heat in the earth's mantle.

Scientists think that liquid-like rock in the upper mantle moves in very slow convection currents. Rock in the earth's mantle is very hot, but some parts are cooler than others. Cooler rock is denser and tends to sink. This pushes up hotter rock, forming a convection current.

Convection currents in the mantle are very, very large. The diagram shows what they might look like. The liquid rock in the mantle is thick. As it moves, it affects the crustal rock above it. Scientists think that the currents in the mantle move the plates of the crust. The plates move very slowly. For example, the North American plate is moving only two centimeters each year. Other plates may move as much as 15 centimeters a year. Even though this movement is slow, it has caused many of the earth's features to form.

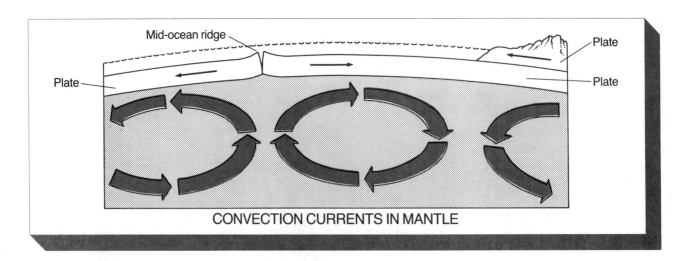

CONVECTION CURRENTS IN MANTLE

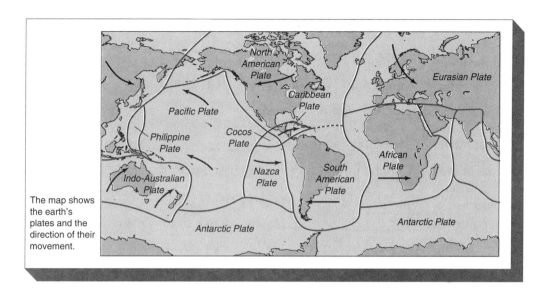

The map shows the earth's plates and the direction of their movement.

To Do Yourself   What Causes Convection Currents?

You will need:

A heat source, 2 Pyrex beakers, water, food coloring, dropper, heat-resistant pad and gloves

Caution: Use great care when heating anything! ALWAYS wear heat-resistant gloves when handling hot objects. Place hot objects on a heat-resistant pad, NOT on a desk or table top.

1. Fill the beakers three-quarters full with tap water.
2. Heat one beaker until the water boils. Remove it from the heat.
3. Carefully release 2 drops of food coloring onto the surface of the water in each beaker.

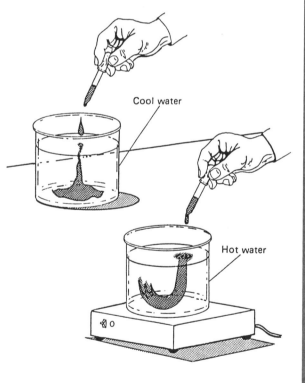

Cool water

Hot water

When liquids are heated, convection currents are set up. The swirls of food coloring in the heated water show the currents. When released in cool water, the food coloring sinks. Hot rock in the earth's mantle also moves in convection currents.

Questions

1. Draw what happened in each beaker.

2. How is the beaker of hot water like the earth's mantle? _____

_____

Review

I. Fill in each blank with the word that fits best. Choose from the words below.

slowly   heating   convection   mantle   cool   plates   liquid

plumes   rapidly   crust

One way that heat moves in gases and liquids is by _____, which

produces currents in the fluid. Such currents happen when one part of a fluid

is _____ and another part is hot. One place such currents are

found is the top part of the _____. Hot melted rock forms rising

_____ that move very _____. This movement

is transferred to crustal _____.

II. Circle the underlined word that makes each statement true.

A. Convection currents probably exist in the earth's (crust/mantle).

B. The North American plate moves about two (centimeters/meters) a year.

C. Heated magma (rises/sinks) if it is surrounded by cooler magma.

D. The force that moves the plates is the (heat from the mantle/current in the ocean).

III. Answer in sentences.

Scientists think the mantle sometimes acts like a solid and sometimes like a liquid. In what way does the mantle act like a liquid?

_____

_____

_____

Review What You Know

A. Use the clues to fill in the blanks below.

1. Moving pieces of the crust
2. The part of the ocean where the Marianas Trench is found.
3. Wegener's name for the supercontinent
4. Formed the Hawaiian volcanoes
5. Deep part of the ocean
6. Valley found along the mid-ocean ridge
7. Part of the continent that is underwater

8. The _____ ridge
9. Kind of current that transfers heat
10. An extinct underwater volcano

11. The _____ Deep is the deepest part of the ocean

12. A circular pattern is called a _____ current.
13. An ocean with hotspots
14. The tallest mountains in the world

1. P __ __ __ __ __

2. __ L __ __ __

3. __ A __ __ __ __ __

4. __ __ T __ __ __ __

5. __ __ E __ __ __

6. __ __ __ T __ __ __ __ __ __

7. __ __ E __ __

8. __ __ __-__ C __ __ __

9. __ __ __ __ __ __ T __ __ __

10. __ __ __ __ O __ __ __

11. __ __ __ __ __ N __ __ __

12. __ __ __ __ __ __ I __ __

13. __ __ __ __ __ __ C

14. __ __ __ __ __ __ __ S

B. Write the word (or words) that best complete each statement.

1. _____ According to continental drift, the continents were once **a.** one land mass **b.** smaller than today **c.** covered by water

2. _____ Which of the following did not support Wegener's idea? **a.** Similar fossils are found on different continents. **b.** The ocean floor is solid. **c.** The continents fit like pieces in a jigsaw puzzle.

3. _____ The idea that the crust is broken into pieces that float on the mantle is the theory of **a.** continental drift **b.** plate tectonics **c.** convection

4. _____ Collisions of plates carrying continental rock form **a.** mountains **b.** trenches **c.** mid-ocean ridges

5. _____ As mountains wear away, they float **a.** higher in the mantle **b.** lower in the mantle **c.** in the ocean

6. _____ When two plates collide, the lighter rock of one plate **a.** rides over the heavier plate **b.** slides under the heavier plate **c.** forms a rift valley

7. _____ The deepest parts of the ocean are **a.** rift valleys **b.** shelves **c.** trenches

8. _____ When a plate moves, the hot spot below it **a.** moves **b.** does not move **c.** becomes an island

9. _____ A seamount is a(n) **a.** mountain peak on an island **b.** mid-ocean ridge **c.** an extinct underwater volcano

10. _____ A mid-ocean ridge forms where two plates are **a.** separating **b.** colliding **c.** joining

11. _____ The part of a continent that continues underwater is a(n) **a.** island **b.** shelf **c.** ridge

12. _____ A rift valley is found at **a.** a hot spot **b.** the center of a plate **c.** a mid-ocean ridge

13. _____ Along a rift valley, lava **a.** is never found **b.** pushes plates apart **c.** cools slowly

14. _____ The part of the ocean floor closest to the mid-ocean ridge is **a.** hardest **b.** oldest **c.** youngest

15. _____ The heat within the earth's mantle moves by **a.** convection currents **b.** collisions **c.** waves

C. Apply What You Know

1. Look at the diagram on page 79. Then answer the questions.

   a. Where is the sea floor forming? _____

   b. Where is a trench forming? _____

   c. Where is magma rising to the surface? _____

   d. Where is the sea floor older, at B or C? _____

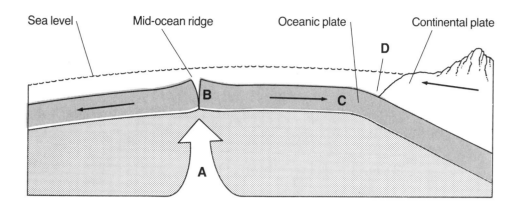

2. Explain why the eastern and western parts of Iceland are moving farther apart.
3. How are the Himalayas and the Alps alike?
4. Why are the deepest ocean trenches found in the western part of the Pacific Ocean?

D. Find Out More

1. Use a relief map or a globe to find the highest and lowest places on earth. Find out how these places relate to the edges of the plates.
2. Find magazine articles about recent volcanic eruptions in Hawaii.
3. Do some research to find out about the hot springs in Iceland. Find out if such springs are found in other parts of the world. Plan a report or a poster illustrating your findings.

A. Label the layers of the earth on the diagram. Then answer the questions using the name of the correct layer.

Layers of the Earth

1 _____

2 _____

3 _____

4 _____

How would you describe each layer of the earth?

1. Where features such as mountains, plateaus, and plains are found

_____

2. The layer in which convection currents form _____

3. This layer consists of moving plates _____

4. The liquidlike layer through which secondary earthquake waves cannot pass_____

5. The solid inner layer _____

B. Complete the statements that follow each diagram.

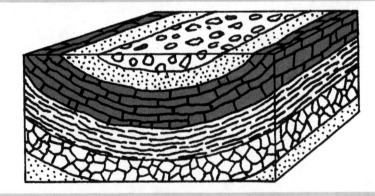

1. This downward curve of folded rock is a(n) (anticline/syncline).

_____

2. When the rock layers curve upward, a(n) (anticline/syncline) is formed:

_____

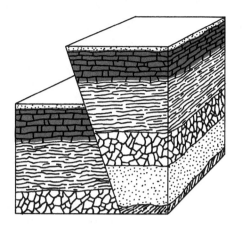

3. Along this fault, one side of the ground (rose/sank). _____

4. This movement forms (volcanoes/mountains). _____

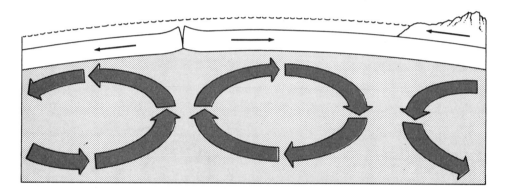

5. This type of current is found in the (mantle/crust). _____

6. This current causes the (oceans/plates) to move. _____

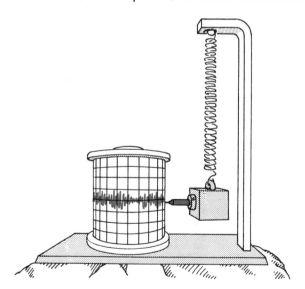

7. This instrument is used to detect (earthquakes/trenches).

_____

8. The part of the instrument that moves is the (pen/paper).

_____

UNIT

4

ROCKS
AND MINERALS

What Are Minerals?

Exploring Science

Panning for Gold. In the 1850's, the old west was a land of opportunity. Pat McLaughlin and Peter O'Riley were two men hoping to "strike it rich." They were panning for gold in Nevada.

First they dug a large hole to hold water. Then they would fill their pans with sand and soil and wash this material in the water. The lighter material would wash out of the pans. The heavier material stayed in the bottoms of the pans. After several washings, the only thing left in the pans were some bright pebbles. These pebbles were gold!

While McLaughlin and O'Riley were working, Henry Comstock came up to them. Comstock was a lazy man who was not above lying. He told the two men that he owned the land on which they were working. He offered to let them keep working there if they would agree to give him half of all the gold they found.

McLaughlin and O'Riley believed Comstock

and agreed to his deal. They kept digging and panning. Every place they dug, they hit the same soft, black rock. Another miner from California recognized the black rock. He had a chemist test it. The black rock was mostly silver. The silver was chemically combined with sulfur, making it look black.

The California miner talked Comstock into selling his rights to the land. He paid 10 dollars down and agreed to pay 9,990 dollars later. Comstock thought he had finally hit the jackpot.

The deposit came to be known as the Comstock Lode. It turned out to be the richest silver mine in history. Billions of dollars worth of silver and gold were mined there. Henry Comstock had really cheated himself.

● McLaughlin and O'Riley could see the gold in the rocks. Why couldn't they see the silver?

This man is panning for gold in a California stream.

Minerals of the Earth's Crust

The gold and silver that the miners discovered are **minerals.** A mineral is a solid natural substance that does not come from anything living. The crust of the earth is made up of about 2000 minerals. Some, like gold and silver, are valued for their beauty. Other minerals contain materials needed for building or for other industries. The earth's minerals are an important resource. They must be used wisely. Once minerals are used up, they cannot be replaced.

All matter is made up of atoms. The kinds of atoms in a substance, and the way those atoms are arranged, is the **chemical composition** of that substance. Each mineral has its own special chemical composition. No two minerals have exactly the same chemical composition. This explains why each mineral has its own set of **properties,** or characteristics.

Some minerals, such as gold and silver, are **elements.** An element is a substance made up of only one kind of atom. Other minerals are **compounds.** Compounds are chemical combinations of two or more elements. Compounds have different properties than the elements they are made up of. For example, the black rock of the Comstock Lode was a compound made up of silver and sulfur. The black rock did not look or behave anything like either of those elements.

There are 88 elements found naturally on earth. Some elements occur by themselves in the crust. Most elements, however, are combined in compounds. These compounds make up most of the crust's minerals.

The graph shows the 8 elements that make up 98 percent of the weight of the earth's crust. The most plentiful element is oxygen. The second most common is silicon. Oxygen and silicon can combine in many different ways. They form quartz (KWORTS) and other minerals. Quartz looks like glass. Millions of tiny quartz particles form the sand on a beach. You may even have a chip of quartz in your wristwatch.

Oxygen and silicon combine easily. Together they combine with elements such as aluminum, iron, and calcium to form minerals. All the minerals that contain silicon and oxygen are called **silicates** (SIL-i-kits). The silicates are the most important mineral group on the earth. They make up most rocks. The table shows some of the silicates as well as other minerals and their compositions.

Do you recognize any other elements from the graph? Aluminum and iron are two common metals. They, too, combine with oxygen to form compounds. The compounds they form are examples of mineral **ores.** Ores contain useful amounts of metals.

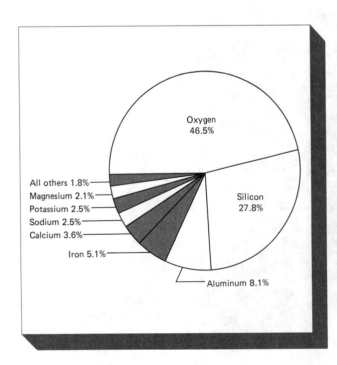

Oxygen 46.5%

Silicon 27.8%

All others 1.8%
Magnesium 2.1%
Potassium 2.5%
Sodium 2.5%
Calcium 3.6%

Iron 5.1%

Aluminum 8.1%

Quartz crystals are easy to identify by their characteristic shape.

Some Familiar Minerals

Mineral	Composition
Gold	Element
Sulfur	Element
Calcite	Compound of calcium, carbon and oxygen
Pyrite	Compound of iron and sulfur
Silicates Quartz	Compound of silicon and oxygen
Hornblende Feldspar Mica	Compounds of silicon, oxygen, and metals

Review

I. Fill in each blank with the word that fits best. Choose from the words below.

silicon   elements   minerals   properties   compounds   ores   oxygen   pyrite

There are over 2000 different _____ found in the earth's crust.

Substances that have only one kind of atom are called _____. Most

minerals are in chemically combined forms called _____. An important

group of minerals is the silicates, formed from _____ and

_____. Minerals that contain useful metals are called _____.

II. Circle the underlined word that makes each statement true.

   A. (Most/All) minerals are compounds.

   B. (A compound/An element) has atoms that are all alike.

   C. The most plentiful (element/mineral) on the earth is oxygen.

   D. Oxygen and (silicon/aluminum) form quartz.

III. Answer in sentences.

   How can there be 2000 minerals when there are only 88 naturally occurring elements?

   _____

   _____

   _____

What Are Crystals?

Exploring Science

Three Giant Crystals. Allan Caplan was astonished. He stared at the picture that the mineral dealer had given him. Could topaz crystals really grow to such size? Caplan was on one of his many journeys to the jungles of Brazil, South America. There, under the lush growth of the rain forest, lay some of the earth's most magnificent gems.

Caplan had been going to Brazil for years to buy beautiful mineral crystals. When he told people back in the United States about some of the minerals in Brazil, they didn't believe him. They knew of Brazilian emeralds and diamonds. But no one had heard of a giant topaz with smooth faces.

In the past, Caplan had been to the mines himself. He had seen workers take large crystals out of the ground. So he trusted the mineral dealer. He bought three giant crystals without seeing them. Caplan returned to the United States and waited for the crystals to arrive.

In Brazil, the gems were wrapped in jungle vines and packed in crates. The crates traveled by train, and then by boat.

Months later, the three crystals arrived. When the crates were opened, Caplan couldn't believe his eyes. The largest crystal was a beauti-

This giant topaz is one of the largest natural crystals ever found.

ful golden color—and it was huge! It was too big for a person to get both arms around. All three crystals were sent to museums. You can see the largest one at the American Museum of Natural History in New York City.

● Scientists think the large topaz crystals started forming over 100 million years ago. What does the length of time it took them to form have to do with their size?

Mineral Crystals

Topaz is a silicate mineral that contains aluminum. Because of their beauty, pieces of topaz are used in making jewelry. All pieces of topaz may not be the same size, but they all have the same shape. This naturally formed geometric shape is called a **crystal.** Each side is a face.

Every mineral has a characteristic crystal shape. Topaz forms crystals that are like prisms. Rock salt, or **halite** (HAY-lit), forms cube-shaped crystals. If you look closely at salt you can see the tiny cubes.

Crystals form under various conditions. Sometimes, minerals are dissolved in water. When the water evaporates, the minerals that remain form crystals.

Mineral crystals also form when hot magma cools underground. If the magma cools rapidly, small crystals are formed. If cooling takes place slowly, atoms arrange themselves into larger crystals. If magma is left undisturbed for thousands of years, almost perfect crystals, like the giant topazes, may form. Usually something occurs to disturb the formation of crystals. Uneven temperatures, impurities, and other mineral crystals forming in the same place disturb crystal growth. Most crystals are not perfect.

To Do Yourself   How Can You Grow a Crystal Garden?

You will need:

2 charcoal briquettes, ¼ cup water, ¼ cup noniodized salt, ¼ cup laundry bluing, 1 tablespoon ammonia, food coloring, mixing bowl, shallow bowl

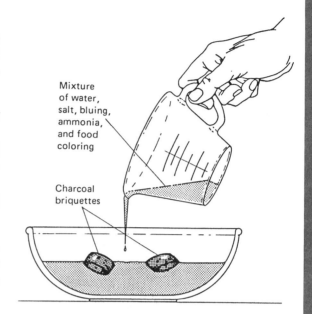

Mixture of water, salt, bluing, ammonia, and food coloring

Charcoal briquettes

1. Place both briquettes in a clean shallow bowl.
2. Mix the liquids in the other bowl. Add food coloring if you like. Pour the mixture slowly over the briquettes.
3. After a few days, you will have a crystal garden.

Most minerals are made of crystals. These crystals have a special shape. The shape is determined by the way in which the atoms of the mineral are arranged.

Questions

1. What crystal shape can you find in your garden? _____

2. What two crystals do you use in food almost every day? _____

Review

I. Fill in each blank with the word that fits best. Choose from the words below.

crystal   halite   magma   face   prisms

A naturally formed geometric shape is a _____ . Rock salt, or _____ , forms cube-shaped crystals. Crystals form underground when hot _____ cools. Each side of a crystal is called a _____ . Topaz forms crystals that are like _____ .

II. Answer in sentences.

Why are most crystals not perfect? _____

_____

How Can You Recognize Minerals?

Exploring Science

Beachcombing. Imagine you are walking along a tropical beach. You search the sand for unusual rocks, shells, or whatever else the tide has washed ashore. A bright sparkle from a small rock catches your eye. Could it be something valuable?

You pick up the rock and examine it more closely. It looks like it is all one mineral, although it is broken on one side. The break exposes a smooth, flat edge. The mineral is clear, but has a slightly yellow tinge. Using your trusty magnifying glass, you can see that before the rock broke, it was a crystal with eight sides.

Now you are excited. You look around for a piece of quartz. There are lots of those on the beach. Now you try to scratch the piece of quartz with the small rock. Using the magnifying glass, you see that the rock has made a tiny scratch on the hard quartz. There are only a few minerals that will scratch quartz. You may be onto something interesting here.

If the beach is in certain parts of Africa or Brazil, you have good reason for excitement. You have probably found a diamond, the most valuable of all gems.

● Brazil and Southern Africa have similar mineral deposits. What can explain this similarity? (Hint: Think back to Unit 2.)

Recognizing Minerals

Chances are you will not find a diamond on the beach. However, you are likely to find other minerals just about anywhere. How can you tell what you have found? Geologists use a number of properties, in addition to the shapes of crystals, to identify minerals.

COLOR: Sometimes you can identify a mineral by its color. Azurite is usually blue. But minerals can be tricky. Many different minerals are the same color. Also, a small amount of some different mineral can be mixed in. The different mineral is called an **impurity.** An impurity can change the color of a mineral. Just the tiniest bit of an impurity can make the usually colorless quartz appear pink, green, violet, or some other color.

STREAK: The **streak** of a mineral is the color it leaves when the mineral is rubbed on a white piece of rough tile called a **streak plate.** No matter what impurities may be in the mineral, the streak is usually the same color as it is for the pure mineral. Sometimes the color of a mineral's streak is different from the color of the mineral itself. Streak is a more reliable identification than color.

LUSTER: **Luster** refers to how a mineral reflects light. *Metallic* and *nonmetallic* are words used to describe the luster of minerals. The typical shine of metal knives, forks, and spoons is a metallic luster. Types of nonmetallic lusters are named for common substances with that luster—waxy, silky, and glassy. A nonmetallic luster with no shine at all is called dull.

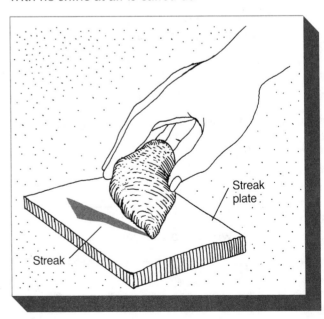

Streak plate

Streak

CLEAVAGE. **Cleavage** is the tendency of a mineral to split along straight surfaces, or planes. Planes of cleavage may be in one, two, or three directions. Mica peels in thin sheets, like slices from a loaf of bread or flakes of crust from a pastry. Its cleavage is in one direction. You learned that halite forms cubic crystals. Halite also shows cleavage in three directions. The planes of cleavage in halite are at right angles to one another.

FRACTURE. **Fracture** refers to breaking without cleavage. A fracture is irregular, but some fractures show a characteristic pattern. For example, the fracture of many minerals has a circular pattern.

HARDNESS. Hardness is a very useful property in mineral identification. The hardness of a mineral is found by doing a "scratch" test. In this test, you find out what the mineral will scratch and what will scratch the mineral. The results of a scratch test are compared with the minerals in **Moh's Scale of Hardness.** In this scale, ten minerals are given "hardness" numbers. Talc, the softest mineral, is 1 on the scale. Diamond, the hardest mineral, is 10. A mineral of higher number can scratch all the minerals below it on the scale. For example, topaz (8) will scratch minerals 1 through 7 on the scale. It will be scratched by corundum and diamond.

Many minerals have several properties in common. But each mineral has its own **set** of several properties. No two minerals have the same set. Therefore, the set of properties is used to identify the mineral.

Mohs' Hardness Scale

Hardness	Mineral	Test
1	Talc	Can be scratched with fingernail
2	Gypsum	Difficult to scratch with fingernail Cannot scratch a penny
3	Calcite	Cannot be scratched with fingernail Can scratch a penny Can be scratched by a penny
4	Fluorite	Cannot scratch glass Can scratch a penny
5	Apatite	Can scratch glass with difficulty Difficult to scratch with glass
6	Orthoclase	Can scratch glass very easily Difficult to scratch with steel knife
7	Quartz	Cannot be scratched with steel knife Difficult to scratch with file
8	Topaz	Can scratch quartz Cannot scratch corundum Can be scratched by corundum
9	Corundum	Can scratch topaz Cannot scratch diamond Can be scratched by diamond
10	Diamond	Cannot be scratched by any mineral Can scratch all substances

To Do Yourself   How Can You Measure Mineral Hardness?

You will need:

A penny, small knife, steel file, your fingernail, some common minerals such as quartz, feldspar, calcite, and talc

1. First use your fingernail to scratch each of the minerals. Then try the other objects in this order: the penny, the knife, and the steel file. **Caution: Always handle sharp objects with great care!**

2. In the table below, record the object that first scratched each mineral.
3. Then compare your results with the table in your book.

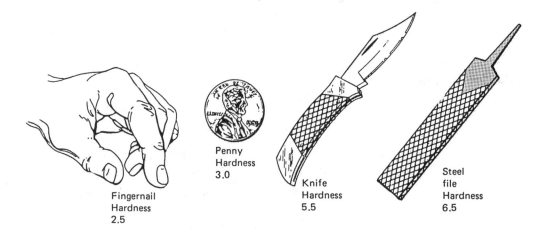

Fingernail
Hardness
2.5

Penny
Hardness
3.0

Knife
Hardness
5.5

Steel
file
Hardness
6.5

Data Table

Mineral	Object that scratches it	Hardness Number
quartz		
calcite		
feldspar		
talc		

Questions

1. Which mineral was the hardest? _____

2. Which mineral was the softest? _____

3. Did your results match the hardness from the Moh's scale? Why? Why not? ____

_____

Review

I. Fill in each blank with the word that fits best. Choose from the words below.

streak   sulfur   glassy   fracture   scratch   quartz   cleavage

You find a clear mineral with a _____ luster. A piece breaks

off irregularly, so it has _____ . It seems to

_____ most other minerals, so it is very hard. The mineral

is probably _____ .

II. Match the tests in column A with the mineral property in column B.

A	B
_____1. Scratch with another mineral	**a.** luster
_____2. Rub on a special plate	**b.** hardness
_____3. Break the mineral	**c.** fracture or cleavage
_____4. Observe how it looks	**d.** color of streak

III. Answer in sentences.

Geologists identify minerals with great certainty by using chemical tests and careful measurements in the laboratory. Why do you think they still make use of the simple tests that you have learned in this lesson?

_____

_____

_____

What Is a Rock?

Exploring Science

A Palace of Rock. It is quiet, except for the wind. The setting sun turns the sandstone cliffs a golden color. It may be Colorado today, but you feel as though you have stepped back in time.

Over 800 years ago, many people lived within these stony walls. It is known as Cliff Palace. On a natural shelf carved from a sandstone cliff, the Pueblo (PWEB-loh) Indians built this rocky home. It was a safe, sheltered place.

The sandstone shelf was worn away and split in some places. Because the sandstone was in layers, loose pieces could be used as blocks.

The blocks were used to build walls for the 200 rooms of the palace.

The rooms are empty now. The Pueblos left Cliff Palace about 1300 A.D. No one knows why. Only the rocks remain, as they have for centuries, in their stony silence.

● Which seems more likely to be true?

A. The Pueblos left Cliff Palace because of earthquakes and volcanoes.

B. The Pueblos left Cliff Palace because food became scarce.

Cliff Palace is in Mesa Verde National Park in Colorado.

Minerals Into Rocks

Cliff Palace was built on solid rock above ground. There were loose rocks scattered nearby. More rock was buried beneath the surface. Much of the earth's crust is covered by rock.

A **rock** is made of one or more minerals. **Sandstone** is made mostly of quartz. The color of sandstone can vary. It can be golden yellow, red, or brown. Impurities or other minerals mixed with the quartz produce the different colors. All samples of sandstone show the layers from which this rock formed.

Granite (GRAN-it) is another common rock. It differs from sandstone in several ways. For one thing, it does not appear in layers. Another difference is that granite is made of three or more minerals, including quartz, feldspar, and mica. The amounts of each mineral can vary. Some granite has a lot of feldspar. It looks pink. Granite with more mica in it will look shinier. Granite and sandstone are widely used as building materials.

Granite is the rock that makes up most of the earth's continents. The ocean floors and parts of the continental crust are made of rock called **basalt** (buh-SOLT). Like granite, basalt contains feldspar. It also contains dark-colored minerals, such as **augite** (AW-jyt) and **olivine** (OL-uh-veen). These minerals give basalt its dark color.

Marble is a familiar rock used in buildings and sculpture. It can be polished to form a smooth surface. Marble is mostly calcite. The streaks of color in marble are produced by different impurities.

Marble, granite, basalt, and sandstone are examples of rocks that have formed in different ways. In the next three lessons you will learn how each kind of rock is formed.

Granite contains three or more minerals.

Marble is often used for works of art.

Review

I. Fill in each blank with the word that fits best. Choose from the words below.

feldspar   different   minerals   layers   metallic   mica

A rock is made of one or more _____. The same kind of rock may

contain _____ amounts of the same mineral. Granite and basalt both

contain the mineral _____. Sandstone shows the _____ from

which it formed.

II. Identify each of the following. Write *R* for rock or *M* for mineral.

A. _____ basalt   **E.** _____ granite

B. _____ quartz   **F.** _____ sandstone

C. _____ marble   **G.** _____ feldspar

D. _____ augite   **H.** _____ calcite

III. Answer in sentences.

Marble, sandstone, and granite are all used as building materials. State a characteristic of each rock that makes it desirable for building.

How Did Rocks Begin?

Exploring Science

A Walk on Giant's Causeway. Irish folktales of long ago are filled with colorful stories of giants roaming the earth. When people first saw the huge columns of rock jutting out near the Irish Sea, they thought the rocks looked like steps fit for a giant. They named the steps Giant's Causeway. A causeway is a walkway or bridge.

Giant's Causeway is a group of rocky columns, each with a regular six-sided shape. It looks like a pile of huge, unsharpened pencils sticking out of the water.

How did the rocky pile form? About 50 million years ago, the Atlantic Ocean was forming. Cracks opened on the earth's crust. Magma came up from below. On the surface, lava spread out in sheets. As the lava cooled, it began to crystallize into basaltic rock. But the basalt cooled unevenly. Deep cracks formed in a regular pattern. The six-sided columns of basalt were the result.

● A place called Devil's Postpile in California has hundreds of tall, six-sided columns. What do you think they are made of?

The Giant's Causeway is made of basalt. The six-sided columns are familiar features of this rock.

Igneous Rocks

The basalt rocks of Giant's Causeway are **igneous** (IG-nee-us) rocks. Igneous comes from the Latin word for *fire*. Igneous rocks form in two ways: from molten magma cooling within the earth's crust; or from red-hot lava cooling on the earth's surface. Do you see how igneous rocks got their name?

If a rock cools underground, it cools slowly. The ground traps the heat. The minerals in the melted rock form crystal patterns as they cool. So rocks like granite and **gabbro** (GAB-roh) that cool underground have large crystals. These crystals give the rocks a coarse, grainy texture. Granite usually looks gray with specks of pink and black. It has many light-colored minerals. It is a familiar rock that is used in many buildings. Gabbro has darker-color minerals. It looks black. (Remember the 3 G's: granite and gabbro form in the ground.)

Rock that forms at the earth's surface cools quickly. Such rock contains small crystals. A rock having the same light minerals as granite, but which forms *above* ground, is called **rhyolite** (RY-uh-lyt). Basalt is a rock with the same dark minerals as gabbro but it forms above ground. Both rhyolite and basalt have small crystals. These small crystals give them fine-grained textures.

At active volcanoes, some hot lava cools so fast that no crystals form. **Obsidian** (ub-SID-ee-un) is an example of a rock that forms this way. Obsidian looks like black glass. It is sometimes called "volcanic glass." **Pumice** (PUM-is), another volcanic rock, is so light that it floats on water. Pumice is full of tiny holes. The holes are made by gases trapped inside as the rock cooled.

Igneous rocks may be very new or very old. The newest rocks come from lava cooling near active volcanoes. The oldest rocks on earth are igneous rocks formed about four billion years ago.

Obsidian has no crystals. It is also known as "volcanic glass."

The holes in pumice were made by gases escaping as the rock cooled.

Where Igneous Rocks Form

Texture	Below the Surface	At the Surface
Light-colored Minerals	Granite	Rhyolite
Dark-colored Minerals	Gabbro	Basalt

To Do Yourself   Why Do Igneous Rocks Have Different Size Crystals?

You will need:

Alum, 2 Pyrex beakers, hot water, stirring rod, heat-resistant gloves and pads

Caution: Use great care when heating anything! ALWAYS wear heat-resistant gloves when handling hot objects. Place hot objects on a heat-resistant pad, NOT on a desk or table top.

1. Carefully pour equal amounts of hot water into the beakers.
2. Add alum and stir. Continue adding until no more alum will dissolve.
3. Place one beaker in a refrigerator or other cold place.
4. Place the other beaker in a warm place.
5. Observe the size of the crystals in the beakers the next day.

When the hot rock cools quickly, small crystals form. When magma becomes trapped underground and cools slowly, large crystals form.

Questions

1. Which beaker has larger crystals. Why? _____

_____

2. Why doesn't obsidian have crystals? _____

_____

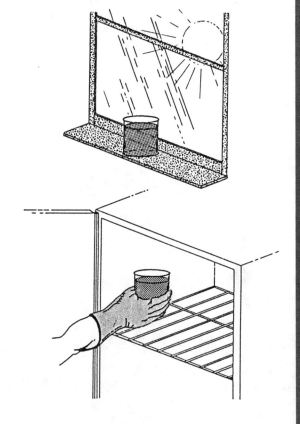

Review

I. Fill in each blank with the word that fits best. Choose from the words below.

basalt   coarse-grained   crystals   igneous   granite   fine-grained   glass

Rocks that form from the cooling of magma or lava are called _____.

Rocks that form underground, such as _____, have a _____

texture and large crystals. Rocks such as _____ form above ground

and have a _____ texture. Obsidian also forms from lava above

ground, but has no _____.

II. Place the following names in the correct place in the table: **granite, basalt, gabbro, rhyolite.**

	Light Minerals	Dark Minerals
Form from lava		
Form from magma		

III. Answer in sentences.

Name and describe two rocks that you might find near a volcano.

_____

_____

_____

How Are New Rocks Made?

Exploring Science

A Piece of Chalk. What is powdery, white, and found in the classroom? The answer is easy—chalk. But do you know that the chalk you write with may be 100 million years old?

The story of chalk starts 100 million years ago. Shallow seas covered much of the earth. Tiny plants and animals lived in the seas. One group of tiny animals was the **foraminifera** (for-uh-MIN-uh-fur-uh). These small animals had round shells made of **calcium carbonate** (KAL-see-um KAR-buh-nayt). When the foraminifera died, they sank to the sea bottom.

After many years, the sea bottom became covered by a layer of shells. In some places the layer was 200 meters thick. Later, other materials were deposited over the shells. The weight of these materials pressed down on the shells. Ever so slowly, the shells turned into a soft rock. It may be a piece of this rock you use to write your name on the board.

● Which of the following is most likely to be true?

A. Shells are changed to chalk by the pressure of overlying materials.

B. Shells are changed to chalk by the evaporation of seawater.

The famous White Cliffs of Dover are made up of the remains of tiny sea animals.

Sedimentary Rocks

The shells that piled up on the ocean floor were **sediments** (SED-uh-munts). Sediments are bits of material that settle to the bottom of bodies of water. Sediments may also be deposited on land by ice, wind, or water. Chalk is a **sedimentary** (SED-uh-MEN-tuh-ree) rock. Much of the top layer of the earth's crust is made of sedimentary rock.

Limestone and coal are other rocks formed from the remains of living things. Different types of limestone form in different ways. Coal is formed from ancient plants. Over time, bacteria and pressure act on the layers of plants. Eventually, only the black carbon remains.

Sedimentary rock can form in another way. Remember that salt crystals, or halite, remain after salt water evaporates. Some forms of limestone are produced in a similar way. The mineral calcite may be dissolved in a liquid. When the liquid evaporates, the calcite sediment forms limestone.

Most sedimentary rock forms in a third way.

Over a long period of time, a rock formation may be worn down into small particles. A layer of these particles may be built up. Other minerals, dissolved in water, seep in between the particles. When the water evaporates, the minerals are left behind. These minerals "glue" the particles together to form sedimentary rock. If the particles are grains of sand, sandstone will be formed. If the particles are tiny pieces of clay, the sedimentary rock **shale** will be formed.

You can sometimes see the layers that form sedimentary rock, especially near water. Sediment is deposited on the bottom of a lake. As the years pass, other layers are deposited on top of it. Each layer presses down on the ones beneath. After thousands of years, the result is rock in a pattern of stripes. A scientist looking at the stripes can "read" how long it took the rock to form.

This rock shows alternating layers of shale and sandstone.

To Do Yourself   How Can You See Plants 100 Million Years Old?

You will need:

A student microscope, a slide, diatomaceous earth

1. Sprinkle a few grains of diatomaceous earth on a slide. Examine the slide under the microscope.
2. Look for symmetrical shapes. These are diatoms.

Diatoms are algae, microscopic plants that live in fresh and salt water. Millions of years ago, billions of diatoms died. They sank to the bottom of the seas. Over the years, their silica walls became light, porous rock. Today diatomaceous earth is used for filters, abrasives, paints, and other products.

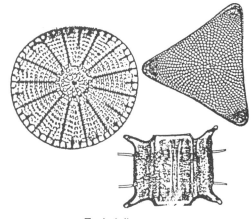

Typical diatoms

Questions

1. What shapes did you find? Draw them. _____

2. Why do you think only the skeletons of the diatoms remained? _____
   _____

3. How can living things form sediments? _____
   _____

Review

I. Fill in each blank with the word that fits best. Choose from the words below.

granite   water   limestone   coal   igneous   ice   sedimentary

shells   sandstone   explode   evaporate

Rocks that form from layers that collect over time are _____ rocks.

The layers are often from small pieces carried by _____, wind, or

_____. _____ is formed from ancient plants. Some

forms of _____ are produced by layers of _____

from sea animals. Other types form when liquids _____ and leave

mineral layers behind. Most sedimentary rocks, like _____, form

when small pieces of rock are glued together.

II. Identify how each of the following rocks formed. Use the letters **LT** if it
formed from living things; **E** if it formed from evaporation; **G** if it formed by
being glued together; and **N** if it formed from none of these. Some rocks may
be formed in more than one way.

A. _____coal   D. _____shale

B. _____limestone   E. _____basalt

C. _____halite   F. _____sandstone

III. Answer in sentences.

The remains of plants and animals are often found in sedimentary rock.
Explain why.

_____

_____

_____

Lesson Seven

How Do Rocks Change?

Exploring Science

Finding Liquid Rock. Even as a young girl growing up in a big city, Anita Harris always liked exploring the outdoors. After studying geology, she took an interest in digging up very old remains, or fossils, that looked like teeth. She found that the fossils were different colors—white, yellow, brown, and black. The color depended on how much the fossils had been "cooked" by the heat and pressure under the ground. Anita often found these fossils near **petroleum** deposits. Petroleum is crude oil. Hundreds of things are made from it, including heating oil, gasoline, plastics, even lipstick. Petroleum is a valuable resource.

Petroleum is made by the same heat that "cooks" fossils. When remains of plants and animals are heated to a high temperature, they turn into a black liquid, petroleum. The liquid moves through the **porous** (POR-us) rock around it. Porous rocks have tiny holes, or pores, that liquids can pass through. When the petroleum reaches a layer of hard rock, the petroleum can no longer travel. It remains trapped between rock layers until someone finds it.

For over 100 years, looking for petroleum deposits has been a major aim of research in geology. Now those toothlike fossils that Anita Harris found have proven useful, wherever those fossils are found, petroleum is likely to be trapped.

● Which of the following is the most likely reason why petroleum is often called "black gold"?

A. Petroleum contains a lot of gold.
B. Petroleum is very valuable.

Metamorphic Rocks

Heat and pressure inside the earth's crust can change the remains of living things into petroleum. They can change the way fossils look. Even rocks can change.

For rocks to change, there must be more pressure than just the weight of the rocks above. The great pressure that occurs when the crustal plates move is also needed. This squeezes layers of rock into folds. Great heat is produced by the pressure also.

The pressure and heat in the earth cause several types of changes in rock. Pressure can make rocks get harder and look shinier. Heat can cause minerals to melt and form bands of new compounds. Large crystals may grow. New layers may form.

The sedimentary rock shale is changed to **slate** by heat and pressure. Slate is harder than shale and has thin layers. Other rocks change to **schist** (SHIST). Schist has layers thick enough to see easily. **Gneiss** (NEYES) is a rock with even thicker layers.

Schist is a very common type of metamorphic rock.

This piece of slate shows that the original sediments were deposited in layers.

This piece of gneiss from North Carolina clearly shows bands of different minerals.

Not all rocks form layers as they change. For example, limestone becomes marble. The impurities that were in the limestone may now look like bands of color. Limestone is mostly calcite. The marble is *still* calcite. The mineral content of a changed rock remains the same.

Each of these rocks change from one kind to another. A word for change is **metamorphosis** (met-uh-MOR-fuh-sis). Rock formed from other rock under heat and pressure is called **metamorphic** (met-uh-MOR-fik) rock.

The original rocks on the earth were igneous rocks. Over billions of years, some igneous rocks were worn down into sediments. Some of these sediments formed sedimentary rocks. Some original igneous rocks were changed by the pressures of moving plates. They became metamorphic rocks. So at different times, the same rock may have been igneous, sedimentary, or metamorphic. The way that rocks are changed from one kind to another is called the **rock cycle.**

The Rock Cycle

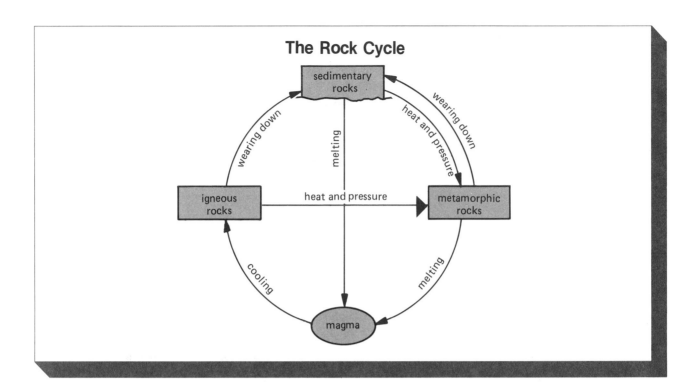

To Do Yourself   In What Kind of Rock Can Oil Be Found?

You will need:

Oil, several types of rock, such as sandstone, shale, and granite, an eyedropper, newspaper

1. Cover your working surface with newspaper. Place the rock samples on the paper.
2. Place a drop of oil on each rock.
3. Wait a few minutes and then observe what has happened to the oil.

In the ground, oil travels up through porous rock. When it reaches nonporous rock, the oil may become trapped. A pool of oil forms between the two rock layers.

Questions

1. Which rocks are porous? How do you know? _____

_____

2. If you wanted to find oil, what kinds of rock would you look for? Why?

_____

_____

103

Review

I. Fill in each blank with the word that fits best. Choose from the words below.

sedimentary   **petroleum**   **crustal plates**   **metamorphic**   **rock cycle**
heat

Great pressure in the earth's crust is caused by movements of the

_____ . The pressure causes _____ .

Together, these forces can change rocks, producing _____
rocks. Rocks changing from one type to another is known as the

_____ .

II. Identify the following rocks as igneous, sedimentary, or metamorphic. Use the letters **I, S,** or **M.**

A. ____ granite   E. ____ gneiss

B. ____ limestone   F. ____ shale

C. ____ marble   G. ____ slate

D. ____ basalt   H. ____ schist

III. Answer in sentences.

A crystal of quartz may be part of granite, sandstone, and the metamorphic rock quartzite. Trace how that same crystal could be found in all three rocks at different times.

_____

_____

_____

Review What You Know

A. Hidden in the puzzle below are 15 science terms. Use the clues to help you find the terms. Circle each term in the puzzle. Then write each name on the line next to its clue. Read up, down, left, or right.

```
M E T A M O R P H I C O L O
T N E S O R E O I G O D B I
R D A N T F U V C N M K R S
S T R E A K W Q L L P H J I
N I L F H B E U E X O I S L
C R Y S T A L X A Y U G E I
E O L O S D Y T V A N N T C
T L U S T E R N A R D E A A
I O S E O N V I G P N O R T
N C O P U M I C E B G U N E
A N O L H A R D N E S S I P
R H G A B B R O E S L O M Q
G T S E D I M E N T A R Y R
```

1. A rock that is changed by heat or pressure _____

2. A substance made up of several elements _____

3. The smallest particle of an element _____

4. A dark igneous rock formed underground _____

5. The characteristic shape of a mineral _____

6. Rock formed in layers _____
7. Characteristic of a mineral that may be different from its streak

_____

8. Splitting along straight surfaces _____

9. "Fire" rocks _____
10. Mineral formed by a combination of oxygen and silicon.

_____

11. May be described as metallic, glassy silky. _____

12. An important source of metals _____

13. The property measured by the Moh's Scale _____
14. The color a mineral leaves when it is rubbed across a plate.

_____

15. A light, porous igneous rock _____

B. Write the word (or words) that best completes each statement.

1. _____ Most of the earth's minerals are **a.** compounds
    b. elements **c.** gold ores

2. _____ Substances composed of one type of atom are
   a. elements **b.** compounds **c.** minerals

3. _____ The most plentiful element in the earth's crust
   is **a.** silicon **b.** oxygen **c.** silicate

4. _____ A very common silicate is **a.** halite **b.** sulfur
   c. quartz

5. _____ A crystal of halite is made up of **a.** sodium
   atoms **b.** chlorine atoms **c.** sodium ions and chlorine ions

6. _____ The rock that forms the ocean floor is
   a. granite **b.** basalt **c.** limestone

7. _____ The characteristic that is least useful in
   identifying a mineral is **a.** cleavage **b.** color **c.** hardness

8. _____ Two mineral characteristics that may or may not
   be the same are **a.** luster and streak **b.** cleavage and luster **c.** color and
   streak

9. _____ The softest mineral is **a.** talc **b.** topaz
   c. diamond

10. _____ A mineral that breaks along straight lines has
    a. cubic crystals **b.** fracture **c.** cleavage

C. Apply What You Know

Place the following rocks in their proper places in the table below.

marble   sandstone   granite   shale   schist   basalt

Types of Rock

IGNEOUS	SEDIMENTARY	METAMORPHIC

D. Find Out More

1. Start your own rock and mineral collection. Pick up interesting samples
   and place them in a box. You may want to use the sections of an empty
   egg carton. Use this book and other guides to identify each sample. Make
   a label for each rock and mineral you can identify.
2. A local museum may have a display of rocks and minerals. Make a report
   on the display for the class.
3. The school or local library may have books on growing crystals. Try to
   grow different types of crystal shapes.
4. Choose one mineral or gemstone and find out about it. Where is it found?
   Why is it valuable?
5. Find out if any mining or quarrying is carried out in your state. What ores,
   minerals, or rocks are taken from these mines? Prepare a report on the
   mines and their importance.

Careers in Earth Science

Finding and Using Mineral Resources. Minerals found in the earth are one of our greatest resources. They provide us with metals, such as copper and aluminum. You find beautiful gems among minerals. But you also find the raw materials for construction and other industries. Because minerals are so important, some scientists specialize in locating them.

Petroleum Geologist. Petroleum geologists look for petroleum. Petroleum, or crude oil, is the starting material for gasoline and fuel oil, as well as for plastics and cosmetics. Geologists use many different techniques to search for oil and natural gas. Near a drilling site, they may examine a sample of rock for its petroleum content. Or they may work with computers to map the location of petroleum deposits over a large area.

Petroleum geologists may work for oil or mining companies, a bank, a land developer, or the federal government. They study geology in college and often have advanced degrees.

Gem Cutter. Mineral crystals are often valued as gems. Crystals of gem quality must be cut properly to show their beauty. That is the job of the gem cutter. A gem cutter cuts, shapes, and polishes precious gems. Working with a revolving saw covered with diamond dust, the cutter forms the edges of the precious stone. A shaping wheel gives the gem its facets, or flat polished faces. Needless to say, the gem cutter must be able to use these tools with great skill. Gem cutters get their skills on-the-job or from technical training.

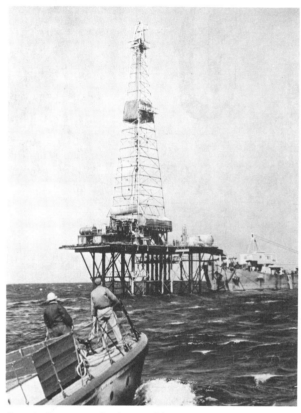

A petroleum geologist on his way to an offshore drilling rig in the Gulf of Mexico.

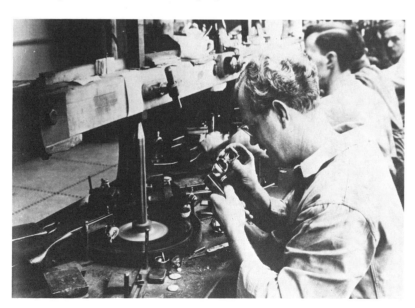

A diamond polisher at work. After a gem is cut, it must be carefully polished to bring out its beauty.

UNIT

5

EROSION AND WEATHERING

Lesson One

How Does Land Wear Away?

Exploring Science

Hiking Through Time. A perfect vacation spot should have great scenery. But energetic visitors to Arizona's Grand Canyon can get much more. By hiking down into the canyon, they can travel back through time.

The Grand Canyon is so big that it can easily be seen from a high-flying plane. Its winding path cuts more than one kilometer into the earth's crust. From the rim of the canyon, tourists stare down at its steep, rocky walls.

Almost every day, hikers take to the trails that zigzag down into the canyon. Along the way they pass layer after layer of red, yellow, and brown rock. The colorful sandstone and shale reflect the sunlight. The farther down the trail one goes, the older the rock layers become.

Several hours after leaving the rim of the canyon, hikers can hear the roar of the Colorado River. The Colorado River carved this canyon. More than a million years ago, movement of the crustal plates forced the Colorado Plateau to rise. As the land moved up, the river wore down the sandstone rock, carving out the canyon. At the bottom, the rock of the canyon walls may be two billion years old.

Camping may be set up along Angel Creek, a stream that feeds into the Colorado River. To protect this desert wilderness, only a handful of campers are permitted to stay each night. At sunrise, it's time to start the long hike back. The twisting trails are about six times longer than the vertical height of the canyon. By mid-morning, the sun is already blazing. The hikers rest for a moment in small patches of shade. Soon they reach the rim of the canyon. They are tired, but

It is hard to believe that this innocent-looking river carved out the Grand Canyon.

they have had an adventure they won't soon forget. They can look back at the canyon with wonder and pride.

● Many rock layers of the Grand Canyon are sedimentary. The bottom layers are not. What kind of rock might the bottom layers be? Explain your answer.

Running Water Causes Erosion

The Colorado River has worn a deep path through the rocks of the Colorado Plateau. This path is the Grand Canyon. There are other deep canyons in the plateau where other rivers have cut down through the rocks. The entire area has never received much rainfall. If it had, much of the land would have washed away. The only moving water has been in the rivers. The rivers caused **erosion** (i-ROH-zhuhn) that changed the shape of the land. Erosion is the wearing down and carrying away of the land. Moving water is a very important cause of erosion.

Moving water can cause erosion in several different ways.

Water pushes loose rock and soil along the river. If you have ever lifted a pail full of water, you have an idea of how heavy water is. Water is heavy enough to move rocks along with it. If there is enough fast-moving water, it can move large, heavy rocks.

Rocks moved by water can loosen other rocks along the way. The rocks carried along by the river hit the sides and bottom of the river. As rocks collide, small bumps and sharp edges break off. Rubbing the rough parts of rocks in this way is called **abrasion** (uh-BRAY-zhuhn). Abrasion causes rocks to get smaller and smoother.

Moving water lifts, cracks, and loosens rock in its path. The water lifts the rocks and gets into cracks. As pieces are removed, the cracks get wider and deeper. The bottom, or **bed**, of the river gets deeper. As the sides, or **banks** of the river erode, the river gets wider.

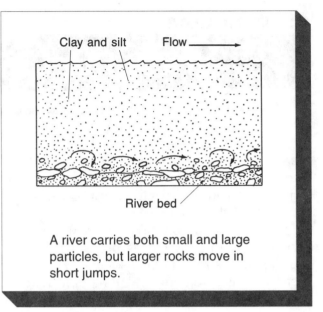

A river carries both small and large particles, but larger rocks move in short jumps.

Water dissolves many minerals in rock. Halite, remember is "rock salt." Halite and other minerals found in rocks may be dissolved as water rushes over the rocks. Eventually most rivers empty into the ocean, carrying with them the dissolved minerals.

This view of the Grand Canyon clearly shows the horizontal layers of rock that make up the canyon walls.

To Do Yourself How Does Running Water Cause Erosion?

You will need:

Soil, pitcher of water, disposable roasting pan, sink (or waterproof container), books, scissors

1. Using the scissors, cut a small notch at one end of the pan.
2. Add soil to the pan, leaving about 5 to 10 centimeters of the pan uncovered at the end near the notch.
3. Place the pan near a sink or a waterproof container. Prop up one end of the pan with a book.
4. Pour a gentle stream of water onto the soil. Observe the result.
5. Pour the water more quickly in a second trial. Observe the result.

Questions

1. How does moving water cause soil erosion? _____
2. What differences did you observe between the first and second trials?

_____

3. Repeat with the pan propped up higher. What do you observe?

_____

Review

I. Fill in each blank with the word that fits best. Choose from the words below.

wider   water   deeper   erosion   longer   land   rocks   abrasion

Moving water causes _____, wearing down and carrying away

the _____. Even large _____ are carried by swift

water and smoothed by _____. Gradually a river gets

_____ and _____.

II. Match each statement in column **A** with its effect in column **B**.

A	B
_____1. Water moves faster.	a. Rocks get smaller.
_____2. Water lifts rocks from the river bottom.	b. Some minerals are dumped into the ocean.
_____3. Rocks collide with each other.	c. The river gets deeper.

111

How Do Rivers Age?

Exploring Science

Missing Parts of the Mississippi. You probably know of Mark Twain's tales about Huck Finn and Tom Sawyer. In his book, *Life on the Mississippi*, Twain made an unusual prediction. He said that by the year 2625, Cairo (KY-roh), Illinois and New Orleans, Louisiana would be one city. What did he mean?

The Mississippi River connects the two cities. Twain knew that the Mississippi has a long, curvy path. Once in a while, the river takes a shortcut across one of its curves instead of going around it. The path of the river shortens. Twain calculated that the Mississippi of his day was 242 miles shorter than it had been 176 years before. If the path of the river continued to shorten at that rate, the river would be less than 2 miles long by the year 2625! The streets of Cairo would join those of New Orleans.

Of course, Twain was exaggerating. Also, his calculation was not right. But, a cutoff can shorten a river overnight. However, over many years, rivers develop giant curves that add to their length. This process is very slow and hard to observe.

● Even if the path of the Mississippi does change in length, does the distance between the cities change? Explain your answer.

Mark Twain

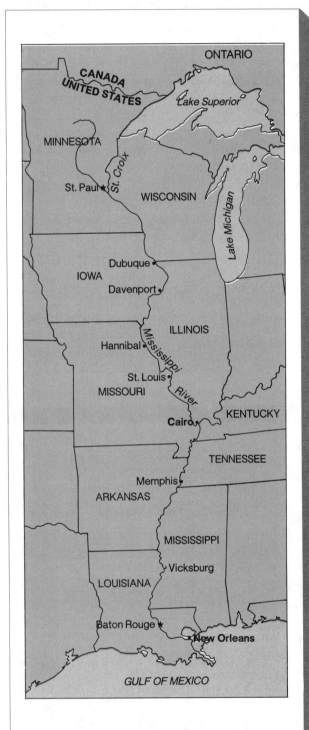

The winding course of the Mississippi River runs the full length of the U.S.

From Young Stream to Old River

The Mississippi River is the longest river in the United States. From its beginning, or **head,** to its end at the Gulf of Mexico, it curves back and forth like a snake. The winding Mississippi is considered to be an old river.

Rivers, like people, go through stages of youth, maturity (muh-CHOOR-ih-tee), and old age. Each stage of a river's life has certain characteristics that help to identify it. For example, a young river flows fast and straight. The valley formed by a young river is narrow with steep sides.

A mature river flows more slowly than a young river. It also follows a more winding path. The valley of a mature river is fairly wide, with gently sloping sides. In old age, a river winds slowly back and forth as it flows along its path.

The age of a river is not measured only in years. A river may be at different stages at different points along its path. This means that one section of a river may be in a youthful stage, while another section of the river is old. Let's look at a river that shows all three stages as it flows along its course.

A river usually forms in a region where it is getting a steady supply of water. When it rains, or when snow and ice melt, some of the water sinks into the ground. If it rains or snows hard enough, some water runs along the surface. This moving surface water is called **runoff.**

Runoff erodes a path along the ground. Where runoff is fairly steady, this path becomes a stream. Along a mountain slope, several small streams may join to form a river. This junction of small streams becomes the head of the river.

A river flowing down a steep slope flows fast and straight. This is a young river. The faster the water flows, the faster it erodes its bed. The banks of the river do not erode as fast as the bed. The valley formed by a young river takes the shape of a *V.* If the river flows over large rocks, rapids and waterfalls are formed. Rapids and waterfalls are features of a young river.

Once the river leaves the steep, mountainous region, it flows onto an area of lower ground. As the land becomes less steep, the speed of the river slows down. It does not erode its bed as quickly. Instead, it starts to erode its banks. The

Waterfalls, like Yosemite Falls shown here, are features of young rivers.

river becomes wider, and its path begins to wind back and forth. Its valley becomes *U*-shaped. This part of the river is in the mature stage.

Usually, the farther you get from the head of a river, the flatter the land becomes. The river moves more and more slowly. The curves in its course become larger. The river winds from one side of the valley to the other. The river valley becomes a wide, flat plain. These features are those of an old river.

So, a river can be young, mature, and old, all at the same time. It all depends on where along its course you view the river.

Rivers also grow old with time. Over thousands of years, a river wears away the rocks in its path. It smooths over waterfalls. It widens its valley. The older a river gets, the gentler its path from high ground to low ground becomes. The diagram compares a young river with an older one.

Wherever a river slows down, it drops sediment. If one side of a river flows more slowly than the other side sediment will be deposited on the slow side. This means that sediment builds up along one bank. The river flows around this built-up sediment and begins carving, or eroding, the opposite bank. As a river ages, it forms more of these curves, or **meanders** (mee-AN-durs).

Meanders go back and forth across a wide, flat river valley. Sometimes a river cuts off one of its curves. It was these cutoffs that Twain observed. The calm water that remains in the cutoff meander forms an **ox-bow** lake.

Near its end, the river flows across level land. Many rivers, like the Mississippi, empty into the sea. Others empty into larger rivers or lakes. The place where the river empties is called the **mouth** of the river.

When a river meets the calmer water of a lake or sea, it slows down very quickly. The river drops the sediment it was carrying. These sediments build up around a river's mouth to form a

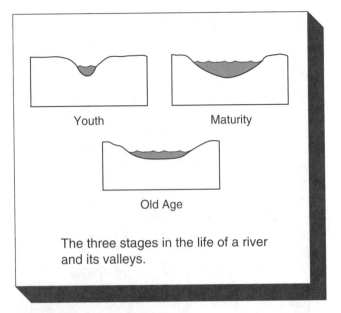

Youth   Maturity

Old Age

The three stages in the life of a river and its valleys.

An old river follows a winding course. The curves are called meanders.

A triangular-shaped deposit of sediment called a delta often forms near the mouth, or end, or a river.

deposit called a **delta** (DEL-tuh). Many, although not all, river deltas are roughly triangular in shape. The term "delta" comes from the Greek letter Δ. As you can see, this letter is shaped like a triangle.

As a river gets very old, its valley gets wider and flatter. In time, the land may become so flat that the river stops moving. It may become a lake or swamp, or it may dry up completely. When a river stops flowing, it is no longer a river. The stages of the river's life have come to an end.

Review

I. Fill in each blank with the word that fits best. Choose from the words below.

quickly   slowly   river   runoff   V-shaped   wider   meanders waterfalls

Flowing water from rain or snow, called _____, collects in streams

that join and form a _____. In its youth, a river has a _____

valley. As it ages, the river flows more _____ and its valley gets

_____. An old river may have many _____.

II. Unscramble the letters to find the parts of a river. Then describe each part.

A. UTHOM _____

B. KANB _____

C. ARDEMEN _____

D. LEADT _____

III. Draw an old, meandering river that forms a delta at its mouth. Label the drawing.

What Causes Beaches?

Exploring Science

A $3-Billion Finger in the Dike. Do you remember a story about a brave Dutch boy? He saved the Netherlands by using his finger to plug a hole in a dike. Most of the Netherlands is below sea level. Dikes are walls that protect the land from the sea. A small leak in a dike can quickly erode into a large hole. In the story, the boy stopped this erosion until help arrived.

Now there is a new twist to that old story. The Dutch have built a $3-billion barrier as large as an Egyptian pyramid. Its job is to protect the dikes from erosion by storm waves. In 1953, before the barrier was built, high storm waves crushed the old dikes. About 50 thousand houses were washed out to sea. Much precious farmland was lost, too. Today, with the clang of a steel gate, the Dutch can keep the sea away from the dikes. No holes can form from the erosion of the dikes. So the story of the brave Dutch boy can remain a story.

● Why would a small hole in a dike erode into a larger hole?

Beaches and Erosion

You have probably seen ocean waves. A wave is an up-and-down, or *vertical*, movement of water that travels through the sea. The combination of up-and-down with forward produces a circular movement in the water. (This circular motion will be discussed in a later chapter.) Waves form far out from shore and come crashing in on the beach. Then the water flows swiftly back toward the sea.

The driving force that moves a wave toward the shore is the wind. The stronger the wind, the faster, and usually the larger, the waves. The faster the waves, the more erosion they can cause.

As you have learned, moving water is a very important cause of erosion. Sometimes large waves erode the shoreline by carrying away sand or soil. Waves have pounded shorelines for millions of years. Why haven't these waves washed away the entire continents?

In time, these rocks will be broken down into grains of sand by the pounding waves.

While waves do carry material away from the land, they also deposit material on the land. The water in an incoming wave may carry sand, seashells, or small rocks. When the wave hits the shore, some of this material is deposited. The weaker, outgoing flow of water removes lighter material from the shore. Gradually, the water washes away the finer grains of soil and sand. It leaves behind larger grains of sand. The waves have formed a sandy **beach.**

During a storm, waves are larger and move faster than usual. Storm waves may carry away more material than they leave behind. A severe storm, such as a hurricane, may wash away an entire beach.

Waves may build up one beach while eroding another beach. In most areas, the wind does not blow directly toward the shore. The waves hit the shore at an angle. As a result, a **current** is produced. A current is a horizontal movement of water in one direction. A current that moves

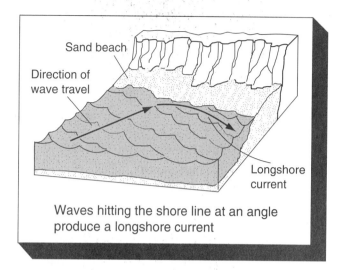

Waves hitting the shore line at an angle produce a longshore current

parallel to the shoreline is called a **longshore current.** Longshore currents move sand along those beaches they flow beside. These currents often deposit sand on any part of the shore that sticks out into the ocean. The beach is built up at those places.

To Do Yourself   How Does a Beach Change?

You will need:

Sand, gravel, water, disposable roasting pan, clear plastic wrap

1. Place a layer of sand and gravel in the pan.
2. Add water to the pan to a depth of about 1 centimeter. Cover the pan with plastic wrap to prevent spilling.
3. Tilt the pan toward one end. Observe what happens to the sand and gravel.

Waves can carry heavy particles into shore and form a beach. Lighter particles may be carried out on the weaker, outgoing wave. During a storm, waves may move a large portion of the beach offshore.

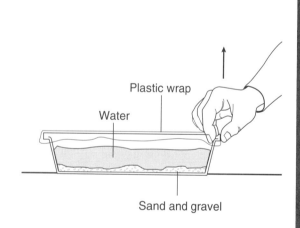

Questions

1. How were the sand and gravel moved by the water? _____

   _____

2. Does the speed of the water affect the way the sand and gravel are deposited?

   How? _____

3. How is your model like an actual beach? _____

Review

I. Fill in each blank with the word that fits best. Choose from the words below.

> **sand   beach   wave   current   erode   clay   circular**
>
> **longshore current   horizontal**

Winds cause water to move in a(n) _____ motion called a wave. Waves can both build up and _____ the shoreline. Since waves take away small particles and leave _____, a _____ is formed. A _____ can build up the shoreline by depositing more sand on a point of land that sticks out into the ocean.

II. Write **T** if a statement is true. If it is false, change the underlined word or phrase to make it true.

A. _____ A <u>wave</u> is a horizontal movement of water.

B. _____ Storm waves may <u>erode</u> a beach.

C. _____ Waves usually hit the shoreline <u>at an angle.</u>

D. _____ A <u>storm</u> current deposits sand at one end of a beach.

III. Answer in sentences.

Why are many beaches sandy?

_____

_____

_____

How Do Waves Change the Shoreline?

Exploring Science

The Risk of Island Living. The warning to evacuate had come too late. The bridge leading to the mainland was already blocked. In Galveston, Texas, 55,000 people were trapped on their island. Within a few minutes, the fury of hurricane Alicia (uh-LISH-uh) was upon them.

Winds blew out the windows of beach houses. Giant waves swept through buildings as if they were cardboard. It would take billions of dollars to repair the damage.

Every year, the threat of hurricanes from the Gulf of Mexico returns. Why is Galveston prone to storm damage? Galveston is a **barrier island** (BAR-ee-ur EYE-lund). It is a thin strip of sand between the Gulf of Mexico and a quiet bay. The people of Galveston built a high sea wall to protect their island from storms. On that August day in 1983, however, the wall was not enough to keep Alicia out.

There are almost 300 barrier islands along the east coast of the United States. They are like a string of pearls hugging the coast from Maine to Texas. Over recent years, more and more people have been attracted to their beautiful beaches. Many islands that were once wilderness are now dotted with homes. But barrier islands are unstable places in which to live. The people of Galveston know that fact only too well.

● Some of the barrier islands are still wilderness areas. Do you think these islands change, too? Explain your answer.

Islands, Bars, and Hooks

Barrier islands are created by waves. Let's take a closer look at wave action. In a wave, remember, water moves in a circular motion. Close to the shore, where the ocean water becomes shallow, the bottom of the wave hits the ocean floor. This causes the wave to "break," or topple over, forming a **breaker.** Breakers move fast and carry sand with them.

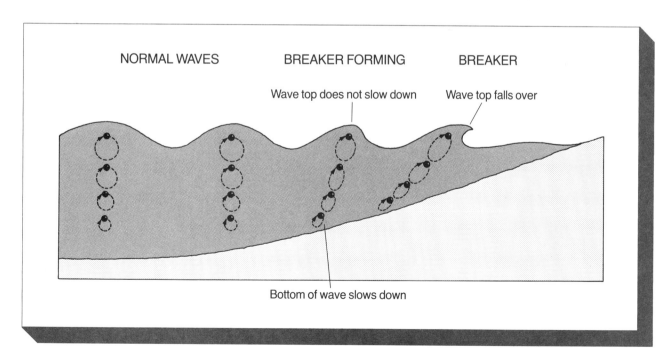

NORMAL WAVES   BREAKER FORMING   BREAKER

Wave top does not slow down   Wave top falls over

Bottom of wave slows down

If the water at a beach is shallow, the waves break far out from the shoreline. The fast-moving breakers roll onto the beach. When the water flows back to the sea, it carries sand with it. This sand is carried back to where the waves are breaking. After a while, this sand piles up. It forms an underwater **sandbar** off shore. In time, the sandbar may become large enough to form an island. Such an island forms a protective barrier for the shoreline. The water between the island and the shore is calm, with no big waves. This part of the ocean is called a **bay,** or **lagoon** (luh-GOON).

Barrier islands are large sandbars. Galveston Island in Texas is an example of a barrier island. Atlantic City, New Jersey, and Miami Beach, Florida, are cities built on barrier islands. During a storm at sea, barrier islands are the first areas to be hit by large storm waves.

Sometimes, one end of a sandbar is connected to shore. In this case, the end that extends out into the ocean is called a **point.** Over time, more and more sand may be deposited. When this occurs, the point extends farther and

The shoreline feature shown here is a hook.

farther into the ocean. If it is out far enough, offshore currents will act on the sand. The currents will strike the end of the point at an angle. Soon a **hook** will form. The photograph shows an example of a hook.

Review

I. Fill in each blank with the word that fits best. Choose from the words below.

point   sandbar   breaker   barrier island   lagoon   hook

A fast-moving wave, a _____ , deposits sand off shore.

Over time, an underwater _____ forms. When it is larger,

this formation is called a _____ . The calm water between

the island and the shore is a _____ .

II. Circle the underlined word that makes each statement true.

A. A breaker forms where water is (deep/shallow).

B. A sandbar connected to the shore forms a (point/breaker).

C. Currents pushing the sand at a point form a (bay/hook).

III. Answer in sentences.

How does a barrier island act like a barrier?

_____

_____

_____

Lesson Five

How Does Wind Change the Land?

Exploring Science

Black Sunday. In Beaver, Oklahoma, they call April 14, 1935 "Black Sunday." Sunday started as a warm, pleasant spring day. But then it came across the plains. "It" was an enormous cloud of dust.

One farmer remembers it as "a boiling wall of dirt, horizon to horizon, several thousand feet high. It overran a house and came rolling on. Birds were flying before it, looking desperate. Then it was on me. Cold, total darkness. I sat there for 40 minutes."

It was as dark as night. Chickens thought it *was* night. They went to sleep! Meanwhile, far out to sea, sailors saw the dust clouds. Oklahoma and parts of Texas were hardest hit by the clouds of dust. A reporter named the area "the dust bowl."

After Black Sunday, many farmers left Oklahoma and headed for California. But some stayed behind. Those that stayed changed some of their farming methods. They all knew the disaster another Black Sunday could bring.

● The dust bowl actually began to form years before Black Sunday. What conditions do you think contributed to the disaster?

Scenes such as the one shown here were common during the dust bowl days.

Erosion by the Wind

You have seen how moving water can shape the land. Moving air, or wind, can also change the land. In the 1930's, wind picked up the dry, loose soil all over the dust bowl region. Some of the dust may have been carried as far as New England.

A desert is the place to see the most dramatic action of the wind. In the desert, winds blow sand into piles called **dunes.** Dunes can grow to a huge size as they move along the desert. Some dunes take on a shape that shows the direction of the wind.

In other cases, all the sand may be blown away from an area by the wind. This process is called **deflation** (dih-FLAY-shun). When all the sand is gone, the desert floor, or **pavement** is visible. Desert pavement is made of many flat rocks that fit snugly together. It actually looks like a stone walkway.

Other obvious marks of wind erosion can be seen on rocks. Wind can toss sand grains as high as a meter above the ground. This wind-blown sand scratches and wears away the nearby rock. The rock may eventually take on a shape similar to the "mushroom rock" in the photograph.

When desert winds blow, they carry the finer sand grains very long distances. These fine grains, called **loess** (LOH-es), may be deposited in huge piles. Some parts of China are covered with many meters of yellowish loess. This loess comes from the Gobi (GOH-bee) Desert. The yellow loess that is deposited in the water gives the Yellow River and Yellow Sea their names.

These sand dunes are in a desert region of Saudi Arabia.

Most of the sand has been blown away from this desert region, leaving the rocky pavement.

These strange formations of rock and soil in Alberta, Canada, were produced by wind erosion. Natives of the area call them "Hoodoos."

To Do Yourself   What Causes a Sandstorm?

You will need

Shoe box, sand, plastic straw, pencil, water, safety glasses

1. Add enough sand to a shoe box to make a layer about 1 centimeter deep.
2. Using a pencil, punch a hole in one end of the shoe box. Insert the straw into the hole.
3. Blow gently through the straw. **Caution: Wear safety glasses. Do not inhale when straw is in the sand.** Observe what happens.
4. Wet the sand slightly and try the activity again.

Both wind and water shape the land. Wind can pick up sand and form dunes. The sand and rock particles carried by the wind can erode other rock.

Questions

1. What happens to dry sand when the wind blows? _____

2. Does wind move wet sand? _____

Review

I. Fill in each blank with the word that fits best. Choose from the words below.

loess   dunes   scratch   deflation   deposit   pavement

The wind shapes the desert sands into _____ . It can also

blow away all the sand, leaving the bare desert _____ . The

blowing sand particles can _____ rocks, giving them

strange shapes. Wind can carry fine particles, called _____ ,
long distances.

II. Circle the underlined word that makes each statement true.

A. Particles of sand are (larger/smaller) than particles of loess.

B. Wind blows away all the sand from an area in a process called
(abrasion/deflation).

C. The finer the grains, the (longer/shorter) the time that they are carried by
the wind.

III. Answer in sentences.

In a sandstorm, a person standing up can see and breathe normally. Why?

_____

_____

_____

What Causes Landslides?

Exploring Science

The Mountain That Walked. Engineers told everyone that the dam was safe—and they were right. But one part of the dam rested on "the mountain that walks." Italians had given Monte Toc this nickname because its rocks and soil moved by themselves. What would happen if the mountain "walked" into the water behind the dam?

On the night of October 9, 1963, Monte Toc began to move. Tons of mud and rock moved down its slopes, forming a landslide. Landslides like this one had given Monte Toc its nickname. But this landslide landed in the water collected behind the dam.

The mass hit the lake with such force that water shot up over the dam and into the river valley below. In the narrow valley, the water picked up speed and started a second landslide. The water pulled rocks and soil from the walls of the narrow gorge and pushed them toward the town below. A wall of water, rocks, and mud sped across the wider river valley below and up the far slope. This second landslide destroyed a town and killed 2600 people. It was all over in just seven minutes.

This accident is considered the worst dam-related disaster of all time. But the dam itself was not involved. The engineers were right, the dam could withstand great pressure without cracking. But the mountain "walked" over the dam and caused the landslide that wiped out the town.

● Do you think that Monte Toc has sides with a gentle slope or a steep one? Why?

Mass Movement and Weathering

A landslide is an example of the sudden movement of rocks and soil down a slope. Any such movement, caused by gravity, is known as **mass movement.**

The steeper the slope, the greater the mass movement. How much mass movement has taken place can be seen at the base of the slope. The pile of broken rock at the bottom of a slope or steep cliff is called **talus** (TAY-lus). Talus can also form when water carries material down a slope.

On gentle slopes, mass movement takes place slowly. If the top layer of soil is loose, it may move downhill inches at a time. This movement is called **creep.** Creep causes a row of fence posts to lean.

How does soil and loose rock form in the first place? They form as a result of **weathering.** Weathering is the breaking down of rock by factors, or agents, in the environment. Water is the most important agent of weathering.

There are two classes of weathering—**mechanical** (muh-KAN-ih-kul) **weathering** and **chemical weathering.** In mechanical weathering,

Talus at the base of the Grand Canyon.

larger pieces of rock are broken into smaller pieces. The rocks do not change. They are just smaller.

In chemical weathering, the rock *does* change. Chemical change is discussed in the next lesson.

One example of mechanical weathering is **frost action.** When water freezes, it expands, or takes up more space. Water gets into tiny cracks and pores in rocks. In cold weather, this water freezes. As it expands, the ice widens the cracks and pores in the rock. If the water freezes and melts several times, the rock may split.

Rocks are usually made up of different minerals. Each mineral in a rock behaves differently. Some minerals expand more than others when heated. Because different minerals act differently, layers of a rock may crack, or split off. This kind of weathering is called **exfoliation** (eks-foh-lee-AY-shun).

The tilt of these headstones in an old cemetery has been caused by soil creep.

To Do Yourself   What Happens When Water Freezes?

You will need:

Plastic container with lid, water, freezer

1. Completely fill the plastic container with water. Put the lid on the container.
2. Place the container in the freezer overnight.
3. Remove the container from the freezer.

When water freezes, it expands. The water that seeps into the cracks of rock freezes when the temperature goes down. The force of the expanding water can widen the cracks. This type of mechanical weathering can change great expanses of rock into crumbly soil.

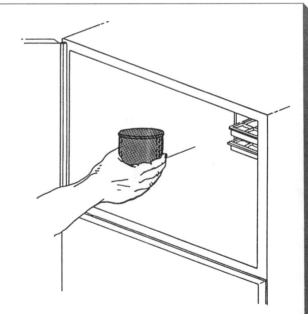

Questions

1. What happens to the container when the water froze? _____

_____

2. How can freezing water break down rock? _____

_____

Even plants and animals can help rocks to weather. Plant roots can spread into tiny cracks of a rock. The pressure of the growing root can cause the rock to split. Animals, even earthworms, dig through soil and soft rock. The holes they leave in the soil expose rock below the surface to the agents of chemical and mechanical weathering.

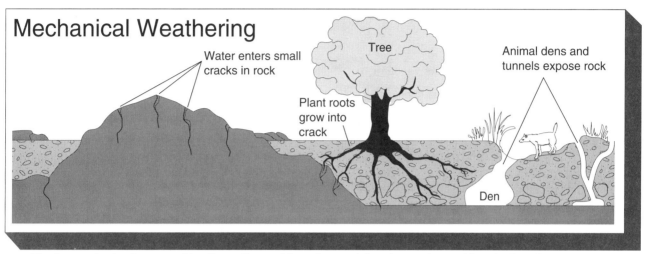

Mechanical Weathering

Water enters small cracks in rock

Tree

Animal dens and tunnels expose rock

Plant roots grow into crack

Den

Rocks can be broken apart by the actions of freezing and thawing water and by plant roots.

Review

I. Fill in each blank with the word that fits best. Choose from the words below.

**creep   smaller pieces   gravity   cracks   talus   sand   water
heat   living things**

The action of _____ , _____ , and

_____ can cause the mechanical weathering of rock. This

process breaks down rock into _____ . A pile of broken

rock at the bottom of a slope is called _____ . This pile

shows that _____ has caused the mass movement of loose
rock.

II. Match each process with evidence that we can see.

	Process		Evidence
_____	1. Creep	a.	Talus at cliff bottom
_____	2. Sudden mass movement of rock	b.	Large rocks break into smaller pieces
_____	3. Mechanical weathering	c.	Bending trees on slope

III. Answer in sentences.

What does *weather* have to do with *weathering?* _____

_____

_____

How Are Caves Formed?

Exploring Science

The River to Hades. For thousands of years, people have known that there is something unusual about the Timavo (TIM-ah-voh) River. The river begins in the mountains of Slovenia. After it flows about 50 kilometers, it vanishes. The ancient Romans said that it became a river in Hades (HAY-deez), the underground world. Today, people believe that the Timavo reappears in Italy.

To prove that the vanishing Slovenian river and the river in Italy are one and the same, an experiment was done. Eels were marked and released into the Timavo River in Slovenia.

Sure enough, some of the marked eels showed up in Italy. The river obviously flows underground. In some places it flows more than 300 meters below the surface.

Since the experiment with the eels, even more of the Timavo River has vanished. Scientists predict that the entire river will disappear someday. Then there will no longer be a river to Hades.

● What kind of rock allows underground rivers to form? Explain your answer.

Chemical Weathering

How does the Timavo River get underground? The answer is weathering. You have learned how water can break up rock. It can freeze and expand in the cracks of a rock. These effects, remember, are part of *mechanical* weathering.

When water contains acids, however, it can break down rock in a different way. Acids can combine with the minerals of rocks. They can change the composition of the rock. The action of an acid or minerals in a rock is an example of **chemical weathering.**

The most dramatic effects of chemical weathering are produced by a weak acid. **Carbonic (kar-BON-ik) acid** is formed when carbon dioxide gas is dissolved in water. Every time you exhale, you add carbon dioxide gas to the air. Volcanic eruptions also contribute carbon dioxide.

Carbon dioxide dissolves in rainwater. The weak carbonic acid that forms finds its way into the groundwater. This acid can completely dissolve the mineral calcite. Limestone is made up almost entirely of calcite. Rainwater, always slightly acidic from carbon dioxide, flows down cracks in limestone and dissolves it. After a very long time, a cave may form. The Timavo River disappears into one of these underground caves.

The limestone "icicles" on the ceiling of this cave are stalactites. When stalactites and stalagmites meet, a column is formed.

Inside a limestone cave, calcite makes some strange and beautiful formations. Water containing calcite drips from the roof of a cave. The water evaporates. Deposits of calcite are left behind. Deposits called **stalactites** (stuh-LAK-tyts) hang from the roof of the cave like icicles. Calcite **stalagmites** (stuh-LAG-myts) rise up from the floor of the cave.

Caves sometimes weaken the ground above them. The roof of the cave may collapse. The ground sinks in, creating a **sinkhole**. If a sinkhole has no outlet, it may fill with water and form a pond or lake.

Another acid that produces chemical weathering is **sulfuric** (sul-FYOOR-ik) **acid.** Sulfuric acid is found in a form of pollution known as **acid rain.** It is the main cause of chemical weathering of marble statues, monuments, and buildings. It can even harm living things.

Acids are not the only cause of chemical weathering. Air is about one-fifth oxygen gas. Oxygen combines with minerals, especially those that contain iron. When iron and oxygen combine, they form a familiar compound—rust. Rust weakens a rock and speeds up its weathering.

This stone monument, called Cleopatra's Needle, shows the effects of chemical weathering.

To Do Yourself   How Can You Tell if a Rock Contains Limestone?

You will need:

Rock samples, medicine dropper, vinegar (or lemon juice), newspaper

1. Cover your work surface with newspaper.
2. Place your rock samples on the newspaper.
3. Using the medicine dropper, place a few drops of vinegar (or lemon juice) on each rock sample. Observe the results.

Rocks that contain limestone will bubble when the vinegar (or lemon juice) touches them. The vinegar (or lemon juice) reacts with calcium carbonate and releases carbon dioxide gas.

Questions

1. Did any of your rock samples bubble when vinegar (or lemon juice) was dropped on them? What did the test tell you about the samples? _____

_____

2. How are caves formed in limestone rock? _____

_____

Review

I. Fill in each blank with the word that fits best. Choose from the words below.

dissolved   caves   limestone   acid   carbonic   oxygen

In a common type of chemical weathering, minerals are _____ by

acids. _____ acid dissolves calcite, a mineral in the rock

_____. This process forms underground openings in rocks called

_____. Sulfuric acid is the cause of _____ rain.

II. Match the terms in column **A** with their descriptions in column **B**.

A	B
_____1. stalagmite	**a.** sunken area above a cave
_____2. sulfuric acid	**b.** combines with minerals and forms rust
_____3. sinkhole	**c.** found in acid rain
_____4. oxygen	**d.** deposit of calcite in a cave

III. Answer in sentences.

The chemical weathering of some rocks turns them a dull red. What process causes this type of weathering.

_____

_____

_____

Where Does Soil Come From?

Exploring Science

Soil Making. One day, the express mail brought Sally a package. Opening it she found a long instruction book, a wooden box that needed to be put together, a quart of what appeared to be dirt, and a cardboard carton filled with a hundred or so small, wiggly red worms. Sally was delighted. "Just what I wanted!" she cried.

Following the instructions, Sally put the box together and filled it with torn-up strips of newspaper, which she sprinkled with water. Then she poured the "dirt"—really, worm food—over the dampened paper strips. Finally, she put the worms in the box.

She kept the box in her kitchen. Every day Sally put coffee grounds, peels, egg shells, carrot scrapings, damaged lettuce leaves, and other plant waste into the box, along with enough water to keep everything damp, but not wet. The number of worms multiplied and the "garbage" quickly disappeared. In its place, the box became filled with a light brown material that smelled like fresh soil, not like decaying garbage. Sally, and her worms, were making soil.

After a few months, Sally emptied the box into a rough-mesh sifter and shook what went through the mesh into her garden. Anything that did not go through the sifter, including many worms, went back into the box. Sally was ready to start making her second batch of soil.

● What do you think happened to the "garbage" in the box? Why?

Soil

Clay and sand are particles found in **soil**. Soil is made of weathered rock and the decayed remains of living things, like the "garbage" in Sally's box. Soil differs from place to place, but it is a precious natural resource everywhere.

Sandy soil has fairly large particles through which water passes quickly. Soil containing clay holds water, forming thick mud. Soil with some clay and some sand is called **loam** (LOME). Loam is usually the best soil for farming. Decaying plants and animals make loam an even better soil for farming.

Imagine slicing through the earth's crust as you would through a layer cake. The icing on the cake is like the top layer of soil, the rich, dark **topsoil**. In topsoil, decay bacteria and worms have broken down the remains of plants and animals into **humus** (HYOO-muhs).

Beneath the topsoil is the **subsoil**. This layer may have more clay materials than the topsoil. It is generally lighter in color. Below the subsoil is a mixture of soil and rock. The lowest layer is the solid **bedrock**.

The most important factor in determining what kind of soil an area has is climate. In hot, humid areas, soil forms quickly. Frequent rainfalls wash, or **leach,** soil minerals into lower layers.

In areas like the American west, there is little rainfall. Many of the minerals remain in the upper layer of soil. These dry areas, therefore, usually have fertile soil.

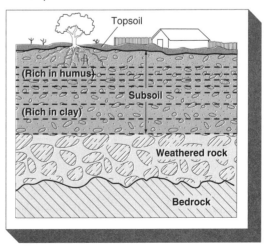

To Do Yourself   What Is Soil Made of?

You will need:

Soil samples, white paper, magnifying glass, plastic bags or small cups

1. Collect samples of soil from different places near your home or school. Place the samples in a plastic bag or cup.
2. Spread each sample out on a sheet of white paper.
3. Use the magnifying glass to examine each sample.

Questions

1. What did you find in the soil samples?

_____

2. Are all the samples the same? _____If not, what made the

difference? _____
3. What part of soil do you think is most important for growing plants? Explain.

_____

Review

I. Fill in each blank with the word that fits best. Choose from the words below.

subsoil   rock   leached   living things   loam   humus

Soil is formed from weathered _____ and the remains of

_____. The best soil for farming is usually _____

with lots of _____. Soil that forms where there is much rainfall

tends to be _____.

II. Match the terms in column **A** with their descriptions in column **B**.

A	B
_____1. subsoil	a. decaying plants and animals
_____2. humus	b. layer beneath all soil
_____3. bedrock	c. half sand, half clay
_____4. clay	d. layer below topsoil
_____5. loam	e. has small particles

What Are Glaciers?

Exploring Science

In the Deep Freeze. On September 19, 1991 a pair of German hikers, Helmut and Erika Simon, on the Smilaun Glacier of the Tyrolean Alps discovered the frozen and mummified remains of a body that had apparently been trapped in the ice for more than 5000 years. The age of the body was not clear at first. It had to be hacked out of the ice with ski poles and ice picks by mountain climbers and people searching for evidence of foul play. The elevation was about 3210 meters. Newspapers in the U.S. soon dubbed the remains the "Iceman."

Scientists believe the Iceman was probably taking cattle to the mountains to graze one fall day about 5000 years ago. He broke his bow and went up the mountain to cut a new one and some new arrows. A sudden storm trapped him. He hid in a crack in the rocks and ate some meat and berries he brought with him. The snow continued and covered his hiding place. He froze to death.

The snow kept piling up. It did not melt the next summer. The Iceman became frozen into the Smilaun glacier, where he stayed until he was found.

● Why was the Iceman found at the end of summer?

Glaciers

A glacier, remember, is a moving mass of ice. Glaciers form wherever more snow falls each winter than melts in the summer. Snow builds up year after year. The top layers press down, turning the lower layers to ice. Snow cannot flow, but ice that is under pressure can. When the mass of ice becomes heavy enough, gravity moves it downhill. A glacier is on the move.

All parts of a glacier do not move at the same speed. The center moves faster than the sides. The parts that touch the valley walls move more slowly. This uneven movement causes the brittle surface of the glacier to crack. These cracks are known as **crevasses**.

Glaciers move forward, or advance, in the winter. In the summer, they "retreat," that is, they melt at their forward edge. The Smiluan glacier was in its summer retreat when the Iceman was discovered. The Smiluan glacier is an example of a **valley glacier**. These glaciers form in the valleys of high mountains.

Glaciers near the North and South Poles are much larger than valley glaciers. Near the poles it is below freezing most of the year. The snow never melts completely. Most of Greenland and Antarctica are covered by huge **continental**

This close-up view of a valley glacier on the slopes of Mount Hood, in Oregon, shows the many cracks and crevasses in its surface.

glaciers, or **ice sheets.** These ice sheets cover millions of square kilometers of land. And the ice is thousands of meters thick!

Many glaciers end at or near the ocean. When a glacier moves forward into the ocean, large chunks of ice break off and fall into the water. These pieces of floating ice are called **icebergs.**

This large chunk of ice is only the "tip of the iceberg." Most of the iceberg is hidden below the surface of the water.

Review

I. Fill in each blank with the word that fits best. Choose from the words below.

moves forward   valley   retreats   pressure   continental   gravity

In high mountains, a _____ glacier may form.

_____ changes snow layers to ice and _____

causes them to flow. A glacier _____ during the winter and

_____ in the summer.

II. Circle the underlined word that makes each statement true.

A. Greenland and Antarctica are covered by (valley/continental) glaciers.

B. Glaciers that end in the sea form (ice sheets/icebergs).

C. In the summer, a glacier (retreats/moves downhill).

III. Answer in sentences.

Describe the conditions needed for a glacier to form.

_____

_____

_____

How Do Glaciers Change the Earth?

Exploring Science

The Birth of Another Island. Do you remember Surtsey, the island that was born in fire? Here is the story of another island, one that was born in ice. In some ways, it's birth is as strange as that of Surtsey, but the island itself may be a lot more familiar.

Hundreds of thousands of years ago, giant glaciers moved south from regions that are now part of Canada. During those Ice Ages, glaciers advanced and retreated several times. Each time the glaciers advanced, they picked up rock and soil. The rock and soil, frozen into the lower layers of ice, was carried along by the glaciers. When they retreated, the glaciers left behind the rock and soil they had carried. The largest piles were left at the southern edges of the glaciers.

Along the east coast of the U.S., glaciers reached as far south as what is now New York City. As the front edge of the glaciers melted, a pile of material about 200 kilometers long was deposited. Today, that soil and rock is some of the most valuable real estate in the United States. It is Long Island, an island born in ice.

● What type of glacier do you think produced Long Island?

Long Island, New York, is about 193 kilometers long and as much as 37 kilometers wide. This large area of land is a terminal moraine, left behind by a huge contental glacier that once covered much of northern North America.

The Effects of a Glacier

If you live in the northern part of the United States, continental glaciers probably once covered your area. As the climate warmed up, the glaciers melted and retreated toward the north.

The land still shows evidence of its once icy covering. Glaciers carried huge boulders that scratched and eroded the rocks beneath. The heavy ice scooped out deep depressions in the land and formed lakes. Glaciers moved through valleys, making them deeper and wider and giving them a U-shape.

As a glacier moves, it picks up rocks and soil. These materials are deposited when the glacier melts. The material dropped by a melting glacier is called **till.** Till can produce different formations.

Piles or ridges of till are called **moraines** (muh-RAYNS). The largest deposits, called **terminal moraines** are left where the leading edge of the glacier stopped. Long Island is a terminal moraine.

Groups of low hills called **drumlins** (DRUM-lins) are also left by retreating glaciers. Drumlins are shaped like upside-down canoes. They point in the direction that the glacier moved.

Water from a melting glacier may form streams inside the glacier itself. The streams pick up till as they flow. When the glacier melts, till is deposited in the winding shape of the stream. These snaking hills are called **eskers** (ES-kers).

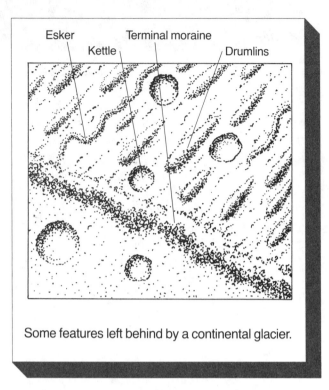

Some features left behind by a continental glacier.

Chunks of ice sometimes break off the glaciers. The ice becomes covered with till. When the ice melts, the till collapses, forming a large hole called a **kettle.** Kettles usually fill with water to form lakes.

Drumlins, eskers and kettles are features of a land once covered by ice. They give the land a rolling appearance.

Glacial till. The ridge of rock and soil in the lower right of the picture is lateral (side) moraine left at the edge of the glacier as it melted.

To Do Yourself   How Do Glaciers Cause Kettles?

You will need:

Pie pan, soil, ice cube

1. Fill the pie pan with soil.
2. Press an ice cube firmly into the soil.
3. Let the ice cube melt.

   Kettle lakes are features left behind by retreating glaciers. Lake Ronkonkoma, the largest lake on Long Island, is a kettle lake.

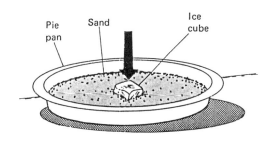

Questions

1. What happened in the soil when the ice melted? _____

2. How is your model like a real kettle lake? _____

Review

I. Fill in each blank with the word that fits best. Choose from the words below.

erode   till   moraine   retreated   advanced   drumlins   kettles   terminal

During the Ice Ages, glaciers _____ and _____

several times. Glaciers produce many changes in the land: the rocks they carry

can _____ other rocks; they leave behind deposits of rock and

gravel called _____. A deposit left by the edge of a melting glacier

is a _____. Low hills that point in the direction of the glacier's

movement are called _____.

II. Match each feature in column A with its description in column B.

A	B
_____ **1.** moraine	**a.** glaciated river valley.
_____ **2.** eskers	**b.** hole made by glacial ice
_____ **3.** U-shaped valley	**c.** low, winding hills
_____ **4.** kettle	**d.** ridge of deposited till

III. Answer in sentences.

Glaciers are often called "rivers of ice." How are glaciers like rivers? How are they different?

Review What You Know

A. In the blanks, write in the words that fit each definition. Then use the numbered letters to spell out the answer to the riddle below.

1. Line of material left by a glacier.
2. The mechanical and chemical breakdown of rock.
3. Curve in an old river.
4. The end of a river.
5. The decayed remains of living things found in soil.
6. Slow movement of soil down a slope.
7. Water from snow or rain.
8. Sand blown into a pile.
9. Fan-shaped deposit at the end of a river.
10. Thick mass of ice.
11. Top layer of soil.
12. Wearing down and carrying away of land.
13. A wave that has toppled over.
14. Pile of rocks left by glaciers.
15. Horizontal movement of water.

1. __ __ __ __ __ __
                     8

2. __ __ __ __ __ __ __ __ __ __
   4   18

3. __ __ __ __ __ __ __
      13

4. __ __ __ __ __
      23   6

5. __ __ __ __ __
   12

6. __ __ __ __ __
         22

7. __ __ __ __ __ __
            7   11

8. __ __ __ __
         10

9. __ __ __ __ __
   15   3

10. __ __ __ __ __ __ __
    5   19

11. __ __ __ __ __ __
    1   13

12. __ __ __ __ __ __
            16   9

13. __ __ __ __ __ __ __
    14

14. __ __ __ __
    2

15. __ __ __ __ __ __
    20   21

Riddle: When is a river lazy?

Answer: $\underline{\hphantom{x}}$ $\underline{\hphantom{x}}$ $\underline{\hphantom{x}}$ $\underline{\hphantom{x}}$ $\underline{\hphantom{x}}$ $\underline{\hphantom{x}}$ $\underline{\hphantom{x}}$ $\underline{\hphantom{x}}$ $\underline{\hphantom{x}}$ $\underline{\hphantom{x}}$
  4   12   21   8   19   1   4   23   10   2

$\underline{\hphantom{x}}$ $\underline{\hphantom{x}}$ $\underline{\hphantom{x}}$ $\underline{\hphantom{x}}$ $\underline{\hphantom{x}}$ $\underline{\hphantom{x}}$ $\underline{\hphantom{x}}$ $\underline{\hphantom{x}}$ $\underline{\hphantom{x}}$ $\underline{\hphantom{x}}$ $\underline{\hphantom{x}}$ $\underline{\hphantom{x}}$ $\underline{\hphantom{x}}$ $\underline{\hphantom{x}}$.
  5   17   3   7   20   18   9   11   13   6   16   14   22   15

B. Write the word (or words) that best completes each statement.

1. _____ Water causes a great deal of erosion when it is
   a. still **b.** moving **c.** deep

2. _____ The valley of a young river is usually **a.** wide
   b. U-shaped **c.** V-shaped

3. _____ A river delta is made of **a.** sediment **b.** talus
   c. loess

4. _____ A longshore current can make a beach
   a. shorter **b.** longer **c.** higher

5. _____ When a wave can no longer complete its full
   motion, it forms a **a.** breaker **b.** sandbar **c.** hook

6. _____ A large sandbar may become a(n) **a.** ox-bow
   lake **b.** lagoon **c.** barrier island

7. _____ The calm water between a barrier island and the
   shore is a **a.** barrier beach **b.** hook **c.** lagoon

8. _____ If the wind blows sand off a desert floor, the
   feature that becomes visible is called **a.** dune **b.** pavement **c.** terminal
   moraine

9. _____ A soil that contains both clay and sand is
   a. loam **b.** loess **c.** humus

10. _____ The movement of rock and soil by gravity is
    called **a.** talus **b.** terminal moraine **c.** mass movement.

11. _____ Two agents of chemical weathering are **a.** heat
    and cold **b.** acids and oxygen **c.** heat and water

12. _____ Soil that forms in an area where there is little
    rainfall tends to be **a.** more fertile **b.** all humus **c.** all clay

13. _____ Pieces of a glacier that fall into the ocean are
    called **a.** kettles **b.** icebergs **c.** caverns

14. _____ A feature not made by a glacier is a(n)
    a. drumlin **b.** esker **c.** stalagmite

15. _____ Underground caverns are most likely to form in
    areas where the bedrock is **a.** granite **b.** lava **c.** limestone

C. Apply what you know.

Label the parts of the diagram below. Then answer the questions.

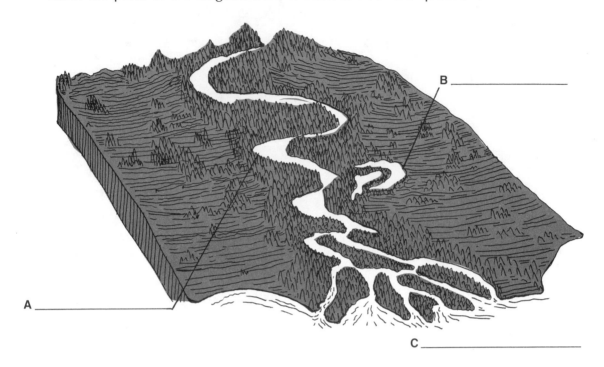

B _____

A _____

C _____

a. At what stage of its life is the river in the diagram?

_____

b. What are some of the ways in which water causes the erosion of a river

bed?_____

D. Find Out More

1. Use plaster of Paris and paint to make a model of an old river valley. What are the features of an old river? Display your model in the classroom.
2. Many river deltas have been photographed by satellites in space. Find pictures of the deltas of the Nile River and the Mississippi River. How are the deltas similar? How are they different?
3. What happens when a river overflows its banks? Do some research about the harmful and helpful effects of this overflowing.
4. Surfers are always looking for the perfect wave. What kinds of conditions produce waves that are good for surfing? Do some research about where the best places for surfing are and what conditions make these places so good.
5. Mammoth Caves, Kentucky, the Luray Caverns, Virginia, and Carlsbad Caverns, New Mexico, are three well-known cave sites in the United States. Find out more about one of these unusual places. What are some of the unusual formations found there?
6. Take a soil sample near your home or school. You may be able to have it tested by your local agricultural agent or at a nearby college. Find out what its mineral content is and how fertile it is.

Summing Up
Review What You Have Learned So Far

A. Identify each diagram. Choose from the terms below.

cave   moraine   mid-ocean ridge   trench   fault   breaker   crystal
soil layers

1_____

2_____

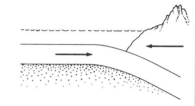

3_____

4_____

5_____

6_____

7_____

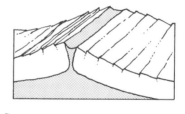

8_____

B. Circle the underlined word that makes each statement true.

1. Rocks that have been changed by heat and pressure are (igneous/metamorphic).
2. The large supercontinent from which present continents came is called (Pangaea/Himalaya).
3. The earth's crust is made of over 2000 (elements/minerals).
4. The element that combines with silicon to form quartz is (hydrogen/oxygen).
5. The repeating pattern of atoms produces (luster/crystal).
6. The mineral mica splits into thin sheets. This property is an example of (cleavage/fracture).
7. Mineral crystals formed below the earth's surface are usually (small/large).
8. The continents are made mostly of (granite/basalt).
9. Volcanoes and earthquakes often occur near (plate boundaries/barrier islands).
10. A characteristic that helps identify a mineral is (size/hardness).

141

UNIT

6

THE OCEANS

What Have We Learned About Oceans?

Exploring Science

The Challenger Voyage. One of the most famous voyages in science was sailed by the exploring ship, the *H.M.S. Challenger*. This British ship was sent around the world in 1872. It helped people learn about huge spaces that had never been explored before. Those huge spaces were the oceans.

In 1872, people did not know the answers to such questions as "How deep is the ocean?" "Do fish live on the ocean floor?" or even "Why is the sea salty?"

The voyage of the *Challenger* gave the first true picture of the depths of the oceans. Scientists put weighted nets over the side of the *Challenger*. These nets were used to collect samples from the ocean floor. The scientists kept records of the depth and temperature of the water. They also studied the ocean currents.

The *Challenger* traveled for over three years. It returned to Britain with a collection of plants and animals, with samples of the ocean floor, and with bottles of seawater.

The scientists aboard the *H.M.S. Challenger* were pioneers. Since that voyage, many other scientific voyages have added to our knowledge of the oceans often drilling into the crust beneath them.

● In Unit 1 you learned about the skills used by scientists. Which of these skills did scientists on *H. M. S. Challenger* use?

Over 100 years ago, the *H.M.S. Challenger* sailed the world's oceans in search of facts about those vast, largely unexplored regions of our planet.

The Making of the Ocean

Oceanography (oh-shee-uh-NOG-ruh-fee), the study of the oceans, is a young science. Only since the voyage of the *H. M. S. Challenger* in the 1870's have the oceans been studied in great detail by scientists. Much has been learned about the oceans since that first voyage. For one thing, scientists have changed their minds about how the oceans formed.

The older idea of how the oceans formed was based on the idea that the earth was originally very hot. While earth cooled, light elements were pushed upwards, forming a hot atmosphere that included water vapor among the gases. When earth cooled enough, the water vapor became liquid rain. Low places on earth's surface became the oceans.

Today scientists think that earth formed from cool smaller bodies; although they produced melting heat when they collided. Earth also contained more radioactive elements early in its history. These elements provided enough heat to melt the planet, leading to what geologists call the "Big Burp." At that time, gases were released and the first oceans formed from rain. Since then, however, ocean water has been steadily lost as it combines with iron or other elements to form compounds. But volcanoes have brought new water to the surface, replacing the amounts lost. If replacement water were not released as water vapor by the volcanoes, the oceans would become much smaller and perhaps dry up completely.

Ocean basins are more than just low places on the crust. Oceans occur because geologic processes make new crust at rift valleys. The crust is hot and thick near the rift valleys, making long ridges. As the crust is pushed away from the ridges, it cools and becomes thinner. Continents are mostly older crust that has piled up away from the ridges, so they are thicker. The thin new crust becomes the floor of an ocean.

	Old Ideas About the Ocean	**Present Ideas About the Ocean**
Origin	Rain formed as the earth cooled, filling low-lying areas.	Volcanoes released the water trapped in rock. This water filled low-lying areas.
Age	The floor of the ocean is the same age as the continents—about 4.5 billion years old.	The oldest known part of any ocean floor is only about 200 million years old.
Nature of Floor	The floor of the ocean is like the continents, only lower. Also, the deep floor is very flat.	The crust under the ocean is much thinner than the crust under the continents. Also, it is made of different minerals. Earth's tallest mountains are located on the deep ocean floor.
Stability	Shallow seas may be formed by land rising or sinking, but the deep ocean is a permanent feature of the earth.	New ocean floor is constantly forming at mid-ocean ridges. Old ocean floor is disappearing at the edges of crustal plates. Trenches form where the floor is sliding below the plate.

Review

I. Fill in each blank with the word that fits best. Choose from the words below.

**wrong   the same as   4.5 billion   right   200 million   different from
oceanography**

The science of _____ is a little more than 100 years old. During that time, we have learned that most of the early beliefs about the

oceans were _____ . Today we know that the floor of the

ocean is not older than _____ years. In many ways, the

oceans are _____ than the continents.

II. Tell whether each statement is an old (**O**) or a new (**N**) idea about the oceans.

A. _____ The floor of the deep ocean does not change.

B. _____ There are very tall mountains under the sea.

C. _____ Parts of the ocean floor are sinking, and great trenches are forming.

D. _____ Most ocean water came from the original atmosphere of the earth.

III. Answer in sentences.

A few hundred years ago, it was common to believe in mermaids and giant sea monsters. Why?

_____

_____

_____

What Are Currents?

Exploring Science

The River in the Sea. Within the Atlantic Ocean, there flows a great river. This river contains five times as much water as all the land rivers of the world combined. This river in the sea is called the **Gulf Stream.**

The Gulf Stream is 50 kilometers wide. It flows at more than 5 kilometers per hour. Because the water in this river is usually a different color than that of the ocean, the Gulf Stream stands out clearly. The water in the Gulf Stream is much warmer than the surrounding water. Many fish and other creatures that live in warm water travel in the Gulf Stream.

The Gulf Stream flows north along the eastern coast of the United States. Just south of Cape Cod, in Massachusetts, it swings to the east and crosses the Atlantic Ocean. Ships sailing from the United States to Europe, travel in the Gulf Stream. Aided by the current, they cross the Atlantic Ocean much faster than if they had taken a shorter route. On the return trip, ships stay out of the Gulf Stream. Sailing westward in the Gulf Stream would be like trying to paddle a canoe upriver.

● Labrador and the British Isles are about the same distance north of the equator. However, winters in Labrador are much colder than winters along the British coast. Why?

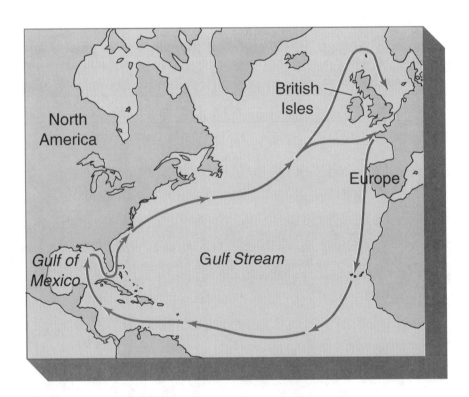

Waves, Tides, and Currents

There are many "rivers" similar to the Gulf Stream flowing in the oceans of the world. The flow of these rivers is just one of several different kinds of movement of ocean water. Some other regular motions of ocean waters include waves, tides, and currents.

WAVES. Recall from the lesson on beach erosion (page 116) waves are circular movements of water. The movement of water as a wave is usually started by strong winds. Particles of water receive some of the wind's energy and change it into energy of their own. As the diagram shows, water particles in a wave move in a circle. Some of the energy of these particles is passed on to nearby water particles. These nearby particles also start to move in a circle, forming another wave.

Once waves start to move, they travel long distances across the ocean. Waves that reach shore on a calm day were probably started by strong winds hundreds of kilometers away. Not all waves are caused by wind. Waves can be caused by earth movements, such as earthquakes and volcanoes.

TIDES. The waters of the ocean move up and down twice a day. These motions are called tides. Tides are mainly caused by the moon. The moon exerts an attraction, or pull, on the earth and its waters. You will learn more about tides when you study the moon.

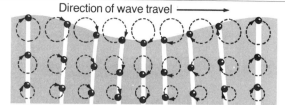

Direction of wave travel ⟶

HOW WATER WAVES TRAVEL

Water particles (black dots) move in circles, giving the wave an up-and-down motion that travels forward. The wave moves through the water; the water particles stay in their "orbits."

CURRENTS. "Rivers" in the ocean, such as the Gulf Stream, are called currents. Ocean currents are caused by **planetary** (PLAN-ih-ter-ee) winds. Planetary winds are huge belts of wind that blow steadily in the same direction all the time. These winds are not the same as the local winds that cause waves.

In the next lesson you will learn more about ocean currents and how they move.

To Do Yourself   **How Does the Rotation of the Earth Affect Ocean Currents?**

You will need:

A globe, washable paint, disposable container (or newspapers)

1. Set up the globe in a disposable container. Or place it on a washable surface covered with newspaper.
2. Pour a little paint on the top of the globe. Observe the path of the paint in the Northern and Southern Hemispheres.
3. Clean the globe. Pour paint on the top of the globe again. This time, spin the globe slowly from west to east (counterclockwise). Make a record of the path of the paint in both hemispheres.

Questions

1. How does the paint move when the globe is still? _____

2. What is the path of the paint when the globe is spinning? _____

_____

3. What effect does the earth's rotation have on the ocean currents? _____

_____

Review

I. Fill in each blank with the word that fits best. Choose from the words below.

tsunamis   waves   tides   winds   currents   landslides

Most of the movement of water in the oceans is caused by

_____ . Ordinary _____ are caused by
storms at sea. Winds that blow from the same direction almost all the time

produce _____ in the sea. _____ are
caused by the attraction of the moon.

II. Match each term in column **A** with its description in column **B**.

A	B
1. _____ currents	**a.** Water moves up and down every few seconds.
2. _____ tides	**b.** Water moves up and down twice a day.
3. _____ tsunamis	**c.** Water moves in the same direction for a great distance.
4. _____ waves	**d.** Water is set in motion by earthquakes.

III. Answer in sentences.

The waves on a beach are unusually large all day. Explain what might produce
large waves for such a long period of time.

_____

_____

_____

Lesson Three

What Causes Ocean Currents?

Exploring Science

A Problem Child. The **Peru Current** flows up the west coast of South America. This current is very cold. Penguins have followed this current north from Antarctica. They now live on islands near the equator. Many fish that live in cold water are found in the Peru Current. The penguins feed on these fish.

In some years, a warm current called El Niño (The Child) also comes to the west coast. When this happens, many fish swim deeper, looking for the cold water they prefer. Some fish move to another part of the ocean. Some die from the change in water temperature. The birds and sea mammals that eat the fish must also leave—or starve.

Until recently, it was thought that El Niño affected only the coast of South America. In 1982, however, the situation changed. El Niño arrived in July—six months earlier than usual. It stayed until late in 1983. During that time, El Niño changed the weather around the world.

India and Australia suffered great droughts, while California had floods. Many ocean species were lost because of changes in the temperature of the water.

Scientists learned during El Niño what the cause of the change was. The temperature in the southern Pacific is warmer than normal. The high temperature expands the sea water, making this part of the ocean higher than the edges. Warm water begins to flow "downhill" toward the edges. The Peru Current is at the eastern edge of the southern Pacific, so it gets a big dose of warm water. Warm water is lighter than cold water, so the water from the middle of the ocean flows over the current. An El Niño is born.

● Which seems more likely to be true?

A. Penguins could not live near the equator without the Peru Current.

B. Penguins could live near the equator without the Peru Current.

These South American penguins depend on the Peru Current for their food supply.

149

Currents: Above and Below

You have learned that ocean currents are started by winds that tend to blow in the same direction all year. But the water does not follow the direction of winds very far. The rotation of the earth turns the currents. It causes them to move in a circular pattern.

Find the South Pacific on the map. Winds blow from east to west along the equator. They start a current in the warm water of the Pacific, south of the equator. The current moves in the same direction as the wind—from east to west. Then, the force of the earth's rotation causes the current to turn left, or south, as it reaches Asia and Australia. When the current reaches Antarctica, it turns left again, toward the east. As the current moves through the Antarctic, it be-comes cold. Finally, the current turns left again, carrying cold water north as the Humbolt Current.

Look at the map again. Notice that most surface currents start near the equator. They move west along the equator, then begin to turn. In northern oceans, the currents turn right, in a **clockwise** circle. That is, they move in the same direction as the hands on a clock. In southern oceans, currents move left, or **counterclockwise,** in the opposite direction of the hands on a clock.

So far, you have been reading about surface currents. Far below the surface of the sea, there are other currents. These currents are caused by differences in density. **Density** (DEN-sih-tee)

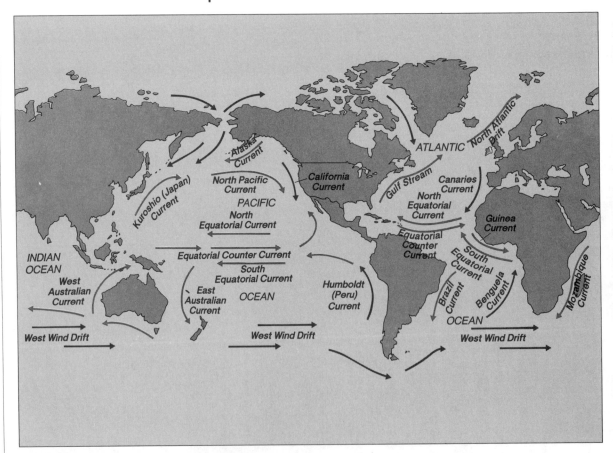

Important Ocean Currents

Black arrows show cold ocean currents.
Colored arrows show warm ocean currents.

is the amount of matter in a given space. Cold water is denser than warm water. Salty water is denser than fresh water. This means that a bottle filled with salty water will weigh more than a bottle the same size filled with fresh water.

Ocean water near the poles is much saltier than sea water near the equator. When water freezes, the ice is fresh water and all the salt stays behind in the liquid water. Water near the poles is not only salty, but also cold. This cold, salty water is so dense that it sinks to the bottom. Warmer, less salty water moves toward the poles to take its place. The cold, salty water spreads away from the poles, forming undersea currents called *density* currents.

Evaporation is another process that takes fresh water away—in the form of vapor—and leaves salty water behind. If warm sunlight causes evaporation near the surface, the salty water will sink and form a density current. The most amazing of these currents flows out of the Mediterranean Sea past the Rock of Gibraltar, and sinks to the bottom of the North Atlantic. There is a giant underwater waterfall where the salty water flows out of the Mediterranean.

The Mediterranean region is famous for its warm, sunny weather. Few rivers flow into the sea to freshen up the water that is left after evaporation. Thus Mediterranean water becomes very salty. People swimming in the Mediterranean notice the dense water makes it easier to float than in the waters of the Atlantic. Even though the water is warm, it is so salty that it is dense enough to flow across the bottom of the Atlantic.

Will all the water eventually flow out of the Mediterranean? No. When a current flows in one direction, a second current flows in the opposite direction. The second current replaces the water carried away by the first current. This second current is called a **countercurrent**. The undersea current that flows out of the Mediterranean has a countercurrent flowing above it. This countercurrent flows from the Atlantic Ocean into the Mediterranean. Every surface current, such as the Gulf Stream, has a countercurrent flowing beneath it.

To Do Yourself   How Does a Difference in Density Produce Currents?

You will need:

Large jar, small jar, funnel, food coloring, water, salt

1. Fill the small jar with water. Add as much salt as needed to dissolve a few drops of food coloring.
2. Add water to the large jar until it is about half-full.
3. Use the funnel and carefully pour the dyed salt water very slowly into the large jar. Observe the results.

Dyed Salt Water

Questions

1. Which is more dense, salt water or fresh water? How do you know? _____

   _____

2. What happens when salt water and fresh water meet? _____

   _____

3. How could you change the activity to test what happens when warm water meets cold water? _____

Review

I. Fill in each space with the word that fits best. Choose from the words below.

denser   **counterclockwise**   **clockwise**   **turn**   **start**   **warmer**
Mediterranean Sea   **Arctic Ocean**   **Gulf of Mexico**

The rotation of the earth makes currents _____ . In

northern oceans, currents move in a _____ direction.

Currents under the sea are caused by water that is _____
than the water through which they move. One undersea current in the

Atlantic Ocean starts in the _____ because of evaporation.

A current that started in the _____ as a surface current
would sink when it reached warm water.

II. Decide what type of current is described in each statement. Choose from the following: Undersea currents (**U**), surface currents (**S**), or both (**B**).

A. _____ It moves over great distances.

B. _____ It is started by the winds.

C. _____ It is caused by differences in density.

D. _____ It has a countercurrent.

III. Answer in sentences.

The Gulf Stream is turned to the east by the force of the earth's rotation. In which direction is its countercurrent turned?

_____

_____

_____

What Is the Ocean Floor Like?

Exploring Science

Skiing Up a Volcano. *Alvin,* a tiny undersea vessel, was off on another trip to the ocean floor. Its mission was to explore a seamount in the North Atlantic, off the coast of New England. The seamount was an old volcano. Its top was 2,000 meters below the surface of the ocean.

Fifteen minutes after the dive began, *Alvin* was surrounded by blackness. The lights inside the vessel attracted a swordfish. The pilot, Larry Shumaker, quickly turned off the lights. He had learned that swordfish would attack *Alvin* if the lights were left on.

Finally, *Alvin* settled onto the ocean bottom. Using its skis, *Alvin* could easily move along the ocean floor. It could even climb the slope of the seamount. At the top, Larry used *Alvin's* mechanical arm to scrape away a black coating from the seamount. The seamount was made of coral, the skeletons of tiny animals that once lived on the seamount.

After gathering some of the coral, *Alvin* returned to a ship waiting on the surface. Another mission had been completed.

● Coral needs light to grow. But no light reaches a depth of 2,000 meters in the ocean. How did coral grow on the top of the seamount?

The *Alvin* preparing for another "sight-seeing" tour of the ocean depths.

The Floor of the Sea

Long ago, sailors believed that the ocean had no bottom. Today, because of electronic devices and vessels like the *Alvin,* we have accurate maps of much of the ocean bottom. On that bottom are plains, mountain ranges, volcanoes, and plateaus. In some ways, these features are very different from similar features on land.

On land, plains are flat, quiet areas. Ocean plains, 4 or 5 kilometers below the water's surface, are also very flat. But scattered over these plains are the remains of volcanoes. Most of these old volcanoes are **seamounts**—mountains that do not reach the surface. In the past, the seamount rose above the water's surface. But erosion made the top flat.

At the edges of the deep plain, the sea bottom rises rapidly. This rise is the **continental slope.** The top of the continental slope gently rises up to the continents. This area is the **continental shelf.** There is nothing on land to match the sharp rise from a deep plain to the continental shelf, less than ¼ kilometer below the surface of the ocean.

Another important feature of the ocean floor is the **mid-ocean-ridge.** This is the world's largest mountain range. But it has not formed in the same way as the mountain ranges on land. The mid-ocean-ridge has formed at places where tectonic plates are moving apart. Most undersea earthquakes occur along the mid-ocean-ridge.

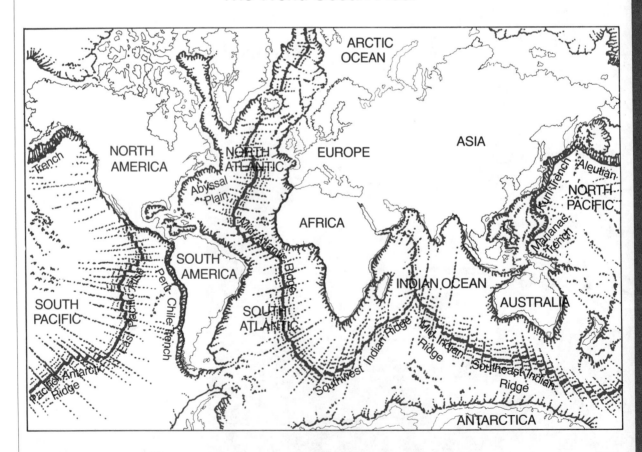

The World Ocean Floor

To Do Yourself

How Can We Use Sound to Find the Depth of the Ocean?

You will need:

Pencil and paper

Sound travels through water at about 1400 meters per second. When sound hits an object, like a wall or the ocean floor, it bounces back. We can use these facts to find the depth of the ocean.

Suppose a sound is sent to the bottom of the ocean. It returns 1 second later. Then the depth of the ocean at that point is 700 meters. It took the sound 1 second to make a "round trip." Therefore, it took ½ second to reach the bottom and ½ second to return. By multiplying the time of the one-way trip by the speed of sound in water, the distance that the sound traveled can be found.

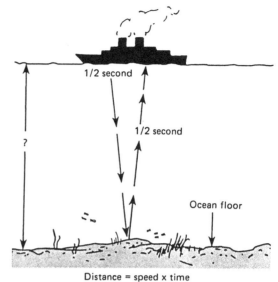

Distance = speed x time

Distance = 1400 meters per second
x 1/2 second

Distance = 700 meters

Questions

1. Suppose you were searching the ocean for buried treasure. At the site of the treasure, you send down a sound wave. It returns ½ second later. How deep is the treasure? _____

Review

I. Circle the underlined word that makes each statement true.

A. Plains in the sea show the remains of many (volcanoes/earthquakes).

B. The world's largest mountain range is the (continental shelf/mid-ocean-ridge).

C. Undersea earthquakes occur at (seamounts/the mid-ocean-ridge).

D. The mid-ocean-ridge was formed where tectonic plates (pushed together/moved apart).

E. The continental slope rises sharply from the (deep plains/continental shelf).

II. Answer in sentences.

What are seamounts? Why do many seamounts have flat tops?

_____

_____

_____

What Are Undersea Canyons?

Exploring Science

The Power of Rock. The Grand Canyon, formed by the Colorado River, is famous. Near New York City there is a canyon almost as large. The Hudson River Canyon is 3 kilometers deep and 300 kilometers long. It is not as well known as the Grand Canyon, however, because it is under the sea.

When the Hudson River Canyon was discovered, no one knew how it had formed. It was too deep to have been formed by the Hudson River. In 1929, a clue was found. An earthquake occurred near Newfoundland. Large amounts of sediment slid down the continental slope. As the sediment fell, it mixed with water. The force of this mixture was tremendous. It broke telegraph cables on the floor of the Atlantic Ocean. One of the broken cables was nearly 500 kilometers from where the slide began.

Geologists now think that over thousands of years, similar slides formed the Hudson River Canyon. The power of rocks and sand suspended in water is one of the most powerful agents of erosion under the sea.

● Why does water carrying small suspended particles flow down undersea slopes?

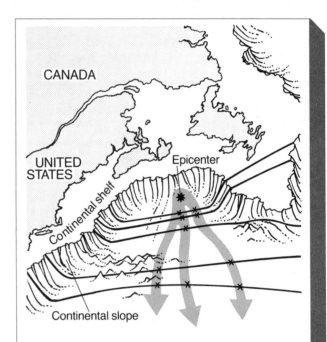

The 1929 earthquake south of Newfoundland set currents of muddy water moving. These currents (arrows) snapped several underwater telephone cables, some over 500 km from the epicenter.

The Grand Canyons of the Sea

The Hudson River Canyon is one of the many **submarine canyons** (SUB-muh-reen KAN-yuns) in the continental shelf. Submarine canyons play a major role in moving sediment from the continents into the deep oceans.

Sediment from a continent can be found thousands of kilometers from shore. Rivers, tides, and winds deposit sediment onto the continental shelf. This sediment builds up. Eventually, it forms a thick layer. Then, suddenly, part of the layer near a canyon collapses.

When this layer collapses, the sediment mixes with water and forms a thick soup-like mixture. Because the mixture is denser than the

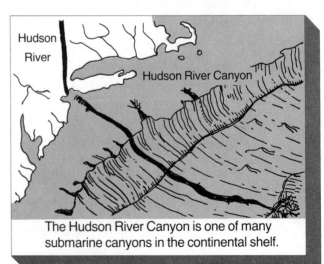

The Hudson River Canyon is one of many submarine canyons in the continental shelf.

surrounding water, it flows more rapidly down the canyon. Along the way, it erodes the walls and floor of the canyon. This makes the canyon larger.

When the mixture reaches the mouth, or end, of the canyon, it may be moving more than 50 kilometers per hour. As it shoots out of the canyon, the mixture spreads far across the flat, deep plain. The sediment gradually settles.

A second kind of ocean "canyon" is the trench. A trench, remember, forms where one tectonic plate slides under another plate. Trenches have very steep walls. Found in the deep ocean, trenches are much deeper than the deep plain.

A third kind of ocean "canyon" runs down the middle of the mid-ocean-ridge. It is called a **rift.** It is deep and V-shaped. Today we know that rifts occur where tectonic plates move apart. New ocean floor forms at the rifts.

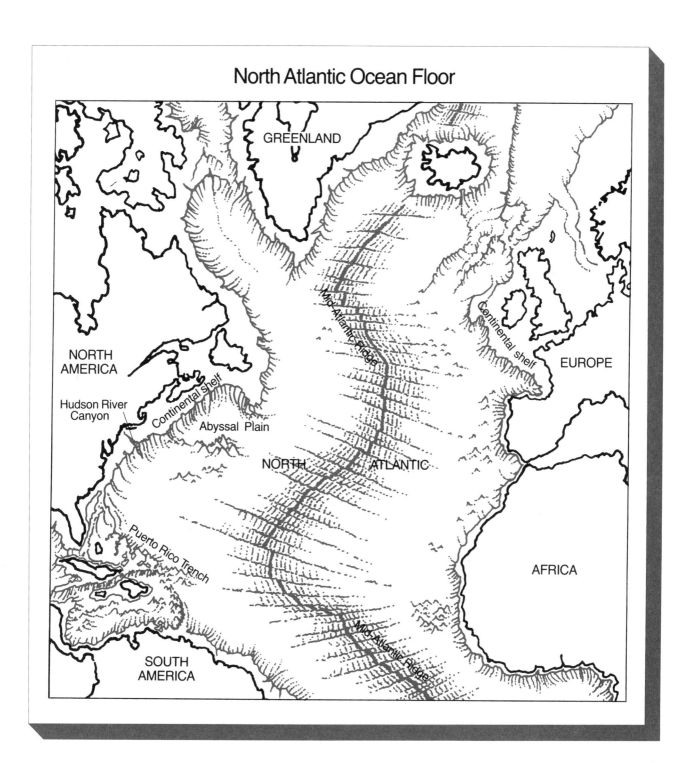

North Atlantic Ocean Floor

To Do Yourself How Does a Mud Slide Cause a Submarine Canyon?

You will need:

Pan balance, two identical jars, soil, water

1. Fill one jar with water.
2. Add water and soil to the second jar to make a thick "soup." Make sure both jars are filled to the same level.
3. Place the jars on the pans of the balance.

Sediment is a mixture of sand, small stones, organic material, and other tiny particles. This mixture "rains" down on the bottom of lakes, rivers, and oceans.

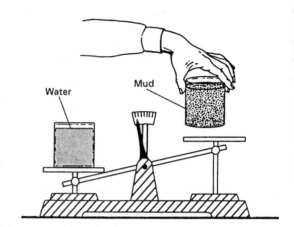

Water

Mud

Questions

1. Which is heavier, water or mud? How do you know? _____

2. Do you think mud slides can be dangerous? Why? _____
3. How would you make a model of a submarine canyon formed by a mud slide?

_____

Review

I. Match each term in column **A** with its description in column **B**. You will use some terms more than once.

A		B
trench	_____	1. Tectonic plates moving apart form a canyon.
rift	_____	2. Dense sediment-filled water carves a canyon.
submarine canyon	_____	3. The sinking of part of the ocean floor forms a canyon.
	_____	4. A canyon found on the continental shelf.
	_____	5. Lowest of all canyons.

II. Answer in sentences.

How did sediments from land get to deep plains thousands of kilometers from shore?

_____

_____

Lesson Six

How Does the Sea Floor Spread?

Exploring Science

Life on Another World. Your ship descends through blackness. Suddenly, you see a column of black smoke. It's even darker than the blackness around you. The column of smoke rises, coating everything in a thick black substance.

The temperature outside your ship rises rapidly as you near the smoker. You use the ship's robot arm to pick up samples of the black substance. Later, you find that the substance contains many heavy metals and the element sulfur.

Upon closer study, you find tiny creatures living on the sulfur. These creatures thrive at temperatures of 250° C and at pressures 265 times the air pressure found at the earth's surface. Feathered worms, some more than 3.5 meters long, live on the sulfur-eaters. So do giant clams. There are even crabs near the smoker. They eat anything they can find, including the "feathers" on the worms.

What planet are you exploring? Earth! The black smoker and its unusual creatures are deep in the ocean. They are in areas where new sea floor is forming.

Strange life forms, such as these tube worms, flourish in areas around smokers.

● Why are temperatures near a smoker very high?

Hot Vents in the Sea

In 1979, *Alvin* was diving off the west coast of Mexico. It was exploring a rift known as the East Pacific Rise. *Alvin* found a strange world that had never been seen before. There were black smokers and white smokers. As *Alvin* approached one of the black smokers, the plastic rod that held its outside thermometer began to melt! *Alvin* quickly backed away.

Smokers are **vents,** places where hot water is rising through the ocean floor. Vents have been found wherever undersea rifts have been explored.

How are vents formed? Seawater moves through cracks in the crust. The water is heated by magma that has worked its way into the crust. The water becomes extremely hot. It can dissolve minerals that cannot be dissolved by

This pillow lava formed near a vent in the ocean floor.

cooler water. When the hot water finds an opening to the surface, the opening becomes a vent. Whether the vent is a black smoker or a white smoker depends on the minerals that are dissolved in the water.

As the hot water leaves the vent, it mixes with cold water at the bottom of the sea. As the water cools, it can no longer hold the dissolved minerals. The minerals leave the water and coat the area around the vent.

On another trip to the rift, *Alvin* made another important discovery. It found fields of **pillow lava.** When hot lava meets cold seawater, it cools and forms shapes that look like pillows. This discovery proved that lava had been flowing into the ocean at a rift valley.

To Do Yourself   How Does a Submarine Submerge?

You will need:

A small plastic shampoo bottle, rubber stopper with hole, rubber tubing, gauze pad, knife, water, sink

1. Carefully cut off the end of a small plastic bottle. **Caution: Always handle sharp objects with great care!**
2. Place a gauze pad over the opening. Keep the pad in place with a rubber band.
3. Push the rubber tubing into the hole of the stopper. Place the stopper in the bottle. You have just made a submarine.
4. Sink the submarine in a container of water.

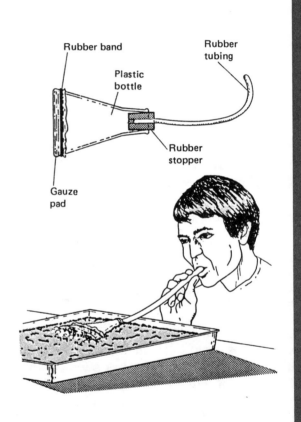

Blowing into the tube forces water out of the bottle and brings the submarine back to the surface.

When a submarine dives below the surface, air is forced out of special tanks and water is drawn in. To surface, the air is forced back into the tanks. By regulating the amount of air and water in the tanks, a submarine can control the depth of its dives.

Questions

1. Can the principle of the submarine be used to raise sunken ships? How?

_____

_____

2. What difficulties might a submarine have at great depths?

_____

_____

Review

I. Fill in each blank with the word (or words) that fits best. Choose from the words below.

seamount   rift   continental slope   vents   pillow lava   minerals

gases

Smokers were discovered by exploring a _____ . These

smokers are _____ in the ocean floor. The smoke is

produced as _____ leave the water of the smoker. When
hot rock pours through the cracks in the sea floor, it cools and forms

_____ .

II. Answer in sentences.

Living things around a black smoker get energy from sulfur. Where does the
sulfur come from?

_____

_____

_____

III. Answer in sentences.

Pillow lava has been found in other places besides the sea floors of rifts.
Where else would you expect to find pillow lava?

_____

_____

_____

What Are the Ocean's Resources?

Exploring Science

A Bed of Lumps. The *Prospector* (PROS-pek-tur) was out in the Pacific. Special cameras aboard the ship scanned the ocean floor. Television screens let workers keep an eye on what the cameras were viewing. Soon, an area densely packed with dark lumps came into view.

These lumps, or **nodules** (NOJ-ools), are found only on the ocean floor. In some places, there are millions of nodules. The nodules consist mostly of the metal manganese. They also contain iron, cobalt, copper, and other metals.

At one time, the metals in the nodules were dissolved in the seawater. For some reason, the metals **precipitated** (prih-SIP-ih-tayt-id), or separated, from the water and formed nodules. Scientists have estimated that 6 million tons of these metals precipitate every year.

Ships like the *Prospector* have mapped locations of important nodule beds. Now "vacuum-cleaner" ships are being developed to pick up the nodules.

● Why do people want to mine the nodules?

Manganese nodules on the ocean floor.

Mining the Sea

The nodules on the ocean floor may someday become an important source of metals. Even today, the resources of the oceans are important. Seawater provides some minerals. Other minerals are mined from the ocean floor.

The mineral halite has been mined from seawater for thousands of years. One important use of halite is to flavor food. Then, we call it salt! It is easy to mine halite from seawater. The water is enclosed in a shallow pond. When the water evaporates, almost pure halite is left behind.

Another important resource from the sea is fresh water. In some countries, fresh water is very scarce. People in those countries get some of their fresh water by removing salt from seawater.

At present, not many resources are taken from the sea floor. It is very expensive to process them. Petroleum and natural gas are two exceptions. Some parts of the continental shelf are mined for their large deposits of these fuels.

Many of the important minerals on land were actually formed in the oceans of long ago. One example is found on the island of Cyprus (SY-prus) in the Mediterranean. Cyprus has large deposits of copper. People have mined these deposits since prehistoric times. Long before that, Cyprus was part of the ocean floor. It was a smoker, the site of a vent in a rift. Copper dissolved in the hot water of the smoker precipitated where Cyprus is today.

Oceans can be "mined." This plant removes salt from the ocean water, producing fresh water and salt.

Review

I. Fill in each blank with the word that fits best. Choose from the words below.

**copper   minerals   natural gas   gold   petroleum   salt   vents
mid-ocean**

The ocean contains many _____ . Halite, which we call

_____ , is taken from sea water. Two resources taken from

the ocean floor are _____ and _____ .

Mineral deposits on land sometimes originated at the _____
rifts.

II. Match each word in column **A** with its description in column **B**.

A	B
_____ copper	**a.** Obtained when sea water is evaporated.
_____ halite	**b.** Found in lumps scattered on the ocean floor.
_____ manganese	**c.** Mined on Cyprus since prehistoric times.

III. Answer in sentences.

The sea floor contains many minerals but few are mined. Why?

_____

_____

_____

A. In the statements below, terms from this unit have been scrambled. Unscramble the capital letters to find a list of interesting information about the oceans.

_____ 1.

The science of (**1**) PNARECAHOGOY is fascinating.

_____ 2.

In the sea there are great rivers called (**2**) RENTRUCS.

_____ 3.

Some that flow deep below the surface are caused by differences in (**3**) TESYIND.

_____ 4.

North of the equator they tend to flow (**4**) SLICKCOWE.

_____ 5.

Beneath the sea there are submarine (**5**) NYASONC, (**6**) MEANSTOSU, and deep (**7**) SCRETHEN.

_____ 6.

_____ 7.

_____ 8.

In the (**8**) STRIF of the mid-ocean (**9**) DIRGE are (**10**) STEVN.

_____ 9.

_____ 10.

_____ 11.

These are surrounded with (**11**) LOPLIW lava and may feature a black or white (**12**) KREMOS surrounded by strange forms of life.

_____ 12.

B. Write the word or phrase that best completes each statement.

1. _____ Scientists believe that water in the early oceans came from **a.** rain **b.** volcanoes **c.** rivers

2. _____ Compared with the continents, ocean floors are **a.** older **b.** the same age **c.** younger

3. _____ The strong winds of storms are the cause of
   a. waves **b.** tides **c.** currents

4. _____ The movement of the water in the ocean up and
   down twice a day is a **a.** tide **b.** current **c.** countercurrent

5. _____ Steady winds that blow from the same direction
   cause **a.** tsunamis **b.** currents **c.** tides

6. _____ The rotation of the earth causes currents to
   a. start **b.** stop **c.** turn

7. _____ Most surface currents start near the **a.** poles
   b. equator **c.** Gulf Stream

8. _____ South of the equator, currents are turned
   a. north **b.** clockwise **c.** counterclockwise

9. _____ Compared with fresh water, salt water is
   a. denser **b.** colder **c.** warmer

10. _____ The tops of seamounts are **a.** above water
    b. underwater **c.** under magma

11. _____ The sharp rise near the edge of the oceans is the
    continental **a.** shelf **b.** slope **c.** ridge

12. _____ Flowing sediment mixed with water is the cause
    of undersea **a.** trenches **b.** rifts **c.** canyons

13. _____ A rift is formed where two plates are moving
    a. together **b.** apart **c.** downward

14. _____ An ocean trench forms when a tectonic plate
    slides under **a.** a canyon **b.** another trench **c.** another plate

15. _____ The area around a deep-sea vent is often coated
    with **a.** minerals **b.** halite **c.** petroleum

16. _____ Halite is **a.** copper ore **b.** salt **c.** fresh water

17. _____ Petroleum is often found in the **a.** continental
    slope **b.** continental shelf **c.** mid-ocean ridge

18. _____ Lava that flows into sea water forms shapes like
    a. rivers **b.** pillows **c.** ridges

19. _____ Earth's crust is thinnest at **a.** abyssal plains
    b. seamounts **c.** mid-ocean ridges

20. _____ Manganese is sometimes found in the form of
    a. nodules **b.** pillow lava **c.** petroleum

C. Apply What You Know

Study the drawing of an imaginary ocean. Label the numbered parts. Choose from these labels.

mid-ocean-ridge   **rift**   **seamounts**   **continental shelf**   **submarine canyon**

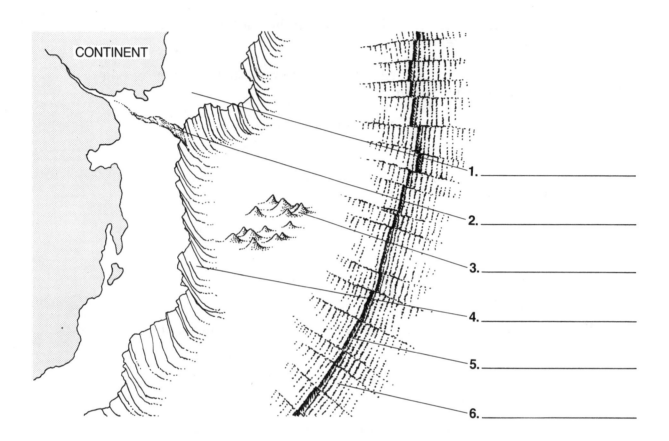

CONTINENT

1. _____
2. _____
3. _____
4. _____
5. _____
6. _____

D. Find Out More

1. Find out more about the voyage of *H. M. S. Challenger.* What was its route around the world? What scientists were aboard? What did it discover? Make a map of the route and do a report for the class.
2. If you have been to the seashore, share your experiences with the class. If possible, bring in some of the things found on a beach and display them. Use a map of ocean currents to try to guess where the objects might have come from.
3. Use modeling clay to make a map of the floor of a typical ocean basin. Show such features as the continental shelf and slope, a submarine canyon, a mid-ocean ridge, a rift, a seamount, and a trench.
4. Deep ocean vents are fairly recent discoveries. Scientists are still learning more about them. Look in recent magazines for articles about vents and the unusual life forms around them. Collect pictures of vents and make a display poster for the classroom.

Careers in Earth Science

Working With the Ocean. The oceans are important to all of us. They provide us with food, minerals, and even oxygen. Although the oceans are vast, they can be changed easily. So far, most of the changes have not been good, either for the oceans or for people.

If you enjoy natural surroundings, you might want to work with the ocean. Today, people who study the oceans and those who use them are working together to protect this great resource of earth.

Environmental (en-vy-run-MEN-tul) **Officer** Much of the life in the oceans is found in the shallow areas near the shore. Many fish and shellfish hatch in these waters and then move out into the open ocean. These shallow areas, however, are often the places that people pollute. They are also being filled in and used for building sites.

State and federal governments hire environmental officers to protect these areas. Some of the officers make sure that laws are not broken. Many of these jobs require a high school education, with no further training. Other officers have studied biology for two to six years in college. These workers check the condition of living things in the water. They also take water samples for chemical analysis.

Environmental officers who patrol the oceans must enjoy being outdoors. They must also be able to work alone much of the time.

Marine biologist. The information gathered by environmental workers may be examined by a marine biologist. A marine biologist needs a college degree followed by at least four years of graduate school. Marine biologists spend a lot of time in the library, reading about what other scientists have learned. Of course, they can also be found at the shore, on the ocean, or below its surface, observing for themselves.

This marine biologist is measuring the temperature of the surface water in a section of the Java Sea.

This environmental worker is checking water purity.

UNIT

7

THE EARTH'S HISTORY

How Did Life Start?

Exploring Science

Life From Space. Scientists have been able to trace how living things on earth have changed over billons of years. But they have not been able to "see" the very first step. How did life on earth begin?

Most scientists think that the earth was the setting for the processes that began life. They think that certain chemicals came together and became organized into the first forms of life. Not everyone agrees that life started here. Some scientists think that life began somewhere else in the universe, then found its way to earth. Perhaps tiny living things, protected by hard shells, traveled through space. They might have floated to earth like specks of dust.

Today, high-flying planes collect dust from space. These planes are equipped with sticky collectors on their wings. The collectors are sent to scientists who examine the dust. Some of the dust does come from space. But no evidence of life has been found in the space dust.

Perhaps earth's living things arrived here on space rocks that sometimes land on its surface. Astronomers have found many chemicals like those used by living things in such rocks.

Scientists continue to look for ways in which life could have come from space. Most scientists, however, still believe that life started here on earth.

● Some scientists say that believing life came from space does not really solve the problem of *how* life began. Explain what they mean.

The Beginning of Life

The earliest fossils are of life forms that lived in the oceans. This fact led scientists to believe that life began in the oceans. This theory starts with the atmosphere or the oceans full of simple molecules. By some means, these molecules were used as building blocks to

Scientist Stanley Miller

make more complex molecules. Perhaps lightning provided the energy needed for this change to take place in the early atmosphere. The complex molecules would then collect in the oceans to make a sort of chemical "soup." Or perhaps high-energy light formed complex molecules in the ocean itself.

Once the more complex molecules were formed, they had to make copies of themselves. Exactly how or why this copying process started is not clear. But, once the process started, life could get its start. In order for anything to "live," it must be able to make a copy of itself—to reproduce.

For many years, the "chemical soup" theory was accepted by just about all scientists. However, in recent years some scientists have been working on a new hypothesis. This hypothesis is based on the idea that "life" actually began in beds of clay. Not life as we know it, but certain life processes. Namely, the ability of patterns to make copies of themselves. Under certain conditions, patterns in clay molecules can reproduce. They can make copies of themselves. Some scientists think that this process may have provided a framework upon which life started. Complex molecules eventually developed from the simple reproducing patterns.

Review

I. Fill in each blank with the word that fits best. Choose from the words below.

lightning   oceans   copy   clay   chemical "soup"   fire

Until recently, almost all scientists believed that life began in the _____

Energy to start life might have come from _____ or high-energy light.

The early oceans were thought to be sort of a _____. A more recent

hypothesis states that life processes began in _____. In order for any

thing to live, it must be able to make a _____ of itself.

II. Answer in sentences.

What fact led to the theory that life began in the oceans?

_____

_____

_____

Lesson Two

How Are Fossils Formed?

Exploring Science

Discovering a Dinosaur. The first of the animals we know as dinosaurs walked the earth about 200 million years ago. Fossils of these curious creatures have been found all over the world. Yet, it wasn't until 1822 that people even suspected that such animals had ever lived.

One spring day in that year, Dr. Gideon Mantell, a physician in Sussex, England, went to call on a patient. Since the weather was pleasant, the doctor's wife, Mary Ann, went along for the ride. While Dr. Mantell was with his patient, Mary Ann Mantell took a walk. As she passed a pile of rocks, she noticed that one of the rocks contained something dark and shiny. Mary Ann Mantell inspected the rock and found that it contained huge teeth. She showed the rock to her husband. They agreed that nothing like these teeth were known.

The Mantells examined the rocks more closely. They found some very large bones. Dr. Mantell identified the fossils as the remains of a giant plant-eating reptile. Almost 20 years would pass before the word *dinosaur* was invented. The word dinosaur comes from the Greek and means "terrible lizard."

● How do you think Dr. Mantell could tell from the teeth that the animal was a plant-eating reptile?

Forming Fossils

The dinosaur teeth that Mary Ann Mantell found were **fossils** (FOS-uls). Fossils are the remains, or traces, of plants and animals that lived long ago. Most of what we know about life in the past comes from the study of fossils.

Most animals and plants do not form fossils when they die. Their soft parts are eaten or broken down by decay bacteria. Hard parts, such as shells, bones and wood, are gradually worn away by rain and other agents of erosion.

On land, fossils form when bodies become frozen in glaciers or become buried in places like swamps and tar pits. The covering of ice, sand, mud, or dirt protects the body from decay. Many more fossils form in seas and lakes than on land. Plants and animals that die in water settle to the bottom. There, the bodies become buried by constantly falling sediments.

Many fossils do not contain any parts of the original plants or animals that formed them. Preserved footprints are fossils. Imprints of ancient plants are often found in beds of coal.

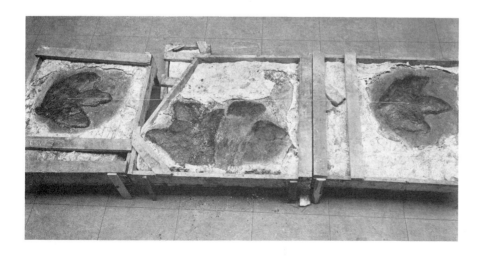

Even though they do not contain any parts of the original creature, these dinosaur tracks are fossils. Each footprint is almost 1 meter across.

Two common types of fossils are *casts* and *molds*. Suppose an animal with a hard shell dies and is buried in mud or sediment. The soft parts of the animal will decay quickly. But the hard shell will leave an **impression** in the mud. This impression is in the shape of the shell. Even if the shell dissolves, the impression will still be there. If the mud turns to sedimentary rock, the shape of the animal becomes a **mold.**

Sometimes a mold becomes filled with minerals dissolved in water. The water evaporates and leaves the minerals behind in the mold. These minerals harden to form an exact copy of the original animal. This copy is called a **cast.**

Can you tell the difference between the casts and the molds in this group of fossils?

To Do Yourself   How Can You Make Fossils?

You will need:

Plaster of Paris, mixing can, water, wooden stirrer, disposable aluminum cake tin, vegetable oil, objects to make imprints

1. Mix some plaster of Paris in a mixing can. Follow the directions on the package.
2. Pour the mixture into a disposable aluminum cake tin.
3. Coat the objects to be "fossilized" with a thin layer of cooking oil. Press the objects into the plaster of Paris.
4. Let the plaster harden.
5. After the plaster is hard, remove the object.

Examine the "fossil" you have created. Fossils can be found in rocks, soil, and on the ocean floor. Some fossils are actual remains of a plant or animal. Other fossils are their imprints.

Questions

1. How can fossils help us find the date when certain land features were formed?

_____

_____

2. Why are the soft parts of a plant or animal not usually found as fossils?

_____

_____

Review

I. Fill in each blank with the word that fits best. Choose from the words below.

swamps   traces   seas   buried   hard parts   molds

A plant or animal must be _____ before it can become a

fossil. Most fossils form at the bottom of _____ . Animals

trapped in _____ may also become fossils. A fossil may not

be the actual remains of a plant or animal, but its _____
are preserved in stone.

II. For each statement, write *fossil* if the event described would be likely to
produce a fossil. Write *not* if the event would not be likely to produce a
fossil.

A. _____ A saber-toothed cat is trapped in a tar pit.

B. _____ A lion kills an antelope on a grassy plain.

C. _____ A hard-shelled sea animal dies and sinks to the
bottom of the sea.

D. _____ A worm makes a burrow in the sea bottom. The
burrow fills with sand and is covered with
sediment.

E. _____ An apple is buried when a dog digs a hole next
to an apple tree.

F. _____ A fern falls to the bottom of a swamp and is
covered by mud.

III. Answer in sentences.

What kind of information can be learned from a single fossil tooth?

_____

_____

_____

How Has the Earth Changed?

Exploring Science

Reading a Stack of Rocks. William Smith lived in England about 200 years ago. As a boy, he became interested in rocks and fossils. Later, he worked as a surveyor and helped build canals. His work gave him the opportunity to study rock formations in many parts of England.

Smith noticed that sedimentary rocks were formed in layers. One layer was stacked on top of another. He reasoned that the layer at the top must be the newest, or youngest layer. The deeper the layer, he said, the older it is.

But rock layers in one place may be very different from rock layers somewhere else. Near London, Smith found a certain kind of clam fossil in a layer near the top of a stack. He found an identical clam fossil more than 100 kilometers away. The second fossil was in a very deep layer.

Was the second fossil a lot older than the first? "No," said Smith. "Layers that contain the same fossils are the same age." It was a while before people realized the importance of Smith's discovery. Today he is known as the father of English geology.

● Fossils of an ancient fish and an ancient plant were found in the same rock layer. What conclusions can you make about when these two life forms were alive?

Eras, Periods, and Epochs

Long before scientists were able to tell how old a rock was, they could tell that some rocks were older than others. Because of the work of William Smith, scientists learned to identify different rock layers or rock formations by the fossils that they contained.

Different kinds of plants and animals have lived at different times in earth's history. Fossils of these plants and animals are found in layers of sedimentary rocks. If the layers have not been disturbed, younger layers are on top of older layers.

In some places, upper layers of a rock formation may have been eroded away. Earthquakes or other strong forces may have folded or overturned rocks, so that young layers are actually *under* older layers. Despite such changes, the fossils in the layers remain.

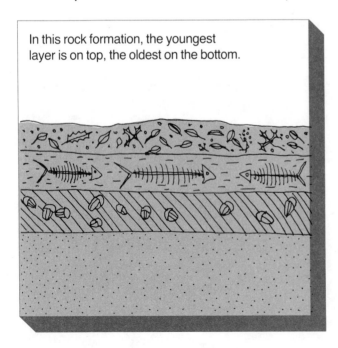

In this rock formation, the youngest layer is on top, the oldest on the bottom.

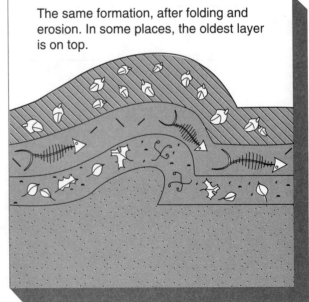

The same formation, after folding and erosion. In some places, the oldest layer is on top.

Young layers of rock contain fossils that are like plants and animals we know. Old layers have fossils unlike living things of today. Using fossils, it is possible to separate earth's history into parts, much as we separate time into hours, minutes, and seconds.

Earth's history goes back a very long way — $4\frac{1}{2}$ billion years. The time span since the earth's beginning is known as **geologic** (jee-uh-LOJ-ik) **time.** Geologic time is divided into longer parts called **eras.** Each era is divided into shorter parts, called **periods.** Some of the periods are further divided into **epochs** (EP-uks).

These divisions of geologic time were originally based on fossil evidence. Today, it is possible to tell how many years ago each time division started and how long it lasted.

Geologic Time Divisions

ERA	Period	Epoch
		Epoch
		Epoch
		Epoch
	Period	Epoch
		Epoch
		Epoch
		Epoch
		Epoch

Review

I. Fill in each blank with the word that fits best. Choose from the words below.

epochs   eras   earthquakes   layers   fossils   erosion   periods

When rock _____ have similar fossils, they are the same age. The history of the earth is divided by geologists into great lengths of time called _____. These lengths are further divided into _____, which are divided into _____. These divisions of time were established by using _____.

II. Write **T** if the statement is true. If it is false, change the underlined word to make the statement true.

A. _____ Scientists used layers of <u>sedimentary</u> rock to tell how old the rock is.

B. _____ Sometimes <u>erosion</u> can cause younger layers to be below older layers.

C. _____ Fossils that look the <u>most</u> like plants and animals of today are the oldest.

How Can We Tell the Age of a Rock?

Exploring Science

A Question of Age. At one time, many people believed that the earth had originally been part of the sun. In 1846, Wlliam Thomson used this theory to determine the age of the earth.

Thomson measured the temperature of the sun and the temperature of the earth. He reasoned that the earth had been cooling since it had separated from the sun. Thomson studied the work of other scientists. He learned the rate at which a large cannon heated and cooled. He applied this rate to the earth. His calculations showed earth to be about 100 million years old.

Geologists didn't agree with Thomson. They said that 100 million years was not enough time for the earth to form. A longer period of time was needed for rivers to cut canyons in plateaus. More time was needed for ocean floors to form, and then to rise into great mountain ranges. Still more time was needed for mountains to wear down into plains.

Later, scientists discovered an accurate "clock" that could be used to measure the age of the earth. This clock is **radioactivity** (RAY-dee-oh-ak-TIV-ih-tee), a process in which certain

In 1846, William Thomson (Lord Kelvin) calculated the age of the earth.

elements give off particles and energy. Using radioactivity, scientists have found that the earth is 4.5 billion years old.

● Why did Thomson and other scientists believe that the earth had once been part of the sun?

Using Radioactivity to Date Rocks

Some of the earth's elements are radioactive. Uranium is such an element. Radioactive elements are not stable. They break down, or **decay,** to form stable elements.

Each radioactive element decays at a steady rate. The rate is different for each radioactive element. The rate of decay is not changed by temperature, pressure, light, chemical action, or any other factor.

The rate at which a radioactive element decays is called its **half-life.** For example, a form of uranium called uranium-238 has a half-life of 4.5 billion years. This means that at the end of that many years, half of any sample of uranium-238 will have decayed. It will have become a stable

form of lead called lead-206. The remaining half of the sample will still be radioactive uranium-238. In another 4.5 billion years, half of that remaining uranium (one-fourth of the original sample) will have changed into lead.

Half-life can be used to date rocks—to find their ages. To do this, scientists compare the amount of radioactive element in a rock with the amount of decay product. The more decay produced, the older the rock. For example, a rock containing uranium-238 but no lead-206 would be a new rock. In a new rock, no uranium has had time to decay. A rock that contained equal amounts of uranium-238 and lead-206 would be 4.5 billion years old.

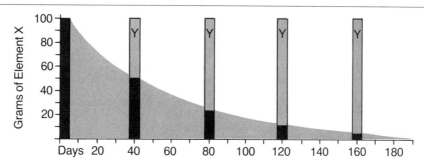

Element X (represented by the black bars) has a half-life of 40 days. It decays to element Y (the pink bars). There are 100 grams of element X at the start. How many grams of X after 80 days? How many grams of Y at that time?

Review

I. Fill in each blank with the word that fits best. Choose from the words below.

all   combine   decay   half   radioactive   stable

Uranium-238 is an example of a _____ element.

Lead-206 is an example of a _____ element. Radioctive

elements break down, or _____ . The time it takes for

_____ of the radioactivity of an element to disappear is
used in measuring the age of rocks.

II. A bar of pure uranium-235 weighs 10 grams. The uranium has a half-life of 713 million years. It decays to stable lead-207.

    A. _____ How much uranium will be left after 713 million years?

    B. _____ What will be the ratio of uranium-235 to lead-207 after 713 million years?

    C. _____ How much uranium will be left after 1,426 million years? (Hint: the ratio of uranium to lead will be 1:3).

III. Answer in sentences.

How old is the earth? How do scientists know its age?

_____

_____

_____

What Was the Earliest Life Like?

Exploring Science

Fossil Ice Cream Cones. Life existed on Earth 3.5 billion years ago. How do we know? Scientists have found fossils. Most fossils from very early times in Earth history are of one-celled algae. This algae is usually found in colonies, or "mats," having thousands of these tiny plants.

Bits of sediment became trapped in these algae mats. Slowly, layer-by-layer, these algae mats and sediments built huge structures called **stromatolites** (stroh-mah-TOH-lytes). The stromatolites often took strange shapes. Some looked like upside-down ice cream cones. These cones were as tall as a five-story building.

For many years, scientists thought that stromatolites had disappeared from the earth long ago. Then they discovered a rich bed of stromatolites in Hamelin Pool, a part of Shark Bay, off the West coast of Australia. Why are these formations so abundant in Hamelin Pool but rare elsewhere?

The water in Hamelin Pool is very salty. Algae can live in it, but animals that would normally eat the algae cannot. Without natural enemies, the algae thrives.

In some ways, conditions in Hamelin Pool are like those found in ancient oceans. Billions of years ago, no animals existed. Algae grew undisturbed. So, stromatolites had time to develop.

● Would you expect to find stromatolites in waters off the coasts of the United States. Explain your answer.

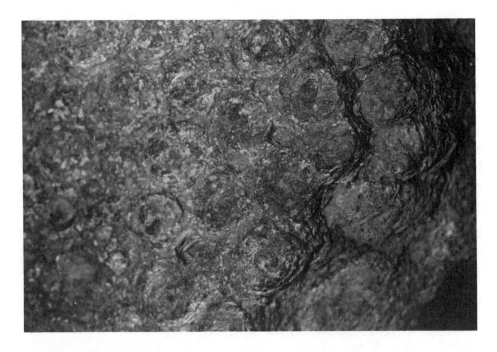

The stromatolites shown here are very similar to those that thrived in the oceans billions of years ago.

Precambrian Time

Recall from Lesson 3 that the time span since earth's beginning is called geologic time. Geologic time is divided into eras, periods, and epochs. Geologists needed some sort of chart, or scale, to show what was happening during the divisions of geologic time. So they developed the **geologic time scale.** This scale is based largely on fossil remains.

The divisions of the geologic time scale were based on fossils found in different rock layers. When the geologic time scale was invented, mostly between 1822 and 1879, there was no way to tell the age of any fossil layers. As early as 1835, however, geologists realized that the fossils in some layers were less advanced than those in others. At that time, the least advanced fossils known were found in a rock layer in the part of Great Britain known as Wales, which is southwest of most of England. Scientists of that time used Latin, and Cambria (KAM-bree-uh) is the Latin name for Wales. So they named the layer of fossils and the Period when the fossils had been alive the **Cambrian Period.**

For a long time after that, no fossils that were less advanced than those of the Cambrian Period were found. Geologists began to speak of **Precambrian** (before Cambrian) **time** as the long stretch of time before fossils appeared. Later, when radioactive dating had been developed, it was found that the Cambrian Period started almost 600 million years ago. Thus, Precambrian time lasted for almost 4 billion years, more than six times as long as the time since the start of the Cambrian.

More than a hundred years after the Cambrian Period was named, geologists began to find fossils in Precambrian rocks. These fossils include stromatolites and other simple life forms. Today, Precambrian time is divided into two eras.

The earliest Precambrian era is the **Archean** (ahr-KEE-uhn) era. Archean means "ancient," or "beginning." The Archean era starts with the oldest known rocks, about 4.6 billion years ago. The earliest evidence of life is from this era. All traces of life this early are of very simple bacteria and one-celled plants.

The second era of Precambrian time is the **Proterozoic** (proht-uhr-uh-ZOH-ik) era. Proterozoic means "earliest life." This era began about 2.5 billion years ago. It lasted until the start of the Cambrian period. During this era, such animals as sponges and jellyfish appeared.

Geologic Time Scale

Time	Era	Period	Epoch	Years Before Present
Phanerozoic	Cenozoic	Quaternary	Recent	11,000
			Pleistocene	1.6 million
		Tertiary	Pliocene	5 million
			Miocene	24 million
			Oligocene	37 million
			Eocene	58 million
			Paleocene	66 million
	Mesozoic	Cretaceous		130 million
		Jurassic		190 million
		Triassic		249 million
	Paleozoic	Permian		290 million
		Carboniferous		350 million
		Devonian		395 million
		Silurian		425 million
		Ordovician		500 million
		Cambrian		570 million
Precambrian	Proterozoic			2,500 million
	Archean			4,600 million

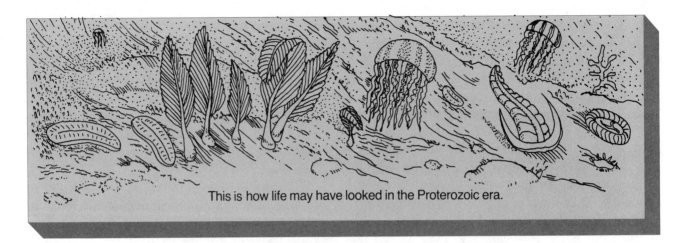

This is how life may have looked in the Proterozoic era.

To Do Yourself   Does Primitive Life Still Exist?

You will need:

Water from an established fresh water fish tank, microscope, glass slides, cover slip, dropper, pencil and paper

1. Using the dropper, remove a drop of water from the filter of the fish tank.
2. Place the drop on a glass slide. Cover with a cover slip.
3. View the slide under low magnification. Draw what you see.
4. Using a coverslip, carefully scrape the sides of the fish tank for algae.
5. Place the scrapings on a slide. Cover with a cover slip.
6. View the slide under low magnification. Draw what you see.
7. View the algae under higher magnification. Draw what you see.

Tiny one celled life forms belong to a group called Protists. These were the first animals and are the simplest. They should be moving rapidly under the microscope. Green boxlike structures are algae. These are among the first green plants.

Questions

1. What differences did you notice in your drawings of the algae?_____

_____

2. How do you know if the organisms you saw under the microscope were alive?

_____

Review

I. Fill in each blank with the word that fits best. Choose from the words below.

Cambrian   **Precambrian**   **algae**   **Proterozoic**   **stromatolites**   **rocks**

The earliest part of Earth's history is called _____ time.

One division of this time span is the _____ era. Among

the oldest known fossils are mats of _____ called

_____ .

II. Match each term in column A with its description in column B. You will use the terms more than once.

A	B
a. Archean era	_____ 1. Means "ancient" or "beginning"
b. Proterozoic era	_____ 2. Ended with Cambrian time
	_____ 3. Earliest era of Earth's history
	_____ 4. Began 2.5 billion years ago
	_____ 5. Earliest known fossils formed
	_____ 6. Sponges and jellyfish appeared
	_____ 7. Means earliest "life"

III. Answer in sentences.

Precambrian time was once one division of the geologic time scale. Why was it divided into eras? On what was the division based?

_____

_____

_____

.

When Did Animals With Shells Appear?

Exploring Science

A Soft Life Becomes a Hard Rock. It is fairly easy to find fossils of ancient sea animals that had shells. Fossils of animals without shells are not as easy to find. This is because the soft parts of dead creatures are usually broken down by decay bacteria.

Decay bacteria need oxygen to live. Are there places without oxygen where decay bacteria cannot live? What kind of fossils would form in such a place?

About 500 million years ago, a shallow sea covered part of Canada. There was a layer of water with very little oxygen at the bottom of that sea. Sloping upward from this layer was a steep mud bank. Many animals lived in this mud.

Every so often, some of the mud slid to the bottom of the sea, carrying animals with it. Once at the bottom, the animals died because there was not enough oxygen. The animals—even soft ones—were covered with mud in water that protected against decay. Most became fossils.

Many fossils have been found in the rocks formed from this mud. Some are fossils of animals with shells. But many more are fossils of animals that did not have shells.

● Soils in tropical areas dissolve bones and teeth faster than soils in colder climates. How would this fact affect the fossil record?

Oceans Filled With Invertebrates

By the beginning of Cambrian time, 600 million years ago, the seas were filled with life. There were many types of **invertebrates** (in-VUR-tuh-brits). These are animals without backbones. There were also many kinds of algae. But there was still no life on land.

Early in Cambrian time, animals with shells developed. The shells gave these animals important advantages. Shells protect animals from being eaten. They protect the soft bodies from drying out if the animals are exposed to air. Shells also make it possible for animals to grow to a large size. Soft body parts are attached to the shell and are supported by it.

Trilobites (TRY-luh-byts) were the most common shelled animals. They were so common that the early Cambrian is sometimes called the Age of Trilobites. Trilobites were relatives of today's lobsters. Most trilobites were small, but they came in many different forms. Some had large heads; others had tiny heads. Some had a dozen eyes; others had no eyes at all. If attacked, a trilobite curled up. Its hard shell protected its soft body.

Trilobites lived in the seas for hundreds of millions of years. Then they became **extinct** (ik-STINGKT). When a plant or animals can no longer be found on earth it is extinct.

This trilobite lived in seas that covered what is now New York state more than 300 million years ago.

To Do Yourself   What Makes a Shell Hard?

You will need

Any beach shell (clam, mussel, oyster), vinegar, large jar

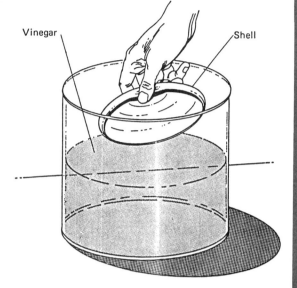

1. Place the shell in the jar or beaker. Completely cover the shell with vinegar.
2. Observe the shell every day.

   Clams, mussels, scallops, and oysters are among those animals classified as mollusks (MOLL-usks). These animals have hard outer shells that protect their soft bodies. These shells are mostly calcium, which make them hard.

Questions

1. What happened to the shell after a few days? _____

2. How are human bones similar to mollusk shells? _____

Review

I. Fill in each blank with the word that fits best. Choose from the words below.

Precambrian   Cambrian   clams   trilobites   lobsters   extinct

The first animals with shells appeared in _____ time.

The most common shelled animals were _____ .

They existed millions of years before becoming _____ .

II. Write T if the statement is true. If it is false, change the underlined word or words to make the statement true.

1. _____ An animal that no longer exists is said to be <u>extinct.</u>

2. _____ There was no life that we know of <u>in the seas</u> 600 million years ago.

3. _____ Animals without <u>shells</u> are called invertebrates.

III. Answer in sentences.

What are some advantages of having a shell?

_____

_____

How Did Life Develop on Land?

Exploring Science

On the Run. Between 450 and 500 million years ago, the first fishes appeared. They were small creatures called **ostracoderms** (OS-truh-koh-durms). They had no jaws. They used their toothless mouths to suck food up from the mud on the ocean bottom.

Ostracoderms had heavy, bony armor. But this armor was of little use against some of the creatures that shared their ocean home. Most dangerous of all were the water scorpions. At that time, they were the largest animals on earth. They were as large as a human being, with huge claws and sawlike mouths. These scorpions could rip the little ostracoderms apart.

Those terrible water scorpions are now extinct. But fish populate all of today's seas. How did they survive? They were able to swim much faster and more efficiently than the scorpions. They had big advantages over the scorpions. They were **vertebrates** (VUR-tuh-brayts), animals with backbones.

● Do you think several ostracoderms could have attacked and killed a water scorpion? Explain your answer.

Animals With Backbones

The development of the skeleton was an important turning point in the history of life. A skeleton has a long column of bone, called a **backbone.** Other bones, as well as muscles, are attached to the backbone.

A skeleton provides less protection than a hard shell. But it enables an animal to move easily. An animal that can move quickly does not need as much protection.

Fish were the first animals with skeletons. They had another advantage, too. Their bodies had a protective covering of **scales.** Scales are a good way to have a hard coat without losing the ability to move easily.

At about the time that fish were beginning to fill the sea, some plants were moving onto land. The first land plants were small and leafless. From these early plants, giant ferns and other tall plants developed.

One early group of fish used their fins to "walk" on the ocean bottom. These fish began to crawl on shore to find food. Gradually, over millions of years, they developed lungs. This allowed them to breathe air, and spend more time out of the water. About 395 million years ago, the first **amphibians** (am-FIB-ee-uhns) appeared. Amphibians are born with gills, but develop lungs as adults. They spend their adult life on land.

Development of amphibians.

The next major advance among animals was an egg that had a shell. Such eggs can be laid on land. The shell protects the egg. The first animals to lay shelled eggs were the **reptiles.** This group of animals became very successful. They took over all parts of the environment. Some swam in the seas, others flew. Among the best known and most widespread of all the reptiles were the dinosaurs. Dinosaurs of all shapes and sizes thrived during the Mesozoic era.

During the Mesozoic era, dinosaurs and other reptiles ruled the land, sea and air.

Review

I. Fill in each blank with the word that fits best. Choose from the words below.

on land   **lungs**   **dinosaurs**   **skeletons**   **reptiles**   **in water**   **scales**

trilobites   **amphibians**   **fish**

Fish could move more easily than earlier animals because they had

_____ and _____

instead of shells. Amphibians are born _____ and

live _____ as adults. The first animals to lay eggs with

shells were the _____ . Included in this group are the

_____ .

II. Match each term in column **A** with its description in column **B.** You will use some terms more than once.

A	B
fish	_____ **1.** First animals with skeletons.
amphibians	_____ **2.** Some learned to fly.
reptiles	_____ **3.** Included the dinosaurs.
	_____ **4.** Descended from fish with lungs.
	_____ **5.** Laid eggs that had shells.
	_____ **6.** First animals with skeletons to live on land.

Why Do Animals Become Extinct?

Exploring Science

What Happened to the Dinosaurs? In 1980, a team of scientists led by Walter Alvarez found a thin layer of clay. It was located between the last layer of rock that contained dinosaur fossils and the first layer after the dinosaurs had become extinct. Alvarez asked his father, a famous physicist, to see if there was anything unusual about this thin layer.

There was. Luis Alvarez found that the clay was rich in iridium (i-RID-ee-uhm). This is a rare metal on Earth, but it is common in the rest of the universe. The Alvarez team thought that something from space must have brought the iridium to Earth.

Perhaps a comet or meteorite brought the iridium. If so, it must have been large, because the iridium layer was found all over the Earth.

Could a large object from space have killed the dinosaurs? If so, how?

One idea was that dust from the impact could have filled the whole sky, cutting off light. Earth would be dark and cold. Plants and other food would disappear. The giant dinosaurs, used to warmth and a plentiful food supply, might have died if that happened.

Others thought of different reasons that such an impact could make the dinosaurs extinct. Soon most scientists believed that the Alvarez team was right about the giant impact.

● Do you think that most ocean plants and animals also became extinct because of the impact? Why or why not?

Changes in Past Life

There are many theories that try to explain why dinosaurs and other living things became extinct. At one time, scientists thought that it was a matter of competition for food. Today many scientists do not think that competition alone is a good explanation.

Dinosaurs came in all shapes and sizes, ranging from about the size of a dog to over 25 meters long.

Some scientists believe that plate tectonics may explain why dinosaurs died out. Major movements of the earth's plates cause great changes to take place. Earthquakes, volcanoes, and "tidal waves" on a worldwide scale could cause changes in life forms. Changes in climate can also take place. These changes in climate can also take place. these changes could cause cold-blooded reptiles to die. Or, their sources of food could die, causing the dinosaurs to starve.

Many major changes in life forms seem to happen at the same time. This has been clear ever since people began to date fossils. In fact, the end of one era and the beginning of another is always marked by a big change in fossils. Almost every era ended with a **mass extinction**. This was a time when many forms of life suddenly ceased to exist.

For example, geologists think the "Cretaceous (kri-TAY-shus) extinction" marked the end of the dinosaurs. It also saw the end of all flying reptiles and reptiles that lived in the sea. Many other forms of life became extinct at that time.

Today, most scientists think that the Cretaceous extinction was caused by a giant meteorite. Could the same kind of event have caused other mass extinctions? The greatest mass extinction of during all of geologic time came at the end of the Permian Period, about 250 million years ago. There is some evidence that this extinction was also caused by a large object from space.

A smaller mass extinction took place at the end of the Ice Age, only 10 thousand years ago. Large mammals of the kind hunted by humans all became extinct at once. There is no evidence that anything from space caused this extinction. Some scientists think that human hunters were the cause.

Review

I. Fill in each blank with the word that fits best. Choose from the words below.

250 million   ocean   extinct   meteorite   10 thousand   successful

Most evidence shows that dinosaurs died out after the earth was hit by a(n)

_____. Most geologic eras ended when many types of life

forms became _____. The greatest mass extinction in geologic

time occurred _____ years ago.

II. Write **T** if a statement is true. If it is false, change the underlined word to make the statement true.

A. _____ Dinosaurs died out at the time of the Permian extinction.

B. _____ No other creatures died out when the dinosaurs did.

C. _____ Most eras ended with a mass extinction.

III. Answer in sentences.

Some geologists suggest that a change in sea level could cause a mass extinction. How do you think this type of change would affect plants and animals?

_____

_____

_____

When Did Mammals and Birds Appear?

Exploring Science

Missing Links. In 1989, Philip Gingerich (JIN-juh-rik) found the fossil of a whale with legs and feet. Although it lived in the water, it had not lost its legs completely. This animal lived in the Eocene (EE-uh-seen) Epoch, about 40 million years ago. It demonstrated that the ancestors of whale lived on land.

Gingerich had found a "missing link,"—a connection between a modern whale and its ancestors. Scientists continue to look for missing links in the history of many animals. For some animals, the fossil record is fairly complete.

One animal for which we have a detailed fossil record is the horse. The first horses appeared in the early Cenozoic era. These horses were about the size of a small dog. They had four toes on each foot. Over millions of years, the horses became larger, and the number of toes was reduced to three.

About 25 million years ago, grasses first appeared and began to thrive. Horses became grazers. Those horses with longer legs had definite advantages over those with shorter legs. Long-legged horses could run faster to escape their enemies. They could also cover more ground in search of food. The long-legged horses survived and reproduced.

Starting in the **Pleistocene** (PLY-stuh-seen) epoch, horses had feet with only one toe. Those horses were very similar to the ones we know today.

● Bats are mammals that can fly. Do you think that bats had ancestors that could not fly? Explain.

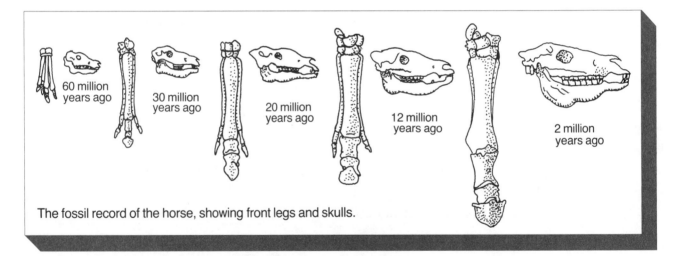

60 million years ago

30 million years ago

20 million years ago

12 million years ago

2 million years ago

The fossil record of the horse, showing front legs and skulls.

The Rise of Warm-Blooded Animals

Both whales and horses are **mammals** (MAM-uls), animals that give birth to live young. Mammals appeared more than 200 million years ago—earlier than the dinosaurs. The first mammals were very small. They looked very much like the reptiles from which they descended.

Birds also descended from reptiles. They appeared at about the same time as the dinosaurs. Like mammals, they were not very successful until after the Cretaceous mass extinction.

What helped mammals and birds survive the mass extinction? For one thing, mammals and birds are warm-blooded animals. This means that their body temperatures are the same all the time, even when the air temperature changes. These animals have outer coverings that help them to control their body temperatures. Mammals have fur or hair. Birds are covered with feathers.

Reptiles, amphibians, and most fish are cold-blooded animals, although there is evidence that at least some dinosaurs were warm-blooded. Cold-blooded animals do not have a built-in way to control body temperature. Their body temperature changes with that of their environment. So, if the environment becomes too cold or too hot, and the creatures cannot move to a new environment, they will most likely die.

Warm-blooded animals have another edge over cold-blooded animals. Warm-blooded animals can be active at night, even when temperatures are quite cold. This means that they can hide from their cold-blooded enemies during the day and hunt for food at night.

After the mass extinction, new mammals and birds filled the environment. Ten million years later, many of these creatures were similar to animals we see today. But life is always changing. What do you think life will be like in another 10 million years? Do you think another mass extinction is possible?

To Do Yourself Are Feathers Good Insulation?

You will need:

Two thermometers, aluminum foil, incandescent lamp, feathers or down, scissors

1. Cut a two inch square of foil with the scissors. **Caution: Use great care when working with sharp objects.** Ball the foil around the bulb of each thermometer.
2. Leave the thermometers under an incandescent lamp until the temperature stabilizes. Record the temperature.
3. Turn off the light. Place several layers of feathers or down around the bulb of one of the thermometers.
4. Compare the heat loss from each thermometer over the next few minutes.

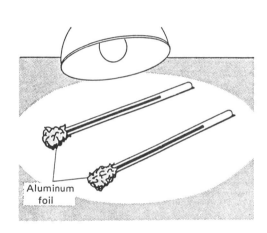

Aluminum foil

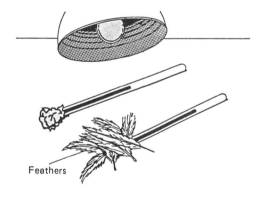

Feathers

Birds and mammals are warm-blooded animals. Warm-blooded animals have special features that help keep their body temperatures more or less the same. Because of these features, a warm-blooded animal's temperature will stay the same when the temperature outside changes. Birds have feathers to keep them warm in winter. Mammals have fur or hair to help keep warm.

Questions

1. Which thermometer lost heat first? Why? _____

_____

2. What other materials might make good insulation? Explain your answer. _____

_____

Camelops

Woolly mammoth

Saber-tooth cat

• What animals of today do these prehistoric animals resemble?

Review

I. Fill in each blank with the word that fits best. Choose from the words below.

warm-blooded   hair   wings   feathers   cold-blooded   heat   scales

Most fish, amphibians, and reptiles are _____. Birds and

mammals are _____ . A mammal's body is covered by

_____ . A bird is covered by _____ .

These structures make it possible for animals to hold_____.

II. Circle the underlined word that makes each statement true.

A. The first mammals developed (before/after) the first birds.

B. The temperature of a reptile is controlled by the reptile's (body/environment).

C. The temperature of an ostrich is controlled by the ostrich's (body/environment).

III. Answer in sentences.

Why were mammals and birds able to survive the Cretaceous mass extinction?

_____

_____

_____

What Caused the Ice Ages?

Exploring Science

A Monster from the Past. In the spring of 1846, a group of Russians was mapping northern Siberia. The icebound land around them was flooded. Unusually warm weather had melted much of the ice. The ground, however, remained frozen. It had been frozen since the last ice age. (It is still frozen today.)

Suddenly, the people saw a monster floating in the water. It looked alive! But it was dead—and frozen. They tied a rope around it and dragged it ashore.

Here is what one of the people wrote to a friend: "Picture an elephant with a body covered with thick fur. The tusks were two and a half meters long, thick and curving. The beast was fat and full-grown. Under the outer hair there was a brown wool. The giant was well-protected against the cold."

The animal was a **woolly mammoth.** Warm weather had freed it from its icy grave. These large creatures, often 4 meters tall, had been common in the ice ages. We know of them not only from fossils but also from cave paintings. Early people made drawings of woolly mammoths on the walls of their caves.

● Few animals besides the woolly mammoth have been found preserved in ice. How would you explain this?

Woolly mammoths roamed the countrysides of Europe and Asia before the last ice age.

The Ice Ages

Only 12,000 years ago, the earth was gripped by an ice age. During this time, temperatures all over the earth fell. Siberia was covered by sheets of ice hundreds of meters thick. The ice covered much of Europe and parts of North America. What caused this **ice age?**

191

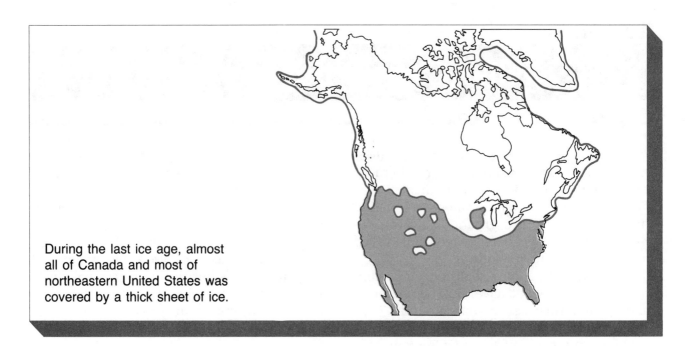

During the last ice age, almost all of Canada and most of northeastern United States was covered by a thick sheet of ice.

There were ice ages even before life began on earth. There have been three major ice ages since. These happened about every 250 million years. The appearances of the ice ages seem too regular to be due to chance.

Scientists have a theory to explain what causes ice ages. The earth travels in a path called an **orbit** around the sun. The orbit changes in a regular pattern. Also, the earth is tilted in its orbit. This tilt changes over many years. Lastly, the earth wobbles slightly as it moves around the sun. Changes in the orbit, tilt, and wobble could all affect world climates. Since these changes occur regularly, climates should also change regularly. Evidence from ocean cores supports this theory.

The last group of ice ages caused many changes in the northern hemisphere. In one of the most important developments, people arrived in North America.

Review

I. Fill in each blank with the word that fits best. Choose from the words below.

250 million   12,000   glacier   orbit   ice age

The geologic record shows a(n) _____ at regular

intervals. These intervals are about _____ years apart. There

is evidence that the cause is related to changes in the _____
of the earth.

II. Answer in sentences.

How could changes in the earth's position lead to an ice age?

III. Answer in sentences.

One theory says that an ice age can start when two plates collide, causing many volcanoes to erupt at once. How could erupting volcanoes cause an ice age?

Review What You Know

A. Each of the following riddles can be answered with one of the main terms or topics from the lessons of this unit. Write your answer on the line.

1. _____ I work on everything, trying to bring things together. Although you cannot see me, I got the sun and planets started. I keep them in their proper paths today. What am I?

2. _____ I was the soup that nobody ate;
My home was the sea and not the plate.
I really got started up in the sky
From lightning and gas—now, what am I?

3. _____ I am not alive, but I look like something that once did live. I am solid as a rock. What am I?

4. _____ I am found at the end of a sentence, but I am made of epochs. What am I?

5. _____ I am known for dating, but I don't go out for billions of years. If I were not active, I might have a full life instead of half of one.

6. _____ I was one of the early ones in the shell game, but I am out of the game completely today. I guess my age—Cambrian— got to me. What am I?

7. _____ I lead two lives. Among animals with skeletons, I am the only one who can breathe underwater at the start. Then I come up for air for the rest of my life. What am I?

8. _____ I used to be a big deal in my time. But something came up about 65 million years ago, and I haven't been around since. What am I?

B. Write the word or phrase that best completes each statement.

1. _____ A star is formed when a ball of gas develops high temperature and   **a.** volume   **b.** gravity   **c.** pressure

2. _____ Planets that form closest to a star will be made of   **a.** rock   **b.** gas   **c.** ice

3. _____ A fossil forms only when the body of the dead plant or animal is   **a.** covered   **b.** dissolved   **c.** eaten

4. _____ Many fossils are formed in   **a.** forests **b.** prairies   **c.** swamps

5. _____ The longest time division of the following is **a.** epoch   **b.** period   **c.** era

6. _____ If sedimentary rock has not been disturbed, the top layer will be   **a.** folded   **b.** youngest   **c.** oldest

7. _____ An element that decays into another element is
   a. a fossil   **b.** stable   **c.** radioactive

8. _____ Life on Earth began during the   **a.** Cambrian era
   b. Archean era   **c.** Protozoic era.

9. _____ The most common shelled animals during the
   Cambrian period were   **a.** clams   **b.** trilobites   **c.** oysters

10. _____ Cambrian time started   **a.** when life on Earth
   began   **b.** when solid rocks formed   **c.** about 600 million years ago

C. Apply What You Know

   Study the drawings of early life forms below. Label each one. Choose from
   these labels.

   ice age creature   Proterozoic life   dinosaur   trilobite

   1. _____   2. _____

   3. _____   4. _____

D. Find Out More

   1. Sometimes fossils can be seen in the walls of limestone or sandstone
      buildings. See if you can find any fossils in building walls in your town.
      Report on the results of your search.
   2. The ice age left signs of its presence all over the northern part of the
      United States. If you live in an area once covered by the glaciers, try to
      photograph some of the glacial features. These may include scratched
      bedrock, gravel deposits, lakes, certain kinds of hills or ridges, large rocks
      that have been left behind by melting ice, and so forth.
   3. Use the school and local libraries to do research on dinosaurs. Prepare a
      report for the class.

SUMMING UP
Review What You Have Learned So Far

A. Study the illustrations. Then write the names of the objects on the lines. Choose from the objects below.

dinosaur   vent   crystal   anticline   trench   mammal

1. _____   2. _____

3. _____   4. _____

5. _____   6. _____

B. Each statement below refers to the illustration having the same number as the statement. Circle the underlined word or phrase that makes each statement true.

1. This feature can form because the interior of the earth is (cold/hot).
2. This feature forms where two plates are (coming together/moving apart).
3. When a liquid cools (slowly/quickly), the particles that form take on this special arrangement.
4. This feature forms where two plates are (coming together/moving apart).
5. An outer shell (preserved their remains/protected their eggs).
6. This creature is (warm-blooded/cold-blooded).

UNIT

8

CLIMATE AND THE ENVIRONMENT

Lesson One

How Do Days Change in Length?

Exploring Science

Ancient Calendars. The Maya (MAH-yuh) lived in Central America long before Columbus and other Europeans came to the New World. The daily lives of the Maya were ruled by the calendar.

A calendar is a system for keeping track of time. To make a calendar, you need to know the exact positions of objects in the sky. The Maya had observatories (ub-ZUR-vuh-tohr-ees) from which they studied the sky. They learned when a certain group of stars was at the lowest and highest points of its yearly path through the sky. They traced the paths of the moon and the planet Venus. From their accurate observations, the Maya made a calendar.

Other early calendars were made of giant rings of stone. The stones were set up by people who lived about 5000 years ago. One such ring in England is called Stonehenge (STOHN-henj). The stones were put in precise places. They mark the seasons and can be used to predict eclipses. Today at Stonehenge, you can watch the sun rise over the Heelstone on the first day of summer.

● Why would it be important for ancient people to know when summer would begin?

Stonehenge, England. These stones are all that is left of an ancient astronomical calender. The largest stones in this group weigh about 25 metric tons and were moved a distance of almost 500 kilometers to their present position.

Day and Night

The earth moves in a path, or **orbit**, around the sun. One complete trip, or **revolution** (rev-uh-LOO-shun), takes 365¼ days, or one year. As the earth moves around the sun, it spins, or **rotates,** on its **axis** (AK-sis). The earth's axis is an imaginary line running through the center of the earth. The ends of this axis are the North and South Poles. One complete spin of the earth takes 24 hours, or one day.

The spinning of the earth causes day and night. It is daytime on the side of the earth facing the sun. It is nighttime on the side of the earth facing away from the sun.

Since the earth makes one complete spin every 24 hours, you would think that day and night would be equal in length every day. However, this is not the case. In the summer, days are long and nights are short. In winter, days are short and nights are long. Why do the hours of daylight and darkness change throughout the year?

The reason why daylight hours change in length is that the earth's axis is not straight up-and-down, or vertical. It is tilted. It is tilted at an angle of 23½ degrees from the vertical. The axis is always tilted in the same direction. The north end of the axis is always pointed at the same spot in space. In fact, it is always pointed towards the North Star.

About June 21, the North Pole of the earth's axis is tilted toward the sun. This date marks the longest day of the year in the Northern Hemisphere. On the same date, the Southern Hemisphere is tilted away from the sun. It is the shortest day of the year there.

Six months later, the earth has moved to the opposite side of its orbit. Around December 22, the North Pole of its axis is tilted away from the sun. This is the shortest day of the year in the Northern Hemisphere. What is happening on this date in the Southern Hemisphere?

Twice a year, neither hemisphere is tilted toward the sun. On about March 20 and September 23, the sun is directly over the equator. On these dates, day and night are equal in length everywhere on earth.

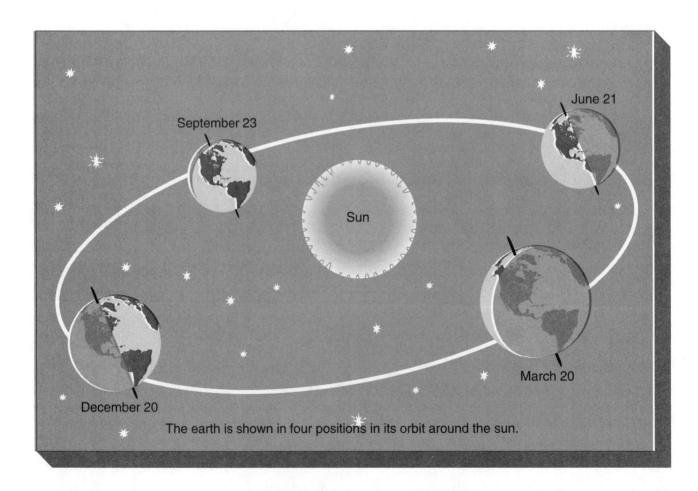

September 23

June 21

Sun

March 20

December 20

The earth is shown in four positions in its orbit around the sun.

Review

I. Fill in each blank with the word that fits best. Choose from the words below.

seasons   long   short   tilted   length   position   spins

As the earth travels around the sun, it also _____ on its

axis. The axis of the earth is _____ . These two factors

affect the _____ of day and night. The hemisphere that is

tilted toward the sun will have _____ days and

_____ nights.

II. Write T if a statement is true. It it is false, change the underlined word to make the statement true.

A. _____ When the North Pole is tilted toward the sun, the Northern Hemisphere has <u>long</u> days.

B. _____ June 21 is the longest day of the year in the <u>Southern Hemisphere.</u>

C. _____ <u>Twice</u> a year, daylight and night are equal everywhere on earth.

III. Answer in sentences.

Imagine a planet that travels around a sun, but does not spin. Does the planet have day and night? Explain.

_____

_____

_____

What Causes the Seasons?

Exploring Science

Invisible Light. Have you ever seen a rainbow? Did you wonder what causes the colors? In the 1600s, young Isaac Newton thought the colors could come from sunlight. He experimented with an angled piece of glass called a **prism** (PRIZ-um). When he sent sunlight through the prism, it separated the white light into the colors of the rainbow.

Newton's experiment showed that sunlight was made from different parts. But it wasn't until 200 years later that still another part of sunlight was discovered. William Herschel, an astronomer in England, wondered about how light energy can change temperature. Herschel used a prism to break sunlight into colors and watched what happened when his thermometer was placed in different colored light. He found that temperature warms faster in red than in violet. As a control, he held the thermometer next to the red end, outside the light. To his surprise, the temperature rose even faster than it did in the light.

Herschel had found the first known invisible radiation. It is called **infrared** (in-fruh-RED) **light,** or infrared radiation. Most of the warmth we feel from sunlight comes from invisible infrared light.

● Do you think there is also invisible radiation just outside the violet end of the rainbow made by a prism? Why or why not?

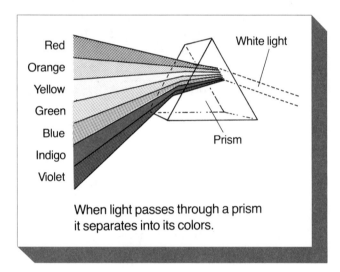

When light passes through a prism it separates into its colors.

Sunlight on the Earth

In Lesson 1 you learned that the earth's axis is tilted. This tilt causes the hours of daylight and darkness to change throughout the year as the earth moves around the sun. The tilt of the earth's axis also causes the change of **seasons.**

Recall that June 21 is the longest day in the Northern Hemisphere. On that date, the North Pole of the earth's axis is tilted toward the sun. Thus, the Northern Hemisphere receives the most direct rays of the sun. The sun's energy is more concentrated in the Northern Hemisphere. June 21 is the first day of summer there.

On that same date, the Southern Hemisphere is tilted away from the sun. The sun's rays strike the earth there at a slant. The energy of the sun is spread out over a larger area for a shorter period of time each day. June 21 is the shortest day of the year in the Southern Hemisphere—the first day of winter.

JUNE 21

The earth continues to travel around the sun. The days get shorter in the Northern Hemisphere and longer in the Southern Hemisphere. On about September 23, the sun is directly over the equator. Day and night are equal—12 hours each—everywhere on earth. This is the first day of autumn in the Northern Hemisphere. What season is starting in the Southern Hemisphere?

Three months later, the earth has completed half its trip around the sun. On about December 22, the North Pole of the earth's axis is tilted away from the sun. The sun's rays strike the Northern Hemisphere at a slant. The first day of winter has arrived.

From this day on, the days will become longer in the Northern Hemisphere and shorter in the Southern Hemisphere. On about March 20, the sun will again be directly over the equator. Day and night will be equal everywhere. It is the first day of spring in the Northern Hemisphere. Finally, June 21 rolls around again. The earth has completed its trip around the sun. A year has gone by. It is the first day of summer again.

To Do Yourself

Which of the Sun's Rays Are Most Concentrated, Direct or Indirect?

You will need:

Flashlight, cardboard, graph paper, tape, pencils (2 colors)

1. Tape a sheet of graph paper to a piece of cardboard. Draw an X near the center of the graph paper.
2. Shine a flashlight directly at the x on the graph paper from a distance of about 1 meter. With a pencil, trace the outline of the lighted area on the graphpaper.
3. Tilt the cardboard at an angle of about 45° away from the flashlight. Repeat Step 2, using a colored pencil to trace the outline of the lighted area.
4. Count the number of squares inside each traced area. Record your results below:
   Direct rays _____
   Indirect (slanted) rays _____

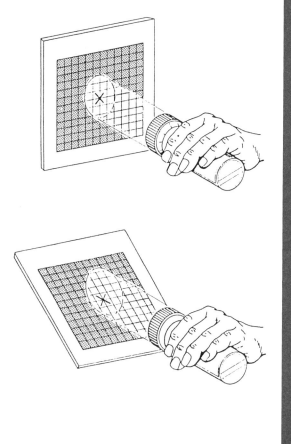

During summer in the Northern Hemisphere, the sun is actually farther from the earth than it is during the winter. Because the sun's rays strike the Northern Hemisphere more directly in summer, temperatures are warmer than in winter.

Questions

1. Which light rays were more concentrated (covered a smaller area)? _____
2. When it is winter in the Northern Hemisphere, what season is it in the Southern

   Hemisphere? Why? _____

Although Earth is tipped only 23.5°, the angle at which the Sun's rays strike a particular place is not 23.5° most of the time. Earth is a great ball, after all. If the Sun is directly overhead at one place on Earth, it is much lower in the sky everywhere else on that hemisphere.

The more atmosphere through which the Sun's rays must pass, the less energy from the Sun reaches the surface. Thus, when the Sun is at a low angle in the sky, its rays do not warm the surface as much as when it is at a high angle.

If the Earth were not tilted, sunlight would never reach the poles at all. But the 23.5° tilt allows the Sun to shine over the poles for 6 months each year. Even so, the highest altitude observed for the Sun from the poles is only 23.5° at noon.

Further south, the height of the Sun at noon is higher. The Sun is higher in the northern hemisphere on June 21 than on any other day, but for most of the Earth the Sun is never directly overhead. In the United States only Hawaii is so far south that the Sun is directly overhead at noon at any time of the year. In the rest of the United States, the highest altitude of the Sun is always less than 90°.

Review

I. Fill in each blank with the word or words that fits best. Choose from the words below.

less   more   directly   at an angle   summer   winter

In the Northern Hemisphere, the time between about December 22 and March

20 is _____. During that time, sunlight strikes the hemisphere

_____. Thus, the energy of the sun is spread out over a larger area and

provides _____ heat.

II. You measure the height of the sun at its highest point in New York City. Tell which measurement was made on December 22 and which was made on June 21.

A. _____ The angle between the horizon and the sun is 72°.

B. _____ The angle between the horizon and the sun is 27°.

III. Answer in sentences.

If the earth did not tilt, would there be seasons? Why or why not?

_____

_____

_____

How Are Places on Earth Located?

Exploring Science

Landmarks at Sea. In the northern hemisphere, one of the most familiar stars in the sky is the North Star. It is also a very useful star. Because it is directly over the North Pole, it shows people in the Northern Hemisphere which way is north.

Early sailors learned that stars could be used as "landmarks" at sea. For example, by measuring the height of the North Star above the horizon, the sailors could tell how far north of the equator they were.

The early sailors, however, did not have an accurate way to find their east-west position. Many ships and sailors were lost because they could not locate their positions. As late as 1707, a British fleet miscalculated its location and went aground. Two thousand sailors died. In 1713, the British Navy offered a cash prize to anyone who could develop a way to determine the east-west positions of ships at sea.

The prize was won by John Harrison in 1765. He developed accurate clocks, called **chronometers** (kruh-NOM-ih-turs), that could be used at sea. The difference between noon on a ship at sea and noon at Greenwich England, told a ship's east-west position.

● At noon in Greenwich, England, the sun is at its highest point in the sky. At the same time, where would sailors in the middle of the Atlantic see the sun?

A John Harrison chronometer.

Latitude and Longitude

Being able to locate one's position on land is as important as it is at sea. Any position on earth can be determined using a system of imaginary circles. To use this system, you must know that a circle is measured in degrees. A circle contains 360 degrees (360°). Half a circle has 180°, one-quarter of a circle has 90°, and so on.

The circle around the earth halfway between the poles is the **equator.** Other imaginary circles can be drawn north and south of the equator.

The distance north or south of the equator is called **latitude** (LAT-ih-tood). The equator has a latitude of 0°. The distance from the equator to a pole is one-quarter of a circle. Therefore, the North Pole has a latitude of 90° north. The latitude of the South Pole is 90° south. A city halfway between the equator and the North Pole,

such as Montreal, has a latitude of 45°N.

Another series of circles can be drawn around the earth from north to south. These circles, which all pass through the poles, measure **longitude** (LON-jih-tood). Longitude describes east-west position. The 0° longitude line is called the **prime meridian** (muh-RID-ee-un). The prime meridian runs from the North Pole, through Greenwich England, to the South Pole. The other half of this circle, halfway around the world, has a longitude of 180°. Points west of the Prime Meridian have west longitudes up to 180°. Points east have east longitudes up to 180°.

To describe a position on the earth's surface, give its latitude followed by its longitude. For example, the location of Washington, D.C. is 39° N 77° W.

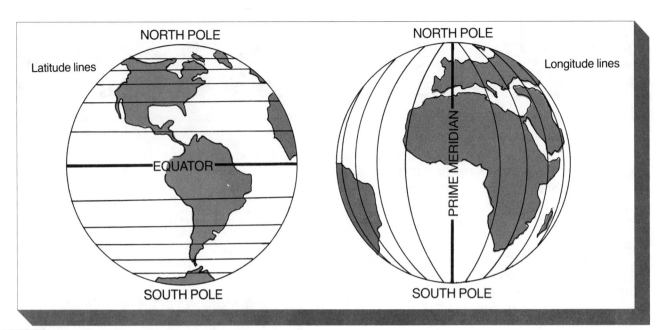

NORTH POLE

Latitude lines

EQUATOR

SOUTH POLE

NORTH POLE

Longitude lines

PRIME MERIDIAN

SOUTH POLE

To Do Yourself   How Can You Find Your Latitude?

You will need:

Plastic drinking straw, protractor, string, steel washer, globe or map, tape

1. Tape the bottom edge of a protractor to a plastic drinking straw. Tie one end of a piece of string to the protractor at the "0" mark. Tie a washer to the other end of the string.
2. Look at the North Star through the straw. Read the angle at which the string crosses the protractor. Subtract this angle from 90°. The difference will tell you your latitude.
3. Check your results on a globe or map. The device you made in this activity is a crude sextant (SEKS-tunt). Sextants are accurate instruments that help sailors find their latitude while at sea. Navigational tables and chronometers are used to find longitude.

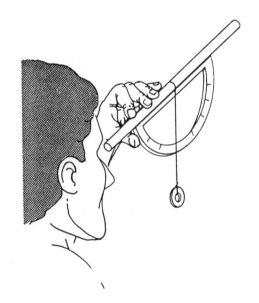

Questions

1. What are some disadvantages of using a sextant for finding latitude? _____

_____

2. What does knowing your latitude tell you? What other information must you

know to pinpoint your position on the earth's surface? _____

_____

Today it is not necessary to use a chronometer to find your position at sea—or on the land either. In the space age, satellites are used to show the exact position of any point on Earth. At any time, two or more of the satellites in the **Global Positioning System (GPS)** are "visible" from every point on Earth. While you usually cannot see them with your eyes, a small radio can detect their signals. The radio is combined with a computer in a GPS locator.

The computer uses the radio signals to determine where the locator is in relation to the satellites. In its memory is the information needed to tell exactly where the satellites are in space. When all the information is combined, the GPS locator knows exactly where in Earth it is. For you to find out, all you need to do is to turn on the locator. It will give you its position in terms of latitude and longitude. It is accurate to within a few feet.

Review

I. Fill in each blank with the word or phrase that fits best. Choose from the words below.

North Pole	longitude	prime meridian	90°	180°	360°
South Pole	latitude	equator			

The position of points on earth is measured in degrees

of _____ and _____ . The

_____ is at 0° latitude. The _____ is at

90°N. The _____ is at 0° longitude. The highest possible

latitude is _____. The highest possible longitude is

_____ .

II. Answer in sentences.

Three locations are given on a map showing an island with buried treasure. Which two locations are wrong? Explain.

A. _____ 20°N 210°W

B. _____ 20°N 140°W

C. _____ 140°N 20°W

_____

_____

_____

How Does Latitude Affect Climate?

Exploring Science

The Year Without a Summer. In New England, people still talk about the year they call, "eighteen hundred and froze to death." In June of 1816, it snowed as far south as Bennington, Vermont, and Utica, New York. On July 5, Maine had ice "as thick as window glass" on ponds and in rain barrels. On August 20, there was a hard frost in Keene, New Hampshire. Two days later, another frost hit New Haven, Connecticut.

Why was it so cold in New England in 1816? In 1815, Mount Tambora, a volcano in Indonesia, erupted. It put more dust into the at-mosphere than any other eruption had done in 10,000 years. The dust decreased the amount of sunlight reaching the earth. Temperatures all over the world dropped. Places far from the poles had weather that was typical of places much closer to the poles. For example, the temperatures in New Haven that summer were like summer temperatures usually found 1000 kilometers to the north.

● Is it really true that New England had no summer in 1816? Explain.

Latitude and Temperature

The people of New England were surprised by the summer weather of 1816. After years of living there, they knew that snow and ice are not expected in July and August. Observing the weather of an area over a long period tells you what kind of **climate** (KLY-mit) the area has. Climate can be called a long-term pattern of weather. An area's climate includes information such as its average annual temperature and its average annual **precipitation** (prih-sip-ih-TAY-shun). This precipitation may be in the form of rain, snow, or sleet.

The climate of an area is affected by many factors. The most important factor is latitude. The mouth of the Amazon River, for example, is on the equator. It is very hot there all year round. As you move closer to the South Pole, temperatures fall. The South Pole is at 90°S. Why do temperatures change with latitude?

Look at the diagram. At the equator, the rays of the sun strike the earth directly. The average temperatures, therefore, are usually high. Because the earth's surface is curved, the closer you get to the poles, the more the rays hit at an angle. When rays hit at an angle, remember they are spread out. The same amount of energy heats up a larger area. Thus, near the poles, average temperatures are low.

Near the equator, day and night are about the same length all year. As you move toward the poles, the length of day and night changes during the year. When a place has long days and short nights, the sun heats it for a longer time. Under reverse conditions—short days and long nights—the place receives less heat. Places with unequal amounts of daylight and night have cold seasons and hot seasons. Winter temperatures can be very cold. Summer temperatures can be very hot.

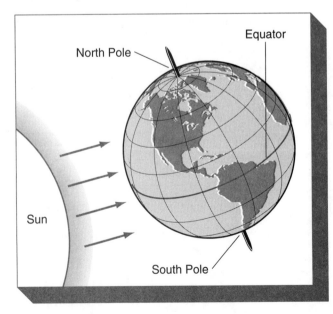

Although the angle of the Sun's rays is determined mostly because Earth is round, Earth's tilt also has an effect. When either spring or fall starts, day and night are equal all over the planet. It is an equinox (EE-kwuh-nahks), or "equal night."

But at the first day of summer or winter, day and night are only equal at the equator. Then the difference between the length of day and the length of night increases as you go away from the equator. At the poles, however, day and night are still equal—six months of each!

Review

I. Fill in each blank with the word or words that fits best. Choose from the words below.

latitude   north   tilted   round   winter or summer   longitude
south   equinox   equator   poles   spring or fall

The most important factor affecting climate is _____. In the

Southern Hemisphere, temperatures get colder as you go _____. Except

for regions near the equator, the sun's rays strike the Earth at an angle

because the Earth is _____. Near the _____, daylight and

night are always of equal length. Elsewhere, they differ in length most of the time

because the Earth is _____. When day and night are equal everywhere

on Earth, it is an _____ and the start of the seasons _____.

II. Arrange the following locations according to their temperatures in the month of June. Use numbers from 1 (warmest) to 4 (coldest).

A. _____ New York City

B. _____ Antarctica

C. _____ 1°N 89°E

D. _____ 89°N 1°E

III. Answer in sentences.

The Earth's orbit is not an exact circle. In January, the Earth is closest to the sun. Why isn't it summer all over the Earth during that month?

_____

_____

_____

How Does Altitude Affect Climate?

Exploring Science

Higher Means Colder ... Up to a Point. If you want to cool off, climb a mountain. As you go up, the temperature goes down. For every 150 meters of altitude, the temperature drops 1°C. In the U.S. Rockies, some mountains are over 4000 meters high. Their tops are always covered with snow. Even in summer, it doesn't get warm enough for the snow to melt.

Does the temperature keep dropping all the way to the edge of the atmosphere? In the 1890s, Teisserenc de Bort studied the atmosphere near Paris. He attached thermometers and other instruments to kites. The kites were on strong wire, and the wind carried them several kilometers into the sky. The wires often broke, and the kites and equipment fell to the ground. So, de Bort switched to balloons. By 1902, he was able to show that the air stopped getting colder above 11 kilometers. The next layer, which he named the **stratosphere** (STRAT-uh-sfir), is warmer.

● In some places near the equator, there is ice and snow all year around. In what kind of places would you find these conditions?

Even in summer, the peaks of these mountains in Colorado are covered with snow. Can you explain why?

Altitude and Temperature

The air that we breathe is part of the Earth's **atmosphere** (AT-muhs-fir). The atmosphere is a mixture of gases, mostly nitrogen and oxygen. There are several different layers of atmosphere, however. They extend to an altitude of over 100 kilometers.

The layer people normally live in is at the bottom of the atmosphere. In this layer, the temperature becomes colder with altitude. Above this layer is the warmer layer called the stratosphere. The stratosphere will be discussed further in the next lesson.

Why does it get colder with altitude in the lowest level of the atmosphere? The main reason is that warm air near the surface loses pressure as it rises. Just as a tire heats up because of increased air pressure when it is pumped, air that loses pressure becomes cooler. This effect accounts for much of the cooling in the lower atmosphere.

The second reason is that the lower atmosphere is heated from the bottom up. Even though the Sun's energy reaches the upper atmosphere first, the lower atmosphere gets little heat from above.

About one-third of the Sun's energy is reflected back into space. About one-fifth of the Sun's energy is kept in the upper atmosphere, which is heated by that process. Nearly a half of the Sun's energy reaches the lower level of the atmosphere. Nearly all of that energy passes on through that lower layer without heating it. The part of the Sun's energy that heats air when it passes through was kept in the upper layers.

Sunlight does not heat air because the air is transparent. When the light hits solid ground or the water of the ocean it does not go very far.

Even in the clearest part of the ocean, all of the energy of sunlight has been captured by a depth of 70 meters or so. Nearly all of this energy becomes heat.

Land or sea that has been warmed by sunlight radiates energy back into the air. But the energy is infrared radiation, not visible light. Some of the molecules in the atmosphere are not transparent to infrared radiation. They are heated by it. The molecules that are heated by infrared radiation include carbon dioxide, water vapor, and methane. Although these are only a small part of the air, they account for most of its heat. This heat is said to come from the **greenhouse effect,** and gases such as carbon dioxide are called **greenhouse gases**.

Not only does the radiation come from below, but also the greenhouse gases are more common at the bottom of the atmosphere.

To Do Yourself   **What Kinds of Surfaces Absorb Heat Best?**

You will need:

2 empty coffee cans, 2 thermometers, aluminum foil, black construction paper, cellophane tape, knife

1. Cover one coffee can with aluminum foil (shiny side out). Tightly wrap a piece of black paper (or cloth) around the second can and tape it in place.
2. Use a knife to cut an "X" in the center of each the plastic coffee can lid. **Caution: Handle sharp objects with great care.** Place the lids on the coffee cans. **Carefully** insert a thermometer into each can through the "X" in the lid. Tape each thermometer in place so that it does not touch bottom of the can.
3. Place both cans in direct sunlight. After one hour, compare the temperatures of the air in the 2 cans.

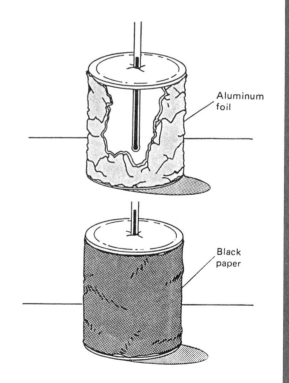

Aluminum foil

Black paper

Questions

1. Which can absorbed more heat? Why? _____

_____

2. Why is light-colored clothing more popular than dark-colored clothing in tropical

climates? _____

_____

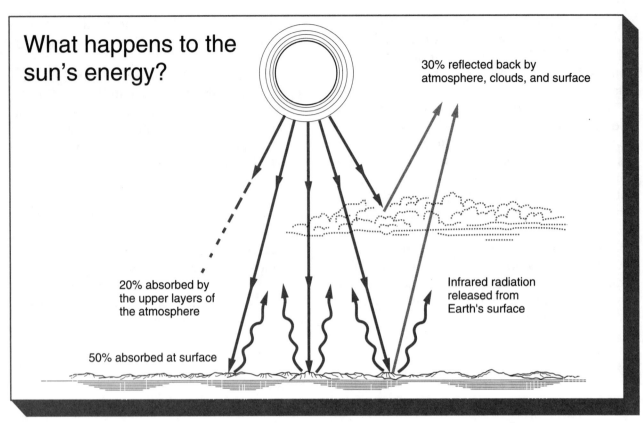

What happens to the sun's energy?

30% reflected back by atmosphere, clouds, and surface

20% absorbed by the upper layers of the atmosphere

50% absorbed at surface

Infrared radiation released from Earth's surface

Review

I. Fill in each blank with the word that fits best. Choose from the words below.

cooler   layers   increases   nitrogen   warmer   decreases
carbon dioxide   surface

Most of the atmosphere is _____ and oxygen. The atmosphere

consists of several _____. In the lowest, temperature becomes

_____ with increasing altitude. One reason is that air cools when

pressure _____. Sunlight passes through the lower layer but heats

the _____. In turn, this produces energy in a form that can be

kept in the air by _____.

II. Write **T** if a statement is true. If it is false, change the underlined word to make the statement true.

A. _____About <u>one-quarter</u> of the sun's energy reaches the Earth's surface.

B. _____The Earth is usually <u>colder</u> than the air directly above it.

C. _____Some of the heat from the sun that reaches the Earth is <u>radiated</u> into the air.

What is Earth's Atmosphere?

Exploring Science

Danger from the Sun. Early in the 1930s the Du Pont company began selling a new gas their chemists had created. The best feature of the gas was that it did not react with other materials, so it could be safely used for many purposes. After the first aerosol spray can, known as the "bug bomb" because it sprayed insecticide, was invented, manufacturers turned to the new gas and similar gases to use in all kinds of sprays—deodorant, hair spray, shaving cream, paint, cleanser; the list was endless.

Then in 1974 two scientists, Sherwood Roland and Mario Molina, recognized that there was a major problem. Because the gases used in spray cans did not react, they traveled all the way into the stratosphere unchanged. There the gases encountered radiation from the sun that broke them apart. One part of the gas, the element chlorine, then destroyed **ozone** (OH-zohn)—the gas that in the stratosphere traps much of the energy from the sun.

The energy trapped by ozone is not visible light and it is not infrared radiation. It is the radiation that is beyond the violet part of the rainbow. This radiation is called **ultraviolet** (ul-truh-VY-uh-lit). If the ozone layer is lost from the stratosphere, ultraviolet radiation could reach Earth's surface in great amounts. It could be enough to kill plants and to cause humans to develop the disease skin cancer.

At first, few believe Roland and Molina. But scientists devised experiments to measure ozone in the stratosphere and found that Roland and Molina were right. Other scientists measured ultraviolet radiation at ground level. They found this radiation growing greater, especially near the north and south poles.

Now governments became concerned. In 1987 they came together to solve the problem. Soon the whole world agreed to stop making the gases. Other gases could be used instead. Du Pont and other companies developed replacements. The whole world had a problem. The whole world got together and solved it.

● Why do you think it took so long before people recognized that the spray gases injured the environment?

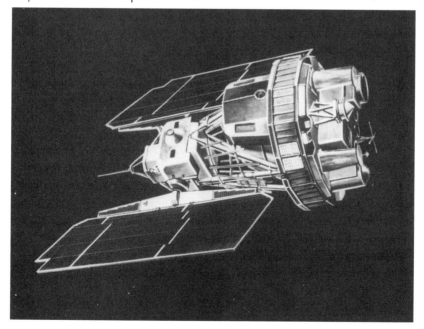

The TOMS satellite measures the ozone layer.

The Layers of the Atmosphere

Recall that Earth is surrounded by a mixture of gases—its atmosphere. Nitrogen gas makes up almost four-fifths of the atmosphere. Oxygen makes up about one-fifth. There are also small amounts of other gases, including the greenhouse gases such as water vapor, carbon dioxide, and methane. Ozone is found in the stratosphere; but some ozone is also produced by air pollution at ground level. Near the ground, ozone causes smog that is harmful to plants and animals.

The atmosphere is composed of several layers, each with its own mixture of gases. The layer closest to the surface of Earth is the **troposphere** (TRAHP-uh-sfir). Nearly all the water vapor is in this layer, so clouds, wind, rain, and other features that make up weather form in this layer.

Throughout the atmosphere, the number of molecules of gas in a given volume, which is reflected in air pressure, decreases steadily. This change accounts for some of the differences between the layers. The troposphere gradually becomes colder with altitude.

At about 11 kilometers, the temperature stops falling and begins to become greater. This is the lower boundary of the stratosphere. Although the air pressure continues to lessen, the mole-cules in the stratosphere take energy from sunlight. In the process, oxygen is changed to ozone and the ozone traps the ultraviolet light. Both processes heat the stratosphere. Unlike the troposphere, which is warm at the bottom and cold at the top, the stratosphere is cool at the bottom and warmest at the top. This is because it is heated from above.

Beyond the stratosphere lay two more layers—the **mesosphere** (MES-uh-sfir) and the **thermosphere** (THUR-muh-sfir)—that have very few molecules for a given volume. The mesosphere is cold, but sunlight heats the thermosphere.

Radiation from the sun and from outer space changes many of the molecules in these layers into ions. Ions are particles that carry electric charges. The region in which ions form is called the **ionosphere** (EYE-ahn-uh-sfir).

The ionosphere can reflect radio waves. This property is very important for some kinds of radio. An AM or shortwave radio wave that hits the ionosphere is reflected back toward Earth. Waves that are reflected at an angle can reach receivers hundreds or even thousands of kilometers away from the transmitter. People all over the world exchange messages using short-wave radio waves bounced off the ionosphere.

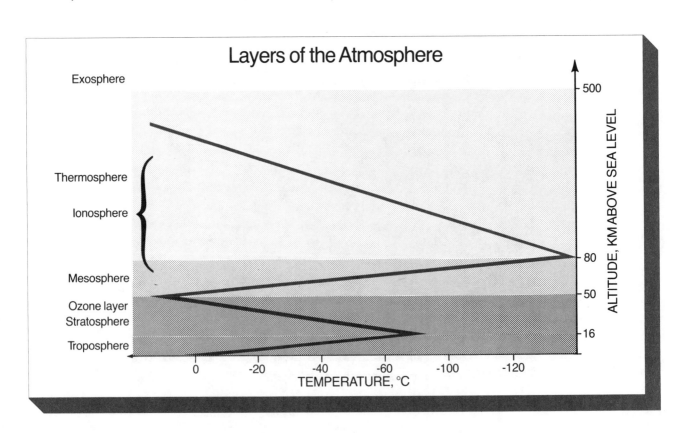

Review

I. Fill in each blank with the word that fits best. Choose from the words below.

ions   oxygen   ozone   weather   layers   thermosphere   rises   falls
troposphere   ionosphere   mesosphere   stratosphere   nitrogen

The most common gas in the atmosphere is _____. The atmosphere

is made up of several _____. The _____ is nearest to earth.

Most of earth's _____ forms in this layer. As you go higher, the next

layer is the _____. In this layer, sunlight changes oxygen to

_____ and the temperature _____. The layer of the atmosphere

that is very cold is the _____. Radiation from outer space strikes

the _____ first, and is one of the causes of the formation of

_____ in the top two layers of the atmosphere.

II. Circle the underlined word or words that makes each statement true.

A. The temperature of the troposphere is greater at the (bottom/top).

B. The density of the atmosphere is greatest (at the bottom of the troposphere/in the troposphere).

C. The ionosphere is caused by (radiation/temperature).

D. Ozone in the atmosphere absorbs (ultraviolet radiation/infrared radiation).

E. In the ionosphere, there are many particles with (ultraviolet light/electrical charges).

III. Answer in sentences.

How is the ionosphere useful to people?

_____

_____

_____

What Causes Winds?

Exploring Science

Crossing the Atlantic. Christopher Columbus set sail from Palos, Spain, on August 3, 1492. Although he wanted to reach the East Indies by sailing west, Columbus didn't head west right away. Instead, he headed southwest.

Columbus was in charge of three sailing ships. Sailing ships need a push from the wind to move. Usually, winds do not blow westward off the coast of Spain. But Columbus had heard that there were steady winds near the Canary Islands, 1300 kilometers southwest of Spain.

Indeed, the winds were there, blowing steadily from the northeast. On September 1, Columbus' ships left the Canary Islands with the help of those winds. They sailed west across the Atlantic. On October 12, the men spotted land in the Caribbean Sea.

After exploring the area for three months, Columbus had to face a problem. How could the fleet return home? They couldn't take the same route. The winds that had carried the ships west across the Atlantic would prevent them from sailing east.

This time, Columbus sailed northeast to go east. He made the right decision. North of the Caribbean, he found winds that carried the ships back to Spain.

● The Vikings discovered North America centuries before Columbus. Sailing from Scandinavia, they landed near 60° N latitude. What does this tell you about winds farther north?

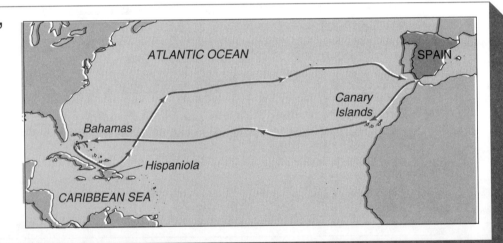

Columbus' First Voyage

ATLANTIC OCEAN

SPAIN

Canary Islands

Bahamas

Hispaniola

CARIBBEAN SEA

Winds Around the World

Columbus was a very skillful sailor. It would have taken more luck than skill to return the ship to Spain if the winds of earth did not follow a certain pattern. Look at the diagram. It shows the major wind patterns north and south of the equator. Winds form these patterns because of the unequal heating of the earth's surface and the earth's rotation.

As air is heated, it expands. It becomes less dense. As air cools, its particles move closer together and the air becomes more dense. At the equator, the sun is almost always directly overhead. The heated air in this area expands. Cool, denser air flows toward the equator and underneath the warm air. A circular flow of air is set up.

As the warm air is pushed up over the equator, it cools. It spreads out and flows toward the poles. At about 30° latitude, the air has cooled so much that it begins to sink. At the earth's surface, some of it flows back toward the equator where it is warmed again. This kind of continuous air flow is called a **convection cell**.

You might expect movement within the cell to be along a north-south path at the surface. But the earth's rotation turns the air flow. In the Northern Hemisphere, the flow turns to the right. In the Southern Hemisphere, the air flow turns to the left.

The winds that form in this cell are called the **trade winds.** In the Northern Hemisphere, trade winds blow *from* the northeast *to* the southwest. In the Southern Hemisphere, the winds blow *from* the southeast *to* the northwest. It was the trade winds that brought Columbus from Spain to the Caribbean.

Another cell develops at each of the poles. Air is chilled at the poles. It sinks and flows toward the equator. At 60° latitude, the air warms and rises. Again, the flow near the surface is turned by the earth's rotation. Like the trade winds, these polar winds flow from an easterly direction. They are called the **easterlies** (EE-stur-lees).

Between latitudes 30° and 60°, another cell forms. Air that rose over the equator sinks at 30°. Some of this air becomes part of the trade winds. Some of it flows toward the poles. This poleward flow rises at 60°. Near the surface, the earth's rotation turns this poleward flow so that it blows from west to east. These winds are called the **westerlies** (WES-tur-lees).

Between cells, there are regions with very little wind. The equator is between two cells. The region of calm at the equator is called the **doldrums** (DOHL-drumz). North and south of the equator at 30° latitude are the **horse latitudes.** These regions of little wind got their name during the time when ships carried horses from Europe to America. If a ship was caught in these belts of no wind, sailors would have to throw horses overboard to save food and drinking water.

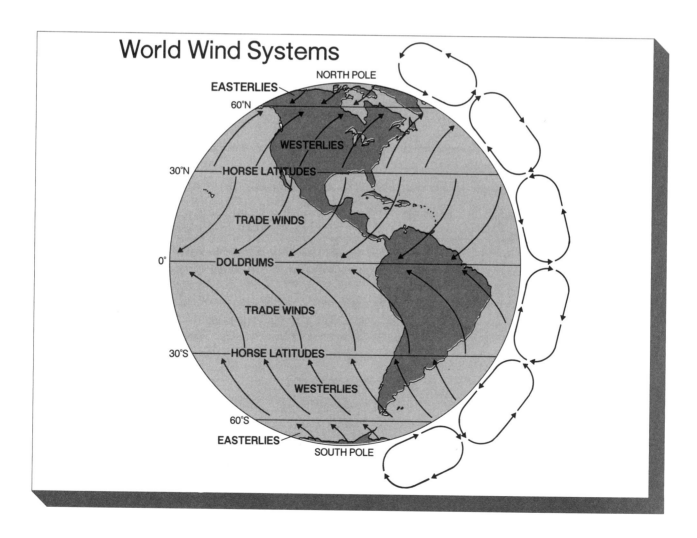

World Wind Systems

To Do Yourself — What Are Convection Currents?

You will need:

Convection box, candle, matches, piece of rope

1. Using a match, start a short piece of rope (or cloth) burning. **Caution: Use extreme care when dealing with fire.** Once the rope is aflame, blow out the flame to produce a smoky material. Hold the smoking material over both chimneys of the convection box. Record your observations.
2. Light the candle. Hold the smoking material over the chimney that is not over the candle. Record your observations.

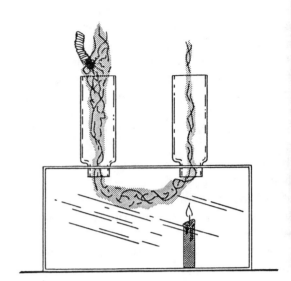

Questions

1. If you blew out the candle, would a convection current still be present? Explain.

   _____

2. Land and water do not heat evenly. How does this uneven heating cause breezes to

   blow? _____

   _____

Review

I. Fill in each blank with the word that fits best. Choose from the words below.

   trade winds   **easterlies**   **doldrums**   **horse latitudes**   **northeast**
   southeast

   If you travel north from the equator, you enter the wind belt called the

   _____ . In the Northern Hemisphere, these winds blow

   from the _____ . A region of calm at the equator is the

   _____ . Regions of little wind, 30° north and south of the

   equator are called the _____ .

II. Answer in Sentences.

   Sally, who lives in New York, hears that a baseball game in St. Louis has been rained out. She tells her family to expect rain in the next day or two. Sally often makes similar predictions. She is right about as often as professional weather forecasters. What is the secret of Sally's method?

How Do Local Winds Form?

Exploring Science

A Lesson From the Chief. A Russian writer was visiting the Yakut (yah-KOOT), the people who live in Arctic Siberia. A fierce wind was blowing. The Yakut called this wind the Chief. The force of the wind blew the stuffing from between the logs of the cabin. Even indoors, the writer could feel the Chief. Still, he wanted to go outside. The Yakut told him not to try it. "The Chief will not like it," they said.

The writer insisted. The Yakut agreed to let him go on one condition. He must have a long strap fastened around his waist. The people inside the cabin would hold the other end of the strap.

The writer described what happened. "I was flung violently to the ground. The air was full of sleet that whipped against my face. In an instant, my cheekbones were frozen. I could not see at all. Where was the door? If my friends had not held the strap, I could not have got back. I just managed to crawl in."

● A wind such as the Chief seems destructive. What good things do you think winds can do?

Breezes and Monsoons

You know how **global winds** form. These are the major wind patterns in the Northern and Southern Hemispheres. There are also **local winds** that affect smaller areas. Some local winds, like the Chief, are so well known that people have named them.

Like global winds, local winds form because of uneven heating of the earth's surface. One kind of wind forms near oceans and large lakes. During the day, the land heats up faster than the water. The air above the land rises. Because the air molecules spread out, cooler air from above the water flows toward the land to take the place of the air that has risen. This movement of air creates a **sea breeze.** At night, the land cools off more quickly than the water. Now, the cooler air over the land flows toward the water. A **land breeze** begins to flow. Like global winds, these local winds are named for the direction from which they start.

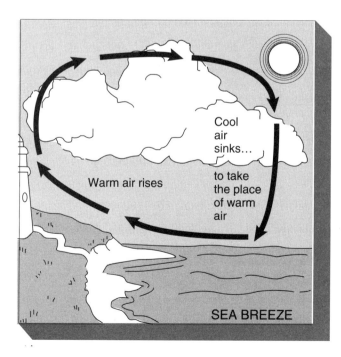

Warm air rises

Cool air sinks… to take the place of warm air

SEA BREEZE

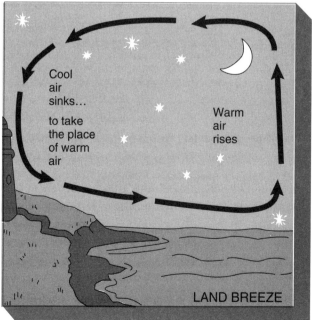

Cool air sinks… to take the place of warm air

Warm air rises

LAND BREEZE

Monsoons (mon-SOONS) are land and sea breezes on a giant scale. Monsoons change with the seasons. They occur in places that have cold winters and warm summers.

Monsoons are common in central Asia. There, the land gets very cold in winter. All winter long, a cold, dry wind flows from central Asia over India toward the Indian Ocean. It is the **winter monsoon.** By May, the sun has warmed the land. Cool, wet air from the ocean flows toward India and central Asia. When it reaches land, heavy rains result. This **summer monsoon** is eagerly awaited, because the rains cool the land and provide needed water.

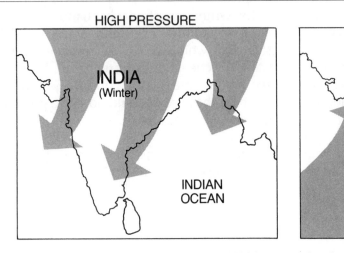
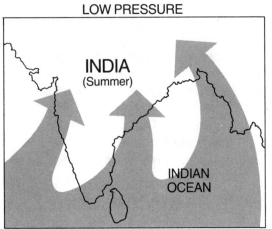

India's monsoons. Which season is rainy, winter or summer?

Review

I. Fill in each blank with the word that fits best. Choose from the words below.

day   night   monsoon   spring   sea   land   seasons   summer

When the land is cool and the sea is warm, a breeze blows from the

_____ toward the _____ . This

movement usually occurs during the _____ . A large-scale

wind of the same type is called a _____ . This type of wind

changes with the _____ .

II. Write **T** is a statement is true. If is is false, change the underlined word or words to make the statement true.

A. _____ A <u>sea</u> breeze forms when the land is warmer than the sea.

B. _____ <u>Winds</u> form because the Earth's surface is not heated evenly.

C. _____ A <u>winter</u> monsoon flows from the ocean toward the land.

III. Answer in sentences.

Do you think the Hawaiian Islands have monsoons? Explain your answer.

What Are the Climates of Earth?

Exploring Science

Its a Record! You may have heard a local weather reporter announce, "Today is the hottest day on record." But your town has probably never had weather records like the following:

The Coldest Places on Earth. At the Soviet Antarctic Station of Vostok, the temperature dropped to -89.4°C in 1983. On the average, however, another place in Antarctica is colder. At the Pole of Cold, the average annual temperature is -57°C, 8° colder than the South Pole.

The Hottest Places. In the Libyan desert, El Azizia reached 58°C in the shade in 1922. In Dallol, Ethiopia, the average annual temperature is 34.5°C, making it the hottest place in the world year-round.

The Wettest Places. On the island of Reunion in the Indian Ocean, 1.88 meters of rain fell in a single 24-hour period in 1952. In 1861, 26.47 meters of rain fell during a 12-month period in Cherrapunji (CHAIR-ah-PUNJ-ee), India. This was an average of more than 7 centimeters each day. The place with the highest amount of rainfall is Mawsynram (mah-SIN-ram), India. Mawsynram receives an average of 11.87 meters of rainfall each year.

The Driest Places. In parts of the Atacama Desert of Peru, it has not rained for at least 400 years.

● How do winds and mountains affect which places are wet and which are dry?

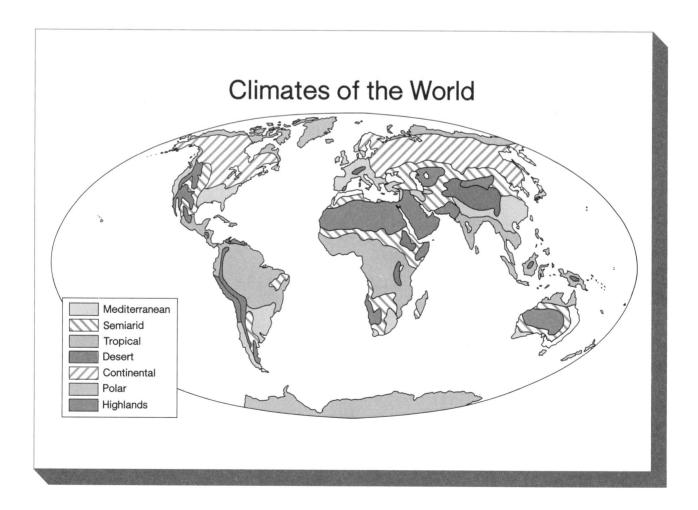

Climates of the World

Legend:
- Mediterranean
- Semiarid
- Tropical
- Desert
- Continental
- Polar
- Highlands

Climates of the World

Different regions of earth have different climates. Temperature and rainfall are the most important elements of climate. Let's look at the most common types of climate.

TROPICAL. The region near the equator is called the tropics. **Tropical climates** are hot and wet. Most of Hawaii has a tropical climate. Some tropical areas are wet all year round. Others, like the southern tip of Florida, have much less rain.

SUBTROPICAL. **Subtropical climates** are usually found between the latitudes of 30° and 40°. They are not as hot or as wet as the tropics. The southeastern United States has a subtropical climate.

MEDITERRANEAN. The climate of Italy and Greece is called **Mediterranean**. In this type of climate, summers are warm and dry, while winters are warm and wet. Much of southern California has a Mediterranean climate. Northern California and the upper west coast near the ocean have a **marine** climate that is moist and moderate all year.

DESERT. Some dry climates have almost no rainfall at all. These are **arid**, or **desert**, **climates**. Many places with arid climates are hot during the day and cool at night. Parts of the western United States have an arid climate. In other dry climates, there is a short wet season. This climate is called **semiarid**. The western part of the Central Plains is semiarid.

CONTINENTAL. In **continental climates**, summers are warm and winters are very cold. Rain falls during the summer. During the winter, it snows. Much of the northern part of the United States, especially the northeast, has a continental climate.

POLAR. Close to the poles the average temperature is below freezing all year long. Most of the ground is covered with ice or snow. **Polar climates** are quite dry. Parts of Alaska have a polar climate.

HIGHLAND. Remember, temperatures fall as you climb above sea level. **Highland climates** are found on high mountains and plateaus which are cooler than nearby lowlands. In the United States, the Rocky Mountains and parts of Alaska have highland climates. Even some places near the equator have a highland climate. Mauna Kea, a mountain in Hawaii, has a highland climate. Sometimes, in the winter, Mauna Kea is covered with snow.

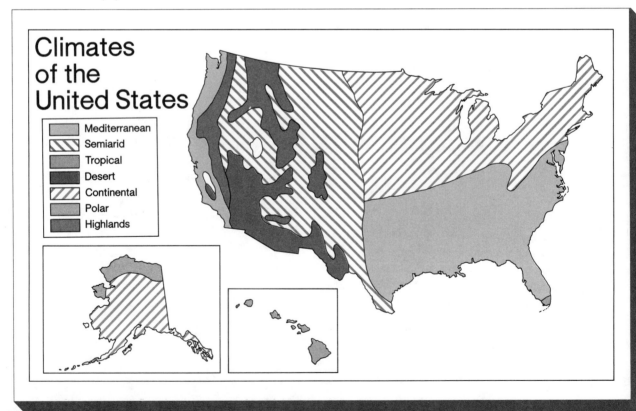

Climates of the United States

- Mediterranean
- Semiarid
- Tropical
- Desert
- Continental
- Polar
- Highlands

Review

I. Fill in each blank with the word that fits best. Choose from the words below

continental   **desert**   **highland**   **rainfall**   **altitude**   **wet**   **warm**
cold   **temperature**

Two important elements of climate are _____ and

_____ . The northeastern part of the United States has a

_____ climate, with _____ summers

and _____ winters.

II. Match each climate in column **A** with its description in column **B**.

	A.		**B.**
1.	_____ tropical	**a.**	Summers are dry. Winters have some rain. Temperatures are warm but not hot.
2.	_____ Mediterranean	**b.**	It is very cold all year. Almost all the ground is covered with ice or snow.
3.	_____ desert	**c.**	Temperatures may be hot during day and cold at night. Almost no rain falls all year.
4.	_____ continental	**d.**	There is rain in the hot summer, snow in the cold winter.
5.	_____ polar	**e.**	It is hot and rainy all year.

III. Answer in sentences.

Why do tops of mountains have a different climate than nearby low areas?

_____

_____

_____

A. Hidden in the puzzle are words related to climate. The clues in the statements will help you. Write the correct word on the line next to its clue. Then circle the word in the puzzle.

```
S  O  M  T  U  N  D  R  A  C  E  L  L
T  A  O  D  O  L  D  R  U  M  S  W  A
R  I  N  E  T  O  B  D  E  S  E  R  T
A  C  S  D  A  F  J  U  P  E  Y  S  I
T  R  O  P  I  C  S  X  A  Q  K  S  T
O  R  O  X  A  L  S  T  E  U  A  T  U
S  E  N  O  N  I  N  F  R  A  R  E  D
P  G  B  I  O  M  E  O  I  T  I  F  E
H  B  A  N  H  A  L  Z  L  O  D  P  H
E  D  I  M  E  T  O  O  C  R  I  E  F
R  G  Y  F  O  E  H  N  S  O  T  L  A
E  M  P  V  U  T  J  E  Y  N  S  O  W
T  U  Z  R  L  O  N  G  I  T  U  D  E
```

1. _____ An imaginary line that circles the earth midway between the poles.

2. _____ Measures the distance, in degrees, east and west of the prime meridian.

3. _____ A region of very little wind near the equator.

4. _____ A land or sea breeze on a giant scale.

5. _____ The layer of the atmosphere where temperature begins to increase with altitude.

6. _____ A form of oxygen that protects the surface of the earth from ultraviolet radiation.

7. _____ The long-term pattern of weather of a region.

8. _____ The main heating rays of the sun.

B. Write the word or words that best completes each statement.

1. _____ The northern hemisphere tilts toward the sun around
   a. December 22   **b.** March 20   **c.** June 21

2. _____ Between June 21 and December 22, the length of daylight in the
   northern hemisphere   **a.** gets longer   **b.** gets shorter   **c.** stays the same

3. _____ The lengths of daylight and darkness are the same about **a.** September 23 **b.** June 21 **c.** December 22

4. _____ The north pole is at **a.** 0 degrees latitude **b.** 90 degrees latitude **c.** 90 degrees latitude

5. _____ Greenwich, England is at **a.** 0 degrees latitude **b.** 0 degrees longitude **c.** 90 degrees longitude

6. _____ Day and night are about the same length all year at the **a.** north pole **b.** south pole **c.** equator

7. _____ Temperature _increases_ with _decreasing_ **a.** longitude **b.** latitude **c.** altitude

8. _____ One of the greenhouse gases is **a.** oxygen **b.** nitrogen **c.** carbon dioxide

9. _____ About one-fifth of the air is **a.** oxygen **b.** nitrogen **c.** carbon dioxide

10. _____ Air temperature goes down as altitude increases until you reach the **a.** troposphere **b.** stratosphere **c.** ionosphere

C. Apply What You Know

1. Study the map of North America. Label each numbered part with the climate found at that place. Choose from these labels

continental   **desert**   **polar**   **subtropical**   **tropical**

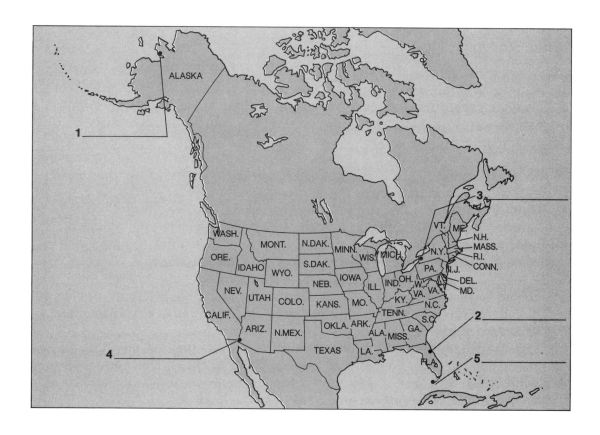

2. Study the diagram of the atmosphere. Label each numbered part. Choose from these labels.

troposphere   **thermosphere**   **ozone layer**   **ionosphere**   **mesosphere**

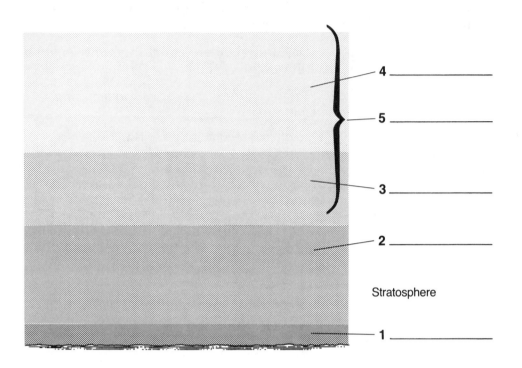

4 _____

5 _____

3 _____

2 _____

Stratosphere

1 _____

D. Find Out More

1. You are the captain of a ship that will sail around the world from New York City to San Fransisco, California. Use what you know about prevailing winds to plan a route heading east and sailing around Africa. Draw the route on a large map of the earth. Mark the parts of the route where you have to worry about lack of wind.

2. Make a graph showing the times of sunrise and sunset in your area for a two-week period. Use the graph to explain the changes in weather that are typical of your climate at this time of year.

3. From the nearest office of the U.S. Weather Service, get the following information for your area: warmest and coldest temperatures, greatest snowfalls, most rain, longest time without rain, and other climate extremes. Make a chart of these records to display in your classroom.

4. Listen to a radio at night for any distant stations you can receive. Make a record of the stations and locate them on a map. Does any pattern emerge? Compare your results with those of your classmates to see who received a broadcast from the greatest distance.

5. Use the library to find out more about local winds that people in a particular area have named. Choose one wind to study. Find out when the wind blows, why it is special, and if there are any local legends about the wind. Prepare a report for your class.

Careers in Earth Science

Living With the Climate. Climates are different in parts of the earth. But people are very much alike. They need to be protected from temperatures that are very hot or very cold. One source of protection is a house.

In many countries, buildings work with the climate. In a tropical monsoon region, for example, people build homes that can withstand heavy rains and protect against heat. But office buildings are also needed in such regions. Today, people design buildings that are comfortable in any climate, from the equator to the North Pole.

Heating/Cooling Engineer. In most places, modern buildings have systems for heating, air conditioning, or both. For each building, there must be enough hot or cold air. Providing too much of either, however, is very costly.

A heating/cooling engineer has learned where and how to install heating and cooling systems. These engineers use mathematics to find the heating and cooling requirements for a room or a building. In addition to a high school education, the job usually requires a year or more of technical school or on-the-job training.

Architect. An architect is a person trained to design buildings. Today, architects must keep many factors in mind—climate is just one of them. A properly designed building will have lower energy bills than one that is poorly designed for the climate. It will also have the space and other necessities for people to work efficiently.

Architects often take special five-year programs in college. Or, they may follow college with two years of graduate study. An architect in the United States must have a license to design buildings.

This architect is designing a floor plan for an office building.

It takes training and experience to know how large an air conditioner is needed and where to install the unit.

UNIT
9

WEATHER

How Does Water Get Into the Air?

Exploring Science

It Sounded Good at the Time. Did you know that scientists are often wrong? Sometimes a scientist has a simple idea to solve a problem. However, the idea often leads to a theory that doesn't work. For example, many scientists tried to explain how water gets into the air. Most of their explanations were wrong.

One idea was that water dissolved in air. People knew that salt could dissolve in water. Although you could no longer see the salt once it was dissolved, you knew it was still there. Perhaps, then, water could be dissolved in air in the same way.

Another idea was based upon tiny bubbles. Soap bubbles float in the air. Maybe tiny bubbles of water rise in the air, too. In 1783, one scientists went so far as to claim that he had seen these water bubbles with a microscope.

Neither of these ideas was correct. In 1802, John Dalton, an English scientist, found the truth. First, water becomes a gas. Then it mixes with the other gases of the air.

● What evidence do we have that water can mix with the air?

Temperature and Humidity

There are many ways to show that water goes into the air. Leave water in an open container. After a few days, the water is gone. It has **evaporated** (ih-VAP-uh-rayt-id). That is, it has changed from a liquid to a gas. The gas has "escaped" into the air.

When you boil water, it becomes steam. You can see steam. Then the steam disappears into the air. The water has changed from a liquid to a gas. This gas is called **water vapor** (VAY-pur). Water vapor is invisible. It mixes with the other gases of the air.

The amount of water vapor in the air is not always the same. It depends on many factors. Temperature is one of the factors. Warm air can hold more water vapor than cold air can hold. For example, a cubic meter of air at 10° C can hold about 9 grams of water vapor. At 25° C, this same amount of air can hold 28 grams of water vapor. These amounts (9 grams and 28 grams) are the most water vapor a cubic meter of air can hold at the given temperatures.

Suppose there are actually 14 grams of water vapor in the air at 25° C. Then the air is holding only half the water vapor it can hold at that temperature. A weather forecaster would tell you that the **relative humidity** (REL-uh-tiv hyoo-MID-ih-tee) of that air is 50 percent. Relative humidity compares the amount of water vapor in the air with the amount of water vapor the air can hold at any temperature.

Can water vapor in the air change back to a liquid? Set a glass of ice water in a warm place. In a few minutes, the outside of the glass becomes wet. Some of the water vapor from the air has changed back to a liquid, or **condensed** (kun-DENST).

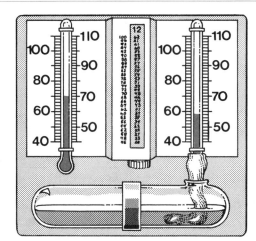

The wet-bulb dry-bulb thermometer is used to measure relative humidity.

Water condenses on the glass because the warm air touching the glass is cooled. The amount of water vapor that that air can hold decreases. The relative humidity of that air goes up. When the relative humidity goes above 100 percent, water vapor in the air condenses to form a liquid.

The temperature at which condensation starts is called the **dew point.** The dew point varies for different samples of air. For example, in very dry air, the dew point is quite low. Since there is not much water vapor present, the air must be cooled to a low temperature before the water vapor will start to condense. On the other hand, in very moist air, the dew point is quite high.

To Do Yourself How Can You Find the Dew Point?

You will need:

Small tin can, thermometer, ice, water

1. Half-fill a shiny tin can with water. Do not use very cold water.
2. Place a thermometer in the water. Slowly add small pieces of ice to the water. **Carefully** use the thermometer to stir the water as you add the ice.
3. Watch the outside of the can closely as you add the ice. As soon as a fine mist starts to form on the surface of the can, stop adding ice. Remove any ice that has not melted and read the temperature of the water. Record this in the data table.
4. Observe the mist carefully. At the moment the mist starts to disappear, read the temperature of the water again. Record this temperature in the data table.

The mist that forms on the can is condensation—moisture from the air in the room. The temperature at which condensation starts to form is called the dew point temperature.

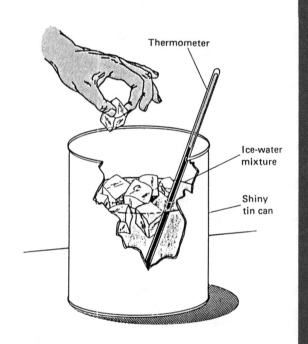

Data Table

Conditions	Temperature
mist starts to form	
mist starts to disappear	

Questions

1. Add the temperatures from Steps 3 and 4 of the activity. Divide the result by 2 to find the average. This average is the dew point temperature for your room at this time. What is the dew point temperature? _____

2. What atmospheric conditions affect dew point temperature? Explain the effect of each condition you list. _____
_____

Review

I. Fill in each blank with the word that fits best. Choose from the words below.

more   **less**   **condenses**   **evaporates**   **relative humidity**

temperature   **steam**   **water vapor**

When water _____ , it changes from liquid to gas. The

gas is called _____ . Warm air can hold

_____ water than cold air. The _____

compares how much water is in the air with how much the air can actually

hold.

II. A cubic meter of air at 10° C holds about 4.5 grams of water vapor. What is
the relative humidity?

_____

_____

_____

III. Answer in sentences.

The relative humidity is 75 percent. The temperature drops from 22° to 20° C.
Does the relative humidity increase or decrease? Explain.

_____

_____

_____

How Does Air Pressure Change?

Exploring Science

The 10-meter mystery. The Greek scientist Aristotle over 2000 years ago was interested in the nature of matter and how it behaves. He knew that the wind—we would say "air"—is matter that fills up all available space. If you try to remove the wind from an enclosed space, it pushes to fill the space up again. Therefore, Aristotle thought that matter must be everywhere. Some other Greek scientists thought that there can be a place with no matter, a place they called the **vacuum** (VAK-yew-wuhm). Aristotle said that the vacuum cannot exist. His saying, "Nature hates a vacuum," became famous.

In the 17th century, the Italian scientist, Galileo, was also interested in matter and vacuums. He observed workers pumping water. Their pumps lifted the water for about 10 meters. Then they had to put the water in a container and use a second pump to lift it any higher. The pumps worked by making a vacuum at the top of the pipe. "Nature hates a vacuum," the workers told Galileo. "so the water rushes up the pipe to prevent the vacuum." Galileo joked to his assistant Evangelista Torricelli that "Nature only seems to hate vacuums less then 10 meters long." He asked Torricelli to study the problem.

After three years, Torricelli solved the mystery. Water would rise only 10 meters because the atmosphere above the water weighs the same as 10 meters of water. A vacuum did not pull the water up the pipe. The weight of the outside air pushed the water up the pipe to fill the vacuum.

● Would a pump at the top of a mountain raise water more or less than 10 meters? Explain.

The Barometer and Air Pressure

Torricelli had correctly decided that the weight of the column of water was important. Its height was not. Working with a 10-meter column of water was very awkward. So, Torricelli switched from water to mercury. Mercury is a much heavier liquid than water. A column of mercury 76 centimeters high weighs the same as a similar column of water 10 meters high. Working with the shorter column was much easier.

Torricelli sealed one end of a narrow tube and filled the tube with mercury. He then lowered the open end of the tube into a dish of mercury and held the tube vertically. The weight of the air on the dish of mercury supported the mercury in the tube.

However, Torricelli found that the height of the mercury column changed from day to day. He knew that this meant that the weight of the air was changing in some way. When the weight of the air increased, it pushed the mercury higher in the tube. When the weight of the air decreased, the height of the column of mercury decreased.

A French scientist named Blaise Pascal set out to test Torricelli's ideas. Pascal measured the length of a mercury column at the bottom of a mountain. The column was 71 centimeters high. He then took the column of mercury to the top of the mountain. There, the column was

Torricelli inventing the barometer.

only 62.6 cm high. This experiment proved that Torricelli was correct. The mercury column fell as the weight of the air around it fell. Torricelli had invented the **barometer** (buh-RAHM-uh-tuhr).

Today, barometers are used to measure **air pressure** as a method to predict weather. Torricelli could not use his barometer to predict weather changes. He did not know how or why air pressure changed from day to day. He also did not know how this change was related to weather.

To Do Yourself   How Can You Measure Air Pressure?

You will need:

Wide-mouthed jar or coffee can, large balloon, wide rubber band, 2 wooden splints (or ice cream sticks), glue, sheet of paper

1. Cut off the neck of a balloon. Carefully stretch the balloon over the mouth of a jar or can. The balloon should fit tightly, like a drum. Use a rubber band to hold the balloon in place.
2. Cut a small square from the end of a wooden splint. Glue the square to the center of the stretched balloon. Allow the glue to dry.
3. Glue one end of a wooden splint to the wooden square. Hold the splint in place until the glue is dry. You now have a simple barometer.
4. Tape a sheet of paper to a vertical surface. Place your barometer so that the end of the wooden splint is right next to the paper.
5. On the paper, mark the level of the splint for several days in a row. Each day, mark the date and the weather conditions.

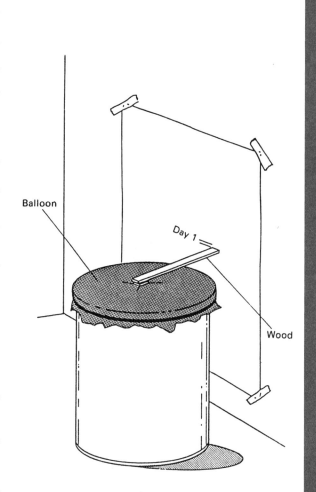

A barometer measures air pressure. Air pressure is closely related to weather conditions. In fair, dry weather, air pressure is generally "high." In cloudy, stormy weather, air pressure is "low."

Questions

1. What causes the level of the wooden pointer on your barometer to move?

_____

2. Did the movement of your barometer agree with the weather conditions? If not, try to explain what might have gone wrong. _____

_____

Air pressure is a measure of the weight of the air at a given time and place. You know that air pressure can change with altitude. How else can it change? When air is heated, it expands. Its particles spread out. Warm air, then, exerts less pressure than cool air.

Moist, or humid, air also exerts less pressure than dry air. This is because particles of water vapor are lighter than some of the particles that make up air. When air contains a lot of water vapor, it is lighter than dry air.

Knowing how air pressure changes can help you use a barometer to predict the weather. When the barometer is high, the air is heavy. It must be cool and dry. When the barometer is low, the air must be warm and moist.

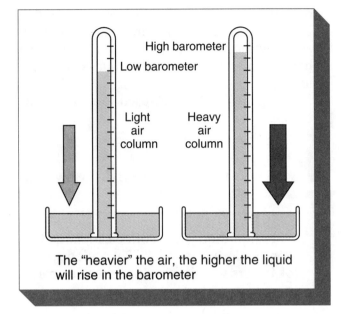

The "heavier" the air, the higher the liquid will rise in the barometer

Review

I. Fill in each blank with the word that fits best. Choose from the words below.

cool   warm   wet   dry   height   weight   rises   falls
barometer   thermometer

Torricelli discovered that a column of mercury was held up by the

_____ of air around it. He had invented

the _____ . When air pressure increases, the column

of mercury _____ . A high reading on a barometer means

that the air is _____ and _____ .

II. Which of the following is lighter?

A. _____ warm air or cool air

B. _____ dry air or moist air

C. _____ high-altitude or low-altitude air

III. Answer in sentences.

A mass of cool, dry air is often called a "high." Explain why this is so.

_____

_____

_____

What Are Clouds?

Exploring Science

The Cloud Namer. Luke Howard worked as a pharmacist in London. In 1803, when he was 30 years old, Howard made a lasting impact on the science of weather. He did something no one had done before. He named the clouds.

Luke Howard had studied Latin in school. He said he had learned so much Latin that he was unable to forget it. So Howard gave the clouds Latin names.

Along with the names, Howard made water color paintings of the clouds. He used the paintings to explain the names. He named clouds that were curled after a lock of hair—**cirrus** (SIR-us) in Latin. Layers of clouds he called **stratus,** from the Latin word for spread out. (Layers of rock are often called strata, too.) He named large single clouds **cumulus** (KYOO-myuh-lus), which means heap. Clouds from which rain comes were **nimbus,** which means shower. All of Howard's names for clouds are still used today.

● Using Howard's system, what would you name a large, single cloud from which rain is falling?

Cloud types: cirrus (top), cumulus (bottom).

Clouds

Howard's cloud names are mainly descriptive. Cirrus clouds are high, thin, wispy clouds. Often the edges of these clouds "curl" upward. Cumulus clouds are white and puffy, like "heaps" of cotton. They are often called "fair-weather" clouds. Nimbus clouds are thick and gray.

Ten different types of clouds occur in nature. To name these clouds, modern cloud researchers have added the prefix *alto-*to some of the cloud names in Howard's system. Alto means "high." For example, high, white, puffy clouds are called *altocumulus.*

Some of the names in Howard's system are used together to name clouds. *Stratocumulus* is one example. What do you think a stratocumulus cloud looks like?

Altocumulus (top) and stratocumulus.

The ten different cloud types are put into groups. The groupings are based on the altitudes of the bottoms, or bases, of the clouds.

Clouds form when water vapor in the air condenses. When air near the surface is heated, it expands and rises. As it rises, it begins to cool and the relative humidity goes up. When the temperature of the air reaches its dew point, tiny water droplets condense out of the air. Clouds are made up of these tiny water droplets. At very high altitudes, clouds may consist of tiny crystals of ice.

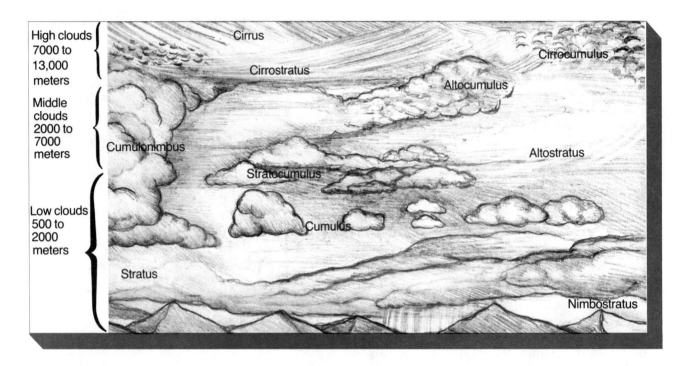

Review

I. Fill in each blank with the word that fits best. Choose from the words below.

cumulus   nimbus   stratus   cirrus   cirro   condenses

Clouds form when water vapor in the air _____ .

The Latin word _____ is used to describe a cloud that is producing rain. The second highest clouds have the word

_____ in their name. The highest clouds

are _____ .

II. Match each cloud in column **A** with its description in column **B**.

A	B
_____ **1.** cumulonimbus	**a.** A very high cloud that looks like a curl
_____ **2.** altocumulus	**b.** A single cloud that produces rain
_____ **3.** cirrus	**c.** A layer of clouds that are not especially high
_____ **4.** stratus	**d.** A single high cloud

What Causes Fog and Smog?

Exploring Science

The Great London Fog. London, England has always been famous for its fog. So, the thick, black fog that fell on the city Thursday, December 4, 1952, was not unusual. By Friday, however, the fog was so bad that conductors had to guide buses through the streets with flares. Moviegoers could not see the screens. An opera was canceled because the singers could not see the conductor.

There were also more serious effects. People began to feel ill. Many had trouble breathing. The fog continued through Saturday. By Sunday, the hospitals were full.

On Tuesday, the Great London Fog was gone. About 4000 people had died from the pollution that came with the fog.

● A fog that lasts all day in London is more likely to occur in December than in July. Why?

The "Great London Fog" of 1952 was so thick that the driver of this mail truck had to be guided by a mailman on foot.

Fogs and Smog

The Great London Fog of 1952 was actually **smog,** a combination of fog and smoke. The dense, black smoke that filled the air came from the burning of coal. Since that time, laws have been passed to lower the amount of coal smoke in the air of London.

London, however, still has foggy weather. The coast of England, remember, is warmed by the Gulf Stream. Warm, moist air from over the water moves in over the cooler land. As the air cools below the dew point, water vapor in the air condenses. **Fog** is the result.

Newfoundland also has London-type fog. Air over the warm Gulf Stream meets air over the cold Labrador Current, producing one of the foggiest places on earth.

Fog can form when the ground cools quickly at night. The cold ground cools the air directly above it. If the air is moist, the relative humidity will rise above 100 percent. Water droplets will condense. This **ground fog** seldom lasts into the day. When the sun begins to warm the air, the relative humidity goes down. The fog "burns off," or evaporates.

Ground fogs are common in valleys and other low areas near rivers or lakes. They usually form on calm, clear nights.

This Los Angeles "smog" is caused by air pollution from automobiles, not by smoke and fog.

Review

I. Fill in each blank with the word that fits best. Choose from the words below.

sea   land   cool   warm   dry   moist   sunlight   smoke   air

Fog forms when _____ , moist air over the sea meets cool

_____ . Ground fogs are formed when the ground cools

the _____ directly above it. If the air is

_____ , water vapor will condense. A combination of

_____ and fog produces smog.

II. For each set of conditions in column **A,** identify the result in column **B.**

A	B
_____ 1. Warm, wet air rises to a height of 1000 meters	a. fog
_____ 2. A community in a valley between two high mountains uses wood-burning stoves in winter.	b. cloud
_____ 3. A cold current is close to a warm coast in summer.	c. smog

III. Answer in sentences.

Why are ground fogs common near lakes and rivers?

What Causes Rain and Snow?

Exploring Science

Are Any Two Snowflakes Alike? You probably know that most snowflakes have six sides or points. If you have ever looked closely at snowflakes, you also know that their shapes can be elaborate. You may even have heard that no two of these shapes are ever alike. Can this be true?

Here are the results of some calculations done by Dr. John Hallet. Dr. Hallet studies the atmosphere. He finds that a snowstorm produces about 1,000,000,000,000,000,000,000 snowflakes. The shape of each snowflake depends on the temperature and humidity of the air.

But these factors change with altitude as the snowflake falls.

Also, each snowflake falls through a different path. The number of possible paths in a snowstorm is 1 followed by 5 million zeros. This means that the chance of finding two identical snowflakes in the same storm, or even hundreds of storms, is close to zero.

● What do you call solids that form characteristic shapes as snowflakes do?

Snowflakes can be found in many beautiful crystal patterns.

Rain and Snow

Water vapor and tiny cloud droplets could remain in the air indefinitely. Yet rain, snow, sleet, and hail are common over most parts of the world. How do the tiny droplets in clouds become rain or snow? Scientists are still not sure of all the steps in the process. But they do have a general idea.

Much of the water that falls from clouds starts as ice. The temperatures in high clouds are low enough for water droplets to freeze. Very tiny particles floating in the air cause water vapor from the air to condense around them. This makes the crystals grow larger. When they be-

come heavy enough, the ice crystals fall. As they pass through lower clouds, or lower layers of the same cloud, they continue to grow. They become snowflakes.

If it is warm near the ground, the snowflakes melt. They fall to the ground as rain. If it is cold near the ground, they fall as snow.

Sleet is frozen rain. Sleet occurs when there is a layer of warm air above a layer of cold air. Snowflakes melt as they pass through the layer of warm air. Then they freeze again as they pass through the layer of cold air near the ground forming small pieces of ice.

Hail forms in very tall cumulonimbus clouds. Strong vertical currents move within these clouds. Raindrops or snowflakes that start to fall through these clouds are carried back up through the cloud by these vertical currents. The flakes, or droplets, freeze into balls of ice. As the ice falls, more water collects around each ball. Again and again, the ice balls are tossed around in the cloud. Finally, many layers of ice have formed around each ice ball. The large ice balls that fall to earth are called **hailstones.** Most hailstones are about 1 centimeter across. However, many larger hailstones have been reported. A hailstone that fell in Kentucky in 1970, was 19 centimeters across!

Hailstone with "growth rings"

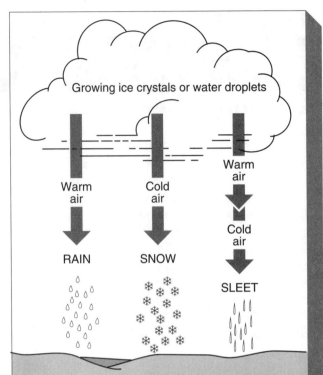

All ice crystals grow as they fall through the clouds. If they reach warm air, they fall to the ground as rain. If the air is cold, the droplets fall to the ground as snow. If they melt in a layer of warm air, then fall through a layer that is below freezing, the droplets fall to the ground as sleet.

Review

I. Fill in each blank with the word that fits best. Choose from the words below.

hail   rain   sleet   ice crystals   snowflakes   vapor

Almost all rain starts our high in the sky as _____ . Tiny crystals that fall through the clouds take water vapor from the air and

become _____ . If they melt and refreeze,

_____ is produced. _____ is formed when vertical currents keep ice in a cloud long enough for layers of ice to form.

II. The following statements describe the steps followed in the formation of rain. Using numbers 1 through 4, indicate the order in which these steps occur.

A. _____ Water freezes and forms ice crystals.

B. _____ The snowflakes reach warmer air and melt.

C. _____ Rising air cools to the dew point and water droplets form.

D. _____ Moist air near the earth's surface is warmed and rises.

How Does Weather Develop?

Exploring Science

A River in the Sky. Near the end of World War II, a group of U.S. planes took off from bases in the Pacific. These planes could fly higher than any other planes produced before this time. At an altitude of about 9000 meters, these bombers met the unexpected. They found themselves surrounded by a fast-moving river of air. The planes were trying to fly "upstream" in this river of air. But the speed of the air matched the speed of the planes. The planes found themselves "standing still" in mid-air.

The river of air was a very powerful wind. Up until that time, no one knew this river of wind existed. Today, we know that this wind is a **jet stream.**

Since that time, other jet streams have been discovered. These fast-moving rivers of air are found at altitudes between 6000 and 12,000 meters. They wind their way around the earth from west to east. Winds in these jet streams may reach speeds of up to 500 kilometers per hour.

● Airliners traveling eastward can cross the United States in less time than those traveling westward. Why?

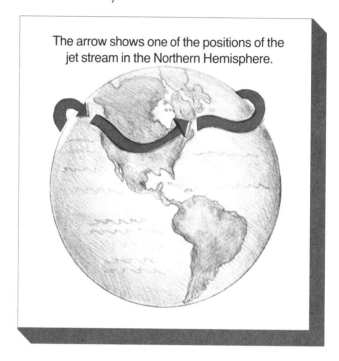

The arrow shows one of the positions of the jet stream in the Northern Hemisphere.

Cold Fronts and Warm Fronts

Jet streams affect weather patterns around the world. Scientists are not sure how these high-speed, high-altitude winds influence air at the earth's surface. It is believed that they tend to "steer" the earth's air masses.

Any time you see or hear a weather forecast, the term **air mass** will probably be mentioned. An air mass is a large body of air in which the temperature and humidity are the same at a given altitude. In other words, in a given air mass, all points at the same altitude will have the same temperature and humidity.

The type of weather you are having depends a lot on the type of air mass that is covering your region. Air masses are named for the part of the globe in which they start, or originate. For example, an air mass that starts near the poles over land will be cold and dry. One that starts near the poles over water will be cold and wet.

Air masses that start near the equator will be warm. If they start over land, they will be warm and dry. If they start over water, they will be warm and wet.

Most weather changes take place along boundaries where two different air masses meet. These boundaries are called **fronts.** A mass of cold air moving into a mass of warm air forms a **cold front.** When warm air replaces cold air, a **warm front** forms. Each kind of front produces its own pattern of weather.

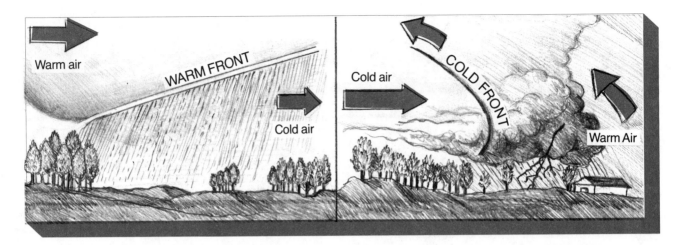

As a warm front approaches, the warm air "rides up" over the colder air. Clouds form as the warm air cools. The first clouds to arrive are high, thin cirrus clouds. As the front gets closer, the clouds get lower and thicker. Then the rain or snow starts. Often it will rain for several hours as the warm front passes.

When a cold front approaches, the heavy, cold air forces the warm air in front of it to rise rapidly. High, towering clouds may form in this rising air. The rain or snow from these clouds may be quite heavy, but does not last long. Soon after the front passes, you will be in a mass of cool, dry air. The sky will be clear.

To Do Yourself   What Can You Learn from Weather Maps?

You will need:

Newspaper weather maps for 14 consecutive days, index cards, glue or cellophane tape

1. Collect weather maps from your local newspaper for at least 14 consecutive days.
2. Cut the maps out and glue them to index cards. Write the date of each map on its index card.
3. Arrange the cards with the oldest map on the top. Hold one edge of the cards and "flip" through the cards from top to bottom. Watch the weather fronts "move" across the U.S.

Questions

1. In which direction do fronts usually move in the U.S? _____

   _____

2. Look at your most recent weather map. What kind of front is to the west of your location? What kind of weather change do you expect to see when this front

   passes? _____

   _____

Warm air, remember, can hold more water vapor than cold air. It is also lighter than cold air. When warm, moist air is surrounded by cooler, drier air, a region of low pressure forms. There are usually several low pressure areas across the U.S. at any given time. Between the low pressure areas, the cooler, drier air presses down. These areas become regions of high pressure.

These **highs** and **lows** are centers of weather systems. They are "steered" by the jet stream and moved by the prevailing westerlies. As these pressure areas move across the United States, they change our weather.

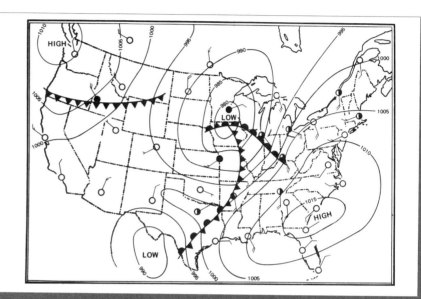

This map shows the pattern of highs and lows across the United States on a given day and the fronts that accompany them.

Review

I. Fill in each blank with the word that fits best. Choose from the words below.

short   long   relative humidity   jet stream   warm front   cold front
low   high

High cirrus clouds moving in from the west generally mean that a

_____ is approaching. You can expect a

_____ period of rain. A line of high, towering clouds is

probably the start of a _____ . You can expect a

_____ period of rain. A warm front is a region of

_____ pressure. Pressure areas are pushed across the U.S.

by the _____ .

II. Circle the underlined word that makes each statement true.

A. It is colder in the northern U.S. when the jet stream is farther (south/north).

B. A long period of rain or snow usually comes with a (cold/warm) front.

C. Fair weather generally comes with a (low/high).

What Causes Storms?

Exploring Science

The Sight of Distant Thunder. Radar was first used during World War II. In England, it helped detect the approach of enemy planes. But its operators thought the radar system had a flaw. They complained that distant storms and airplanes sometimes looked alike on the radar screen.

After the war, radar was changed again. This time it was the distant storms that people wanted to locate. In a few years, there were more than 200 radar weather stations in the United States.

The newest change in radar is called Doppler radar. Doppler radar can find a storm and show the amount of rain the storm makes. It will also be able to show where the storm is heading.

Doppler radar works like the "radar gun" a police officer uses to catch speeding automobiles. But weather radar tracks speeding raindrops instead of cars.

● Give one reason why it is important to be able to predict the weather.

Thunderstorms, Tornadoes, and Hurricanes

It is especially important for radar to detect small, intense storms, such as **thunderstorms**. Thunderstorms are very common. As many as 70 thunderstorms a year occur around the Gulf Coast of the United States.

Many thunderstorms take place in the summer, when large masses of warm, moist air are heated. The heated air rises high into the air. First, a huge, white cumulus cloud forms. As the cloud continues to grow, it gains altitude. It becomes a cumulonimbus cloud. Ice and snow form at the top of the cloud.

Rain pours from the cloud. Strong winds—sometimes strong enough to uproot trees—develop inside the cloud. A thunderstorm is often accompanied by lightning and thunder.

Cumulonimbus cloud

Scientists are not sure why some of the giant cumulonimbus clouds produce lightning. They do know that electric charges can build up inside a cloud under certain conditions. These charges can jump from one part of a cloud to another. They can also jump from the cloud to the ground.

As it passes, lightning heats the air and makes it expand very quickly. This expansion is almost like an explosion. The noise made by the expanding air is thunder.

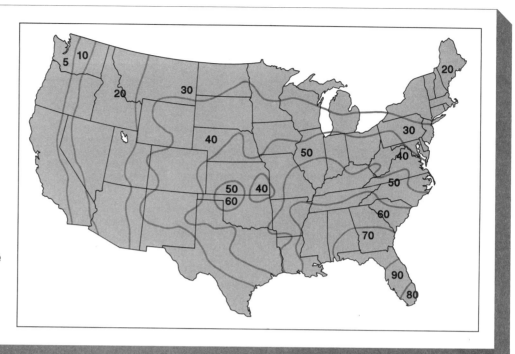

The numbers on this map show the number of thunderstorms that occur in one year.

A thunderstorm may be only a few kilometers wide. Thus, one neighborhood can be having a major storm, while nearby areas still enjoy bright sunshine. The storm may pass in half an hour, but it is not really over. It moves on with the cloud. Like most weather patterns in the United States, the cloud will probably move from west to east.

Some thunderstorms form in lines along cold fronts. Others form over warm land during the day or over warm bodies of water, such as lakes and ponds, at night.

Tornadoes are fairly common in the Central Plains and in the valley of the Mississippi River. These storms generally take place under the same conditions that form thunderstorms. The dark, funnel-shaped cloud is the **tornado.** It seems to hang from a thundercloud.

A tornado starts when warm air comes in from the Gulf of Mexico. A mass of warm air, remember, is a low pressure area. At the same time, much cooler air moves in from the Rocky Mountains. Instead of pushing under the warm air, the cold air mass rides on top of the warm air. The heavier, cool air begins to sink. It squeezes the low, forcing it to rise.

What happens next is not well understood. As the low rises, the pressure drops lower and lower. Inside the low, winds pick up speed.

They may reach 800 kilometers per hour. These whirling winds remove most of the air from the center of the storm. Inside the tornado, the air pressure may be only 70 percent of normal.

Tornadoes are the smallest and most violent of storms. They destroy everything in their short path. Where they touch ground, tornadoes act like a giant vacuum cleaner. The low pressure can cause buildings to "explode." The high winds can pick up cars, tractors, and other objects and fling them many meters away. Fortunately, this most dangerous storm completely disappears within a few minutes.

A tornado is the smallest, yet most destructive, kind of storm.

The swirling clouds around the center of this hurricane are clearly visible in the satellite photograph.

Tropical Storms form over the warm ocean waters near the equator. The air over this water is warm and humid. The air pressure is low. This is a perfect place for storms to form. Once formed, tropical storms move from the equator toward land.

A **hurricane** is a large tropical storm with very strong winds. A hurricane may be 300 to 600 kilometers across. The winds may reach as high as 300 kilometers an hour.

Imagine flying into a hurricane. The first thing you observe is the heavy rain and thick clouds. The clouds grow darker and the winds stronger as you near the center of the storm. In the center, however, the winds and rain stop. The temperature rises. And the sun is visible through thin clouds. The center of a hurricane is called the **eye.** After you pass through the eye, the winds, clouds, and rain start again. On this side of the storm, the winds blow from the opposite direction. In a hurricane, the winds rotate around the eye.

Hurricane winds range from 120 to 250 kilometers an hour. It is these winds that cause so much damage. When a hurricane reaches land, the low pressure in its center causes a rise in sea level. The high sea level, the heavy rain, and the waves pushed by the winds all combine to produce coastal flooding.

Hurricanes always form over warm ocean water. When they travel over land, they soon lose much of their energy. They become severe rainstorms.

An average of 10 hurricanes a year form in the Atlantic Ocean or the Caribbean Sea. Each of these storms is given a name. The names are in alphabetical order and alternate between male and female.

Hurricane winds cause flooding along coastal regions.

Review

I. Fill in each blank with the word that fits best. Choose from the words below.

**cumulonimbus   cirrus   cumulus   cold   warm   rain   lightning
snow**

Thunderstorms develop when a mass of _____ air is
pulled high into the sky. At first, a _____ cloud forms. The
cloud continues to rise, becoming _____ . Inside these
giant clouds, electric charges may cause _____ .

II. Match each event in column **A** with its description in column **B**.

A	**B**
1. _____ A hurricane moves in over land.	a. The area has a heavy rainstorm without much wind.
2. _____ A hurricane has just reached the shore	b. You move from a windy, rainy area into a calm area.
3. _____ A plane is flying through the eye of a hurricane.	c. Sea level and waves are higher than normal.

III. Answer in sentences.

How are tornadoes and thunderstorms alike? How are they different?

_____

_____

_____

How Do You Read a Weather Map?

Exploring Science

A Lifetime of Weather. When George W. Richards was 20 years old, he began to watch the weather for the U.S. government. In return, he received the instruments he needed to measure rainfall, temperature, humidity and wind speed and direction. Richards reported on the weather in Maple Plain, Minnesota.

Each day, Richards checked his weather instruments. He reported on storms, snowfalls, cold waves, heat waves, and dry spells. In fact, he made his reports from Maple Plain for more than 60 years.

One day, Richards was invited to Washington, D.C. So were about 5000 other long-term weather watchers. The occasion was a celebration of the important role they had played in weather forecasting.

All over the country, volunteers like George Richards still keep weather records. Why do they do it? Well, like George said, "I've enjoyed it. When you watch weather close like that, it's exciting."

● Why is the weather in Maple Plain, Minnesota, important to people outside that area?

Weather Maps

Meteorologists (mee-tee-uh-ROL-uh-jists) are scientists who study the weather. These scientists use the data from volunteer weather watchers. They combine this data with information from the National Weather Service. All of this data is used to produce weather maps. These maps are models for the ones shown in newspapers and on television.

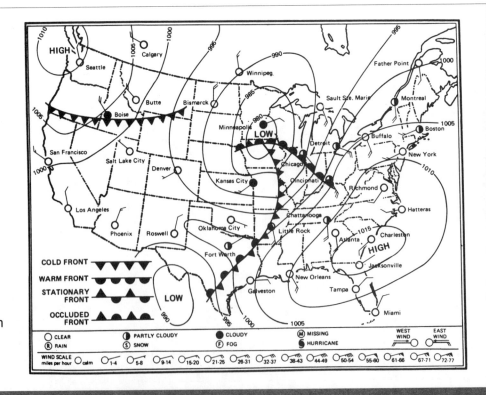

A typical weather map. This map shows highs and lows, fronts, cloud cover, and wind speed and direction at several weather stations across the U.S.

Look at the weather map. It has lines connecting places that have the same air pressure. Normal air pressure at sea level is 1000 millibars. These lines are called **isobars** (EYE-suh-bahrs). Isobars form patterns that show high- and low-pressure areas. These can help a meteorologist predict the weather for the next few days.

Some maps have lines connecting places that have the same temperature. These lines are called **isotherms** (EYE-suh-thurms). Weather maps printed in newspapers often have isotherms. They give the reader an idea of the temperatures all over the country.

Weather maps use special symbols for the following: cold fronts, warm fronts, stationary fronts, wind speed and direction, rain, snow, sleet, fog, and cloud cover. All of these symbols are shown and explained in the **station model**.

Station Model and Some Weather Symbols

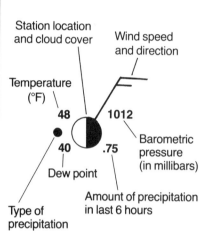

Precipitation		Fronts		Wind Speed	
Fog	≡	Cold Front	▲▲▲▲▲	1-2 knot	
Snow	✳	Warm Front	●●●●		
Rain	●	Occluded Front	▲●▲●▲	3-7 knot	
Drizzle	9			8-12 knot	
Thunderstorm	T<	Stationary Front	▲▼▲▼	13-17 knot	
Cloud Cover				18-22 knot	
Clear ○		1/2 ◑	Overcast ●	23-27 knot	
2/10 ◔		7/10 ◕		48-52 knot	
				1 knot = 1.85 km/hr	

To Do Yourself   How Accurate Are Weather Forecasts?

You will need:

Weather forecasts for 7 consecutive days, actual weather data for the same days

1. Make several charts like the one below.
2. Collect weather forecasts and actual weather data for a period of at least 7 consecutive days. Each day, fill in your chart with the weather forecast for that date and the actual weather that occurred on that date.

Questions

1. Were the weather forecasts accurate? _____

2. Which parts of the forecasts were most accurate? Least accurate? _____

_____

Weather Record

Date	Forecast	Actual
high temperature		
low temperature		
precipitation (amount and type)		
wind (direction and speed)		
general description		

Review

I. Fill in each blank with the word that fits best. Choose from the words below.

isotherms   meteorologists   stationary fronts   symbols   isobars

warm fronts

   Scientists who study the weather are called _____ . In their maps, lines that show places with equal air pressure are called

_____ . Lines that show equal temperature are called

_____ . Most weather maps also have various

_____ for different types of weather.

II. Use the weather map to describe the weather in Clarksville on the day the map was made.

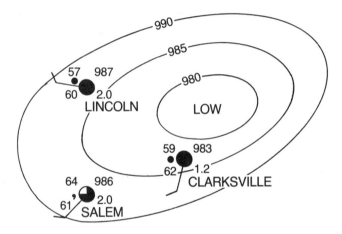

III. Use the weather map to predict what the weather will be like in Clarksville one day later.

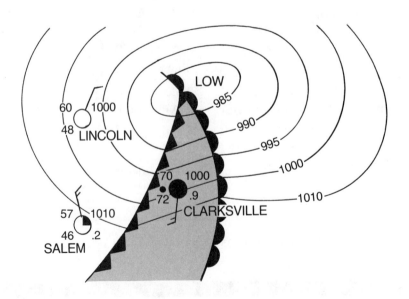

A. Here is a coded message.

$\overline{}_{1}$ $\overline{}_{2}$ $\overline{}_{3}$ $\overline{}_{4}$ $\overline{}_{5}$ $\overline{}_{6}$ $\overline{}_{7}$ $\overline{}_{8}$ $\overline{}_{9}$

$\overline{}_{10}$ $\overline{}_{11}$ $\overline{}_{7}$ $\overline{}_{1}$ $\overline{}_{8}$ $\overline{}_{11}$ $\overline{}_{1}$ $\qquad$ $\overline{}_{7}$ $\overline{}_{10}$

$\overline{}_{12}$ $\overline{}_{13}$ $\overline{}_{8}$

Each of the words defined below is in the same code as the secret message. Fill in each word (one letter per line). Then you will know the code and be able to complete the coded message.

1. Very fast winds circling a small area of very low pressure.

$\overline{}_{14}$ $\overline{}_{5}$ $\overline{}_{6}$ $\overline{}_{8}$ $\overline{}_{15}$ $\overline{}_{16}$ $\overline{}_{5}$

2. A combination of smoke and fog.

$\overline{}_{10}$ $\overline{}_{17}$ $\overline{}_{5}$ $\overline{}_{9}$

3. An area of warm, moist air surrounded by cooler, drier air.

$\overline{}_{4}$ $\overline{}_{5}$ $\overline{}_{18}$

4. A line connecting places that have the same air pressure.

$\overline{}_{7}$ $\overline{}_{10}$ $\overline{}_{5}$ $\overline{}_{19}$ $\overline{}_{15}$ $\overline{}_{6}$

5. Ice pellets made up of several layers of ice.

$\overline{}_{20}$ $\overline{}_{15}$ $\overline{}_{7}$ $\overline{}_{4}$

6. High, thin, wispy clouds with a curled edge.

$\overline{}_{11}$ $\overline{}_{7}$ $\overline{}_{6}$ $\overline{}_{6}$ $\overline{}_{13}$ $\overline{}_{10}$

7. Water in the form of an invisible gas.

$\overline{}_{21}$ $\overline{}_{15}$ $\overline{}_{3}$ $\overline{}_{5}$ $\overline{}_{6}$

8. Frozen rain.

$\overline{}_{10}$ $\overline{}_{4}$ $\overline{}_{1}$ $\overline{}_{1}$ $\overline{}_{14}$

9. Boundary line between two different air masses.

$\overline{}_{12}$ $\overline{}_{6}$ $\overline{}_{5}$ $\overline{}_{8}$ $\overline{}_{14}$

10. Causes heated air to become less dense.

$\overline{}_{1}$ $\overline{}_{2}$ $\overline{}_{3}$ $\overline{}_{15}$ $\overline{}_{8}$ $\overline{}_{10}$ $\overline{}_{7}$ $\overline{}_{5}$ $\overline{}_{8}$

B. Write the word or phrase that best completes each statement.

1. _____ The amount of water vapor in the air compared to the amount the air could hold at that temperature is **a.** relative humidity **b.** air pressure **c.** temperature

2. _____ An instrument used to measure air pressure is **a.** vacuum **b.** isotherm **c.** barometer

3. _____ A cold air mass pushing into a warm air mass forms a **a.** warm front **b.** cold front **c.** stationary front

4. _____ A dark cloud from which rain is falling is a **a.** nimbus cloud **b.** altus cloud **c.** cirrus cloud

5. _____ Clouds that form in low, sheetlike layers are called **a.** cirrocumulus **b.** altocumulus **c.** stratocumulus

C. Apply What You Know

Label the numbered features of the weather map. Choose from the labels below.

cold front   high   isobar   low   warm front

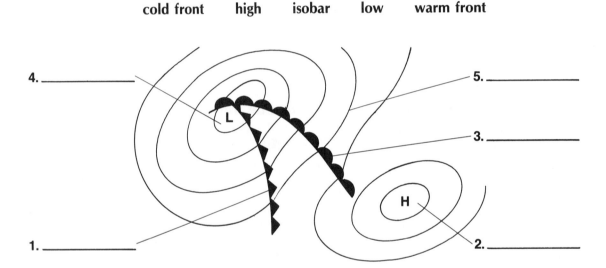

4. _____

1. _____

5. _____

3. _____

2. _____

D. Find Out More

1. Check the weather predictions in your local newspaper. Keep a record. Every day, note the predicted weather. On the following day, see if the prediction was accurate. Keep a record of your findings. Find the ratio of correct predictions to total predictions. Plan a way to show how this ratio changes.

2. Does your area ever have smog? If so, find out the cause of it. If not, try to find out why. Make a smog report to the class.

3. Keep a hurricane log. On a map of the Atlantic Ocean, mark the names and track the paths of all the hurricanes for one year.

4. Write to the nearest office of the National Weather Service. Ask for information about the volunteer weather-recording program. Prepare a report for the class. You may also try to find out if any weather-recording volunteers live in your area. If so, you may be able to get this person to speak to the class about the program.

SUMMING UP:
Review What You Have Learned So Far

A. Study the diagrams. On the line below each diagram, write the name of the object shown. Choose from the terms below.

winter   experiment   volcano   vertebrate   meander   sea breeze

1. _____

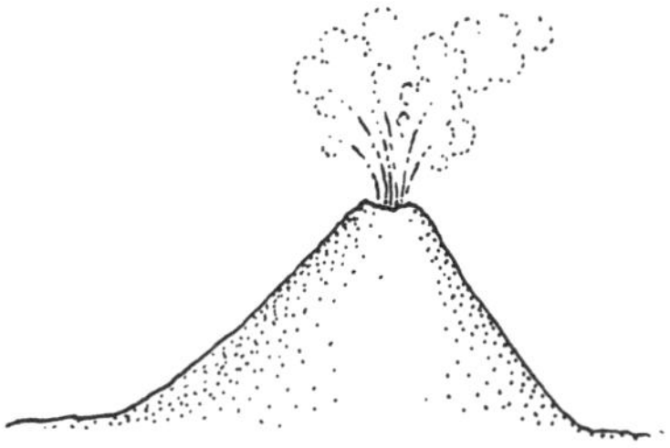

2. _____

3. _____

4. _____

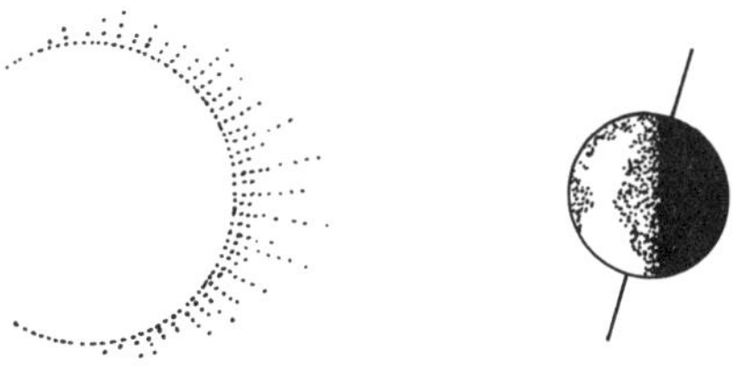

5. _____

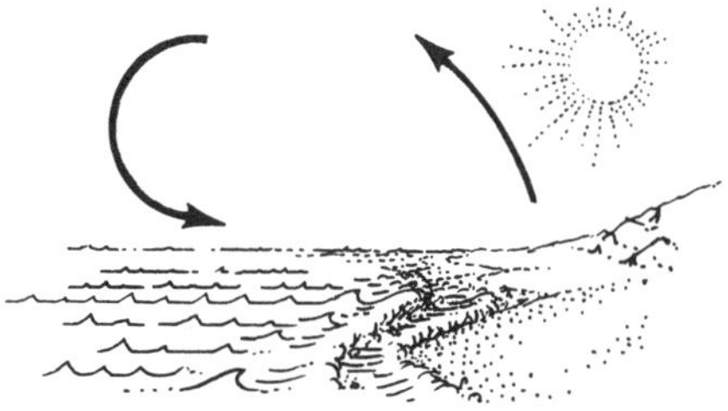

6. _____

B. Each statement below refers to one of the diagrams. The number of the statement is the same as the number of the diagram. Circle the underlined word or phrase that makes each statement true.

1. Using these stakes helped to show something about the (motion/age) of a glacier.
2. The steep sides show that this is a (shield/cinder) cone.
3. A river that shows this feature is (young/old).
4. The first animals to lay eggs on land were (reptiles/amphibians).
5. This diagram shows that seasons are caused by the earth's (tilt/rotation).
6. In this diagram, the warmer area is over the (land/sea).

UNIT
10

THE SOLAR SYSTEM, STARS, AND THE UNIVERSE

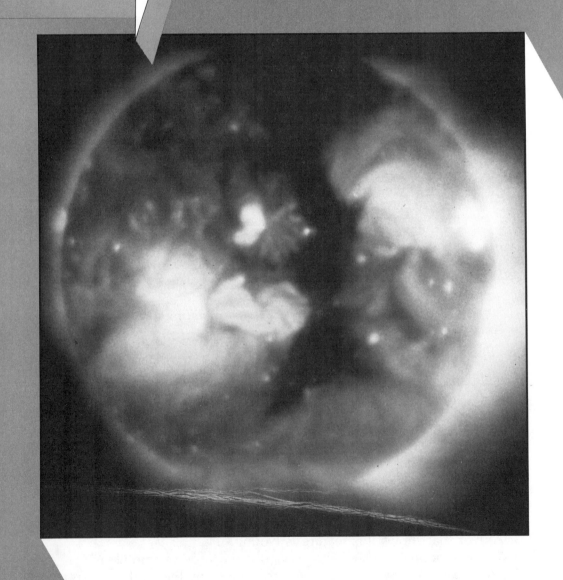

What Is the Solar System?

Exploring Science

Beyond the System. On June 13, 1983, the spacecraft *Pioneer 10* headed into deep space. Until then, no other space flight had ever left the **solar system.** The solar system consists of the sun and the objects that revolve around it.

Pioneer is an old hand at space exploration. It has been traveling through the solar system since 1972. *Pioneer* has studied the planet Jupiter. It has reported, by radio, on the particles that stream out from the sun. If there is a tenth planet in our solar system, *Pioneer* may be the one to find it.

While *Pioneer* does not have any people aboard, it does carry a message. The message shows the nine planets around our sun. It pictures a man and a woman from Earth—the third planet from the sun.

Other spacecraft are also on their way beyond our solar system. One of them carries a record of sounds from Earth. Scientists hope that someday Earth will get some return mail from space.

● Many spacecraft launched before (and after) *Pioneer 10* did not leave the solar system. What do you think happened to them?

Pioneer 10 is the first spacecraft to leave the solar system.

Members of the Solar System

People have begun to travel in the solar system. But it will probably be many years—if ever—before we can make the same trip as *Pioneer 10.*

In the meantime, there is a lot to explore. The solar system is very large. We have been to the moon a few times. The moon is a **satellite** (SAT-ul-lyt) of Earth. A satellite is a body that revolves around a **planet.** A planet is a large body that revolves around the sun. Other planets also have satellites, or moons.

The paths that planets take around the sun are called **orbits.** The paths that moons take around planets are also called orbits. Orbits are very close to being complete circles, however, they are slightly flattened. This slightly flattened circle is called an **ellipse** (ih-LIPS).

No one has traveled to another planet yet.

But we have landed spacecraft on the two planets nearest to Earth—Venus and Mars. In some ways, these planets are much like Earth. In other ways, they are very different.

We have sent spacecraft near Mercury, the planet closest to the sun. Other spacecraft have gone beyond Mars to Jupiter, Saturn, Uranus, and Neptune. The four planets beyond Mars—Jupiter, Saturn, Uranus, and Neptune—are all very different from Earth. The only planet not yet visited is Pluto.

Most of the time, the farthest planet from the sun is Pluto. Its unusual orbit, however, sometimes brings it closer to the sun than Neptune. In fact, when *Pioneer 10* left the solar system, Neptune was further from the sun than was Pluto.

There are other things to see in the solar system besides the planets and their moons. There are small, rocky objects called **asteroids** (AS-tuh-royds) orbiting the sun. Most are between Mars and Jupiter. But some asteroids come close to Earth.

Comets are also members of our solar system. The "dirty snowballs" are made of ice, frozen gases, and bits of rock and metal. Most comets orbit around the sun. Their orbits are very long and flat. Many comets travel great distances beyond the farthest planet.

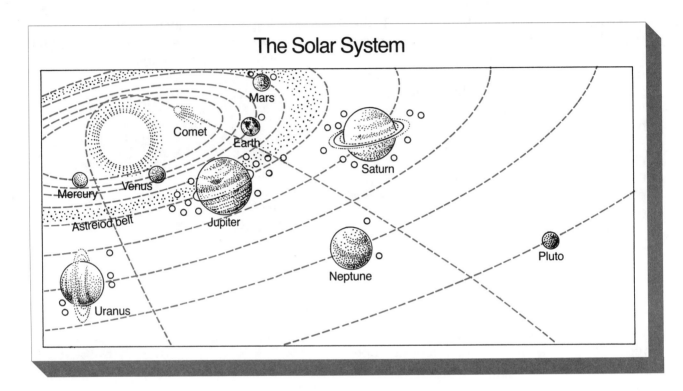

The Solar System

Review

I. Fill in each blank with the word that fits best. Choose from the words below.

**asteroids   Mars   Mercury   comets   Venus   Jupiter   solar system
satellites**

The sun and the planets make up the _____ . The Earth

and other planets have moons, or _____ that orbit around

them. The planets most like Earth are _____ and

_____ . Rocky bodies that orbit between Mars and Jupiter

are called _____ .

II. Use the numbers **1** (closest to the sun) to **9** (for farthest from the sun) to
show the usual order of the planets from the sun.

A. _____ Earth   **D.** _____ Mercury   **G.** _____ Saturn
B. _____ Jupiter   **E.** _____ Neptune   **H.** _____ Uranus
C. _____ Mars   **F.** _____ Pluto   **I.** _____ Venus

Why Does the Moon Change?

Exploring Science

The Rarest Minerals on Earth. We think of diamonds and gold as rare. Yet these are not nearly so rare as some other minerals on Earth. The rarest minerals are found in the samples brought back to Earth from the moon. These minerals were formed under special conditions found on the moon.

Scientists have invented new names for such minerals. One is **tranquilityite** (TRAN-kwuh-lih-tee-eyet). It is named for the Sea of Tranquility, the place where people first landed on the moon. Another is named **armalcolite** (ar-MAL-kuh-lyt), a combination of the names Armstrong, Aldrin, and Collins. Armstrong and Aldrin were the astronauts who took the first steps on the moon. Collins was the pilot of their spacecraft, which was in orbit around the moon.

All of the moon minerals did not come to Earth in the same way. In 1982, scientists in Antarctica found an unusual rock on the ice. It was a moon rock. Scientists believe that a large object struck the moon and blasted the rock from its surface. The rock eventually landed on Earth.

● On the Antarctic ice, scientists also found a rock that they think came from Mars. But they cannot be sure. Why not?

The crew of the Apollo 11 lunar flight mission. They are, from left to right: Neil Armstrong, Michael Collins, and E. Aldrin, Jr. Armstrong was the first human to step on the surface of the moon.

The Earth and the Moon

Compared with distances between planets, the trip to the moon is a short one. The average distance between the earth and the moon is 384,400 kilometers. The moon takes about 27 days to travel once in its orbit around the earth. This motion, remember, is called a **revolution**. As the moon is revolving, it is also spinning on its axis. This motion is called **rotation.** The moon makes one rotation during each revolution. This means that the same side of the moon is *always* facing the earth.

If you look at the moon every night for a month, you will see that it seems to change shape. Look at the diagram. It shows how the shape of the moon changes. Of course the moon does not really grow larger and smaller. These changes, called **phases,** are caused by the positions of the sun, Earth, and moon. We can see only that part of the moon that is in sunlight. When the moon is between the earth and the sun, the side that faces us is dark.

Where did the moon come from? This question remains unanswered. The moon is much closer in size to earth, than other satellites are to their planets. The moon's diameter is more than one-fourth that of the earth. Jupiter and Saturn each have a satellite that is a bit larger than the moon. But these planets are *many* times larger than Earth. Therefore, scientists think that the process that made the moon may have been different from the one that made the other satellites.

To Do Yourself   What Are the Motions of the Moon?

You will need:

Newspaper or almanac with moonrise and moonset times, paper, pencil

1. Using information from a newspaper or almanac, record the times of moonrise and moonset for 7 consecutive days in the table below.
2. If the moon is visible, sketch its shape in the space provided in the table. If it is not visible, give the reason.

Moon Chart

Date	Day 1	Day 2	Day 3	Day 4	Day 5	Day 6	Day 7
Moonrise time							
Moonset time							
Shape of moon							

Questions

1. How much later does the moon rise each day? _____

2. Why does the moon rise later each day? _____
_____

3. How many days will it be until moonrise occurs at the same time as on Day 1?
_____

4. Why does the moon seem to change shape? _____
_____

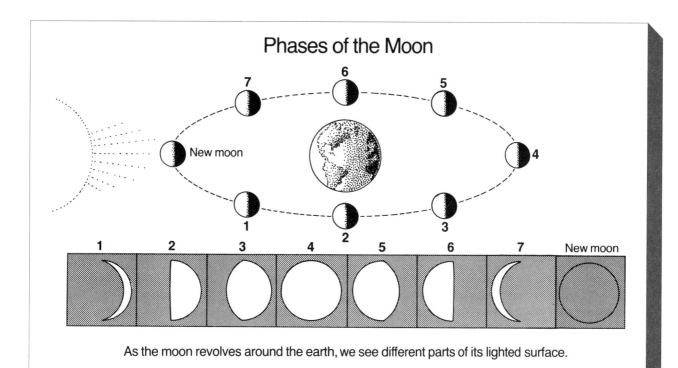

Phases of the Moon

As the moon revolves around the earth, we see different parts of its lighted surface.

Review

I. Fill in each blank with the word that fits best. Choose from the words below.

sunlight   larger   smaller   the same   different   revolution
phases   rotates

As the moon travels around the earth, it also _____

on its axis. The moon always keeps _____ side facing

Earth. Changes in the shape of the moon are called _____ .

They are caused by changes in the _____ that reaches
the moon. Scientists think that the moon is different from other satellites

because it is _____ than expected.

II. Tell the phase of the moon in each statement.

A. _____ The earth is between the sun and the moon.

B. _____ The sun, earth, and moon form a right angle with
earth at the corner.

C. _____ The moon is between the sun and the earth.

III. Answer in sentences.

The earth rotates as the moon revolves around it. If you are on the side of the
moon facing earth, will the earth show phases? Why or why not?

Lesson Three

What Causes Eclipses and Tides?

Exploring Science

An Eclipse in Siam. Perhaps you have seen a play or movie about the king of Siam. The story is based on the life of King Mongkut. Mongkut was king of Siam, now called Thailand, from 1850 to 1868. He brought an English woman to his palace to teach his children about the world beyond Siam. Mongkut also tried to bring scientific ideas to his small Asian country.

The king was an astronomer. He predicted when an **eclipse** (ih-KLIPS) of the sun would take place in Siam. His royal advisors were very upset. They told the king that eclipses could not be predicted. The advisors believed that eclipses occurred when the demon Rahoo ate the sun, the "jewel of the sky." Eclipses were believed to be very bad luck. The advisors said that loud noises had to be made to scare Rahoo away.

King Mongkut invited many people, including astronomers from France, to Siam to view the eclipse with him. The sun disappeared as the king had predicted. A grand celebration was held. Fireworks and cannons were set off. Soon the sun was visible again.

After the eclipse, the king told his advisors that they should pay more attention to science. The advisors pointed out that the fireworks and cannons had probably scared Rahoo away.

Indeed, bad luck did follow these events. While watching the eclipse, King Mongkut had been bitten by a mosquito. The bite infected the king with a fatal disease. He died a few weeks later.

● Do you think that anything happening to the sun, 150 million kilometers away, could cause "bad luck" on Earth?

The Moon's Effects on the Earth

At times, the moon passes directly between the sun and the earth. When this happens, the shadow of the moon falls on the earth. The moon's shadow has two parts. The darker area is the **umbra.** The **penumbra** (pih-NUM-bruh) is the lighter area. People in the part of the earth covered by the umbra will see a **total solar eclipse.** (Solar means "of the sun.") The moon's shadow blocks out the face of the sun. People in the penumbra will see a **partial solar eclipse.**

Starting at the lower left, these "steps" in a total solar eclipse were photographed at seven-minute intervals.

258

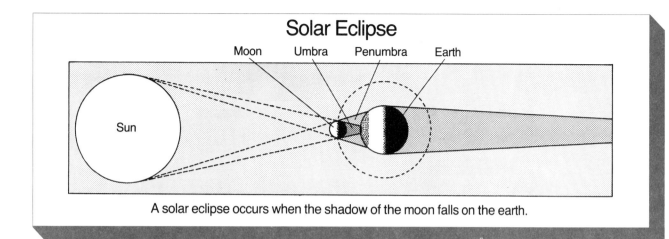

Solar Eclipse

Moon Umbra Penumbra Earth

Sun

A solar eclipse occurs when the shadow of the moon falls on the earth.

Total solar eclipses may happen several times a year. But each one can be seen only from a small part of the earth that is covered by the umbra of the moon's shadow.

On most revolutions, the moon does not pass directly between the sun and the earth. This is because the moon's orbit is tilted.

When the earth moves between the moon and the sun, a **lunar eclipse** takes place. During a lunar eclipse, the moon moves into the shadow of the earth. (Lunar means "of the moon.") The umbra of the earth's shadow is wide. Therefore, lunar eclipses can be seen over a larger area of the earth.

The moon affects the earth more than a few times each year. With some help from the sun, the moon causes the tides to change twice a day. Remember that tides are the rise and fall of waters of the ocean.

The tides are caused by the gravitational attraction between the earth and the moon. The sun pulls on the earth too. But the sun is so far away that its effect on the tides is much smaller than that of the moon.

Under the pull of the moon, the liquid oceans

actually rise. On the side of the earth facing the moon, they bulge out toward the moon. This is a **high tide**. On the opposite side of the earth, the ocean is not pulled as much. The moon pulls the solid earth away from the water a little. Another bulge forms. The result is a high tide on that side of the earth.

The moon's attraction produces two high tides on the opposite sides of the planet. In between the two high tides, the water level is lower. These are the two **low tides**.

A little more than six hours later, the earth has completed one-quarter of a rotation. Now, the parts of the earth that had low tides six hours earlier are having high tides. Those areas that had high tides now have low tides. Because the moon is revolving as the Earth rotates, the time from a high tide to a low tide is about 6 hours, 13 minutes.

When the attraction of the sun and the moon are combined, a very high tide and a very low tide occur. These are called **spring tides**. When the sun and moon form a right angle with the earth, the tides are neither very high nor very low. These tides are called **neap tides**.

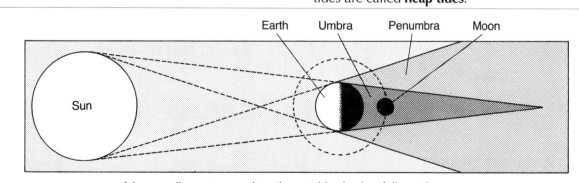

Earth Umbra Penumbra Moon

Sun

A lunar eclipse occurs when the earth's shadow falls on the moon.

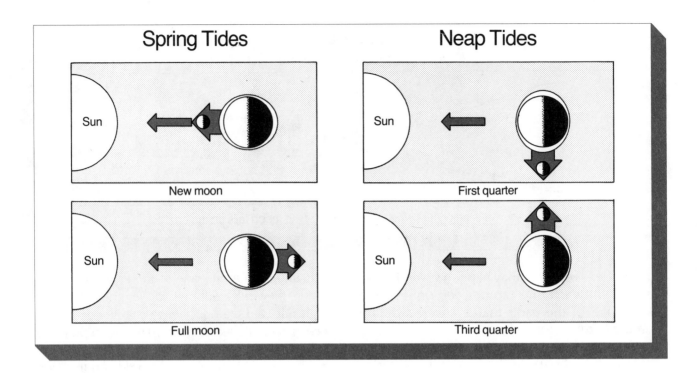

Spring Tides	Neap Tides
New moon	First quarter
Full moon	Third quarter

Review

I. Fill in each blank with the word that fits best. Choose from the words below.

**high   low   neap   spring   gravitational attraction   moon   sun
earthquakes**

When the moon is between the sun and the earth, an eclipse of the

_____ takes place. When the earth is between the sun

and the moon, an eclipse of the _____ takes place. Tides

are caused by the _____ between the earth and the moon.

If it is high tide at one place, it is _____ tide at a point
halfway around the earth. When the sun, moon, and earth are lined up,

_____ tides occur.

II. In what phase of the moon does each of the following occur? (Some may have
more than one answer.)

A. _____ total solar eclipse

B. _____ total lunar eclipse

C. _____ spring tide

D. _____ neap tide

III. Answer in sentences.

The moon rises about 50 minutes later each night. What do you think happens
to the tides?

Lesson Four

What Are the Inner Planets?

Exploring Science

Magellan at Venus. The explorer Magellan is famous for being the first person to lead an expedition that traveled all the way around a planet. But Magellan did not live to complete the first voyage around the Earth in 1519.

The spacecraft Magellan fared much better. Between August 1990 and October 1994 it traveled all the way around a planet 20 times every day. The planet was not Earth, however, but Venus.

The main objective of the spacecraft Magellan was to map Venus using powerful radar. It was so successful that it mapped 99 percent of the planet. We now have better maps of Venus than we do of Earth. The radar maps increased the number of named land features on Venus from about 300 to about 1000. A trillion bytes of data were sent back to Earth in all.

Even when the spacecraft was so crippled by old age that it could no longer perform mapping duties, Magellan proved itself useful. Scientists commanded the craft to commit suicide by lowering itself into the top levels of the atmosphere, so that it could test methods of satellite braking and make measurements of the atmosphere.

● Why might it be easier for a spacecraft to travel to Venus than to Mars?

Mercury, Venus and Mars

The inner planets are Mercury, Venus, Earth, and Mars. Mercury has been visited only once. Any spacecraft traveling near Mercury is pulled by the sun's gravity. When this happens, the spacecraft travels faster and faster. There is no time to observe Mercury.

Scientists found a way to use the gravity of Venus to slow down a spacecraft as it neared Mercury. So *Mariner 10* was able to study the planet. It took photographs of Mercury's surface. It recorded the temperature. *Mariner* found that Mercury has a magnetic field. Scientists think this means that Mercury has a core made of iron.

Large craters, like those on the moon, can be seen on the surface of Mercury. Craters near the poles may contain ice. Mercury has almost no atmosphere. There are no winds and no water to cause erosion. The features of Mercury have probably changed little since they formed.

The surface of Mercury as seen from *Mariner 10.* The insert (right) is a close-up of the crater inside the white square.

Venus is not easy to observe. Thick clouds of carbon dioxide and sulfuric acid cover the planet. Below the clouds, the temperature is over 450° C. The pressure at the surface of Venus is 90 times greater than that on Earth.

Despite these conditions, we do have details about the planet. Soviet landers took the first photographs of the surface. Then they broke down under the great heat and pressure. Later, the U.S. spacecraft Pioneer and Magellan sent radar maps back to the United States.

We now know that Venus is very different from Earth. Its crust does not have floating plates, and much of the crust is geologically new lava flows. Perhaps eruptions of the many huge volcanoes on Venus added the carbon dioxide and sulfuric acid to the atmosphere. The carbon dioxide may explain why the planet is so hot. The gas traps heat from the sun, producing a "greenhouse effect."

Today, we can study a map of Mars made by satellites that orbited the planet. The map shows giant canyons. One canyon is four times deeper than the Grand Canyon of Earth.

The map shows volcanoes. One of the volcanoes, Olympus Mons, is almost three times as tall as Mount Everest. Since the atmosphere of Mars is very thin, there is little erosion. The tall slopes of the volcano do not wear down. There are many channels where water once flowed. There is some water on the planet. It is frozen into the ice caps at the poles.

Scientists think that Mars once had surface water and a thicker atmosphere. They believe that when the volcanoes were erupting, they added water and gases to the atmosphere. After the volcanoes became inactive, the atmosphere leaked away. Mars' gravity was too weak to hold it. The water may still be there. Perhaps it is frozen below the Martian soil.

	Mercury	Venus	Mars
Distance from sun:	57,900,000 kilometers	108,200,000 kilometers	227,900,000 km
Rotation:	59 Earth days	243 Earth days	25 hours
Revolution:	88 Earth days	225 Earth days	687 days
Distance across:	4,880 kilometers	12,104 kilometers	6,787 km
Number of satellites:			2

Review

I. Fill in each blank with the word that fits best. Choose from the words below.

sulfuric acid   carbon dioxide   craters   volcanoes   thick   thin

The atmosphere of Mercury is _____ . Its surface has

many large _____ . Venus is covered with clouds of

_____ and _____ . Its surface has huge

_____ as well as craters.

II. Tell which planet is being described in each phrase.

A. _____Closest to the sun.

B. _____Once had surface water.

C. _____Has a very thick atmosphere.

D. _____May have a core of iron.

E. _____A day is two-thirds as long as an Earth year.

III. Answer in sentences.

Would you expect to find many large craters on the surface of Venus? Explain your answer.

What Are the Outer Planets?

Exploring Science

Planet Ten. Ancient people knew of the planets from Mercury to Saturn. They could see them with their unaided eyes. In 1781, William Herschel, the astronomer, found a seventh planet, Uranus. Scientists knew that Uranus could not be the farthest planet from the sun. If Uranus were the farthest planet from the sun, it would have a different orbit.

In 1846, both Urbain Leverrier in France and J.C. Adams in England, calculated the position of an eighth planet. They soon found Neptune—almost exactly where their calculations said it would be.

Even with Neptune in place, scientists still thought there was something wrong with the orbit of Uranus. Could there be a ninth planet? Astronomers searched for years. Finally, in 1930, Clyde Tombaugh found Pluto.

Does the story end here? Neptune's orbit, like that of Uranus, is not quite what calculations say it should be. And Pluto alone is too small to cause the change. Some astronomers think that there is a tenth planet. The search continues.

● Do you think a tenth planet would be like Earth? Why or why not?

The Outer Planets

The four planets closest to the sun have solid crusts made of rock. These are the **terrestrial planets.** Terrestrial means like Earth. The next four planets are giant balls of gas. The surface of each of these "Gas Giants" is liquid hydrogen. Beneath this surface is an "ocean" of frozen, or solid, hydrogen. If any of these planets contain rock, it is deeply buried. Rock may form a core, but not a crust.

The core of Jupiter may be about twice the size of Earth. Jupiter itself is more than twice the size of all the other planets put together.

The surface of Jupiter is crossed with bands of many colors. A storm, at least 300 years old and 25,000 kilometers long, forms the Great Red Spot. The bands and the Great Red Spot form because the planet rotates so fast. One day on Jupiter is less than half an Earth day.

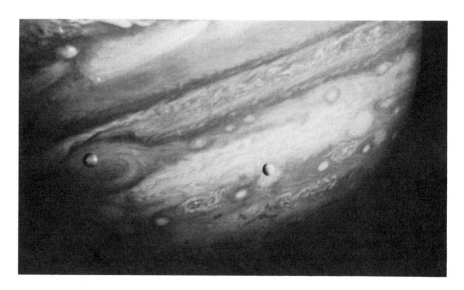

This photograph of Jupiter clearly shows the Great Red Spot. Two of Jupiter's moons are also visible against the surface of the planet.

Close-up photograph of Saturn's rings. *Voyager I* was 740,000 km from the surface of the planet when this picture was taken.

Saturn was a familiar sight even to early astronomers. With the aid of the telescope, Galileo found that Saturn was very interesting. To him, Saturn looked like three planets, not one.

Improved telescopes showed that what Galileo really saw was one planet surrounded by rings. We now know that all of the Gas Giants have rings. The rings of Saturn, however, are by far the most spectacular. That is why astronomers (and the public, as well) were excited when *Voyager 1* visited Saturn in 1980 and *Voyager 2* visited the same planet in 1981.

The close-up photographs from the Voyager cameras showed that the rings are more complex than anyone had thought. There are about 1000 different rings. The rings are not very thick, perhaps only about 100 meters. Two of the rings seem to be twisted together. Strange bands move along other rings.

The rings are not solid. They seem to be made of ice particles. The ice particles are of different sizes, ranging from tiny grains to boulders.

There is another mystery about Saturn. The planet produces three times as much heat as it gets from the sun. This heat, like the rings, has not been fully explained.

Uranus is a typical Gas Giant. While it is much larger than Earth, it is smaller than Jupiter and Saturn. The temperature near the top of its atmosphere is about -200°C.

One of the mysteries about Uranus is its tilt. The planet is tilted so much that it seems to be lying on its side. Perhaps Uranus was once hit by some space object and pushed into its present position.

Uranus and Neptune are very much alike. Both Gas Giants have been visited by Voyager 2—Uranus in 1986 and Neptune in 1989. Uranus and Neptune are about the same size. Both have atmospheres of hydrogen and helium.

One of the differences between Uranus and Neptune is the amount of heat given off by each of the planets. Similar to Saturn, Neptune gives off more heat than expected. Uranus does not.

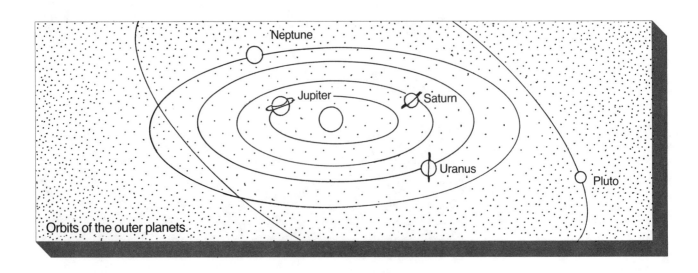

Orbits of the outer planets.

Pluto lies beyond Neptune—most of the time. Pluto is not a giant. It is probably as small as Mercury, the smallest planet. It may be a ball of frozen gas. It has a satellite, but does not seem to have any rings. Because it is so far away, we know very little about Pluto.

Pluto's orbit tilts much more than that of any other planet. Some scientists think, therefore, that Pluto is not a planet at all. Perhaps it was a part of Neptune that broke off and now orbits on its own. Or, perhaps Pluto is a very large, frozen comet.

	Jupiter	Saturn	Uranus	Neptune	Pluto
Distance from sun:	778 million km	1472 million km	2870 million km	4497 million km	5900 million km
Rotation:	10 hours	11 hours	24 hours	22 hours	6 days
Revolution:	12 years	29 years	84 years	164 years	248 years
Distance across:	142,800 km	120,600 km	51,800 km	49,500 km	2290 km
Number of Satellites:	16	18	15	8	1

Review

I. Fill in each blank with the word that fits best. Choose from the words below.

Jupiter   Pluto   Saturn   heat   Neptune   Uranus   cold

The Gas Giants that are farthest from the sun are _____

and _____ . _____ is a ball of frozen

gas. Neptune, like Saturn, is producing more _____ than expected.

II. Tell whether each statement describes Uranus, Neptune, or Pluto.

A. _____ It gives off more heat than expected.

B. _____ Its orbit is tilted more than those of other planets.

C. _____ A "day" is much longer than a day on Earth.

D. _____ It seems to be lying on its side.

E. _____ It may not have rings.

III. Answer in sentences.

The nine known planets can be grouped by size into four pairs with one planet left over. What are the four pairs?

_____

_____

_____

Asteroids, Meteors, and Comets

Exploring Science

The Asteroid Twins. When the asteroid Castalia came about 4,050,000 km from Earth on August 25, 1989, the image obtained using radar looked more like a peanut than a ball. Three years later, in December 1992, the radio telescopes got a better view of another "peanut" asteroid, Toutatis, which was even closer (3,500,000 km). This time the peanut was actually two lumps traveling together. Could most asteroids be twins?

In 1993, the space probe Galileo got close to its second asteroid, having already passed close to asteroid Gaspra. But the new quarry, Ida, was not alone in space. It had a tiny satellite orbiting at a distance of about 100 km. Like asteroid twins, Castalia and Toutatis, Ida's satellite named Dactyl, was probably formed, as fragments from a collision between two larger asteroids.

● Do you think there are any "triplet" asteroids? What evidence would you look for to support your idea?

Asteroids, Meteors, and Comets

Today, over 2000 asteroids are known. There are probably thousands more to be discovered. Asteroids are small, rocky bodies. Many contain metals. Most asteroids orbit in a belt between Mars and Jupiter. Some, however, wander much farther. Some cross the orbit of the earth. Planets and moons have been hit by these wandering asteroids.

Smaller rocks and grains of dust moving through space are called **meteoroids** (MEET-ee-uh-royds). When a meteoroid enters Earth's atmosphere, it heats up from friction with the air. The meteoroid burns up, shooting across the sky with a bright glow. This glowing body is called a **meteor**, or a "shooting star."

Once in a while, a larger meteoroid does not burn up completely before it reaches the earth's surface. The space rocks that hit the ground are called **meteorites** (MEET-ee-uh-reyets). About 500 meteorites larger than an orange fall to Earth each year.

Some scientists think that asteroids and meteoroids are material that are left over from the dust clouds at the beginning of the solar system. Others think that they may be the remains of a collision between two planets.

This giant meteorite struck the earth's surface in Africa. Most meteors burn up in the earth's atmosphere.

Where do comets come from? In 1950, Jan H. Oort, a Dutch astronomer, proposed a very interesting theory. According to Oort, a huge cloud of materials is located several trillions of miles from the sun. The frozen gases, ice, and bits of metal in this **Oort cloud** combine to form comets. Some disturbance, such as the gravitational pull of a passing star, causes a comet to be flung out of the cloud and into an orbit around the sun.

As the comet nears the sun, the heat causes the head of the comet to glow. Some of the gases from the head evaporate. They stream away, forming a bright tail. Energy and particles from the sun make a **solar wind** that "blows" away from the sun. This solar wind causes the comet's tail to always point away from the sun.

A comet gets a little smaller with every trip it makes around the sun. Some of its material gets vaporized by the sun's heat. Many comets orbit the sun every 5 to 10 years. Some fly out of the solar system. Some crash into the sun.

The famous Halley's comet orbits the sun every 76 years. It was named for the English astronomer who predicted its return. Halley's

Halley's comet. The tail of this famous comet consists mostly of gases.

comet was known long before Halley, however. Records of its sighting go back to the year 684. If Halley's comet was last near Earth in 1986, when will it return?

Review

I. Fill in each blank with the word that fits best. Choose from the words below.

meteors   hydrogen   metal   meteorites   meteoroids   asteroids

Most _____ are in orbit between Mars and Jupiter. They are rocky bodies containing some _____ . Smaller particles, or _____ , burn up as they pass through Earth's atmosphere. Any that reach the surface are called _____ .

II. Write **T** if a statement is true. If it is false, correct the underlined word to make the statement true.

A. _____ <u>Meteors</u> appear as bright lights shooting through the sky.

B. _____ Space rocks that hit the surface of the Earth are called <u>asteroids.</u>

C. _____ A small space rock that passes near Earth is a <u>meteoroid.</u>

III. Answer in sentences.

Would it be easier to get metals from an asteroid or a planet? Explain your answer.

What Is the Sun Like?

Exploring Science

Great Solar Flares. The solar wind, which pushes the tails of comets away from the Sun, is propelled by magnetism. Like Earth, the Sun has a magnetic field. The Sun's magnetic field, however, is much stronger and more active. Parts of the magnetic field are so strong that they sometimes break, and magnetic lines of force crack against the Sun like a whip. This knocks great numbers of charged particles from the spot that was whipped into the solar wind. The whipped-up particles fly away in a giant **flare** that often reaches beyond Earth's orbit.

On May 18, 1991, a satellite detected the start of a large flare. But the Sun's rotation moved the flare to the side away from Earth. When the flare returned, on June 1, 1991, it was so strong that it knocked out the flare detector on the satellite. Astronomers saw that there were six separate flares now facing Earth. Particles from these flares reached Earth and were visible as far south as Washington, DC.

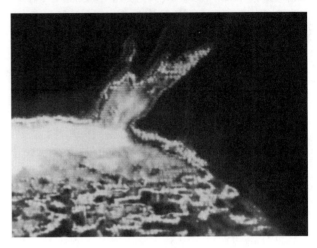

Later that year, another giant flare knocked out electric lines in New England and Canada. The 1991 flares also caused some radio and television interference.

● What kind of particles do you think the magnetic whip could knock off the surface of the Sun? Explain your answer.

The Sun Itself

The sun is a medium-sized star. But in our solar system, it is by far the largest and most important object. The distance across the sun is almost 10 times the distance across Jupiter, the next largest object in the solar system. Nearly 1000 Jupiters could fit inside the sun. The sun's mass is 700 times that of all the planets put together.

There are several parts of the sun that can be seen from Earth. The part that we see most often is the yellow **photosphere** (FOH-tuh-sfeer). During an eclipse, you can see parts of the sun's atmosphere. The **chromosphere** (KROH-muh-sfeer) is the layer above the photosphere. It appears to glow with a red light. The **corona** (kuh-ROH-nuh), forms the outer atmosphere. This thin cloud of gas extends far out into space. Sometimes, great streams of hot gas flare out through these layers of the sun's atmosphere. The flares extend millions of kilometers from the surface.

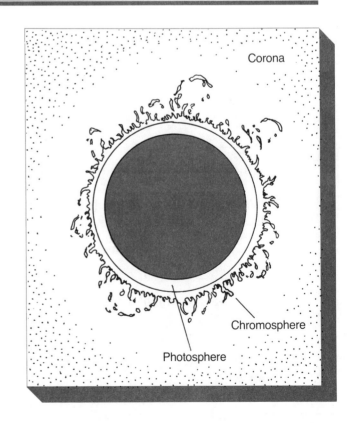

Although many elements can be found on the sun, most of the sun is hydrogen and helium. In fact, helium was found in the sun before it was discovered on Earth.

At the core of the sun, hydrogen atoms combine to form helium. Their combination releases a tremendous amount of energy. The energy from the core moves by convention currents to the surface.

Sometimes dark spots appear on the surface of the sun. These **sunspots** are caused by gases that are cooler than the others around them. Sunspots, like flares, produce effects in the Earth's atmosphere. After sunspot activity leads to a flare, radio, telephone, and electrical service on Earth may be disrupted. This reveals that sunspots are caused by magnetism. The most dramatic effect of sunspots, however, is the formation of the **auroras** (aw-ROWR-uhs). The auroras are colored lights that appear and change in the sky near the poles. The ones in the northern hemisphere are sometimes called "Northern Lights."

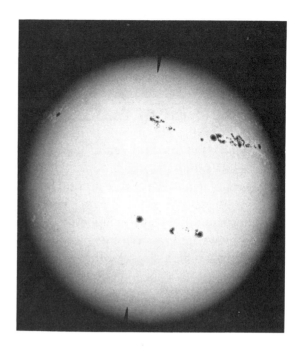

Sunspots. This photograph was taken at the beginning of a period of high sunspot activity.

Review

I. Fill in each blank with the word that fits best. Choose from the words below.

corona   sunspots   hydrogen   aurora   photosphere   carbon

The part of the sun that we see most of the time is the

_____ . Sometimes this is covered by dark areas called

_____ . One part of the sun that we see in an eclipse is

the _____ . Like Gas Giants, the sun has an outer surface

that is mostly _____ .

II. Circle the underlined word that makes each statement true.

A. The sun is a (star/planet).
B. The sun's mass is almost (10/700) times greater than that of the planets.
C. The element (helium/hydrogen) was first found on the sun.
D. The lower atmosphere of the sun is the (chromosphere/photosphere).

III. Answer in sentences.

The sun rotates faster near its equator than it does near its poles. What does this tell you about the composition of the sun?

What Is a Star?

Exploring Science

Little Green Men and the Crab. In 1054, a very bright star suddenly appeared in the sky. Chinese astronomers wrote about it and Native Americans drew pictures of it on the rock walls of canyons. Soon the new star faded. After telescopes were invented, astronomers looked at where the bright star had been. They found a great patch of gas that they named the Crab, because of its shape.

In 1967, an Englishwoman, Jocelyn Bell, found mysterious signals coming from the sky. At first, she and astronomers working with her called the source of the signals LGM, for "Little Green Men." But soon the astronomers guessed that the signals might be coming from the remains of a giant explosion. A star that exploded might leave behind a rapidly rotating body that would send regular radio signals into space. They named such a star a **pulsar,** for the pulsing signals. Various other pulsars were quickly found using radio telescopes. But no one could see a pulsar at first.

One of the newly discovered radio pulsars seemed to be coming from the Crab. Astronomers in Arizona turned their telescopes toward the Crab. There in the middle, was a very small star that blinked very fast. It was the pulsar. This proved that the pulsar explanation was true.

The new star that was seen in 1054 had been the explosion, a kind called a **supernova.** The pulsar and the Crab were the remains of that supernova explosion.

● Why did the Chinese astronomers not know that the supernova was an exploding star? Explain your answer.

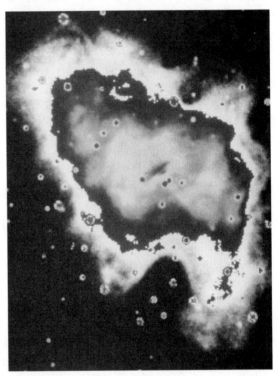

The Stars

The sun and the other stars are large balls of glowing gases. The source of their energy is hydrogen. In the stars, remember, hydrogen atoms fuse and form helium. A tremendous amount of energy is given off every time this **fusion** (FYOO-shun) reaction takes place.

Most stars are not exactly like the sun. Some are very small—only slightly larger than the Earth. These **dwarf** stars are so dense, however, that their mass is as great as the sun's.

Stars with a diameter 100 times that of the sun are **giants.** Larger still are the **supergiants.** Some of these stars have diameters as much as 1000 times that of the sun.

To Do Yourself
How Can You Compare the Sizes of Stars?

You will need:

Straight pin, circle compass, metric ruler, construction paper: red, 18 × 24; orange, 9 × 12, yellow, 9 × 12, scissors

1. Set the compass to draw a circle 16.5 centimeters in radius. Draw a circle on the red construction paper and cut it out. The red circle represents a red supergiant, such as the star Antares in the constellation Scorpio.
2. Draw a circle with a radius of 1.8 centimeters on the orange paper. Cut it out. This circle represents an orange giant, such as Aldebaran in the constellation Taurus.
3. Draw a circle with a radius of 0.6 centimeters on the yellow paper. Cut it out. This circle represents the size of a large yellow star, such as Capella in the constellation Auriga.
4. Place the yellow and orange circles on top of the red circle. Insert a straight pin through the circles. The head of the pin represents the size of our sun, which is a medium-sized yellow star.

There are stars much larger and much smaller than those in your model. For example, to make a model of the star Epsilon Aurigae, you would have to cut out a circle 120 centimeters in diameter! A model of a white dwarf would be 20 times smaller than the head of the pin!

You can actually see one of the differences among stars. Look carefully at the night sky from a dark part of the Earth. Some stars appear very bright while others are dim. The brightness of a star depends on its distance from Earth. A bright star that is very far from Earth will look dim.

Another difference you may notice is color. Some stars look red. Others look yellow, blue, or bluish-white. The color tells you the temperature of the star. If an iron poker is heated, it will first glow red. Then it will become "white hot." The temperature of a star varies in the same way. A red star is cool; a bluish-white star is hot.

Visible light is only a small part of the energy released by a star. Stars give off a range of energy from radio waves to X-rays. The range of energy is called the **electromagnetic spectrum** (ih-lek-troh-mag-NET-ik SPEK-trum). Analyzing the light from stars has helped scientists understand not only stars, but other parts of the universe also.

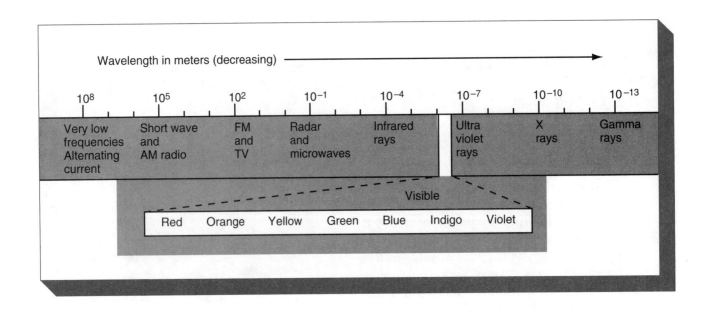

Wavelength in meters (decreasing)

| 10^8 | 10^5 | 10^2 | 10^{-1} | 10^{-4} | 10^{-7} | 10^{-10} | 10^{-13} |

Very low frequencies Alternating current | Short wave and AM radio | FM and TV | Radar and microwaves | Infrared rays | Ultra violet rays | X rays | Gamma rays

Visible

Red   Orange   Yellow   Green   Blue   Indigo   Violet

Review

I. Fill in each blank with the word that fits best. Choose from the words below.

heat   energy   dim   color   red   electromagnetic spectrum brightness

II.   The _____ of a star tells us about its temperature. A very bright star far from the Earth may appear _____ . We learn about stars by studying the _____ they release. The visible light from a star is only one part of a range called the _____ .

Circle the underlined word that makes each statement true.

A. A star that is not very hot is (red/blue).

B. All stars get their energy from (burning/fusion).

C. A star's distance from Earth affects its (brightness/temperature).

D. Visible light is a form of energy between radio waves and (color/X-rays).

III. Answer in sentences.

The sun is often called an "average star." Explain what you think that statement means.

_____

_____

_____

How Far Away Are the Stars?

Exploring Science

A Measuring Stick for the Universe. In 1902, Henrietta Leavitt, joined the Harvard Observatory. Her work included photographing stars. She soon became an expert on the subject, and her standards for star photography are still used today.

Leavitt was particulary interested in stars called **cepheid** (SEE-fid) **variables.** These stars change in brightness every few days. Even today, we don't know why their brightness changes. But Leavitt made an important discovery about the cepheids. She learned that the time it takes a cepheid to change depends on the greatest brightness of the star.

If you know how bright a star really is, you can find out how far away it is. When Leavitt made her discovery in 1912, distances to only a few nearby stars were known. Now it was possible to find the distance to far-off stars. Astronomers had taken the first step toward measuring the universe.

● Is it important to know the size of the universe? Why or why not?

Measuring Distances

At a distance a large bonfire may look as small as a nearby candle flame. Even through the largest telescope, stars look like pinpoints of light. Some are bright and others dim. But you cannot rely on brightness to find out how far away any one of them is.

One way to determine distance is to use **parallax** (PAR-uh-laks). Parallax is the change of position of an object against its background. Try the method for yourself. Use only your right eye to look at an object about 10 or 15 centimeters away. Then look at the object with just your left eye. Did the object seem to change position?

Now try the same thing with an object that is 2 or 3 meters away. Notice that it does not seem to change position as much. The amount of change depends on how far away the object is and how far apart your eyes are.

In 1838, Friedrich Bessel (FREE-drik- BES-ul) used parallax to measure the distance to a star. First he looked at the star from one side of the Earth's orbit. He noted where the star was

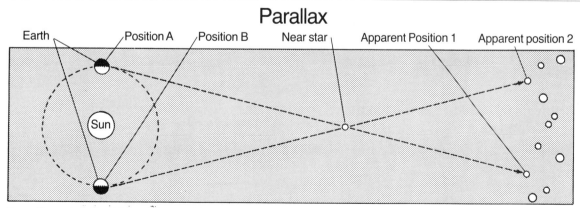

Parallax

Earth, Position A, Position B, Near star, Apparent Position 1, Apparent position 2

Sun

From the opposite sides of the earth's orbit, the position of a nearby star will seem to change when viewed against a background of more distant stars.

against the background of other stars. Six months later, he again noted where the star was. Because the Earth was on the other side of the sun, this was like having his eyes millions of kilometers apart! Then, using geometry, Bessel showed that the star was about 56 trillion kilometers from Earth.

The star that Bessel measured was really nearby, in space terms. But, expressed in ordinary units, like kilometers, its distance was a large number— too large for astronomers to use easily. So they found another unit to describe the distance to the stars. They based their unit on speed of light.

Light travels about 300,000 kilometers per second. In one year, then, light travels 9,460 million kilometers. It would take 6 years for light from Bessel's star to reach Earth. So the distance to the star is expressed as 6 **light-years.** A light-year is the distance light travels in one year.

Parallax can be used to find the distance to stars that are within about 300 light-years of Earth. Beyond that, the stars' relative positions do not change enough to be measured. Henrietta Leavitt's discovery showed how to find the distances to those more distant stars.

Although not all faraway stars are cepheid variables, cepheids are often found in groups of stars that are all roughly the same distance from Earth. Knowing how bright the cepheids are tells about how far away those stars are. The other stars near the cepheids must be about the same distance away as their neighbors.

To Do Yourself   How Can You Measure Parallax?

You will need:

Meter stick, tape, chalk

1. Tape a meter stick to the chalkboard in a horizontal position at about eye level.
2. Stand about 2 meters from the center of the meter stick. Hold a pencil vertically between your eyes about 10 centimeters from your nose.
3. Cover one eye. Observe where the pencil appears to be on the meter stick. Have a student mark that spot.
4. Uncover your eye and cover the other eye. Repeat Step 3.
5. Measure the distance the pencil appeared to move.
6. Hold the pencil at arm's length. Repeat Steps 2 through 5.

Questions

1. How many centimeters did the pencil appear to move when it was held 10 centimeters from your nose? _____ When it was held at arm's length? _____

2. Did the pencil really move? _____ Why did it appear to move? _____

_____

_____

_____

Review

I. Fill in each blank with the word that fits best. Choose from the words below.

    nearby   far away   geometry   Moon   Earth's orbit   parallax
    background

    If you look at the same object from two places, the object will appear to move across the _____ . This method, called

_____ , can be used to find the distance to a star.
You need to make two measurements from different sides of the

_____ . This method only works for stars that are

_____ .

II. The nearest star is about 4 light-years away from Earth. How many kilometers away is it?

III. Answer in sentences.

How can the speed of light be used to measure distance?

_____

_____

_____

How Do Stars Form and Change?

Exploring Science

The Sky Horse. In the constellation Orion, a horse's head appears against a background of stars and faintly glowing clouds. The horse is certainly not like any on Earth. From nose to mane, the head is 3 light-years long!

The horsehead is part of a **nebula** (NEB-yuh-luh), a cloud of cool, dark gas. Within the nebula, changes are taking place. Some of the particles of gas have come together in a clump. The gravitational attraction of the clump brings more material to the growing mass. Heat starts to build and build. When the temperature in the mass is high enough, hydrogen in the mass begins to fuse to form helium. A star is forming.

Scientists think that the Horsehead and other nebulae (NEB-yuh-ly) are the "factories" where new stars are made.

● In some parts of the Horsehead, you can see stars against the dark cloud. What does this tell you about the stars?

Horsehead nebula in Orion.

Birth and Death of an Average Star

Stars form within giant clouds of gas and dust. Most of these stars are medium-sized, like our sun. Let's follow the life cycle of such a star, from "birth" to "death."

Gravity causes particles in the cloud to come together. When a large enough mass has formed, hydrogen atoms start to fuse, or combine, and form helium. This reaction is called **fusion.** Great amounts of energy are given off. A star is born.

The star continues to release energy for millions of years. This energy balances the force of gravity that tends to make the star smaller. At some point, energy starts to build up inside the star. The star starts to expand. It grows larger and less dense. Its surface starts to cool. The star, now glowing with a reddish light, is a **red giant.**

After millions of years as a red giant, the star changes again. The star's supply of hydrogen has run out. It has no more "fuel" to produce energy. The helium in the core has fused to form heavier atoms, like carbon. At this point, gravity causes the star to shrink into a small, tight mass. This collapse cannot be balanced by energy from the core. There is no more fuel. Now glowing with a bluish-white light, the star has become a **white dwarf.**

About 10 billion years have passed since the star was born in the gas cloud. What happens next? Some stars go out in a blaze of glory—they explode. Others, perhaps, just fade out.

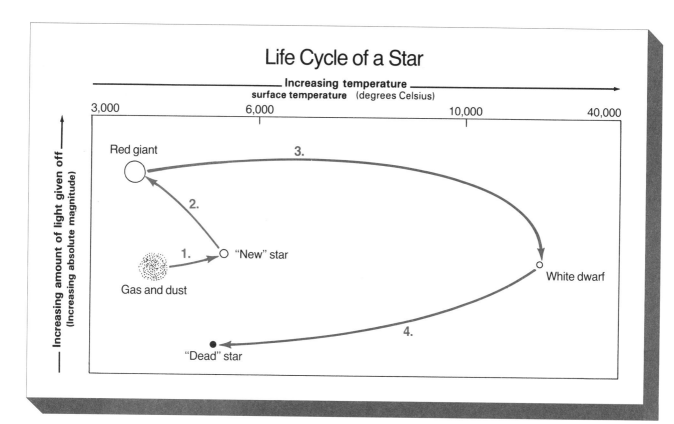

Life Cycle of a Star

Increasing temperature
surface temperature (degrees Celsius)

3,000   6,000   10,000   40,000

Increasing amount of light given off
(Increasing absolute magnitude)

Red giant

3.

2.

1.   "New" star

Gas and dust

White dwarf

4.

"Dead" star

Review

I. Fill in each blank with the word that fits best. Choose from the words below.

fusion   nebulae   friction   red giants   hotter   gravity   cooler

Stars are born in clouds of gas called _____ . As a mass

of gas becomes denser, it also becomes _____ . Eventually,

the reaction called _____ begins. This is the source of
energy for the star. At each stage in its life, the star's energy must balance the

force of _____ or the star will collapse.

II. Use the numbers **1** (first) through **5** (last) to put the following events in order.

A. _____ The star becomes larger, cooler, and red.

B. _____ The cloud becomes hotter.

C. _____ The star becomes smaller and glows bluish-white.

D. _____ A cloud of gas begins to come together under the force of gravity.

E. _____ Atoms in the cloud begin to fuse.

III. Answer in sentences.

It is difficult to discover what happens to a star after it has become a white
dwarf. Why?

What is a Galaxy?

Exploring Science

The Milky Way. The Sun is only one of a great collection of over 200,000,000,000 stars that travel through space together. These stars are known as the **Milky Way**. The stars form a faint band across the sky that looked like a trail of milk to the ancient Greeks. All such collections of stars are called **galaxies** from the Greek for "milky."

Soon after Henrietta Leavitt discovered the connection between cepheid stars and distance, the astronomer Harlow Shapley used this idea to measure the Milky Way. In 1918, Shapley found that the Milky Way was about 120,000 light years across. He found that the Sun was halfway to the edge, 30,000 light years from the center. It takes the Sun 250,000,000 years to travel once around the center as the galaxy revolves.

In 1993, astronomers weighed the Milky Way by measuring how its gravity affected its neighbors. The two closest neighbors are small galaxies called the **Magellanic Clouds**, while the next nearest neighbor, known as **Andromeda,** is larger than the Milky Way. The Milky Way itself has a mass that is about the same as 600,000,000,000 Suns.

In 1994, astronomers were surprised to find that the Milky Way has another close neighbor. The galaxy **Dwingaloo** cannot be seen because of dust from the Milky Way. But it was located using radio waves and photographed with infrared light that can penetrate dust.

● Why are large numbers often called "astronomical"? Explain your answer.

A Universe of Galaxies

When Shapley measured the size of the Milky Way, he thought that the Magellanic Clouds and Andromeda were part of it. Astronomer Edwin Hubble used cepheids to measure the distance to Andromeda and other galaxies. He found that they were much farther away than any of the stars in the Milky Way galaxy. Hubble was the first person to prove that there were galaxies outside the Milky Way, although earlier astronomers had suspected the truth.

A spiral galaxy.

An elliptical galaxy.

Edwin Hubble continued to measure the distances to galaxies. He also studied how galaxies were moving. In 1929, after five years of measuring, he was able to show something astounding. All galaxies are moving away from the Milky Way. Furthermore, the farther away a galaxy is from the Milky Way, the faster it is moving.

Hubble's discovery meant that the universe was getting bigger, or **expanding**. Over the next fifty years, astronomers found convincing evidence that the universe had started in a great explosion, which became known as the **Big Bang**. Since the Big Bang the universe has been expanding. The Hubble Space Telescope, named after Edwin Hubble, can just about see the edge of the universe, somewhere between eight and twenty billion light years away.

To Do Yourself   How Can You Show the Expanding Universe?

You will need:

Large balloon, pieces of cotton, glue, metric ruler

1. Blow up the balloon part way. Twist the neck and hold it closed. Do not tie the neck.
2. Make model "galaxies" by shaping small pieces of cotton. Glue these galaxies to the surface of the balloon.
3. Measure the distance between any two of your galaxies. Blow the balloon up the rest of the way and tie its neck. Measure the distance between the same two galaxies.

Questions

1. What happened to the distance between the two galaxies as the balloon got larger?

   _____

2. What happened to the distance between the rest of the galaxies as the balloon got larger? _____

3. Imagine you were in the center of the balloon, looking out at the galaxies. What would appear to be happening to the galaxies? _____

   _____

Review

I. Fill in each blank with the word that fits best. Choose from the words below.

   stars   farthest   closest   irregular   spiral   dust

   Both the Milky Way and Andromeda are _____ galaxies.

   Galaxies are groups of _____ , gas, and

   _____ . All galaxies move. The _____

   galaxies appear to move fastest.

II. Answer in sentences.

   How did the discoveries of Henrietta Leavitt, Harlow Shapley, and Edwin Hubble tell us more about the universe?

Review What You Know

A. Use the clues to fill in the crossword.

Across
1. The cause of the tides.
3. It has water in the atmosphere.
5. The largest planet.
6. It has clouds of sulphuric acid.
8. It seems to lie on its side.

Down
1. *Mariner 10* found its magnetic field.
2. The twin of Uranus.
4. Its water, if any, is in the soil.
7. Its flares cause disturbances on Earth.

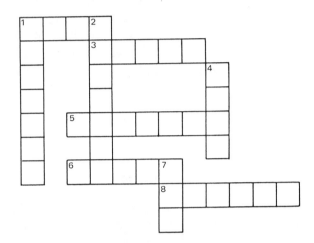

B. Write the letter and words that best complete each statement.

1. _____ The color of a star indicates its **a.** size **b.** distance **c.** temperature

2. _____ The reaction to form helium is called **a.** fusion **b.** friction **c.** gravitation

3. _____ The distance to nearby stars can be found by **a.** parallax **b.** red shift **c.** telescope

4. _____ A light-year is the distance light travels in one **a.** second **b.** minute **c.** year

5. _____ As a medium-sized star ages, it first becomes a **a.** white dwarf **b.** red giant **c.** galaxy

6. _____ The planet that seems to be "lying on its side" is **a.** Mercury **b.** Uranus **c.** Earth

7. _____ The first spacecraft to leave the solar system was **a.** *Apollo 11* **b.** *Sputnik 1* **c.** *Pioneer 10*

8. _____ The sun is **a.** a medium-sized star **b.** a red giant **c.** a bluish-white star

9. _____ All stars get their energy from **a.** burning **b.** fusion **c.** friction

10. _____ A galaxy's distance from the Milky Way affects its **a.** temperature **b.** size **c.** speed of moving away

11. _____ The Milky Way is **a.** a spiral galaxy **b.** an elliptical galaxy **c.** an irregular galaxy

12. _____ The sun seems to be the brightest star because it is the **a.** closest star **b.** largest star **c.** hottest star

13. _____ Space rocks that strike the earth's surface are **a.** asteroids **b.** meteorites **c.** meteors

14. _____ The Great Red Spot is a **a.** small star **b.** storm on Jupiter **c.** volcano on Mars

15. _____ The hottest stars are **a.** yellow **b.** bluish-white **c.** red

C. Apply What You Know

Label the numbered parts of the diagram. Choose from the words below. Then tell which part of the diagram is described in each statement that follows.

asteroids   **Earth**   **Jupiter**   **Mars**   **Mercury**   **Neptune**   **Pluto**
Saturn   **Sun**   **Uranus**   **Venus**

1. _____   2. _____   3. _____

4. _____   5. _____   6. _____

7. _____   8. _____   9. _____

10. _____   11. _____

1. _____ The largest of these was discovered on the first day of the nineteenth century.

2. _____ Its satellite is one-quarter of its size.

281

3. _____ It was the first planet to be visited by the Voyager spacecraft.

4. _____ It seems to be lying on its side.

5. _____ This is a small ball of gases very far from the sun and in orbit around the sun.

6. _____ This hot planet has almost no atmosphere.

7. _____ This has an extinct volcano taller than Mount Everest.

8. _____ Carbon dioxide in the atmosphere causes very high surface temperatures here.

9. _____ Before there were telescopes, this was the most distant planet known.

10. _____ Sometimes this Gas Giant is the farthest planet from the sun.

11. _____ This is the largest member of the solar system.

D. Find Out More

1. Venus is often one of the brightest objects in the sky. Use a newspaper or magazine such as *Natural History* or *Astronomy* to find out when Venus is visible. Observe the planet several times over a period of weeks. Report your observations to the class.

2. Mars has been the scene of many science fiction stories. Use the school or local library to find stories about Mars. Read one of them and make a list of the ways in which the fictional Mars is different from the real one.

3. The *Voyager* spacecraft have traveled to the farthest planets. Collect pictures from these missions from current magazines. Make a poster of the most dramatic sights from the *Voyager* journeys. Make sure you include a picture of the spacecraft.

4. Many of the brighter stars have names. Some of these stars are Aldebaran, Algol, Alpha Centauri, Arcturus, Antares, Barnard's star, Betelgeuse, Capella, Canopus, Deneb, Fomalhaut, Mizar, Polaris, Procyon, Proxima Centauri, Rigel, Sirius, Vega. With another classmate as a partner, find out about these stars. What is special about each star? In what constellation is it found? How did it get its name? You may want to make a poster of the information you find. Or you may choose one or two of your favorite stars and make a report on them for the class.

5. Scientists have been able to describe, in small fractions of a second, the events that took place after the Big Bang. Make a time line for the first few seconds of the universe. Show when matter was first formed, when atoms began to form, and so forth. Under the time line, show how big the universe was during each event.

GLOSSARY

abrasion (uh-BRAY-zhuhn): the breaking apart of rocks into smaller rocks as a result of collisions with other rocks, 110

acid rain: a form of pollution containing sulfuric acid that reaches the earth's surface through precipitation; a major cause of chemical weathering, 129

active volcano: a volcano that has erupted in recent times, 22

air mass: a large body of air in which the temperature and humidity are the same at a given altitude, 239

air pressure: a measure of the weight of the air on a specific area, 231

altocumulus clouds: high, white puffy clouds with a rounded appearance, 233

altostratus clouds: layers of grayish clouds found 2,000 to 7,000 meters above the earth's surface, 234

amphibian (am-FIB-ee-un): a vertebrate that is born in the water, but develops lungs, and spends its adult life on land, 184

anticlines (AN-tih-klyns): upward folds of rock strata, 29

Archean (ahr-KEE-uhn) **era:** in the geologic time scale, the earliest division of Precambrian time, 179

architect: a person trained to design buildings, 225

arid: very dry, 220

armalcolite (ar-MAL-kuh-lyt): one of the minerals brought to the earth from the moon, 255

asteroids (AS-tuh-royds): rocky or metallic bodies smaller than planets that orbit the sun, 254

augite (AW-jyt): a common, dark-colored mineral found in rocks such as basalt, 93

auroras (aw-ROWR-uhs): colored lights that appear and change in the sky near the poles as a result of sunspot activity and solar flares, 269

axis (AK-sis): the line about which a spinning body rotates, 198

barometer (buh-RAHM-uh-tuhr): an instrument used to measure air pressure, 230

barrier island (BAR-ee-ur EYE-lund): a thin strip of sand between open ocean and a quiet bay, 119

basalt (buh-SOLT): a common igneous rock made primarily of feldspar, that makes up the ocean floor and much of the continental crust, 72

batholith (BATH-uh-lith): a large mass of rock that has formed from the cooling and hardening of magma below the earth's surface, 34

bay: a calm body of water between an island, or peninsula, and the shore, 120

beach: the deposit of sand, by waves, along the shoreline, 116

bedrock: the solid layer of rock beneath all of the layers of soil in the earth's crust, 131

breakers: fast-moving waves that carry sand, 119

Cambrian (KAM-bree-un): in the geologic time scale, the period in the early part of the Paleozoic era, beginning about 600 million years ago, 179

canyon: a deep, narrow groove worn into a plateau by fast-moving rivers, 2

carbonic (kar-BON-ik) **acid:** a weak acid that forms when carbon dioxide gas is dissolved in water, 128

cast: a type of fossil formed when minerals fill an impression and harden to make an exact copy of the original organism, 172

Cenozoic (see-nuh-ZOH-ik) **era:** in the geologic time scale, the period of time extending from about 50 million years ago to the present, 188

cepheid (SEE-fid) **variables:** stars that change in brightness every few days, 273

Challenger Deep: the world's deepest spot, located in the Marianas Trench in the Pacific ocean, 62

chemical composition: the kinds of atoms in a substance, 169

chemical weathering: the breaking down of rocks and minerals as the result of a change in their chemical composition, 125

chromosphere (KROH-muh-sfeer): the reddish, central layer of the sun's atmosphere, 268

chronometer (kruh-NOM-ih-tur): an accurate clock that is used to determine longitude, 203

cinder cone: a steep-sided hill or mountain that forms from the piling up of loose rocks and ash that come from a volcano, 25

cirrocumulus clouds: high patches of fluffy, cotton-like clouds, 234

cirrostratus clouds: high layers of white sheetlike clouds, 234

cirrus (SIR-us) **clouds:** high, thin wispy clouds, frequently having curled edges, 233

cleavage: the tendency of a mineral to split along straight surfaces, or planes, 89

climate (KLY-mit): the long-term pattern of weather in a particular area, 206

cold-blooded animals: animals with a body temperature that changes with the temperature of their environment, 189

cold front: a front formed when a mass of cold air moves into a mass of warm air, 239

comet: a body made of ice, frozen gases, and bits of rock and metal that orbits the sun, often in a very long orbit, 254

composite (kuhm-PAHZ-it) **cone:** a volcano formed by the build-up of lava and layers of volcanic ash and rock, 26

compounds: chemical combinations of two or more elements, 84

condensation (kun-DEN-say-shun): the process or result of changing a gas into a liquid, 227

continental climate: a pattern of weather found in areas that have warm summers and cold winters and receive moderate amounts of rain and snow year round, 220

continental drift: a theory which says that the earth's continents are slowly moving as they float in the earth's mantle, 55

continental glaciers: sheets of thick ice that cover continent-sized areas of land, 133

continental shelf: the shallow, sloping land beneath the surface of the ocean, along the coastline of a continent, 68

continental slope: the rapid rise in land from the edges of the deep plain of the ocean floor to the continental shelf, 154

continents (KON-tuh-nunts): large land masses formed of thick crusts, 2

convection cell: movement of a liquid or gas in a circular pattern; caused by uneven heating, 215

convection (kuhn-VEK-shuhn) **current:** a current in a convection cell, 74

corona (kuh-ROH-nuh): the outer atmosphere of the sun, 268

countercurrent: a current that replaces water removed by another current, 151

crater: the opening in the cone of a volcano, 22

creep: the slow downhill movement of soil, 125

Cretaceous (krih-TAY-shus) **extinction:** a period of mass extinction that marked the end of the dinosaurs and many other life forms, 187

crevasse: a large crack, 133

crust: the outermost layer of the earth; the earth's surface, 15

crystal: the naturally formed geometric shape of a mineral, 86

cumulonimbus clouds: large, thick towering clouds that are usually associated with thunderstorms, 234

cumulus (KYOO-myuh-lus): a large, single "puffy" cloud, 233

current: the horizontal movement of water in one direction, 117

decay: the breaking down of a substance into another substance, 176

deflation (dih-FLAY-shun): removal of sediments, such as sand, from an area as a result of wind action, 122

delta (DEL-tuh): the land caused by the deposit of sediment at the mouth of a river, 115

density (DEN-sih-tee): a measure of the amount of matter in a given space (volume), 150

desert: a biome with very little rain, characterized by plants and animals that can survive with very little water, 122

desert climate: a pattern of weather that is very dry, as the result of little rainfall, 220

dew point: the temperature at which condensation starts to take place, 228

dike: a vertical wall of rock formed when magma oozes into cracks across rock layers and hardens, 33

doldrums (DOHL-drumz): the region of calm winds located near the equator, 215

dormant volcano: a volcano that has not erupted in historic times, but still appears capable of eruption, 22

drumlin (DRUM-lin): a low hill, shaped like an upside-down canoe, left by a retreating glacier, 136

dunes: piles of sand made by the wind, 122

Earth: the third planet from the sun in the solar system; the planet we live on, 1

easterlies (EE-stur-lees): polar winds that flow from an easterly direction toward the equator, 215

eclipse (ih-KLIPS): the cutting off of light from one body by another body, 258

electromagnetic spectrum (ih-lek-troh-mag-NET-ik SPEK-trum): the range of energy from radio waves to X-rays, including visible light, 271

element: a substance made up of only one kind of atom, 84

ellipse (ih-LIPS): the slightly flattened circular shape of the planets' orbits, 253

epicenter (EP-uh-sen-tuhr): the point located on the earth's surface right above the focus of an earthquake, 36

epoch (EP-uk): the smallest division of time in the geologic time scale; a subdivision of a period, 174

equator: the imaginary line midway between the poles that divides the earth into northern and southern hemispheres, 203

era: the largest time division in the geologic time scale, 174

erosion (i-ROH-zhuhn): the wearing down and carrying away of land, 110

eruption (ee-RUP-shun): the forcing of substances, such as rocks, lava, and gas, from within the earth to the surface because of a build-up of heat and pressure within the earth, 21

eskers (ESK-kers): hills of till deposited in a winding shape by water flowing under a glacier, 136

evaporation (ih-VAP-uh-ray-shun): the process of changing a liquid to a gas, 227

exfoliation (eks-foh-lee-AY-shun): the process through which layers of rock break, or split-off as a result of mechanical weathering, 126

experiment: a trial that tests a hypothesis, 6

extinct (ek-STINGKT): when an organism no longer exists on earth, 182

extinct volcano: a volcano that is no longer capable of erupting, 22

eye: the calm center of a hurricane, 244

fault: a break in the earth's crust, 33

focus: the place where the movement of the crust begins during an earthquake, 36

fog: particles of condensed water vapor suspended in the air, 235

foraminifera (for-uh-MIN-uh-fur-uh): small, round-shelled tiny animals that lived in the ancient seas, 98

fossils (FOS-uls): the remains, or traces, of plants and animals that lived long ago, 101

fracture: the tendency of a mineral to break irregularly, without cleavage, often leaving a rough surface, 89

fronts: the boundaries between two different air masses, 239

frost action: a form of mechanical weathering that results from the freezing and melting of the water in a rock, 126

fusion (FYOO-shun): the formation of a heavier atom from two lighter atoms, 270

gabbro (GAB-roh): an igneous rock, characterized as having large crystals, that forms from magma cooling within the earth's crust, 95

galaxy (GAL-uk-see): a very large group of stars traveling together through space, 278

geologic (jee-uh-LOJ-ik) **time:** the time span since the earth's beginning, 175

geologic time scale: a chart that shows the divisions of the earth's history in eras, periods, and epochs, 178

geologist: a scientist who studies the earth, 55

giants: stars with a diameter 100 times that of the sun, 270

glacier (GLAY-shur): large, thick mass of ice that moves across land, 4

global wind: the major wind patterns in the Northern and Southern Hemispheres, 217

gneiss (NEYES): a metamorphic rock characterized as having thick layers, 101

granite (GRAN-it): a common igneous rock made up of three or more minerals, including quartz, feldspar, and mica, 92

gravitational attraction (grav-ih-TAY-shun-ul uh-TRAK-shun): the force, or pull, that a large mass has on a smaller mass, 259

great red spot: a storm on the surface of Jupiter, 263

greenhouse effect: a rise in temperature world-wide caused by an increase in the amount of certain gases in the atmosphere, 209

ground fog: particles of condensed water vapor suspended in the air close to the earth's surface, 236

Gulf stream: a current of warm water that travels north from the Gulf of Mexico, along the eastern coast of the United States, then east towards Europe, 146

hail: balls of ice that form in thunderclouds and then fall to the earth, 238

half-life: the amount of time it takes for one-half of a radioactive element to decay into a stable form, 176

halite (HAY-lit): rock salt, 86

harbor waves: strong movement of water in bays or harbors caused by earthquakes and landslides, 42

head: the beginning of a river, 113

heating/cooling engineer: a person who installs heating and cooling systems based upon the specific requirements of a building, 225

high: a region of high barometer pressure, 241

highland climate: patterns of weather found on mountains and plateaus, 220

high tide: the highest point of the rise in the water level of the ocean as a result of the gravitational pull of the moon, 259

hook: a curved portion of a shoreline produced by longshore currents, 120

horse latitudes: regions of little wind at 30° N and 30° S of the equator, 215

hot spot: the place where hot magma continuously rises from the mantle, 65

humus (HYOO-muhs): a substance formed from the decayed remains of plants and animals, 131

hurricane: a large tropical storm with winds greater than 112 km per hour, 119

hypothesis (hy-POTH-ih-sis): an educated guess about the solution of a problem, 6

ice age: a long period of time when the temperature all over the earth falls below normal and continental glaciers advance to cover great areas, 191

icebergs: large pieces, or chunks, of floating ice that break off from glaciers, 134

ice sheets: very large pieces of ice that cover vast land areas; continental glaciers, 134

igneous (IG-nee-us) **rocks:** rocks formed from molten magma cooling within the earth's crust, or from lava cooling on the earth's surface, 95

infrared (in-fruh-RED) **light:** electromagnetic radiation of slightly longer wavelengths than red light, 200

inner core: the solid, innermost layer of the earth, 16

invertebrates (in-VUR-tuh-brits): animals without backbones, 182

ionosphere (EYE-ahn-uh-sfir): the region in the atmosphere in which ions form, 212

isobars (EYE-suh-bars): lines on a weather map that connect places with the same air pressure, 247

isotherms (EYE-suh-thurms): lines on a weather map that connect places that have the same temperature, 247

jet stream: a high-speed, high-altitude current of air that moves from east to west, 239

Jupiter: the fifth planet from the sun in the solar system; the largest planet, 253

kettle: pond or lake formed by a block of ice from a melting glacier, 136

lagoon (luh-GOON): a calm body of ocean water, protected by surrounding islands, 120

lake: a large inland body of fresh water, 2

land breeze: the movement of cooler air from above the land toward water, 217

latitude (LAT-ih-tood): distance north or south of the equator measured in degrees, 203

lava: red-hot melted rock that reaches the earth's surface during a volcanic eruption, 22

leach: the washing of soil minerals into deeper layers of the earth's surface, 131

light-year: distance light travels in one year; an astronomical unit, 274

loam (LOME): soil containing sand and clay in about equal amounts, 131

local winds: wind patterns that are unique to a specific area, 217

loess (LOH-es): very fine grains of soil, 122

longitude (LON-jih-tood): describes east-west position in relation to the prime meridian, 203

longitudinal waves: vibrations, caused by an earthquake, that form when primary waves and secondary waves reach the earth's surface, 39

longshore current: a current that moves parallel to the shoreline, 117

low: a region of low barometric pressure, 241

low tide: the low points of the water level between two high tides because of the gravitational pull of the moon, 259

lunar eclipse: the blocking of light from the sun to the moon by the Earth, 259

luster: the way a mineral reflects light, 88

Magellanic clouds: two small galaxies that appear as fuzzy patches in the night sky of the Southern Hemisphere, 278

magma: melted rock found beneath the earth's surface, 22

magnitude (MAG-nuh-tood): a measure of the amount of energy released by an earthquake, 38

mammals (MAM-uls): warm-blooded animals that have fur or hair and give birth to live young, 188

manganese nodules (NOJ-ools): lumps of densely packed sediment containing the metal manganese found on the ocean floor, 162

mantle (MAN-tul): the layer of the earth that lies between the crust and the core, 15

marble: a familiar metamorphic rock that is frequently used in buildings and sculpture, 93

Marianas (ma-REE-an-us) **Trench:** the world's deepest ocean trench, located in the Pacific Ocean near the Philippines, 63

Mars: the fourth planet from the sun in the solar system, 253

mass extinction: a time when many forms of life suddenly cease to exist, 187

mass movement: the movement of rocks or soil down a slope as a result of gravity, 125

meanders (mee-AN-durs): the large, winding curves along the course of a river, 114

measurement: an observation of how many or how much of something, 5

mechanical (muh-KAN-ih-kul) **weathering:** the breaking down of large pieces of rock into smaller pieces of rock by wind or water, 125

Mediterranean climate: a pattern of weather characterized by warm dry summers, 220

Mercury (mur-KYOUR-ree): the planet closest to the sun in the solar system, 253

mesosphere (MES-uh-sfir): the layer of the atmosphere between the stratosphere and the thermosphere, 212

metamorphic (met-uh-MOR-fik) **rock:** a rock formed from another type of rock under conditions of great heat and pressure, 101

metamorphosis (met-uh-MOR-fuh-sis): to change from one thing into another, 102

meteor: the glow from a meteoroid as it enters the Earth's atmosphere, 266

meteorites (MEET-ee-uh-reyets): space rocks that strike the earth's surface, 266

meteoroids (MEET-ee-uh-royds): small rocks and grains of dust moving through space, 266

meteorologist (mee-tee-uh-ROL-uh-jist): a scientist who studies the weather, 246

Mid-Atlantic ridge: a giant mountain range located beneath the surface of the Atlantic Ocean, 68

mid-ocean ridge: a large mountain range rising from the floor of the ocean, 68

Milky Way Galaxy: a vast collection of stars, of which the sun is a member, 278

mineral: a solid natural substance that does not come from any living thing, 84

Moh's Scale of Hardness: a scale which assigns minerals a number from 1 to 10 based upon a "scratch test", 89

mold: a type of fossil formed when an impression of an organism remains after the organism has decayed, 172

molecule (MOL-uh-kyool): the smallest particle of a substance having all of the properties of that substance, 169

monsoon (mon-SOON): a large scale seasonal wind and rain pattern, 217

moraines (muh-RAYNS): piles or ridges of till, 136

mountain: a large landmass that rises far above the earth's surface, 2

mouth: the end of a river; the place where a river empties into another body of water, 114

nebula (NEB-yuh-luh): [pl. nebulae (NEB-yuh-ly)]: a cloud of cool, dark gas, 276

Neptune (NEP-toon): in the solar system, the eighth planet from the sun most of the time, 253

nimbostratus clouds: low, thick layers of dark gray clouds that produce rain or snow, 234

nimbus: a cloud from which rain falls, 233

normal fault: the sinking of ground on one side of a fault caused by vertical, or up-and-down, movement, 33

observation (ob-zur-VAY-shun): the gaining of information by using one's senses, 5

observatories (ub-ZUR-vuh-tohr-ees): buildings, with large telescopes, used for studying the sky, 197

obsidian (ub-SID-ee-un): a black, glasslike, igneous rock that is formed by fast-cooling lava on the earth's surface, 95

oceanography (oh-shee-uh-NOG-ruh-fee): science dealing with the study of the oceans, 144

olivine (OL-uh-veen): a common, dark-colored mineral found in rocks such as basalt, 93

Olympus Mons: a large volcano on the surface of Mars, 262

Oort cloud: a huge cloud of materials where comets originate, 267

orbit: the path of a planet as it travels around the sun; the path followed by any body as it circles another body, 253

ore: a mineral or combination of minerals that contain a substance, such as metal, which can be mined, 84

ostracoderms (os-truh-koh-durms): the first fishes to appear on earth; jawless fishes that appeared during the Paleozoic era, 184

outer core: the upper part of the earth's core; the outer core lies between the earth's mantle and the inner core, 15

ox-bow lake: a body of water that results from the cut-off meander of a river, 114

ozone (OH-zohn): a form of oxygen that forms a layer in the upper region of the stratosphere responsible for absorbing most of the ultraviolet radiation given off by the sun, 211

Pangea (PANG-gay-uh): the name given to the single land mass that Alfred Wegener believed was made up of all the present continents at one time in the past, 55

parallax (PAR-uh-laks): the apparent change of position of an object against its background due to the change in position of the observer, 273

partial solar eclipse: the blocking out of part of the sun by the shadow of the moon, 258

pavement: the desert floor, 122

penumbra (pih-NUM-bruh): the lighter area of the moon's shadow on Earth, 258

period: a division of time in the geologic time scale; a subdivision of an era, 174

Peru current: a current of cold water that flows up the west coast of South America, 149

petroleum: a fossil fuel, formed from the decaying parts of living things, 101

phases: the different appearances in the shape of the moon as it moves through its orbit, 256

photosphere (FOH-tuh-sfeer): the thin yellow layer of the sun's atmosphere that is most visible from Earth, 268

pillow lava: pillow-shaped lava structure formed when cold seawater cools and hardens hot lava, 160

plains: large, flat areas of land, 3

planet: a large body that revolves around the sun, 253

planetary (PLAN-ih-ter-ee) **winds:** huge belts of wind that blow steadily in the same direction all the time, 147

plate: a large piece of the earth's crust that moves as a unit, 47

plateau (plah-TOH): high, flat regions of land, 2

plate tectonics (tek-TON-iks): a theory which states that the earth's crust consists of several sections that move very slowly as they float on a partly melted layer, 55

Pleistocene (PLY-stuh-seen) **epoch:** in the geologic time scale, the part of the Cenozoic era that began about 1.6 million years ago, 188

Pluto: in the solar system, the planet that is usually farthest from the sun, 253

polar climate: patterns of weather found in regions that are dry and have an average temperature that is below freezing all year, 220

porous (POR-us): having tiny holes, or pores, that liquids can pass through, 101

Precambrian: in the geologic time scale, the time before the Cambrian period, 178

precipitate (prih-SIP-ih-tayt): the separation of a substance, as a solid, from a solution; a solid that has come out of solution, 162

precipitation (prih-sip-ih-TAY-shun): moisture that falls to the earth, 206

predict: to state beforehand what will happen, 6

primary wave (P wave): a vibration caused by an earthquake that travels in a pushing and pulling pattern through the earth, 35

prime meridian (muh-RID-ee-un): an imaginary line running from the North Pole, through Greenwich, England, to the South Pole; the 0° line of longitude, 203

properties: the characteristics, or traits, of a substance or object, 84

Proterozoic (proht-uhr-uh-ZOH-ik) **era:** in the geologic time scale, the second era of the Precambrian time, beginning about 1 _ billion years ago, 179

pumice (PUM-is): a light igneous rock, filled with tiny holes, that forms when gases are trapped within fast-cooling lava on the earth's surface, 95

radioactivity (RAY-dee-oh-ak-TIV-ih-tee): energy in the form of subatomic particles produced as atoms change from one element to another, 176

range: a group of mountains, 2

red giant: a large star with a reddish glow, 276

relative humidity (REL-uh-tiv hyoo-MID-it-tee): a comparison between the amount of water vapor in the air with the amount of water vapor the air can hold at a given temperature, 227

reptiles: cold-blooded vertebrates that lay eggs, 185

reverse fault: the upward movement of ground on one side of a fault, 33

revolution (rev-uh-LOO-shun): the movement of a body in its orbit around another body, 198

rhyolite (RY-uh-lyt): an igneous rock, characterized by small crystals, that forms from the cooling of lava on the earth's surface, 95

Richter scale: a standard of measurement used for determining the magnitude of an earthquake, 38

rift: a V-shaped underwater canyon caused by the moving apart of tectonic plates, 157

rift valley: cracks in the ocean floor caused by the separating of the earth's crust, 71

river: a natural stream of water, 113

rock: a substance made of one or more minerals, 4

rock cycle: the way that rocks are changed from one kind of another, 102

rotation (roh-TAY-shun): the spinning of a body, such as the earth, on its axis, 198

runoff: moving water that runs along the surface of the earth, 113

San Andreas (SAN an-DRAY-uhs) **fault:** a giant crack in the earth's crust that runs through southern California, 35

sandbar: the build-up of sand off shore, 120

sandstone: a type of sedimentary rock made mostly of quartz particles fused together, 92

satellite (SAT-ul-lyt): a body that revolves around another body, especially about a planet, 253

Saturn: the sixth planet from the sun in the solar system, 253

scales: the outer covering of fish and reptiles, 184

schist (SHIST): a metamorphic rock characterized as having thick layers, 101

sea breeze: the movement of cooler air from above the water toward the land, 217

sea-floor spreading: the separation and widening of the crust on the ocean floor, 71

seamounts: extinct underwater volcanoes, or mountains, that do not reach the ocean's surface, 65

Sea of Tranquillity (TRAN-kwuh-lih-tee): the place where people first landed on the moon, 255

secondary wave (S wave): vibrations, caused by an earthquake, that travel in a snakelike pattern, 36

sedimentary (SED-uh-MEN-tuh-ree) **rock:** rock formed from deposits of sediments, such as clay, rock fragments, or pieces of shell, 98

sediments (SED-uh-munts): bits of material, such as rock fragments or pieces of shell, that settle to the bottom of bodies of water, 98

seismic (SYZ-muk) **waves:** vibrations such as those caused by earthquakes, that travel through the earth, 15

seismograph (SYZ-muh-graf) : an instrument used for measuring earthquake waves, 38

semiarid climate: a pattern of weather found in areas that are usually very dry, but have a short wet season, 220

sextant (SEKS-tunt): an instrument used to determine latitude, 204

shale: a sedimentary rock formed from clay, 14

shield (SHEELD) **volcano:** large, wide volcano that forms when lava spreads out over a large area, 26

shock waves: vibrations, such as those created by earthquakes, that travel through a substance, 15

silicate (SIL-ih-kit): any mineral containing silicon and oxygen, 84

sill: a rock formation made by the cooling and hardening of magma between horizontal layers of rock, 33

sinkhole: a large opening in the ground created by the weakening and collapse of a cave, 129

slate: a metamorphic rock formed from the sedimentary rock shale, 101

sleet: frozen rain, 237

smog: a combination of smoke and fog, 235

soil: a loose covering of the earth's surface made from weathered rock and the decayed remains of living things, 131

solar wind: energy and particles from the sun that move away from the sun, 267

stalactites (stuh-LAK-tyts): deposits of calcite that hang from the roof of a cave, 128

stalagmites (stuh-LAG-myts): deposits of calcite that rise up from the floor of a cave, 128

station model: the feature of weather maps that shows the weather conditions in a particular area, 247

stratocumulus clouds: a large, rounded, low cloud having a soft appearance, 233

stratosphere (STRAT-uh-sfir): the layer of the atmosphere above the troposphere and below the mesosphere, 208

stratus: layers of clouds that are spread out, 233

streak: the color a mineral leaves when it is rubbed against an unglazed tile; the color of a mineral when it is powdered, 88

streak plate: the unglazed tile used to find a mineral's streak, 88

strike-slip fault: the horizontal, or sideways, movement of ground along a fault, 33

stromatolites (stroh-mah-TOH-lytes): formations made from the build-up of sediments in mats of algae, 178

submarine canyon (SUB-muh-reen KAN-yun): a canyon found on the continental shelf caused by the rapid movement of dense, sediment-filled water, 156

subsoil: the layer of earth between the topsoil and the bedrock, 131

subtropical climate: a warm and wet pattern of weather common to regions between the latitudes of 30° and 40° north and south of the equator, 220

sulfuric (sul-FYOOR-ik) **acid:** a strong acid formed when sulfur dioxide combines with water; the primary pollutant in acid rain, 129

summer monsoon: a strong warm wind, accompanied by heavy rains that flows from the ocean toward the land during the summer season, 218

sunspots: dark spots appearing on the surface of the sun caused by gases that are cooler than the other gases around them, 269

supergiants: large stars, some with diameters 1000 times larger than the sun, 270

syncline (SING-klyn): a downward fold of rock strata, 29

talus (TAY-lus): pile of broken rock at the bottom of a steep slope, 125

terminal moraines: large piles or ridges of till left where the leading edge of a glacier stopped, 136

terrestrial planets: planets with rocklike crusts similar to Earth's, 263

theory (THEE-uh-ree): an explanation of a scientific idea that has been thoroughly tested and accepted, 6

thermosphere (THUR-muh-sfir): the layer of the atmosphere above the mesosphere, 212

thunderstorm: small intense storms, usually accompanied by thunder and lightning, that form when a mass of warm air is pulled high into the sky, 242

tides: the up-and-down movement of ocean water as a result of the gravitational pull of the moon, 147

till: the rock, gravel, and sand dropped by a melting glacier, 136

topsoil: the rich, dark top layer of the soil; soil containing decayed organic matter, 11

tornado: a dark, funnel-shaped cloud that moves at a high speed, 243

total solar eclipse: the apparent blocking out of the entire face of the sun by the umbra of the moon, 258

trade winds: the constant winds that flow from the horse latitudes toward the equator, 215

trilobites (TRY-luh-byts): most common shelled animal during the Cambrian period; now extinct, 182

tropical climate: a hot and wet pattern of weather common to regions near the equator, 220

tropical storms: storms formed over the warm ocean waters near the equator that move toward land, 244

troposphere (TROP-uh-sfir): the layer of the atmosphere closest to the earth, 212

tsunami (TSOO-nah-mee): giant waves caused by earthquakes in the ocean floor, 41

ultraviolet (ul-truh-VY-uh-lit) **light:** a form of radiation that is beyond the violet part of the rainbow, 211

umbra: the darker area of the moon's shadow on Earth, 258

undersea current: movement of water below the surface of the ocean as a result of density differences, 151

Uranus (YOOR-ay-nus): the seventh planet from the sun in the solar system, 253

vacuum (VAK-yew-wuhm): empty space; a region containing no matter, 230

valley: low area of land between two mountains, 2

vents: places where hot water is rising through the ocean floor, 159

Venus: the second planet from the sun in the solar system, 253

vertebrates (VUR-tuh-brayts): animals with backbones, 184

volcano (vol-KAY-noh): an opening in the earth's crust where hot, melted rock from inside the earth comes to the surface, 25

warm-blooded animals: animals with body temperatures that are about the same all the time, even when the temperature outside changes, 188

warm front: a front formed when a mass of warm air replaces a mass of cold air, 239

water vapor (VAY-pur): water as a gas, 209

waves: circular movements of water caused by winds, 116

weathering: the breaking down of rock by factors, or agents, in the environment, 125

westerlies (WES-tur-lees): winds that form near the horse latitudes and blow in a general west-to-east direction, 215

white dwarf: a small, dense star, formed from a red giant that has used up its hydrogen supply, that glows with a bluish-white light, 276

winter monsoon: a cold, dry wind that flows from the land toward the sea during the colder months, 218

woolly mammoth: an animal, resembling an elephant with fur, that became extinct during the last ice age, 191

Index

Photo Credits